Public Sector Reform in ASEAN Member Countries and Korea

Public Sector Reform in ASEAN Member Countries and Korea

Pan Suk Kim
Editor

Daeyoung Moonhwasa Publishing Company
Seoul, Republic of Korea

Public Sector Reform in ASEAN Member Countries and Korea

Edited by
Pan Suk Kim

ISBN 978-89-7644-386-1
Published by Choon Whan Lim
Daeyoung Moonhwasa Publishing Company
178-2 Chungpa-dong l-ga, Yongsan-gu, Seoul 140-869, Korea
TEL (02) 716-3883, (02) 714-3062
FAX (02) 703-3839
Published on December 30, 2011

Price KR 23,000

Contents

Preface

This book entitled *Public Sector Reform in ASEAN Member Countries and Korea* is the third development of the ASEAN Public Management Forum. ASEAN member countries include Brunei, Cambodia, Lao People's Democratic Republic, Indonesia, Malaysia, Myanmar, Philippines, Singapore, Thailand, and Vietnam. In 2009, the first book entitled *Public Administration and Public Governance in ASEAN Member Countries and Korea* was published and the second book entitled *Civil Service System and Civil Service Reform in ASEAN Member Countries and Korea* was published in 2010.

Public Administration and Public Governance in ASEAN Member Countries and Korea was the first book of its kind to present a comprehensive introduction and analysis of public administration and public governance in ASEAN member countries including the structural change, system transformation, and the development of public administration and the public sector in major Southeast Asian countries. The second book, *Civil Service System and Civil Service Reform in ASEAN Member Countries and Korea*, also serves as a landmark in the study of civil service systems and civil service reform, and presented a rich explanation and in-depth analysis of civil service systems and various reform measures in those countries including major issues in civil service reform as well as the current status and future challenges.

It is intended that this third book on public sector reform will make a timely contribution to the understanding and explanation of public sector reform in ASEAN member countries and Korea. Many Southeast Asian countries are growing rapidly, but the public sector in those countries needs more proactive innovations. Various international organizations including the World Bank show that the governance indicators of Southeast Asian countires was not higher than countries in Western and Eastern Europe, Central and Latin America, and North Africa. The role of the public sector is highly critical for further development in terms of economic growth, social development, public service delivery, and political development. Reform means to put, or change, into an improved form, or condition, to restore public trust and improve government effectiveness. Public sector reform, seeking to improve the system and the structure as well as its performance and service delivery, is greatly needed in many countries of Southeast Asia and many other regions.

In the past, there were not many opportunities for academic exchanges and dialogues in the field of public administration in ASEAN member countries and Korea. Moreover, publications on Asian public administration and the public sector have not been produced well in a common language such as English and not well disseminated in the region as well as in the world. In that regards, a scholarly forum and publication on public administration and public sector could promote more active dialogue and collaborations in the region. Along such a line, the ASEAN Public Management Forum supported by the ASEAN Secretariat and the Korean Ministry of Foreign Affairs and Trade was held at the National Institute of Development Administration in Bangkok, Thailand on July 21-22, 2011. During the forum, active presentations and provocative discussions were made and all presented manuscripts have been thoroughly revised by each author based on comments received for the publication of this book.

Similar to the previous two books, the third book, *Public Sector Reform in ASEAN Member Countries and Korea*, aims to furnish better understanding of public sector reform in ASEAN member countries and Korea, focusing on various reform trajectories and implementation of reform measures. Public sector reform is not simply optional for further development it is absolutely essential for sustainable government effectiveness and economic growth in any country. Accordingly, this book incorporated new collection of manuscripts on public sector reform prepared by leading experts from respective countries in Southeast Asia. In addition, this book includes a chapter on public sector reform in Korea for providing a comparative view on ASEAN member countries and Korea.

In the past couple of decades, we have witnessed major structural, functional and system changes in the area of public administration. The traditional bureaucratic and top down system has been substituted by a more accountable, transparent, and participatory system with the application of information technology and communication (ICT). Moreover, the ongoing economic downturn brought the introduction of the market mechanism into traditional public administration under the name of new public management. Accordingly, various forms of new pubic management have penetrated widely into the global, regional, and local public sectors including Southeast Asian countries and Korea. Criticism against new public management has increased substantially over the years, but NPM has not disappeared from our radar. In the future, we may need a new direction for the development of public administration and value-oriented public administration could become a new alternative in the future.

Leaders in many Southeast Asian countries introduced a broad range of reform measures to deal with the daunting challenges they face, but not all of them are successful or effective. Therefore, the ASEAN Public Management Forum has provided a window for exchanging the experiences and lessons of public sector reform in ASEAN member countries and Korea. I hope such practice to be continued in the future. The theme of this book is an important insight of public sector reform in the Asian region and for other continents. Discussing the reform measures and approaches in those countries not only is timely and important for those countries, but also useful as a reference for other developing nations in the design and implementation of public sector reform. I hope a series of publications on public administration including the first, second and third books can provide a relevant reference and practical tools for sharing experience and lessons in the region and the world.

Lastly, I would like to express my deep appreciation to all participants of the international forums and the series of book publications. Without their active participation and dedication, the publication of this book would be difficult. Furthermore, I would like to thank a number of experts (Mr. Misran Karmain, Mr. Thongphane Savanphet, and Ms. Carla Budiarto) in the ASEAN Secretariat in Jakarta for their continuous support. Last but not least, many thanks go to the ASEAN Cooperation Division of the Ministry of Foreign Affairs and Trade in the Republic of Korea. Especially, I would like to acknowledge that the ROK-ASEAN Development Cooperation Program was very helpful in supporting the forum and its related projects.

Pan Suk Kim

Chapter 1 Introduction

Pan Suk Kim

This book is about reform experiences in Southeast Asian countries. The Association of Southeast Asian Nations (ASEAN) is a geo-political and economic organization of ten countries located in Southeast Asia comprising of Indonesia, Malaysia, the Philippines, Singapore, Thailand, Brunei, Myanmar, Cambodia, Laos, and Vietnam. Its aims include the acceleration of economic growth, social progress, cultural development amongst its members, the protection of regional peace and stability, and to provide opportunities for member countries to discuss their differences peacefully. ASEAN, ever since its establishment in 1967, has been involved in encouraging accelerated economic growth and collaboration in the member of countries in Southeast Asia (see more details about ASEAN at http://www.aseansec.org).

In addition, by broadening its sphere of association, ASEAN has created different arrangements with Korea and other countries out with the organization. The collaboration between ASEAN and Korea has been a useful medium for development, economic discourse, as well as political and cultural sharing. In a way to promote more specific collaboration between ASEAN member countries and Korea, the first ASEAN public management forum was held in 2009, supported by the ASEAN

Secretariat and the Korean Ministry of Foreign Affairs and Trade. It is one part of the major collaboration which aims to serve as a means for collaborative scientific research, and the sharing of new findings in the areas of public administration and governance. So far, the ASEAN public management forum has successfully organized three international conferences and has been able to publish three books in the area of public administration: (1) Public Administration and Public Governance in ASEAN Member Countries and Korea (Kim, 2009); (2) The Civil Service System and Civil Service Reform in ASEAN Member Countries and Korea (Kim, 2010); and (3) Public Sector Reform in ASEAN Member Countries and Korea.

In the current time of globalization, regional collaboration is not only inevitable, but is also a critically important base for new scientific discovery, knowledge dissemination and the addressing major regional and global issues. Moreover, in the knowledge-driven economic and political structure, these collaborative discussions and regional dialogues nurture a learning-and experience-sharing environment to allow the promotion of "first best or second best practices," and create an education and learning platform from "failed practices."

The main theme of this book entitled *Public Sector Reform in ASEAN Member Countries and Korea* is one of the current pressing issues which needs close attention as countries experience economic growth and further development. This book reviews some of the most challenging issues confronting the public sectors in Southeast Asian countries in an era of globalization and localization. The contributors examine the potential and limits of managerial reforms, and the book provides lessons from the experience of implementing public sector reforms in developing countries. How to achieve an efficient, responsive and accountable public sector reform has been the center of debate and research as it touches different disciplines.

The most important point here is that the understanding and implementation of public sector reform is complicated and challenging but the effectiveness and efficiency of the public sector is vital to a country's economic development (World Bank, 2008).

The public sector reforms in the ASEAN member countries are no different from the main ideology of "change" to bring a better performing public sector. The major reform areas in the ASEAN member countries are strategic planning development, civil service reform and human resource development, introduction of rule of law, anti-corruption, and the decentralization of the public sector. Improving the capacity of public employees to improve the professionalism of public management systems yielded relatively higher achievement both in the quality and amount of service provision in those countries. The fight against corruption remains the major concern. From the discussion below, it can be seen that most countries in the ASEAN membership introduced diverse programs hoping to have better government effectiveness and a lower level of corruption in the public sector.

The introduction of e-Government, or use of ICT, is also a major reform program which aims at facilitating public service provision and bringing citizen-oriented service provision to the public sector. Reforming the state institutions and the civil service as a way to improve public service delivery supported by improved human capital and supporting infrastructure can be mentioned as a major factor for the success of more of the reform programs. In terms of public finance management, implementing sound, modern, public finance management supported by electronic systems improved the transparency and accountability in most countries. In addition, the private sector received considerable attention for playing a major role in economic development. This ensures ordinary people's participation and private sector development as well as promoting productivity and competitiveness of the market and the economy in general. Moreover, the reform programs and measures in developing countries have quite ambitious goals aiming to bring a better quality of life, social integration, political stability, eradication of inequalities in society, and institutional capacity for crisis recovery.

This book presents an in-depth analysis of the public sector reform programs that have been implemented in each of the ASEAN member countries, as well as Korea. It has eleven national cases prepared by a number of public administration experts and practitioners in the area of public administration that were presented at the ASEAN Public Management Forum held in Bangkok on July 21-22, 2011. The major aim of this international forum was promoting public sector reform and further collaboration amongst ASEAN countries and Korea. Provocative and critical discussions were made at the international meeting, to ensure the richness of each paper, in terms of academic rigor and practical relevance.

The first chapter presents "Reforming the public sector in Brunei" prepared by David Jones. Brunei has an extensive public sector, funded by revenue from oil and gas production which is by far the biggest sector of the economy. The dominant institution of the public sector is the civil service. Over the years, the need to reform both the public sector in general and the civil service in particular, has expanded and grown. A number of reform initiatives have been launched. These include the application of strategic planning, the enhancement of human resource practices, the fostering of better customer orientation in front-line services, the adoption of e-Government, and the streamlining of business regulations. However, all too often the implementation of these reforms has been slow and inconsistent, whilst other shortcomings of the civil service have yet to be comprehensively addressed. These include the lack of agency autonomy, the proliferation of bureaucratic rules and procedures, the protracted and multi-layered decision-making processes, the excessive paper work, and an old-fashioned financial management system. The paper will consider the reasons for the patchy implementation of the reforms to date and the failure to introduce other much needed reforms. One reason is the stake that civil servants have in retaining the status quo, which has led to a failure to whole-heartedly embrace reform. The other is that certain existing shortcomings in the civil service, that the reform agenda either addresses or may address in the future, are themselves obstacles to the effective implementation of the reforms.

The second chapter presents the "Reforming the Public Sector in Cambodia" prepared by Ngo Hongly and Alain Benicy. Cambodia is a less-developed, post war country. By the time the Khmer Rouge genocidal regime was overthrown in 1979, the institutions of the State had been destroyed and the population decimated. Cambodia's journey is more about rebuilding than reforming the public sector. Following the Peace Accord in 1991 and the first post-war elections in 1993, successive Royal Governments have focused on national reconciliation and winning the peace. There could not be development without peace and no peace without development. The journey to date could be broken down into three phases: a rehabilitation phase (1993-1998), a consolidation phase (1999-2003), and a development phase (from 2004 to date). During the first phase, a new Constitution was promulgated, the Legislative, Judicial and Executive branches of the State were reestablished; the prerequisites for a market based economy and a liberal multi-party democracy were set in place. During the second phase, the machinery of government and required decision-making, implementation and monitoring processes were strengthened.

Because of the in-in strategy followed by the Prime Minister, the national government could exercise its authority over the entire country for the first time in over 500 years. In 2004, the Royal Government adopted a wide-ranging Rectangular Strategy for Growth, Employment, Equity, and Efficiency, which was put into operation as the National Strategic Development Plan 2006-2010 (NSDP). Both were updated in 2009 following the fourth national elections in 2008. The scope of the work is breathtaking, as everything must be done at the same time with limited human, financial and institutional capacity. The pursuit of good governance is at the core of the Rectangular Strategy and the NSDP. It entails four major reforms: the Administrative Reform including decentralization and deconcentration, the Legal and Judicial Reform, the Reform of the Armed Forces and the Fight against Corruption. These are complemented by an extensive set of reforms including the Reform of Public Finance, the Reform of Natural Resources Management, Gender Equity, Health, Education, Trade and Commerce and the strengthening of the private sector as the engine of growth. In spite of an uncertain and volatile world economy, the rapid rate of growth of the Cambodian economy, the reduction in poverty levels and the country's integration into the world attest to Cambodia's success at meeting its objectives of sustainable development and social justice. After a brief description of major cross sector reforms, the paper focuses on the Administrative Reform and its major achievements as illustrative of the approach to reforming the public sector and lessons learned.

The third paper is about "Exploring Public Sector Reform in Indonesia" by Eko Prasojo. Public sector reform is one of the important pillars in Indonesia's current politics, both at national and local government levels. Since 2009, Indonesia has made public sector reform a highest national priority. This paper attempts to provide general elaboration on the public sector reform that has been made and coming agendas in Indonesia, the problems, and how the prospect of reforms would affect future development in Indonesia. The various experiences that Indonesia has in public sector reform can serve as a lesson for other countries. Some of the reforms include, among others, the reorganization of local government, using the ICT in government (e-Government), many agendas of civil service reform, reform of public procurement, reform of public finance management, and reform of government accountability. This paper will also elaborate on some reforms taken in local government in Indonesia. The most important challenges in public sector reform in Indonesia are steering capability and consensus among political leaders.

The fourth paper presents "Public Sector Reform in the Lao People's Democratic Republic" by Suresh Balakrishnan and Khammoune Viphongxay. The Lao People's Democratic Republic (Lao PDR) has been making the transition from a centrally-planned system towards a market-oriented economy, achieving an average economic growth rate of more than 7 percent per annum between 2001 and 2010. This impressive development has, in no small measure, been a result of significant strengthening of the public sector, which plays the main role in accelerating the development of the country, through the use of a strategic mix of policy reforms and programme implementation. This paper first provides a perspective on the country's political and economic evolution, in which reform has taken place, in order to highlight the challenges in the last two decades. This section touches upon the transformation of a revolutionary people's state to a modern rule of law state, as well as the political directions for economic transformation. The paper then proceeds to elaborate the main public sector reform, initiatives and programmes. These reforms include the National Strategic Plans for Governance and other key initiatives for governance and public administration reform. This section discusses the four pillars of reform, namely improving public services, ensuring people's participation, building rule of law and implementing sound public financial management. The discussion in the paper is focused on reforming the state institutions and the civil service as a way to improve public service delivery. The third section analyzes and reflects on the six challenges encountered in the process, which range from the lack of equity in development to the limitations in deploying civil servants in remote areas. The final section presents the five lessons recognized by the Lao administration, which provide the medium term perspective for public sector reform in the Lao PDR.

The fifth paper presents "Public Sector Reform in Malaysia" by Nik Rosnah Wan Abdullah. In light of changing policy priorities in the mid-1980s, there emerged a "paradigm shift" in the Malaysian public sector, with the adoption of market ideology and privatization policy as part of public sector reform. Since then, the Malaysian public sector underwent a major restructuring that brought about enormous change. At the macro level, Malaysia thought that it needed to respond to economic challenges and global uncertainties. The answer was to formulate strategic approaches that link reform of the public sector with its effectiveness and efficiency in promoting economic development fundamental to the needs of the management of a market economy. In essence, the government reformed the public sector to enhance private sector development and to promote productivity and competitiveness whilst at the same time to ensure equity and social justice. The focus was on industrialization as the country's development base and the private sector as the engine of growth, with the government as the enablers.

The sixth paper is about "Public Sector Reform in Myanmar" by Htay Htay Lwin. The public sector, or state sector, is non-private and non-profit oriented in nature, and its role is essential for guiding the market system to operate properly. It is also widely accepted as the sole provider of public goods. However, it is not limited to the production of goods and services by government; its enterprises and provision of services encourage equity and fairness. Consequently, the role of the public sector is significant in socio-economic development and achieving targeted socio-economic policies. Currently, the Government of the Union of Myanmar is initiating the building of a new modern developed democratic nation with five future aspirations; achieving good governance and clean government, the development of democratic practices, the maintenance of justice, improving the efficiency and effectiveness of the public sector, and enhancing the integration among ministries and implementing agencies. The public sector in Myanmar is comprised of government, local authorities, and State Economic Enterprises (SEEs). The local authorities consist of the municipalities and townships serviced by the town and city development committees. The State Economic Enterprises (SEEs) are obliged to contribute to the budget, which is used for financing the working capital and investment. Public sector reform is the government's deliberate and effective attempt for the organization and setting of the public sector. Reform in the public sector is not a new phenomenon. Since the post 1988 period, the Government of Myanmar has implemented various reform measures in administrative, economic and social spheres. Amongst the three branches of the public sector; legislative, executive and judicial, this paper will focus on executive branch of the public sector of Myanmar and its reforms throughout the post 1988 period.

The seventh paper is about "Public Sector Reform in the

Philippines" by Alex B. Brillantes, Jr., and Herisadel P. Flores. The enactment of Republic Act No. 7160, also known as the Local Government Code of 1991, ushered in a new era in Philippine local governance. Through the said law, the country has formally adopted devolution as an approach to public sector reform, granting sub-national institutions a high degree of political and fiscal autonomy. Like all types of reform, the end goal of this policy is to accelerate economic growth and, more importantly, provide a better quality of life for citizens. However, the Code brought about more than just administrative reforms. Several of its most important provisions, such as on the participation of civil society in local development planning, encroaches on the realm of *governance* – almost a full decade before the term became a buzzword in the halls of multilateral development organizations. This paper takes on the challenge of assessing the impact of the Code on the way local government units (LGUs) in the Philippines, and the country as a whole, are governed. Although guided by the concepts forwarded by the proponents of the Worldwide Governance Indicators, this paper is not an empirical study. Rather, it reviews the rich but somewhat fragmented literature on the topic – indeed some of it presented insightful empirical analyses. In doing so, the paper tries to provide a broad overview of the successes and shortcomings in the implementation of this wide-ranging reform policy. The conclusion provides a quick look at national outcomes that can partially be attributed to devolution. It concludes by presenting some policy considerations that may facilitate the continuing process of devolution in the country.

The eighth paper is about "Singapore-Style Public Sector Reforms" by Jon S.T. Quah. Public sector reforms were neglected in Singapore during the British colonial period because the civil service was concerned with maintaining law and order, building public works and collecting taxes. Consequently, the

Singapore Civil Service (SCS) did not play an important role in national development. When the People's Action Party (PAP) government assumed office in June 1959, it inherited a civil service and civil servants with "a colonial mentality" and the problems of a serious housing shortage, high unemployment, widespread corruption, and low economic growth. The PAP leaders realized that they had to change the attitudes of the civil servants by replacing their "colonial mentality" to enable them to contribute to the attainment of national development goals. Accordingly, the Political Study Center was formed in August 1959 to conduct part-time and non-residential two-week courses for senior civil servants to change their attitudes and increase their awareness of Singapore's contextual constraints through their interaction with the PAP leaders. The PAP government's approach to public sector reforms in Singapore is based on this division of labor between the SCS and the statutory boards: the SCS performs the "housekeeping" functions while the statutory boards like the Housing and Development Board and the Economic Development Board were established, respectively, to accelerate the implementation of the public housing program and to promote economic development by attracting foreign investment to Singapore. After initiating comprehensive reform of the SCS in 1959-1960, the PAP government began the fight against corruption with the enactment of the Prevention of Corruption Act in June 1960. The personnel system was also reformed with the decentralization of the Public Service Commission in 1990 and 1995. To minimize the brain drain of the senior civil servants to the private sector, the salaries of civil servants and political leaders were periodically increased from 1972 to 1994, and have been benchmarked to the salaries of six private sector professions since 1995. These six reforms are analyzed and evaluated in this chapter in terms of the problems encountered, the strategies employed to solve these problems, and the effectiveness of the reforms. The chapter concludes by identifying the six lessons of Singapore's experience in implementing public sector reforms, from which other Asian countries can learn.

The ninth paper is about "Public Sector Reform and Governance in Thailand" by Pairote Pathranarakul. This paper examines concepts of governance and reform in the context of sustainable development. The author reviews current and past development strategies and the performance of national economic and social development plans with regards to development administration, changes and sustainability. This paper presents public sector reform and development emphasizing the strategies, progress and outcomes. The development and evolution of public sector reform are discussed and future challenges are addressed. The author proposes a new paradigm for public sector reform with the ultimate goal leading toward sustainability. In addition, the paper concludes that public sector reform and governance should aim for sustaining human well-being. The prime reform outcomes include a better quality of life, social integration, political stability, the eradication of inequalities in society, and the institutional capacity for crisis recovery.

The next paper presents "Reforming the Public Sector in Viet Nam" by Jairo Acuña-Alfaro and Do Thanh Huyen. Public sector reform in Viet Nam is a process that involves characteristics of a single-party-ruled, socialist country. It is large in terms of scale, scope and coverage, involving the entire state apparatus, not only the government as the executive branch. This paper addresses two components of ongoing public sector reforms in Viet Nam, including public administrative procedures and public service delivery. Although these services are increasingly more available, accessible and convenient for citizens, further reforms are needed to improve their quality of performance. Using a novel approach to capture citizens' experiences, this paper provides evidence that professionalism and modernization in public services are needed to enhance convenience of public services, competence of public service providers, and attitude of civil servants towards users of the public services. In addition, the paper argues that areas that need special attention include equitable and fair access for poorer ethnic minorities. In sum, with the support of objective data, the paper argues that an improved level of performance of the public sector in service provision will be achieved through greater involvement of non-state actors, and users of public sector services in the monitoring and evaluation process.

The last paper presents "Major Issues of Government Innovation in South Korea" by Pan Suk Kim and Kil Pyo Hong. During the era of old authoritarian regimes, the issues of reform or innovation were taboo. However, those terms are widely used nowadays as if they are the key to success in business and government. Previous governments that have attempted many reforms are those of Kim Young-Sam, Kim Dae-Jung, and Roh Moo-Hyun and this chapter attempts to review government reform and the methodologies executed during the Roh Moo-Hyun Government from 2003 to 2008. Among many issues, this case will especially look into the matter of government size and efficiency (logic and limits of government innovation based on a market-friendly structural reform, logic and limits of government innovation stressing on personnel and process), the issue of visible innovation and performance (the cost of government innovation, measuring outcome, and effectiveness of the time-lag and policies), and tasks to solve for a more sustainable government innovation (deriving an appropriate size of the government, developing measures for the self-regulating restructuring of the government, and reinforcing the theoretical foundation of government innovation).

All the papers present diverse public sector reform programs, as well as the challenges and bottlenecks to their effective implementation. There are many urgent tasks to transform public administration in developing countries. Major trajectories of public sector reform include civil service reform, anti-corruption initiatives, decentralization and local autonomy, corporatization or privatization, public financial and budgetary reform, regulatory reform (deregulation), informatization (electronic government), public enterprise reform, and public-private partnership (PPP). However, it may not be realistic for government to attempt to initiate all such reform measures at once. Government can choose some of them based on its capacity and a doable sequential framework or roadmap.

Introducing a reform program is relatively easy, but the most critical issue might be a question of how to effectively implement the target programs. In various developing countries, public sector reform has taken place over the years and well written reform documents have been produced. However, one of the most common issues is the fact that "implementation is the challenge." Implementation includes the realization of an application or execution of a new idea, plan, design, model, specification, standard, or policy. In order to effectively carry out a new policy, strong national leadership and political support are also very much needed for effective implementation. Governments need to give due attention to the successful achievements of set outcomes in the proposed reform. A lack of government follow-up has been cited as the main cause of poor performance. Following-up and monitoring are necessary actions in order to facilitate a positive outcome and to ensure that there is a spillover effect into other sectors. In sum, government or agency in charge of reform should take the following actions in order to make successful implementation of public sector reform: (1) share a sense of urgency or crisis, and be alert and proactive for public sector reform; (2) mobilize commitment through joint diagnosis of problems in the public sector by top leaders and key officials; (3) develop a shared vision and communicate the vision with stakeholders (officials, the citizens, the media, civil society, and politicians); (4) generate short-term wins of public sector reform; and (5) constantly evaluate progress of public sector reform measures and adjust the vision and the implementation approach as required.

In the journey towards sustainable public sector reform, governments could face a number of hindrances. Such hindrances for the implementation of public sector reform measures includes lack of adequate institutional capacity and professional skills. Therefore, first of all in the design of reform programs, governments need to set achievable targets rather than setting over ambitious programs that are doomed to fail. Secondly, central and local governments need to make sure that the necessary skills and capacity (i.e., capacity in individual, system, and organizational levels) should be created, or embedded, with a can-do spirit and ownership for sustainable further improvement. Innovative or creative ideas can be borrowed from many development partners and advanced countries, but implementation of such ideas is the sole responsibility of each country, agency in charge, or responsible agent. Lastly, top leader's clear vision and political leadership would also be significantly important for effective public sector reform and other national development programs in many developing countries.

References

ASEAN (2008). *ASEAN Statistical Yearbook*. Jakarta, Indonesia: ASEAN Secretariat.

ASEAN (various years). *Annual Report of ASEAN*. Jakarta, Indonesia: ASEAN Secretariat.

Kim, Pan Suk (2009). *Public Administration and Public Governance in ASEAN Member Countries and Korea*. Seoul: Daeyoung Moonhwasa Publishing Company.

Kim, Pan Suk (2010). *Civil Service System and Civil Service Reformin ASEAN Member Countries and Korea*. Seoul: Daeyoung Moonhwasa Publishing Company.

World Bank Independent Evaluation Group (2008). *Public Sector Reform: What Works and Why?* Washington, DC: World Bank.

Chapter 2 Reforming the Public Sector in Brunei

David Seth Jones

Introduction

Brunei has an extensive public sector, funded by revenue from oil and gas production which is by far the biggest sector of the economy. The dominant institution of the public sector is the civil service. Over the years, as it gradually expanded, the civil service acquired many of the features of a traditional government bureaucracy. These included an extensive payroll, a high degree of centralization, a proliferation of rules and procedures, multi-layered decision-making processes, and a great deal of documentation and paperwork. There was also a lack of strategic planning, little evaluation of performance or service delivery, and limited customer orientation. In addition, at the lower and middle levels of the civil service, operational responsibilities have been handicapped by a shortfall of professional and technical skills.

In recent years, reforms have been implemented to address some of these issues. They include the adoption of strategic planning by government ministries, a greater emphasis on customer service, and the implementation of e-Government. Also part of the reform program has been the reform of human resource practices, including the strengthening of the performance appraisal system, and the expansion of training at all levels of the civil service so as to address the shortfall in management, professional and technical skills. The most recent reform focuses on the streamlining of bureaucratic procedures for businesses. The implementation of the reforms has been patchy. Some have gained traction and resulted in genuine improvements others have had only a limited impact. In addition, there remains scope for further reform to address the shortcomings that continue to characterize the public sector.

The paper will examine the features of the society, economy government, administration and the public sector of Brunei. The paper will then consider the reforms mentioned above, assessing how effectively they have been implemented. It will consider the outstanding challenges that remain in terms of ensuring that the current reforms gain traction and that further reforms are introduced to meet the continuing shortcomings of the public sector.

Society and Economy of Brunei

The population of Brunei is just over 380,000. 67 percent are Malays, 13 percent Chinese, and 10 percent tribal groups with the remainder being expatriates. Brunei has a mixed economy, with the state actively promoting economic development. Many citizens enjoy a high standard of living, with a GDP per head of US$36,225 (US$48,200 at purchasing power parity), the second highest in Asia and slightly below that of Singapore (IMF, 2011a; ADB, 2010: 158). This is largely due to being endowed with large reserves of oil and gas relative to its population size. In addition, the high standard of living of the population is buttressed through an extensive system of social provision. This includes free or subsidized education, health care and housing and price subsidies applied to electricity, fuel, and certain staple food items. Due to the revenues from oil and gas, taxation remains low, the most notable feature of which is the exemption of income earners from personal income tax (Sainah, 2011). Over the last ten years, the Brunei government has assiduously accumulated foreign reserve and foreign asset holdings based on budget surpluses from oil and gas revenue. The foreign assets totaled US $30billion (250 percent of GDP) (Sovereign Wealth Fund Institute, 2011).

Although a modern, affluent society, Brunei has maintained a traditionally ascriptive culture rooted in of the predominant Malay community. Central to this are fine gradations of status based on customary titles and positions at the apex of which is the institution of the monarchy. Brunei has also retained a strong village culture based on close kinship ties, personal bonds and customary deference. At the heart of such traditions is a strong attachment to Islamic values and practices, with widespread observance amongst the Malay community of obligations of devotion, fasting and pilgrimage.

Government and Administration

The System of Government

The system of government in Brunei is monarchal, in which executive power is exercised by His Majesty the Sultan, mainly in his role as Prime Minister. To underline, his centrality to the affairs of state, the Sultan also occupies the portfolios for Finance and Defense. Day to day executive and policymaking responsibilities are undertaken by ministers who are the political heads of the ministries of the civil service. Alongside the executive, there exists a legislative council (LegCo), established in 2004. It consists of 29 members who are either ex-officio members (mainly by occupying a ministerial or senior government post) or appointed by the Sultan (Rosli, 2008; Brunei Resources [BR], 2005a; BG, 2011a). Although Legislative Council is essentially a consultative body, which cannot override executive policy, it is able in its deliberations to raise matters of public concern and draw them to the attention of ministers. It is also responsible for examining and approving the budget and supply bill.

The governing philosophy of Brunei is Melayu Islam Beraja (Malay Islamic Monarchy, commonly called MIB), which blends the monarchal principle of rulership with the upholding of Islamic values and laws, and the preservation of Malay language, culture and traditions. The MIB philosophy is applied in tandem with pragmatic commitments to economic development, administrative efficiency, and modern technology. It is the amalgam of these various element that shapes both the system of government and the wider political culture (BG, 2011b; Sainah, 2001; Othman, 2002).

Public Sector and Government Administration

As mentioned above, the public sector consists mainly of the civil service, comprising 13 ministries and employing 47,000 public servants (25 percent of the working population). Ministries are subdivided into departments and directorates, which number more than 90. In a few cases, ministries are first subdivided into divisions which are then subdivided into departments (BR, 2008). The status of departments varies. For historical reasons, some departments have their own budgets separate from that of the parent ministry, and in many respects, may operate independently of that ministry. These are known as full-pledged departments, examples being the Lands Department and the Public Works Department in the Ministry of Development. Other departments do not enjoy separate budgetary status, and are more closely linked to the parent ministry (BR, 2008).

Several quasi-government bodies also exist such as statutory corporations and government-owned companies, but these form only a minor part of the public sector (IMF, 2011a). Amongst them are the Brunei Economic Development Board, and the Brunei Monetary Authority (both statutory corporations), and the Brunei National Petroleum Company and Telekom Brunei Berhad (both government-owned companies). In addition, there are a number of public-private partnerships, in which the state collaborates with the private sector to promote investment and achieve development goals. The leading and most long standing example is Brunei Shell Petroleum (the main oil producing company), in which Royal Dutch Shell and the Brunei Government each hold 50 percent of the equity.

The civil service and the statutory corporations are well-funded through major revenue flows from the oil and gas industry. Government expenditure comprised about 40 percent of GDP in financial years 2009 and 2010, whilst revenues, which fluctuate from year to year as a result of variations in oil and gas prices, reached 57 percent of GDP in 2010. This is the highest level of public spending and revenue intake in Southeast Asia. More than 90 percent of public revenue is derived from the oil and gas industry (IMF, 2011a). The primary balance was +17 percent of GDP; but for the oil and gas revenue, this would be -28 percent of GDP (IMF, 2011a; IMF, 2011b: 23-26).

Policymaking and senior management are exercised by a well educated elite group of government officers consisting of administrative service officers and special duties officers who work in close collaboration with ministers in the government. Policymaking is undertaken at two levels. The Prime Minister's Office provides overall policy direction in key areas such as public finance, economic planning, energy, social welfare, crime and justice, and security, undertaken by specialist policy sections designated for each of these areas (Prime Minister's Office [PMO], 2011a). This dovetails with specific policymaking and rule drafting that is carried out within the ministries themselves, involving permanent secretaries, their deputies, and major divisional heads and their senior staff. Day to day management of operations and programs is handled by the middle managers in the departments etc., although many operational decision emanate from or are checked by senior administrators, as mentioned below (BR, 2005b; BR, 2005c; BR, 2008). The central responsibilities of financial and human resource management of the civil service are performed by the Treasury in the Ministry of Finance, and the Public Service Department within the Prime Minister's Office (in conjunction with Public Service Commission) respectively (Syohreni, 2008: 7-9).

There are three main organs of public accountability, which are located in the Prime Minister's Office, viz. the Public Service Commission, which is responsible for senior appointments, promotion and discipline in the civil service, the Audit Department, which performs mainly compliance and procedural audits on ministries and departments, and the Anti-Corruption Bureau (International Organization of Supreme Audit Institutions, 2001; Public Service Commission, 2011; Anti-Corruption Bureau, 2011).

The fulcrum of government administration is the Prime Minister's Office. Apart from being the central policymaking agency as mentioned above, it provides coordination for multi-sector programs, and directs the human resource management of the civil service through the Public Service Department. In addition, it monitors the performance and enforces the accountability of ministries and a department through the organs mentioned above, and initiates reforms of public management practices (PMO, 2011a).

Personnel Structure of the Civil Service

The Brunei civil service is divided hierarchically into various schemes of service. These consist of the administrative and diplomatic services, special duties officers, the executive service, various professional and specialist services, such as engineering, accounting, medicine, and education, and a number of support services.

Cross-cutting these services are vertical rankings called divisions ranging from Division 1, the most senior division, to the lowest which is Division 5. Division 1 is small elite of officers at the senior management and policy making levels. Only 2 percent of the government workforce is designated as Division 1 officers. They include heads of ministries, departments and sections. Amongst them are permanent secretaries, deputy permanent secretaries, and directors, director-generals, and commissioners together with their deputies and senior assistants (BR, 2005b; BR, 2008; IMF, 2011b: 18). Division 2 comprises other senior officers numbering 19 percent of government employees. This Division covers the senior ranks of the professional and specialist services and middle ranks of the administrative service, who occupy middle management positions. Division 3, totaling 24 percent of government employees, includes largely the bulk of supervisory staff, as well as a range of junior executive officers, qualified technical officers, administrators, and inspectors. Division 4 numbering nearly 26 percent of government employees, consists mainly of those involved in clerical work. The lowest stratum is Division 5 consisting of routine officers, junior clerks, and those in support services. This is the most numerous divisions, with over 29 percent of the government workforce (BR, 2005b; BR, 2008; IMF, 2011b: 19).

Appointments and promotions in the Brunei civil service are in part determined by merit, as measured by formal educational qualifications and the extent and type of training undergone. These prescribe the entry position of an officer, and also how far he/she may be promoted. However, recognition of merit criteria is balanced in promotional decisions by consideration for seniority in terms of years of service. Officers tend to move up the career ladder by age cohort, with the most senior positions occupied by those in their mid or late career. Given the respect for seniority, no formal scheme of fast-track promotion of so-called "high flyers" exists. In addition, ethnic influence also affects appointments and promotions with the preponderance of officers, including those in the senior ranks drawn from the predominant Muslim-Malay population. There are only a few senior officers drawn from the Chinese community, partly because it comprises only a small section of the Brunei population, and because its members who have a good education often prefer careers in the business sector.

At the heart of Brunei's civil service is the administrative service, which is a distinct and elite scheme of service at the upper level of Division 1. Administrative service officers are generalists who exercise senior management and policy making responsibilities. In terms of academic background they are drawn from a variety of disciplines including humanities and social sciences, business, administrative and policy studies, the sciences and engineering. Administrative officers are appointed to the administrative service, instead of being appointed or attached to a particular ministry, unlike their equivalent in Japan. In fact, during the course of their career, as discussed below, they move from one ministry to another on a frequent basis. Such mobility together with similarity of educational background, tenured employment, engagement in similar types and levels of responsibility, reinforced by a separate and clearly demarcated status, have instilled in the administrative service a shared set of values and a common professional identity (BR, 2005c).

The administrative service is stratified into four grade categories, with each category or grade within the category linked to a particular designation or level responsibility. The lowest category consists of the introductory grades (Administrative Officer Grade 1 and Administrative Officer Special Grade) to which new entrants into the Service are appointed. Above them is the Superscale category, consisting of four grades from Superscale C to Superscale Special. Above the Superscale category is the Group category, comprising three grades. The most senior category is the Permanent Secretary or Grade category, consisting of four grades from Deputy Permanent Secretary to Permanent Secretary (Grade A) (BR, 2005c).

Although there is no formal fast-track promotion as mentioned above, as a matter of practice, most administrative service officers are able to ascend the promotional ladder from the entry grade to the most senior grade in the Group category over a period of 25 years. Many of them will reach this grade before the age of 50. The interval between promotions ranges from 5 years at the lower level to 3 years for the higher posts. Although regular upward movement between and within the Basic, Superscale and Group categories can be expected, thereafter the process becomes more selective, with only the most able chosen to enter the so-called Grade category comprising Deputy Secretary and various levels of Permanent Secretary (BR, 2005c).

On top of satisfactory job performance, the key determinants of promotion of an administrative service officer are the years of service in particular grades, the number of postings in different departments, and attendance at two executive training courses (the last mentioned being required milestones in an officer's career path). Promotion is also facilitated by the fact that grades are not necessarily linked to posts, with the result that any post can encompass more than one grade. Thus an officer's promotion does not always depend upon a vacancy arising in a particular post (BR, 2005c). Whilst most administrative service officers began their career in the service on leaving university, a number of promising officers have been appointed from other schemes of service, such as the engineering and educational services. Although lessening the exclusive nature of the administrative service, mid-career entry has widened the pool of talented and suitable manpower that may be assigned to policy making and senior management roles. Another feature of the career of an administrative service officer is the frequency with which he/she is moved from one ministry or department to another. In the first five years officers may be expected to occupy twelve different posts in different sections and departments, so acquiring a wide ambit of experience (BR, 2005c).

The administrative service exercises crucial influence upon the formulation and administration of policy throughout the different ministries, especially by those officers who are permanent secretaries and deputy secretaries. Administrative service officers below this level, such as directors, as mentioned above, are engaged in policy work too, as well as being responsible for senior level operational matters. Administrative service officers are found in all ministries, working alongside officers of the professional and departmental services, and are normally concentrated in the headquarters and policy planning units of the ministries (BR, 2005c).

In light of the nature and diversity of their work and the frequency with which they are moved from one post to another, administrative service officers can be regarded as generalists, often dealing with matters in which they do not have a trained specialization. In doing so, they may exercise the intellectual abilities of the good all-round generalist, quickly understanding the essential issues, exercising analytical and problem solving skills, and adopting a comprehensive overview of a complex problem. In addition, they often come to possess a breadth of understanding of the policy issues and administrative procedures in government administration, acquired from working in different postings.

The generalist character of senior administration in Brunei is reinforced by the wide spectrum of academic disciplines in which administrative service officers were educated, which includes humanities, social sciences, business studies, law, engineering and science. The Brunei government has avoided the tendency to favor certain disciplines, such as engineering and law, in making senior appointments. This has been evident in some countries, examples being Singapore and Japan.

It should be pointed out that the administrative service does not monopolize the senior management and policymaking positions in the civil service. Occasionally, officers outside the administrative service are appointed to such positions, being designated as special duties officers. The grade structure for these officers is similar to that of the administrative service, although they are noguaranteed the same career advancement as their counterparts in the administrative service. The appointment of special duty officers to the positions mentioned above further adds to the diversity of backgrounds and specialisms at the senior echelons of the Brunei civil service (BR, 2005c).

Recent Reforms of the Public Sector

The Need for Reform

As mentioned in the introduction, the civil service has retained many of the features of a traditional government bureaucracy. These include a high degree of centralization, a proliferation of rules and multi-layered procedures, a great deal of documentation and paperwork, and often protracted processes of decision-making and task implementation. At the middle and lower levels of the civil service, operational performance has been handicapped by a lack of performance incentives, and shortfalls of professional and technical skills. Further failings in the past have been the absence of strategic planning in ministries and departments, little evaluation of their performance and service delivery, limited customer orientation, and the continuation of traditional practices in financial management. As a result, a number of reforms have been or are in the process of being implemented to address these shortcomings and to create a civil service reflecting internationally recognized standards of good governance.

Strategic Planning

One of these reforms was the introduction of strategic planning. From 2003, each ministry and department was required to formulate its own strategic plan. This identified its background, mission, objectives, core business, key initiatives (both current and future), and stakeholders. The plan provided clarification of long-term aspirations, overall purpose and specific roles, which then could be aligned with the national vision as outlined in successive National Development Plans. The strategic plans also indicate policy making and operational processes which require coordination between different ministries and departments, or which could be integrated or reduced due to overlapping or inter related responsibilities (Abas, 2005: 4; MSD, 2007a: 11-12). Essentially, the strategic plans provide a framework to facilitate co-operation between ministries and departments, to reduce duplication and unnecessary work, and to improve public services by identifying the needs of stakeholders and clients.

Customer Orientation

Another key reform has been the Client's Charter, drawn up in 1998. This sets out a framework to guide the way civil servants deal with members of the public on a day-to-day basis. The emphasis is on customer orientation, whereby services to members of the public are delivered in a timely, transparent and empathetic way, taking into account individual needs and circumstances on a case by case basis. As part of the Client's Charter, departments are expected to provide the public with clear guidelines on how forms are to be completed, not to reject incomplete or inaccurately completed forms but to obtain the missing or relevant information in a follow up inquiry, and to set time targets for completing certain procedures. What's more, counter staff are expected to be informative and helpful to members of the public, and to undergo such training in the basic skills required in this role (Abas, 2005: 4; Desar, 2005: 6; MSD, 2007b: 1-16). An example of the emphasis on individual needs under the Client's Charter is provided by the Special Needs Education program of the Ministry of Education. It produces individual progress report on each special needs student, tailors teaching materials and examinations to be compatible with each type of special need, provides individual therapy sessions, and arranges consultation sessions with parents (Ministry of Education, 2010).

To further the objective of the Client's Charter, the Management Services Department, which is in the Prime Minister's Office undertakes research on how administrative reforms can be implemented to improve service delivery, and provides a feedback channel by which the public can convey complaints about public services, which are forwarded to the relevant ministry (MSD, 2011; Desar, 2005: 5-6; Abas, 2005: 7).

To ensure that the momentum in the application of the Client's Charter is maintained, the Client's Charter Auditing Program of

2003 was established, followed by the creation of a Steering Committee on Service Delivery to the Public in 2007. This was a response to the continuing dissatisfaction about the quality of services to the public, which have been voiced in letters to the local press, in direct communications with ministers and officials, and through the feedback channel in the Management Services Department. A particular concern for the Steering Committee, which it seeks to address, are delays in processing applications which involve more than one agency such as occupancy permit application once a building has been constructed, and various business licensed applications, as discussed below (MSD, 2007a: 12-13).

Reforms in Human Resource Management

Another key area of reform in the civil service has been the upgrading of human resource practices with the aim of rewarding merit, and overcoming shortfalls in the competencies and motivation of staff especially at the operational level. This began with the introduction in 1988 of performance appraisal for all grades of officer. The performance appraisal system was enhanced in 1997 by the use of separate forms for management and professional level officers (Division 1 and 2), supervisory and technical officers (Division 3) and operational officers (Divisions 4 and 5).

The appraisal consists of a questionnaire which is completed by the appraising officer, followed by an interview with the appraisee. During the interview, the appraisee can read the comments and ratings made the appraising officer, with an opportunity to reply and indicate agreement or non-agreement. The duly completed appraisal form is then checked for fairness and accuracy by an officer above the level of the appraising officer. Amendments may be made before itis counter-signed by this officer (Normasidah, 2007: 31-32). The appraisal covers a wide range of traits; the importance of each in the appraisal depends upon the level of responsibility of the officer being appraised. For example in the appraisal of management and professional level officers, traits which are important to effective job performance at this level figure prominently in the appraisal. These include knowledge of job, effectiveness of work output and work quality, integrity, supervisory/management ability, problem solving and decision-making abilities, and initiative and innovativeness (MSD, 2007a: 9-10; Normasidah, 2007: 32).

Certain features of the appraisal system are worth noting. One is its open nature, based on the requirements that the appraisee sees the comments and ratings, as mentioned above, and responds accordingly, and discusses various aspects of his/her performance in an interview with the appraising officer. Another feature is the use of percentage ratings for each of the traits on which the appraisee is being assessed, with the average percentage rating taken as his/her overall appraisal score. Percentage scoring is intended to make the appraisal more precise and objective, so that in theory at least high and low performers can be differentiated. A third feature is the use of the appraisal to identify the training needs of the appraisee and to determine the types of training courses from which he/she could benefit (Normasidah, 2007: 32, Public Service Department [PSD], 2011).

To upgrade their competencies and create a strong core of professionalism in the civil service, government officers are required to undergo regular training throughout their career. For most civil servants 100 hours of training per years is mandated. Much of the training, but not all, is provided by the Civil Service Institute (Institut Perkhidmatan Awam, commonly called IPA), which offers a range of courses to enhance management and administrative competencies of different grades of civil servant including senior officers. Typically the courses cover such areas as total quality management, quality control circles, six sigma practices, project management, information systems, and office automation. Each course is targeted to a cohort of civil servants from a particular personnel division (IPA, 2009). IPA is in the Prime Minister's Office, as is the Management Services Department which undertakes research on how administrative reforms can be implemented to improve service delivery (MSD, 2009).

Furthermore, senior and middle managers, mainly administrative service, special duties officers, and senior officers in the professional and specialist services, are required during their career to take an executive training course conducted at the Institute of Leadership, Innovation and Advancement (ILIA) in the Universiti Brunei Darussalam. One course is taken by officers in senior management positions and another by those in middle management positions. Each course exposes the participants to the most recent practices and reforms in policy-making and public management, and entails the completion of research assignments and joint class projects, all relating to policy issues affecting the civil service, economy and society of Brunei. The course is a required stepping stone to further promotion. On completing the course, the middle managers can move up into the Superscale category and the senior managers into the group category (BR, 2005c; ILIA, 2011).

e-Government

In response to its widely acknowledged benefits, e-Government has now become a central priority in the reform agenda of the Brunei government. The benefits include improving public access to a wide range of information concerning public policy and government agencies, and facilitating transactional processes involving the public. This allows applications, claims, returns, inquiries and payments to be submitted and processed on-line. Through e-Government, feedback from the public on matters of policy and public services can be solicited. Within the civil service itself, it can enable information to be gathered and stored on-line, and readily accessed by all ministries and departments through an intranet system.

A commitment was made in 2000 to establish e-Government in Brunei, with an investment commitment of just under Brunei $1 billion (US$700 million) (Abas, 2005: 5-6). Since then limited progress has been made to implement e-Government. A great deal of information has been digitalized, an example being property title registrations by the Lands Department, and ministries and departments have their own web sites. However through those web sites the range of information disseminated, including statistical data, remains modest.

A number of other e-Government initiatives have been started in recent years, which deserve mention. One of them is TAFIS (Treasury Accounting and Financial System) introduced in 2004. This is an on-line function for processing invoices, bills, and payments (including salaries and wages) and for processing and presenting the accounts for each ministry (Abas, 2005: 6). Another initiative is the e-Customs system, established in 2006. It consists of a number of modules, providing on-line services which both businesses and the Royal Customs and Excise Department can avail of. Amongst these are the registration of importers and exporters, submission and processing of import and export applications, submission of cargo manifests, and notification of clearance approvals to importers, shippers and customs officials at the wharfs. The e-Customs system provides too for automatic valuations of import cargoes and calculation of duties payable, which can be automatically sent to the importer, with a facility for electronic payments and receipt issue (Royal Customs and Excise Department, 2011).

Currently being implemented in its pilot stage is the Government Employee Management System (GEMS), which is an internal on-line human resource management system. Through GEMS, civil servants can apply for various benefits, leave and enrollment in training courses, track the stage reached in the processing of the application, and ascertain whether approval has been given. Job applicants can too submit their applications and curriculum vitae on-line. Where necessary requests and applications are automatically forwarded where processing and approval involves different layers and departments. Moreover, it enables appraisal reports and other information about staff to be uploaded, and the data base for each officer to be accessed by all ministries and departments. The intention is to shorten the time taken to submit and handle requests and applications, reduce the steps and paper work required, and to facilitate the retrieval of data in timely and convenient way (PSD, 2011).

Despite the commitments and initiatives already mentioned, much more remains to be done to accomplish a fully operational system of e-Government. The limited progress in implementing e-Government has meant that, as indicated below, much red-tape and time consuming procedures remain in the day to day administration of government agencies. This has given rise to a revamped e-Government plan, known as the e-Government Strategic Plan, 2009-2014, intended to expedite the measures to put e-Government on a more comprehensive footing (PMO, 2011b). The need to expedite e-Government will be considered below as a major reform challenge facing the Brunei government.

Streamlining Business Regulation Processes: the Integrated Business Licensing System

Up to recently, one shortcoming in government administration which had not been tackled, were unwieldy and protracted regulatory procedures that affect doing business. Investors in Brunei have not found regulatory procedures to be amenable to doing business in a number of areas, the most serious being starting a business, and acquiring property rights. This has been a matter of growing concern, being cited as one of the reasons for the slowness in achieving a more diversified economy, the lack of foreign direct investment especially for medium sized businesses and the continuing weakness of the private sector.

In acquiring business registration for starting a business, there is much red-tape that investors have encountered in terms of multiple procedures to follow and approvals or licenses to obtain, as well as extensive paper work and form filling to complete. The World Bank Doing Business survey of 2011 found that there were 15 procedures to follow in starting a business, not counting procedures which are industry specific (such as those in the food industry and construction sector). With so many procedures and approvals required, inevitably delays occurred. According to the same survey, it took 105 days to register a business in the three previous years the figure was 116 days (see Table 1). Brunei's global ranking for ease in starting a business declined from 117 out 178 countries, to 153 out of 183 countries between 2008 and 2010, but did improve to 133 out of 183 countries in 2011 though this is still a low ranking (see Table 1). Brunei's global ranking for overall ease in starting a business has like wise declined each year from 78 out of 178 countries in 2008 to 112 out of 183 countries in 2011 (though the latter figure was a small improvement on the ranking of 117 in 2010) (see Table 1). These measures and rankings suggest that there is scope for significant further improvements in streamlining procedures and cutting red-tape for business start ups. Likewise with respect to renewal of licenses each year, and updating particulars relating to a license, the procedures and paper work involved could be readily reduced (World Bank, 2011).

Table 1. Ease of Doing Business in Brunei Darussalam, 2008-2011

Year	Ease of Doing Business (Rank)	No. of Economies	Starting a Business (Rank)	No. of Days to Start a Business
2008	78	178	117	116
2009	88	181	130	116
2010	117	183	152	116
2011	112	183	133	105

Sources: World Bank (2007; 2008; 2009; 2010).

In response, the government of Brunei is currently implementing reforms to reduce impediments and curtail red-tape in starting and continuing a business by introducing the Business Licensing System (BLS). Although the BLS does not decrease the number of approvals/licenses needed, it allows applications to be processed concomitantly rather than sequentially, reduces the amount of form filling and paper work, and obviates the necessity for managers to visit several government agencies. This is achieved by requiring businesses to complete just a single umbrella business licensing form which can be submitted on line through a single window or one stop shop. This portal is then linked to various government agencies which can then process the application. Likewise, renewal of license and updating particulars of the business relevant to the licenses can be undertaken through the same on line window. It is expected that the various phases in setting up BLS will be completed by the end of 2011 (Ministry of Industry and Primary Resources, 2011).

Combating Corruption

In 1982, the Anti-Corruption Bureau (ACB) was established as a specialist agency to combat corruption. Much of its work has of course involved investigating alleged cases of corruption.

However, in 2003, preventing corruption became a priority as well, with the creation of the Community Relations and Support Services Section, now called the Prevention, Community Relations and Education Division. A key part of its remit is to enhance public awareness of and instill an aversion to corrupt practices. This is undertaken by two units within the division, viz. the Media and Community Relations Unit and the Education and Development Unit, with the focus on training civil servants, educating the public, using the mass media, and disseminating anti-corruption messages through a range of publications. The target groups are front-line civil servants, the youth of Brunei particularly students, village leaders members of non-government and even business organizations in the private sector (MSD, 2007a: 15; ACB, 2011). The centerpiece of the prevention strategy is outreach to schools and colleges undertaken by the Education and Development Unit. It conducts talks and dialogue sessions with students, teachers, and parent-teachers associations, and hosts visits from schools and colleges. It too has developed a component of the national curriculum focusing on corruption, drafting teaching materials and work books for this purpose. These are carefully targeted to the level of understanding of particular age groups of children (ACB, 2011).

Reform Challenges

Substantial scope exists to promote further reform in the Brunei public sector. This entails either: (1) extending or reinforcing reform initiatives already started, but remain too restricted or have not up to the present been satisfactorily implemented, or (2) introducing reforms to address shortcomings of government administration not yet covered in the reform agenda.

Extending e-Government

Although there have been a number of initiatives, progress to create a comprehensive system of e-Government has been slow. This prompted His Majesty, the Sultan, to deliver a Titah in 2010 expressing his concern thus:

> I allowed the implementation of the e-Government strategy since 2000 with a budget of B$1 billion. However, its use so far is still unsatisfactory. Similarly, IT applications, which are to facilitate the public's dealings with the government, are also unsatisfactory, when compared with other countries in the region (PMO, 2011c).

The lack of progress in adopting e-Government is reflected in the scores given to Brunei in the the United Nations Public Administration Programme e-Government Survey Report of 2010. For the main portal, the report accorded Brunei 37 out of a maximum of 138 points, one point given out of 44 for transaction services, and 16 out of 61 for information services. The portals of the individual ministries surveyed fared even worse. For information services, only a few points were awarded (between 2 and 5 out of a maximum of 11; for transaction service hardly any points were awarded. Brunei's overall e-Government ranking was a little more favorable than the above scores suggest being 68th out of 192 countries. However, Brunei still lags significantly behind Singapore ranked 11th with a score of 0.75, Malaysia ranked 32,nd with a score of 0.60, and South Korea, the leading country in the index, with a score of 0.88 please add 0(zero). Brunei's score and rank are just above those of Thailand and Philippines, and its rank is still below what it achieved in 2003 (55th position) (Crosby, 2008; United Nations Public Administration Network, 2010; Borneo Bulletin, 2009).

Further improvements in information services and transactional facilities are needed in three main areas of e-Government, viz. Government-Government, Government-

Citizen, Government-Business. The last mentioned will be further discussed below. One of these areas is e-procurement which has hitherto not been introduced although well-established in neighboring countries. This would involve setting up a procurement portal to disseminate procurement laws and bidding regulations, to publish bid opportunities, to download pre-qualification questionnaires, and bidding documents, to enable on-line registration, pre-qualification and bid submissions, and to announce bid outcomes.

The Need for Continued Streamlining of Business Regulations

A further challenge is the continuing obstacle to doing business posed by bureaucratic regulation, delay and inefficiency. In fact, amongst businesses in Brunei surveyed by the World Economic Forum in 2010, "inefficient government bureaucracy" was listed a third most serious problem impeding doing business (World Economic Forum, 2011: 108). Thus it is necessary to sustain the streamlining of businesses regulations and procedures, which, as mentioned above, began in 2011 through the introduction of BLS. Whilst the BLS is a genuine effort to facilitate the business sector in Brunei, its success depends upon how quickly the various government departments with licensing responsibilities respond to on-line applications for business licenses and registration, and make full use of the on line BLS system. In addition, there remains scope for reducing the number of licenses required for a business to be legally registered. Besides, other aspects of doing business where government regulations and bureaucratic procedures (and also judicial procedures) are still an impediment such as the enforcement of contracts, granting of exports and import permits, and acquiring property rights remain to be addressed.

Reinforcing Implementation of the Client's Charter

The Client's Charter of 1998 and the Client's Charter Auditing

Program of 2003, mentioned above, were significant steps in creating a more customer-oriented public sector. However, the progress in implementation has been limited. The Management Services Department, mandated to carry out the audit in 2003, has reviewed only a few departments to determine what steps have been taken and what impact has been achieved in implementing the Client's Charter. In those that have been audited, only two have achieved a 70 percent compliance with the measures prescribed under the charter. This prompted His Majesty the Sultan in 2010 to state: "The implementation of the client's charter needs to be activated because it is on the government agenda. It is also important to substantiate whether the client's charter is running smoothly and satisfactorily or whether it still has flaws" (PMO, 2011c).

Improving the Implementation of the Performance Appraisal System

As mentioned above, the performance appraisal system has become well-established and major improvements have been made to the appraisal questionnaire. However, weaknesses in implementation have become evident. The main one is the widely followed practice of awarding high or moderately high performance ratings to most staff. This is partly due to the value placed on conflict avoidance and the presence of a unified ethos and continuity of tenure in the civil service. These are underpinned by networks of personal and family ties in the civil service, which are inevitable in view of the large numbers it employs out of avery small working population. Indeed, it is the norm for several members of a family to be employed in the civil service. Further influencing the ratings given to staff is the link between the appraisal and the award of the end of year one month bonus, which depends on achieving a certain overall grade. Given the strong ties, the value placed on work place harmony, and a strong sense of entitlement, ratings are often given with the primary intention of ensuring appraisees receive their bonus. In consequence, the appraisal often does not reflect the variation in ability and motivation amongst staff. As such, it does not serve as an incentive for better performance and fails to provide an adequate basis for promotion based on merit.

Moreover, feedback given by a number of civil servants indicates that some appraising officers do little preparation before an appraisal, and simply follow the appraisal rating and comments made in the previous year, without any thorough review of the performance of staff. The failings of appraising officers are compounded by the dearth of training in conducting appraisals and completing appraisal questionnaires. Another concern is that the appraisal questionnaire is not sufficiently tailored to the specific needs of particular jobs and is largely based on generic measures to assess performance. All this further compounds the mismatch between the ratings given and the performance of staff (Normasidah, 2007).

Strengthening Efforts to Combat Corruption

Whilst corruption is less than in other countries of Southeast Asia (with the exception of Singapore) and the ACB has been diligent and well-focused in combating it, there is scope to enhance anti-corruption laws. One weak area is the absence of legal provisions covering conflicts of interest. Such provisions would require senior officials to declare conflicts of interest in government tenders or in appointments and promotions, and to be excluded from the decision-making process, or to divest of business portfolio where conflict of interest might arise. This is all the more important in view of close family and personal connections within the civil service and between it and outside organizations so as to avoid the risk of nepotism and cronyism. The increased emphasis on meritocracy has though helped to limit family and personal influences. Another weakness is the absence of measures that would enable the ACB to track life-style changes in government officers (which is often evidence of enrichment through bribes and embezzlement), and also to protect whistleblowers who are prepared to divulge information about corrupt dealings.

Reducing the Size of the Civil Service and Decreasing Red-Tape

With a payroll at 25 percent of the workforce, the civil service remains bloated. Whilst it absorbs the surplus in the labor market, expenditure on manpower constitutes an excessive drain on public resources which could be diverted to internal investment. In addition, either as a cause or an effect of such a large payroll, the internal operations and street level services are often characterize by protracted procedures, multi-layered approvals, and extensive and duplicate documentation. Thus, it may be appropriate in the foreseeable future to focus on creating a leaner and more efficient civil service, with less red-tape and more streamlined procedures. One option would be to undertake an audit of all regulations and procedures and to eliminate those which are no longer necessary or which duplicate others. A related reform is to review all jobs, and then identify those with related or substantially overlapping tasks and those in which the tasks are no longer necessary. This could be followed by eliminating tasks and paperwork which are unnecessary and combining jobs with related or overlapping tasks.

However, downsizing the civil service crucially depends on the diversification of the economy and the expansion of the private sector. This would allow school and university leavers in particular, who had hitherto looked to the civil service for employment, to find a job within a private business or public-private partnership. However, given the continuing constraints on private investment, it is likely that any downsizing would have to be a gradual process.

Autonomy and Corporatization

As mentioned above, the public sector in Brunei is highly centralized. This is due to the small size of the quasi-government sector consisting of partially autonomous corporate entities such as statutory authorities and government-owned companies. At the moment, only a handful of such bodies exist. It may be thus suggested that the many professional, regulatory, and technical services, presently provided by ministries and departments, but which require autonomy and flexibility, could be undertaken by statutory authorities. Examples are the services provided by the Lands and Surveys Departments, Brunei, Investment Agency and the Brunei Investment Authority. In addition, agencies such as the Electrical Department, the Post Office, and Water Department, which provide commercial services, could likewise be converted to statutory authorities, and eventually restructured as government-owned companies. As separate corporate entities, such agencies would be free from the constraints of centrally managed budgets and the need to obtain disbursement approvals from the Treasury. They would have flexibility in adapting their internal management structures and in determining their operational priorities. Furthermore, autonomy would be enjoyed in hiring and promoting staff, and setting terms and conditions of employment separate from those of the civil service.

Financial Management

Brunei has retained a traditional system of financial management. Budget allocations within ministries and departments are centrally determined by the Treasury in the Ministry of Finance. It controls spending within ministries and departments, including the apportionment of budget funds amongst different programs, and the transfer of funds from one program to another in the financial; year. Payments to contractors and suppliers and payroll remunerations are processed and approved by the Treasury. Sometimes even minor disbursements require Treasury approval. In addition, traditional cash accounting is still practiced and ministries and departments cannot retain any unspent budget allocation.

A number of reforms in the financial management of the Brunei civil service may be considered. One is to introduce en bloc budgeting, in which ministries and departments would have discretion in apportioning their budgets and transferring funds from one program to another, as well as in processing and approving their own disbursements.

Another reform is the adoption of accrual accounting to replace the conventional cash-based accounting. Accrual accounting, commonplace in private businesses, recognizes non-cash expenditures. These include depreciation costs, capital costs (i.e. the loss of the opportunity to invest money allocated to ministries), imputedrental costs (the loss of the opportunity to lease space occupied by a government office on the rental market), and the recording of expenditure in the years in which goods have been acquired, and services and works undertaken, even though payment may be made in the previous or in subsequent financial year(s). The benefit of accrual accounting is to give civil service managers a true picture of the full cost of day-to-day operations. If accrual accounting was applied in the Brunei civil service, such benefits would give permanent secretaries and departmental heads a more accurate knowledge of costs and thus a greater measure of control over expenditure.

A further reform would be to give ministries and departments an opportunity to retain part of any surplus they have achieved from their budget allocation, as in Singapore. As is conventional practice, any unspent budget allocation to a ministry or department is simply returned to the consolidated revenue account. As a result, spending throughout the year continues to be "lumpy" and uneven. In 2009/10, quarterly spending ranged from a low of 16 percent of yearly total in the first quarter to a high of 37 percent in the fourth quarter. In the two intervening quarters, spending ranged between 24 percent and 23 percent (IMF, 2011a: 25-26). This has been the pattern in previous financial years. A key reason for the biggest share of spending to be undertaken in the fourth quarter is the requirement for ministries and departments, as in many other states, to return unspent allocations to the consolidated fund at the end of the financial year.

Conclusion

The recent reforms implemented in the Brunei public sector and the possible future reforms were and will be shaped by the necessity to downsize the civil service, streamline and decentralize government administration, and create a more prominent quasi-government sector. This involves replacing a highly bureaucratic and centralized system by onethat allows autonomy, minimizes red tape and the burden of regulation, and embraces private sector and customer-oriented practices. Yet major impediments remain to achieving these goals.

One impediment is the small size of the private sector, which at the moment, as mentioned above, is not able to generate the job opportunities to absorb the labor market surplus arising from any downsizing of the civil service. Any reduction in the payroll would of necessity be gradual and be linked to the expansion of job opportunities in the private sector. A second impediment is the lack of private capital to enable the creation of government-linked companies. Such companies are important in the shift to a more decentralized and business oriented public sector.

The third impediment is weaknesses in the implementation of some of the reforms. Whilst commitments are made and initiatives announced, all too often there is insufficient follow up action to ensure the intended results are obtained. Feedback from government officers to the author have highlighted this failure. In fact His Majesty the Sultan expressed concern on this matter stated in a Titah to mark National Day 2010: We want plans to be actually carried out according to schedule, and not merely planned on paper. For example, if there are plans to build a school or mosque, sometimes the causes for delay were due to impediments relating to land regulations, land that has yet to be gazetted and so on.

The Sultan continued:

> If these are the causes, then does this not involve the government? If the government itself has the will, then surely the problem should not be as complicated anymore. But the delay still occurs, why? Are we actually serious or not? If the delay is within the lower hierarchy are the upper level officials willing to "come down to the field" to negotiate? (PMO, 2011c; Ubaidillah, 2010).

In light of the Sultan's Titah, two reasons may be given to explain patchy implementation of the reforms. One reason may be the perception of civil servants at the management and operational level in the Brunei civil service that they have a stake in preserving the status quo. Thus, they may not have the motivation to engage in the types of concrete and sustained action necessary for effective implementation. This attests to Kelman's theory that change in public organizations rests upon the existence of dissatisfaction with the status quo amongst front-line employees. Without that dissatisfaction, resistance may arise amongst such employees that can readily nullify the impact of the reforms (Kelman, 2005).

The second reason for weak implementation of the reforms is that the shortcomings in the civil service which certain of the reforms have sought or may in the future seek to address, may themselves be impediments to implementation. It is evident that that the plethora of rules under which decisions are made (each of which could be an obstacle), lack of coordination between ministries and departments, protracted decision making processes, and multi-layered procedures (where even minor issues are referred up the line even to the highest reaches of government for decision or endorsement) may all undermine or delay the implementation process.

References

Abas, S. (2005). Reform Initiativesin the Civil Service of Brunei Darussalam, paper presented to the Commonwealth Advanced Seminar, Wellington, New Zealand, 21 February-4 March.

Anti-Corruption Bureau (2011). *Background*, Brunei; Brunei Government: Available at http://www.anti-corruption.gov.bn.

Asian Development Bank (2010). *Key Indicators for Asia and the Pacific 2010*(41st ed.), Manila: Asian Development Bank.

Borneo Bulletin (2009). Progress of E-government Initiatives in Brunei Darussalam, *Borneo Bulletin*, 7 November.

Brunei Government (2011a). *System of Government*, Brunei: Brunei Government: Available at http://brunei.gov.bn/government/.

Brunei Government (2011b). *National Philosophy*, Brunei: Brunei Government: Available at http:// brunei.gov.bn/government/.

Brunei Resources (2005a). *The Legislative Council: Majlis Mesyuarat Negara*, Brunei: Brunei Resources.com: Available at http://www.bruneiresources.com.

Brunei Resources (2005b). *The Brunei Civil Service: An Introduction*, Brunei: Brunei Resources.com: Available at http://www.bruneiresources.com.

Brunei Resources (2005c). *The Brunei Civil Service Explanatory Notes on Senior Administrative Officer and Special Duties Officer*,

Brunei: Brunei Resources.com: Available at http://www.bruneiresources.com.

Brunei Resources (2008). *The Brunei Civil Service: Heads of Government Ministries and Departments*, Brunei: Brunei Resources.com: Available at http://www.bruneiresources.com.

Crosby, Mark (2008). *Research Project on Economic Diversification: Summary Report*, Brunei: Centre for Strategic and Policy Studies.

Desar, D. S. (2005). Civil Service Reform and its Challenges: A Case Study of Brunei Darussalam, paper presented to the Commonwealth Advanced Seminar, Wellington New Zealand, 21 February - 4 March.

IMF (2011a). *IMF Executive Board Concludes 2011 Article IV Consultation with Brunei*, Public Information Notice No. 09/74, Washington: IMF.

IMF (2011b). *Brunei Darussalam: Statistical Appendix*, IMF Country Report No. 9/142, Washington: IMF.

Institut Perkhidmatan Awam (2009). *Training Programme*, Brunei: Prime Minister's Office: Available at http://www.ipa.gov.bn.

Institute for Leadership, Innovation and Advancement (2011). *2011 Executive Development Programme for Senior Government Officers*, Brunei: Universiti Brunei Darussalam.

International Organization of Supreme Audit Institutions (2001). *Mandates of Supreme Audit Institutions: Brunei Darussalam*, Vienna: International Organization of Supreme Audit Institutions: Available at http://www.intosaiitaudit.org/ mandates.

Management Services Department (2007a). Country Paper of Brunei Darussalam: Brunei Darussalam's Initiatives toward Developing a Corporate Culture in its Public Service, paper presented to 14th ASEAN Conference on Civil Service Matters, Bali, Indonesia, 29-31 October.

Management Services Department (2007b), Client's Charter—Towards a More Transparent and Accountable Public Service (Brunei Darussalam's Experience), paper presented to 14th ASEAN Conference on Civil Service Matters, Bali, Indonesia, 29-31 October.

Management Services Department (2011). *Tasks and Responsibilities*, Brunei: Prime Minister's Office: Available at http://www.msd.gov.bn/task.htm.

Ministry of Education (2010). *Special Education Unit: Programmes*

& Support Services, Brunei: Ministry of Education: Available at http://www.moe.edu.bn/ web/moe/dept/ coreedu/seu/ progs.

Ministry of Industry and Primary Resources (2011). *Business Licensing System*, Brunei: Author: Brunei: Author http://www.business.gov.bn/.

Normasidah, Abdul Majid (2007). *An Assessment of Performance Appraisal System in Brunei Darussalam's Civil Service: A Case Study at Selected Government Departments*, Unpublished Master of Public Policy Case Study, Universiti Brunei Darussalam.

Othman, Azlan (2008). Govt to Make It Easy to Do Business in Brunei, *Borneo Bulletin*, 12 November.

Prime Minister's Office (2011a). *Prime Minister's Office: About PMO*, Brunei: Government of Brunei: Available at http://pmo.gov.bn/government.

Prime Minister's Office (2011b). *E-Government Strategic Plan, 2009-2014*, Brunei: Government of Brunei: Available at http://www.pmo.gov.bn/pmo1/.

Prime Minister's Office (2011c). *Titah 2010*, Brunei: Author: Available at http://www. pmo. gov.bn /pmo1/.

Public Service Department (2011). *About GEMS: GEMS Functionalities*, Brunei: Brunei Government: Available at http://jpa.gov.bn/gems.

Rosli, Sobrina (2008). A Primer on the Legislative Council of Brunei, *Brunei Times*, 4 March.

Royal Customs and Excise Department (2010). *E-Customs*, Brunei: Ministry of Finance: Available at http://www.mof.gov.bn/English/RCE/Pages/eCustoms.aspx.

Sainah, Hajah Saim (2001). *The Administrative System of Brunei Darussalam: Management, Accountability and Reform*, Brunei: Universiti Brunei Darussalam.

Sainah, Hajah Saim (2011). Social Protection Arrangements in Brunei Darussalam, Faculty of Business, Economics and Policy Studies Discussion Papers, Brunei: University of Brunei.

Sovereign Wealth Fund Institute (2011). *Brunei Investment Agency*, Roseville, CA: Sovereign Wealth Fund Institute: Available at http://swfinstitute.org.

Syohreni, Adi (2008). Recruitment in the Public Sector of Brunei Darussalam: Policy Issues and the Socio-cultural Influences on Employee Recruitment, Unpublished Master of Public Policy Case Study, Universiti Brunei Darussalam.

Ubaidillah, Masli (2010). Carry out government projects on time, *The Brunei Times*, 23 February.

United Nations Public Administration Network (2010). *E-Government Development Knowledge Base*, New York: United Nations Public Administration Network: Available at http:// www2.unpan.org/egovkb-datacenter/CountryView.aspx.

World Bank (2007). *Doing Business 2008*, Washington, DC: World Bank

World Bank (2008). *Doing Business 2009*, Washington, DC: World Bank.

World Bank (2009). *Doing Business 2010: Reforming through Difficult Times*, Washington, DC: World Bank.

World Bank (2010). *Doing Business 2011: Making a Difference for Entrepreneurs*, Washington, DC: World Bank.

World Bank (2011). *Doing Business: Measuring Business Regulations: Brunei*, Washington, DC: World Bank: Available at http://www.doingbusiness.org/ExploreEconomies.

World Economic Forum (2011). *The Global Competitiveness Report 2010-2011*, Geneva: World Economic Forum.

Appendix

Information on the Brunei civil service and public sector isavailable from the following web-sites:

http://www.bruneiresources.com
http://brunei.gov.bn/government
http://www.pmo.gov.bn
www.mof.gov.bn
http://www.csps.org.bn

Chapter 3 Reforming the Public Sector in Cambodia

Ngo Hongly and Alain Benicy

Introduction

On 7 January 1979, the Khmer Rouge regime was finally overthrown and a new national government undertook to rebuild the country from scratch. However, a civil war broke out and the new State was ostracized by the international community. The Peace Accord was reached in 1991 which opened the way to national elections in 1993 and the formation of a coalition government of national reconciliation. Shortly thereafter, the embargo imposed on Cambodia was lifted and inflows of ODAs and FDIs resumed.

The Royal Government of Cambodia (RGC) proceeded to rebuild and rehabilitate the social, physical and institutional infrastructures of the country. The focus was on strengthening peace, stability and security. A new constitution was promulgated on 24 September 1993 to enshrine principles of a liberal pluralist democracy, a market economy and human rights. In March 1994, the Royal Government approved the National Program to Rehabilitate and Develop Cambodia (NPRDC), which set the development strategy and specific short-term and medium term initiatives. The program identified six major thrusts: (1) restructuring the economy (macro-economic management, public sector management, privatization); (2) reforming State institutions (administrative reform, judiciary reform, security reform); (3) developing the rural economy (management of natural resources, agriculture, forestry, fisheries, land); (4) developing human resources (education and health); (5) rebuilding physical infrastructures (irrigation, roads, telecommunications); and (6) sustainable growth of production (agriculture, tourism, industry-energy-mines, environment).

The NPRDC was followed by the first Socio-economic Development Plan (SEDP) and a Public Investment Program which focused efforts and investments for economic development, social justice and poverty reduction. The national budget was unified. Financial planning and control systems were introduced. Check and balance institutions were created. The Civil Service was unified by integrating the administrations of the parties to the Paris Accord into one administration. Progress was constant and systematic on every front from agriculture to equity.

In July 1997 political stability stumbled. The pace slowed as attention focused on restoring political stability. Following general elections in July 1998, characterized as the "Mekong Miracle," a new Royal Government of Coalition was formed in November 1998. The RGC approved a plan of action in February 1999 that was essentially an extension of the SEDP but with an immediate focus on preparing for the long haul. Resources were mobilized, partnerships were formed. A multitude of projects were initiated.

The RGC made significant headway in securing peace, stability and security, and in completing and strengthening the legal, policy and institutional frameworks. The Khmer Rouge administration and armed forces were disbanded and major elements were incorporated into the National Administration and the Royal Cambodian Armed Forces.

The first Governance Action Plan was approved in March 2001. The Strategy to Rationalize the Civil Service was approved in October 2001. An updated Socio-economic Plan 2001-2005 and the National Poverty Reduction Strategy were approved in late 2002, Cambodia committed to the Millennium Development Goals in September 2003. It joined the WTO as a means to develop its market economy and to further governance. Cambodia became a full and active member of a host of international institutions including ASEAN and NAFTA. Government expenditures were contained and real GDP growth was robust reaching 8.5 percent in 2003.

Following the 2003 elections, the Royal Government adopted the Rectangular Strategy for Growth, Employment, Equity and Efficiency to guide its actions during the mandate and approved the National Strategic Development Plan 2006-2010 (NSDP) to facilitate its implementation. Measures were introduced to enhance aid effectiveness and facilitate harmonization and alignment. The focus was on improving the livelihood and quality of life of a rapidly growing population.

The pursuit of Good Governance was at the heart of the strategy. Reforms undertaken as part of the Governance Action Plan were accelerated. The work covered a broad spectrum including: decentralization and local governance, the reform of the market economy, the Legal and Judicial Reform, the Administrative Reform, Public Finance Reform (customs, tax and expenditures), the Anti-corruption Reform, the Gender Equity Reform, the Reform of the Armed Forces, the Land Policy Reform and the Reform of Natural Resources Management.

Between 2004 and 2007, real GDP growth average 11.1 percent a year reaching 13.3 percent in 2005. Inflation was kept under check at below 6 percent a year. Budget revenues increased on average by 26 percent a year. With the advent of the world economic crisis in 2008, the rate of growth reduced from 10.2 percent in 2007 to 6.7 percent in 2008. The reforms were pursued aggressively with each of them achieving important sustainable milestones on which to widen and deepen the reforms. By the end of the 2007, significant progress had been made: (1) peace and security had been established throughout the country and political stability was restored; (2) democracy and human rights were taking hold; (3) deepening and widening State reforms were underway on a broad front; (4) the economy was growing rapidly and poverty was being reduced by one percentage point a year; (5) Cambodia was rapidly integrating into the community of nations; and (6) public services were being restored and made supportive of good governance.

Framework of Public Sector Reform

In 2008, the newly elected Royal Government approved an update of the Rectangular Strategy for Growth, Employment, Equity and Efficiency. The Rectangular Strategy II covers the same areas as the initial strategy. However, priorities and expected results were adjusted to take into account achievements to date.

The scaffolding of it all is good governance: the fight against corruption, legal and judicial reform, public administration reform including decentralization and deconcentration and the reform of the armed forces.

The environments that condition implementation include: securing peace, political stability and social order; establishing development partnerships with stakeholders; ensuring favorable macroeconomic and financial conditions; and integrating Cambodia into the region and the world.

It identifies four growth strategies for sustainable development and social justice: (1) agriculture productivity, diversification and competitiveness including access to markets, land reform and mines clearance, fisheries and forestry reforms; (2) continued rehabilitation and construction of physical infrastructures including the continued restoration of transport infrastructure, the management of water resources and irrigation, the development of energy and power grids, and the development of information and communication technology; (3) private sector growth and employment including attracting private investments, the strengthening of the financial sector, promoting SME's, creating jobs and improving working conditions, and establishing social safety nets; and (4) capacity building and human resource development including enhanced quality of education, improvements in health services, fostering gender equity, and a rational population policy.

Although the Rectangular Strategy identifies four core governance reforms, the quest for good governance permeates every aspect of the strategy. Behavior will change, the capacity of institutions and people will be developed and Cambodian resources will mobilize towards priority needs and duly be accounted for. The Royal Government's approach to State reforms is based on three core principles: (1) securing peace, political stability and security and the necessary conditions for growth and sustainable development; (2) strengthening governance thus improving transparency and accountability the necessary conditions for due diligence and sound public administration; (3) making public services more transparent and responsive, and less bureaucratic.

Public Sector Reform includes the following: administrative reform, the fight against corruption, legal and judicial reform, decentralization and deconcentration, economic and financial reform(incl. the reform of public finances), social development, gender equity, reform of the armed forces, land reform, reform of natural resources management. The Supreme Council for State Reforms chaired by the Prime Minister sets the priorities and steers the reforms. It is supported by the Council for Administrative Reform and its General Secretariat.

Periodic meetings involving representatives from government and development partners provide the means to monitor and report on progress and to set priorities for partnerships. The Cambodia Development Cooperation Forum and the Government Development Partners Coordination Committee meets periodically to review and set Joint Monitoring Indicators (JMIs) to track progress. Both are supported by a network of Technical Working Groups (TWGs) covering reform areas. The TWGs are made of representatives from concerned ministries and development partners. They plan, coordinate and monitor efforts in support of agreed JMIs, and address issues as they arise.

Implementation of Public Sector Reform

Implementation of the Public Sector Reform is proceeding apace. The following is illustrative of progress being made in a few selected reforms that impact all ministries and agencies. It draws on reports made by the concerned reforms in the context of such documents as the NSDP. It is not a comprehensive report on progress made. The next section will expand on the Administrative Reform as a critical part of the Rectangular Strategy.

Fighting Corruption

Fighting corruption requires capacity to effectively manage and enforce related laws and regulations. It also requires eliminating root causes of corruption through transparent processes and administrative procedures. A number of institutions are involved in preventing and combating corruption, including the Anti-Corruption Unit, the National Audit Authority, the Ministry of the National Assembly and Senate Relations and Inspection (MONASRI) and internal audit units in ministries and agencies. Major achievements include the promulgation of the Anti Corruption Law, the strengthening of anti-corruption institutions including the Anti-Corruption Unit, and joining the international forum to fight corruption.

Priorities for the Anti-Corruption Unit are articulated around five interwoven strategies: (1) prevention (enhancing awareness and ethics); (2) strengthening accountability and institutional capacity (avoid conflict of interest, effective implementation of the law); (3) public support and participation (disseminate information, international cooperation); (4) private sector participation (regulatory framework and procedures in support of competition); and (5) law enforcement (investigate and prosecute corrupt individuals). Priorities for MONASRI include the strengthening of law dissemination, inspection and complaints mechanisms, and institutional and human capacity.

The Legal and Judicial Reform

Since 2005, the Council for Legal and Judicial Reform co-chaired by the Deputy Minister and Minister in charge of the Office of the Council of Ministers and the President of the Supreme Court has been implementing a comprehensive strategy and action plan that build on previous achievements. They are articulated around seven strategic objectives: (1) improving the protection of fundamental rights and freedoms; (2) modernizing the legal framework in support of the rule of law; (3) improving access to legal and judicial information; (4) enhancing the quality of legal processes and related services; (5) strengthening judicial services; (6) introducing alternative dispute resolution mechanisms; and (7) strengthening legal and judicial sector institutions.

Significant progress has been made to complete and modernize the legal framework and to enhance the competence and independence of the judiciary. For example, a significant body of laws was promulgated including the Civil Code and the Code of Civil Procedure, the Criminal Code and the Code of Criminal Procedure, and laws on the Statute of Judges and Prosecutor and Code of Ethics. A Model Court program is underway. A network of Centers for Legal Services is operating. Capacity development programs for judicial and legal professionals are fully operational. However, the severe lack of human and financial resources remains a challenge.

Current priorities continue to address the seven strategic priorities with a particular focus on: enhancing competencies, further developing support mechanisms, expanding legal aid, promoting alternative dispute resolution mechanisms and expanding judicial services through the establishment of special chambers (commerce, labor, administration).

Decentralization and Deconcentration

The objective is to promote democratic development at the sub-national level and to bring public service closer to the people thereby promoting local development and reducing poverty. The National Committee for Sub-National Democratic Development (NCDD) chaired by the Deputy Prime Minister and Minister in charge of the Ministry of Interior provides overall direction and coordination for the Reform.

Significant progress has been made with the promulgation of the Organic Law on Administrative Management of the Capital, Provinces, Municipalities, Districts and Khans, and the Law on Elections of Capital City Councils, Provincial Councils, City Councils, District Councils and Khan Councils. Successful elections were held and support programs were introduced to enhance capacity. The National Program for Sub-National Democratic Development (NP-SNDD) 2010-2019 was approved to set the timeframe for the implementation of D&D reforms. The major challenge is to build human resources capacities of sub-national councils so that they could fully assume and take up assigned responsibilities.

Besides developing capacity, another priority is to define and implement the legal and regulatory framework relating to the transfer of power and functions from the national to the sub-national administrations. Ministries will prepare practical action plans to this effect. The framework will be implemented in three phases: the establishment and institutionalization of structures and governance framework; consolidation and improving these structures and developing capacity to implement; and drawing on lessons learned, improve the program to further enhance democratic development.

The Reform of Public Finance

Cambodia has achieved sustained economic growth, macro-economic stability and poverty reduction over the last decade. The increasing diversity of economic sectors and the robust contribution of the agricultural sector were the two main factors for that performance. Tourism, garment manufacture, construction and the financial sectors have been particularly dynamic.

Significant progress was made in implementing the Public Financial Management Reform Program (PFMRP) towards meeting international standards. The Public Financial Management Reform Steering Committee chaired by the Minister attached to the Prime Minister steers the reform. The program activities are grouped in a series of platforms representing real and measurable improvements. Revenues collection and the flow of resources to ministries have improved significantly. Greater fiscal stability has been achieved. Outcomes include: (1) improved revenue policy, forecasting, management and collection; (2) improved budget preparation; (3) improved budget implementation and efficiency; and (4) enhanced institutional and human capacity within MEF and among ministries.

The Royal Government will continue to pursue prudent monetary and budgetary policies in order to consolidate macro-economic and financial stability. It will continue to foster a highly conducive climate for private and public investments so as to strengthen the competitiveness of the Cambodian economy.

The PFMRP will be deepened to further enhance the efficiency of the National Budget as a key tool of development. Priorities include: (1) further improvements in the management of revenues, debts, bank accounts and procurement; (2) further refining budget classification, the chart of accounts and the Financial Management Information System; (3) decentralizing budget implementation and developing related capacity; (4) the empowerment of budget entities managers; (5) the alignment of resources with policies and program priorities; and (6) the enhancement of accountability for results

Improving Performance

This section provides a brief overview of two instruments the Royal Government is currently piloting to improve performance within the Civil Service. It is intended that both will be gradually deployed more broadly overtime.

Performance Management and Accountability System (PMAS)

A performance management and accountability system is a management tool to assist institutions, work units, managers and staff to achieve agreed objectives and expected results; it provides the means to monitor and evaluate progress with indicators; it informs on capacity development needs; and, it generally provides a work environment conducive to performance. The PMAS are instruments to gradually change attitude and behavior within the Administration towards a culture of service and values of loyalty, motivation and professionalism. The PMAS is being piloted in two instruments designed to enhance performance: the Special Operating Agencies and the Priority Operating Costs instrument (POC). The POC is a temporary instrument developed to support the implementation of development arrangements with development partners. It is envisaged that, by the end of 2011, POC schemes covering over 30 projects involving about 10,000 civil servants will have been established. PMA systems are built around the following: (1) position descriptions (Position descriptions establish the responsibilities and duties associated with a particular position, its placement within the organization and reporting relationships. They include a desired competency profile for that position setting standards for staff development); (2) annual work plans (Unit work plans directly relate to the ministry priorities and operational plan. They establish the unit's priorities, the sequencing of deliverables, indicators of performance and expected results. Unit work plans are supported by cascading work plans for sub-units and for each member of staff); (3) periodic performance and accountability reports (Each unit and individual staff member prepares a periodic P&A report specifying achievements, challenges and constraints. Those reports including suggestions for capacity improvements are endorsed by their immediate supervisors); (4) individual annual performance agreement (Each staff memberand their immediate supervisor sign a yearly performance agreement based on the work plan. It specifies priorities, expected results, associated performance indicators and planned capacity development during the upcoming period; and (5) periodic performance appraisal of individuals (Supervisors and their staff meet periodically (at least every six months) to review performance, agree on constraints and means to mitigate them. These appraisals provide information on capacity development needs). It is envisaged that the PMAS will not be linked to performance pay.

Special Operating Agencies (SOAs)

The Special Operating Agencies are distinctive instruments that focus on improving the delivery of public services. They are a group in a series of instruments identified by the Policy on Improving Public Services ranging from traditional ministerial delivery mechanisms all the way to privatization. A Royal Decree provides the necessary legal framework. The Special Operating Agencies are agents of a parent ministry established by the ministry. The SOAs do not have a legal status other than that of the ministry. They are an integral part of that Ministry, but structurally separate to concentrate on a few functions. They are established by sub-decrees based on approved Terms of Reference that define the purpose and functions of the agency, the type and standards of services to be provided, expected results, delegated authorities and reporting obligations. The minister and the SOA Head sign a yearly management contract that defines measurable and evaluable results using indicators of performance. This contract is supported by cascading annual performance agreements between the SOA Head, managers and individual members of staff. The SOAs will produce periodic activity reports (usually yearly) to facilitate monitoring and evaluation by the parent ministry and relevant stakeholders. The format and content of these reports may vary but they must clearly report on all core agreements between the Minister and the SOA Head based on verifiable evidence. The governance regime of the SOA is tailored to enhance effectiveness. Each

SOA is delegated specific authority to enhance its management of financial and human resources. For example, they may be authorized to retain a percentage of user fees to meet operational needs or to hire temporary contractual staff. In return, the SOAs are expected to adopt transparent processes for due diligence and implement core elements of the PMAS: (1) unlike "contracting in/out" schemes, SOAs institutionalize performance and accountability practices through an appropriate legal framework; (2) unlike public enterprises, SOAs have no independent legal status, no financial autonomy and do not compete in the market place; (3) unlike public establishments, SOAs have no independent legal status, they do not have a Board of Directors and their budget is part of the budget of the parent ministry; and (4) unlike decentralization, SOAs do not necessarily involve the delegation of functions to the sub-national level. The Ministry of Health is establishing a network of SOAs in nine provinces involving provincial and district referral hospitals, health centers and health posts covering some 4,000 members of staff of which about 3,200 are civil servants. The Ministry of Labor is deploying the National Employment Agency which covers nine job centers in eight provinces.

Management Reform

Much like the Reform of the Public Sector, the Administrative Reform was more about building than reforming as everything had to be done from scratch. Like the reform of the public sector, it was done in phases: a rehabilitation phase, a consolidation phase and a development phase. The current civil service is barely a decade old. It is the result of amalgamating the administrations of the parties that signed the Paris Peace Accord into a single, unified civil service. The amalgamation was completed in 1999 when the Khmer Rouge administration was integrated following the win-win strategy of the Prime Minister.

The Rehabilitation Phase (1993-1998)

The focus of this phase was to implement elements of the Peace Accord by, for example, creating a unified civil service. In addition, building on earlier efforts by the Government of the State of Cambodia, the newly elected Royal Government proceeded to establish the legal framework and attendant regulations to structure and manage the Civil Service. The Common Statute setting out the particularities of the career system and establishing rights and obligations of civil servants was promulgated in 1994. A body of statutes and regulations to organize the work and to structure ministries and agencies was also promulgated. A first counting of civil servants was completed in 1995 resulting in the elimination of some 10,000 ghosts. Personnel management and control procedures and systems were established for the recruitment, promotion and deployment of staff.

Vast consultations were undertaken to operate aspects of the National Program to Reform the Administration (NPRA). The consultations focused on three interdependent issues: the development of human resources; the remodeling of the civil service; and better motivating civil servants. Papers were prepared to inform on options relating to each issue.

The Consolidation Phase (1999-2003)

Following the 1998 elections, the Royal Government and development partners endorsed in February 1999, the National Program for Administrative Reform (NPAR) which sought to strengthen management practices in the civil service. The Royal Government approved the Strategy to Rationalize the Civil Service in October 2001 which sought to maintain the number of civil servants and to introduce measures to enhance performance and service delivery. Work proceeded to lay the foundations for sustainable reforms: (1) a national census of the civil service was completed in 2001 to determine the composition and distribution of the workforce; (2) the legal framework to regulate the administration was completed (e.g. the Particular Statutes establishing the cadres); (3) automated management tools were introduced: a data base was created, the payroll was automated, a management information system was introduced; (4) new classification and remuneration regimes more conducive to motivation were implemented and human management processes were streamlined; (5) the use of the existing wage envelope was optimized leading to a 44 percent increase in average salaries in the public service; and (6) innovative and flexible tools designed to mobilize and motivate officials such as priority mission groups, targeted allowances and one-stop window offices were introduced.

The Development Phase (2004-2010)

During that period, the focus was on setting the foundations to widen and deepen the reform. The CAR completed a series of studies to inform on the next steps, designed instruments to enhance performance and prepared for their implementation and undertook to formulate a comprehensive policy framework to manage and develop capacity in the Civil Service. Major achievements included: (1) the strengthening of control mechanisms (recruitment, promotion, deployment and retirement); (2) a quintupling of average salary between 2001 and 2010; (3) a new pension and benefits regime; (4) a Policy on the Delivery of Public Services to anchor policies on capacity development and on the management and development of human resources; (5) the design and deployment of instruments such as Special Operating Agencies and the Performance Management and Accountability System to enhance performance; and (6) the publication and distribution of papers and handbooks to inform on public services and the reform.

The Way Forward

The next phase of the reform will be about enhancing performance. The reform is facing difficult challenges: (1) public services must be available when and where needed and meet recognized standards of quality; (2) attitude and behavior of civil servants and the culture of organizations must become citizen centered; (3) to be effective, capacity development must become demand driven, Cambodianized and its management must be closely coordinated; and (4) the civil service should be modernized and its management become more rigorous to enhance performance.

The goal of the new NPAR (2010-2013) is to serve people better for the well-being of citizens and the prosperity of the Nation. Its target is to modernize the civil service into an effective provider of public services. This requires public services that are more transparent, responsive and effective. It also requires civil servants that uphold values of motivation, loyalty, professionalism and a culture of service. Early priorities include: (1) completing the policy framework including finalizing policies on capacity development, on the management and development of human resources, on redeployment and on compensation; (2) designing and implementing a Public Service Quality System to encourage ministries improve the quality and delivery of their services, including the establishment of a code of conduct andusers feedback mechanisms; (3) completing the Governance Action Plan III with a focus on how ministries will improve the quality and delivery of their services to meet set standards of governance and quality; (4) establishing mechanisms to plan, coordinate and monitor capacity development investments; including initiating a training program to enhance management capacity in the use of available resources; (4) finalizing guidelines and conduct training workshops in the use of such instruments as Special Operating Agencies, Performance Management and Accountability System, operational reviews and, generally, in the implementation of the PAR policy framework; and (5) further reforming the compensation system to enhance motivation and performance in ways that respect principles of macro-economic stability, fairness and coherence both within the Civil Service and among State institutions.

The Annex expands on two instruments the Royal Government is currently piloting to enhance performance. Performance Management and Accountability Systems focus on improving the performance of organizational units, teams and individual civil servants. Special Operating Agencies focus on improving the delivery of public services.

Challenges of Public Sector Reform

As for every country in the world, the Cambodian public sector is one of the country's strategic assets for Cambodia to become and remain competitive in today's globalized and uncertain world. The Royal Government has undertaken very broad and deep reforms to transform the country from a centrally planned economy to a market economy, from a one party system to a liberal multi-party democracy, all at once, in dire circumstances following a long period of warand with very limited human and financial resources. Although much has been accomplished to improve the public sector, and much remains to be done, many post-conflict countries have taken longer than one generation to reach the level that Cambodia has reached.

Cambodia now faces a difficult challenge of capacity to continue its journey and accelerate the pace. Human skills and competencies required by both the private and public sector are severely lacking. It is now time for the reform of the Public Sector to concentrate efforts on developing human and institutional capacity to plan, implement and sustain. Resources will need to be better mobilized and used to further develop capacity. Capacity development investments will become demand driven and Cambodianized.

Reformers can draw on a sound base of knowledge and experience to meet this challenge. Key lessons learned include: (1) reforming the State is a political venture about what can be done and sustained that requires unwavering leadership based on a compelling and shared vision; (2) to be sustainable, the reform must be grounded in the country's reality and its capacity to sustain the course on its own; (3) inclusion, broad base participation and commitment are essential to sustainability; (4) change initiatives must be demand driven with early practical and recognizable results; (5) the importance of drawing on others experiences, of making optimal use of available resources and thus of innovation to leapfrog steps; and (6) the difficulty for development partners to align their programming with government priorities.

Conclusion

Under the leadership of the Prime Minister, significant and sustainable progress has been made in a relatively short time to reform the public sector. Yet, as experience around the world shows, modernizing the public sector and making public services more effective can only be work in progress.

Cambodia's journey shows that much can be achieved on a broad front with commitment, dedication and the involvement of all the stakeholders from the political leadership to grass-roots officials, citizens and external development partners. The scope of work accomplished has been breathtaking, as everything had to be done all at the same time with limited human, financial and institutional capacity. The focus is on good governance which is at the core of the Rectangular Strategy for Growth, Employment, Equity and Efficiency and the National Strategic Development Plan.

Progress made to reform the administration under the stewardship of the Chairman of the Council for Administrative Reform illustrates well the scope and depth of reforms in every sector. Public sector reform will increasingly focus on developing human and institutional capacity to implement and sustain change. It will also increasingly rely on the country's own resources and institutions.

References

Cambodian Rehabilitation and Development Board (2006). *Enhancing Development Cooperation Effectiveness to Implement the National Strategic Development Plan*, Cambodia.

Council for Administrative Reform (2009). *Compendium of Information on Public Services Category IV*, Phnom Penh, Cambodia.

Council for Administrative Reform (2010a). *Compendium of Information on Public Services Category I*, Phnom Penh, Cambodia.

Council for Administrative Reform (2010b). *Handbook for Civil Servants*, Phnom Penh, Cambodia.

Council for Administrative Reform (2010c). *Common and Particular Statute of Civil Servant Handbook*, Phnom Penh, Cambodia.

Council for Administrative Reform (2011a). *Compendium of Information on Public Services Category II, V, VI and VII*, Phnom Penh, Cambodia.

Council for Administrative Reform (2011b). *Special Operating Agency Guideline*, 2nd ed. Phnom Penh, Cambodia.

Council for Social Development (2002). *National Poverty Reduction Strategy 2003-2005*. Phnom Penh, Cambodia.

Royal Government of Cambodia (1994). *National Program for Rehabilitation and Development of Cambodia*, Phnom Penh,

Cambodia.

Royal Government of Cambodia (2000). *National Program for Administrative Reform 1999-2003*, Phnom Penh, Cambodia.

Royal Government of Cambodia (2001a). *Governance Action Plan I*, Phnom Penh, Cambodia.

Royal Government of Cambodia (2001b). *National Strategy to Rational Civil Service*, Phnom Penh, Cambodia.

Royal Government of Cambodia (2004a). *Public Financial Management Program I*, Phnom Penh, Cambodia.

Royal Government of Cambodia (2004b). *The Rectangular Strategy for Growth, Employment, Efficiency and Equity Phase 2004-2008*, Phnom Penh, Cambodia.

Royal Government of Cambodia (2004c). *National Program for Administrative Reform 2004-2008*, Phnom Penh, Cambodia.

Royal Government of Cambodia (2005). *Policy on Public Service Delivery, Phnom Penh*, Cambodia.

Royal Government of Cambodia (2006a). *National Strategic Development Plan 2006-2010*, Phnom Penh, Cambodia.

Royal Government of Cambodia (2006b). *Governance Action Plan II*, Phnom Penh, Cambodia.

Royal Government of Cambodia (2006c). *National Operational Guidelines for Development Cooperation Grant Assistance*, Phnom Penh, Cambodia.

Royal Government of Cambodia (2008a). *Public Financial Management Program II*, Phnom Penh, Cambodia.

Royal Government of Cambodia (2008b). *The Rectangular Strategy for Growth, Employment, Efficiency and Equity Phase 2009-2013*, Phnom Penh, Cambodia.

Royal Government of Cambodia (2010a). *National Strategic Development Plan updated 2009-2013*, Phnom Penh, Cambodia.

Royal Government of Cambodia (2010b). *National Program for Administrative Reform 2010-2013*, Phnom Penh, Cambodia.

Royal Government of Cambodia (2010c). *National Program for Sub-National Democratic Development (NP-SNDD 2010-2019)*, Phnom Penh, Cambodia.

Selected Websites

Ministry of Planning: www.mop.gov.kh
Ministry of Economy and Finance: www.mef.gov.kh
Ministry of Interior: www.moi.gov.kh
Supreme National Economic Council: www.snec.gov.kh
Council for Administrative Reform: www.car.gov.kh
Council for the Development of Cambodia: www.cdc.gov.kh
Cambodian Rehabilitation and Development Board: www. cdc-crdb.gov.kh
Council for Legal and Judicial Reform: www.cljr.gov.kh

Chapter 4 Exploring Public Sector Reform in Indonesia

Eko Prasojo

Introduction

Public sector reform has been known and applied for a long time in countries all over the world. In fact, no country may survive without reforming its administration system. Even for developed countries, public sector reform is a never ending process they have to undergo. This is because of continually increasing public demand toward the government's performance, along with the development and the dynamics of the society. Government cannot just stand still, once being faced with sluggish, complicated, inefficient, ineffective, unaccountable and non-transparent state administration. Another reason that makes it even more tremendously important is the external pressure i.e. globalization which makes inter-state competition more competitive than ever. In fact, only countries that have an efficient and effective state administration system can compete with other countries.

Public sector reform or public management reform, therefore, which is a form of transformation of the administration reform (Caiden, 1969; Lee, 1976; Dror, 1976), has become a global movement in all countries, which is also referred to as Global New Public Management (Ingraham, 2001; Pollit, 2000). It can be said then that the advancement that the three Asian giants achieved, namely Japan, China and Korea, is actually a result of a long process of public sector reform. There are some drivers that contributed to public sector reform. Pal and Ireland (2009) explained four drivers of global public sector movement: (1) the popularity of New Public Management and the new spirit it brings to the management of the public sector; (2) the evolution in the international donor community over the 1990s towards an emphasis on the importance of the state and good governance for economic development and social stability; (3) increased global economic competition in 1990s that forced the government to have well designed regulatory and business regime; and (4) and the collapse of the former soviet union and the expansion of the European union to eastern Europe.

Pennings (2010) argued that "The main goals of public sector reform are to reduce costs, increase effectiveness and efficiency in order to make the public sector more business like, 'work better and cost less' and be more client-oriented. Although there are different routes in public sector reform, the focus is on the most dominant one which favours the diffusion of market values in the public sector, so that the operation of public programmes in general, and in public enterprise in particular, is steered by the market mechanism." But reforming public management is not like buying a new car (Pollit, 2003). Political cost of reform is obvious, while the benefit is less certain (Laking and Norman, 2007). Some scholars argued that the main objective of public management reform is the efficiency and effectiveness of public organization (Osborne and Gaebler, 1992; Hood, 1991), while some scholars noted that public management reforms are aimed at improving the performance of organizations in the public sector (Brandsen and Kim, 2010). "This embodies 'a major cultural shift as the old paradigm, which was largely process and rules-driven, is replaced by a new paradigm which attempts to combine modern management practices with the logic of economics, while retaining the core public values'" (OECD, 1998; Samartunge et al., 2008). Other scholars criticized public management reform in some countries because it failed to meet certain public sector principles, especially the principle of accountability, and while overwhelmingly strengthening values and instruments aiding economic and financial considerations, it neglected citizen participation (Boston et al., 1996).

The success of public sector reform depends on various factors in every country. In some countries, reforms stopped merely at the level of political rhetoric. In others, reform could reshape public administration structures, policymaking processes, and administrative practices. Refering to the case of Public Sector Reform in South Africa, Pillay (2008) argued that "the present article postulates that the successful implementation of NPM requires the existence of societal and cultural norms that complement and reinforce the new institutions of public governance." A number of authors noted that in some countries, especially in developing countries, the success of public sector reform is merely independent on removing corruption, increasing accountability and administrative capacity (Pillay, 2008).

Despite new public management's having become a global reform, the ways in which countries have translated it into specific policies and programmes vary. Pollitt (1995: 134) identifies nine main elements of new public management: (1) cost cutting; (2) capping budgets and greater transparency in resource allocation; (3) disaggregating traditional bureaucratic organizations into separate agencies; (4) decentralized management within public agencies; (5) separating the function of providing public services from their purchase; (6) establishing market and quasi-market mechanisms; (7) emphasizing performance management targets, indicators and output objectives; (8) introducing term contracts, performance-related pay and local determination of pay and conditions; and (9) increasing emphasis on service quality, standard setting and customer responsiveness. Hood noted the elements of public sector management as the following: hands-on management, performance measurement, output control, disaggregation and decentralization, competition, private sector management styles, and financial discipline (Hood, 1991: 4-5).

The practices of public sector management in some countries have been introduced and implemented in different elements. To date, in some countries, such as Northern Ireland, public sector reforms outside the civil service have comprised the amalgamation of executive agencies, the structural reorganization of quangos and limited changes in the functions of local councils (Birrell, 2010). In sub-Saharan Africa (Kenya, Zambia, Tanzania), and also Asian Countries like Srilanka, Indonesia, most cases of public sector reform have almost always referred to the civil service reform, with the predominant approach being restructuring and downsizing (Laking and Norman, 2007). In these countries, the civil services have been characterized as oversized, unresponsive, low incentive, and co-opted by the patronage system. In the Netherland's case, public sector reform includes financial reform with the predominant approach on output focused budgeting, personnel reform with the most extensive reform in reducing the number of civil servants and the creation of a Civil Service Corps that encouraged rotation among departments and the professionalization of senior civil servants, and organizational reform with main elements privatization of government services (Brandsen and Kim, 2010). The ways of public sector reform in Korea could be divided into two phases. The first phase was during the Kim Dae-Jung government (1998-2003) with the market as the prominent guiding principle. The objective of the public sector reform in this phase was to create small but efficient and better serving government. The second phase of the reform, led by Roh Moo-Hyun (2003-2008), referred to participation and decentralization (Brandsen and Kim, 2010). Still, South Korea is focusing on civil service reform as the main element of public sector reform (Kim, 2010).

In Indonesia, public sector reform is one of the most important issues. Public sector reform aims to reduce the opportunity and incentive for corruption, collusion and nepotism. Reforming the public sector in Indonesia is a requirement in installing a meritocracy system with adequate pay in a depoliticized public administration, clarifying governance structure, enhancing transparency and accountability in fiscal management, and focusing policy reforms on improving the delivery of government services. The reform of the public sector in Indonesia requires the rule of law, property rights, a meritocratic civil service and internal controls to ensure proper use of public funds. Another most important thing for Indonesia is the reform of public financial management. This includes the establishment of transparent budget formulation, treasury, accounting and auditing systems, and improving other areas of public financial management. The yearly financial cycle must be reformed in order to implement the program planned in a timely manner. A key feature of the modern treasury is that spending, including most extra-budgetary funds and off-budget revenue is held, under a single account, at the country's central bank and that all expenditure transactions are routed through the treasury.

Public sector reform in Indonesia also covered the creation of a system to respond to the weakness of procurement practices. Corruption in procurement wastes scarce government resources that might otherwise be used to fight poverty or improve service delivery to the population. E-Government is a solution in some countries to improve public procurement. This could upgrade the traditional public services to more radical restructuring of citizen and state interaction, and directly involve the citizen in the decision making process within public institutions.

One other important problem in the Indonesian public sector is use of available resources by the government. Questions that should be asked about resource efficiency are: (1) how does the government make efficient and effective use of available economic and human resources; (2) can the government coordinate conflicting objectives into a coherent policy; (3) can the government curb corruption successfully? Existing problems of using optimum resources have normally been reflected both in proposing and implementing of budget. These are, in Indonesia, characterized by mark up, miscalculated, and misallocated. To avoid these problems, the political leadership should introduce and implement performance based budgeting. Corruption eradication, as part of resource efficiency, should include not only coercive action by law enforcement, but also preventative action by creating a new standard of administrative procedures. Currently, the Indonesian Ministry of Administrative Reform is proposing a law about administrative procedures, which is a key instrument in firmly establishing the principle of good governance in Indonesia and accordingly increase efficiency, transparency, and accountability.

Public sector reform should also include citizens as stakeholders in the government. As stakeholders, citizens have important roles to play in combating corruption and improving the quality of government. Under the Indonesian system right now, the role of civil society controlling the quality of public service is very limited. Citizens are still perceived as the object of public service and development, not the subject. Non-governmental organizations on this country are still in the early stages of development or remain closely linked to the state. Citizens are not able to file a complaint to the government if they are not well serviced. Grass-roots initiative that reflects the participation of civil society in public service has failed because of a lack of formal mechanism and access. Understanding how the poor are affected by weak governance and lack of access to services is essential for bolstering citizen involvement. Citizen voice and participation are essential ingredients to improving governance. Indeed, a key goal of governance is precisely to put information in the hands of the public and to stimulate the demand for reforms by providing citizen score cards rating satisfaction with government services.

As part of public sector reform and making the governance works, the civil service reform plays an essential role. This could be started with competitive recruitment, monitoring of actual civil service management practices, development of a pay and development of measurements of the performance of public servants. Building the capacity of the civil service for a truly meritocratic and depoliticized civil service, however, will take time and indeed, the challenges in implementation remain formidable. In national policy, the success of public sector reform is mostly based on the commitment of central government, especially the commitment of the President. Much research has shown that in some regions in Indonesia the public sector reforms are applied through astute government leadership. Unfortunately, the political elites in some regions, demonstrating poor political management, have, on the contrary, triggered further regression. We can assume that the key success factor of public sector reform in Indonesia is the role of leadership.

Approach, Strategy and Content of Public Sector Reform

Public Sector Reform in Indonesia, in fact, has been carried out since the New Order period (1965-1999) through various agendas such as Deregulation and Debureacratization (1984), Decentralization (1974), and the improvement of the quality of Personnel System (1978). These various reform agendas were aimed in increasing efficiency and the effectiveness of the government as well as a way to receive economic growth as soon as possible. Nevertheless, it must be acknowledged that the various reforms were not expected to reinforce government responsiveness towards the interests for the community. This was caused by the approach of President Soeharto, which really stressed the growth of economics and ignored the involvement of the community in the government and the development.

The bigger public sector reform happened in the period after political reform of 1999 that created a more democratic system in politics as well as in the government. The change of the 1945 Constitution, which has been revised four times since the reform in 1999, has created a number of changes on the laws and government regulations aimed to increase democratization, participation, and decentralization in the government's implementation. The laws drafted after the constitutional change have led Indonesia to become a country that provides space for the people to have control over the government. This is meant to prevent the occurrence of authoritarian and centralistic government as happened for 32 years during Soeharto's regime. Some of the new laws that are related to, and influenced by, public sector reform in Indonesia since 1999: (1) Law No. 2 of 1999 on Political Party; (2) Law No. 3 of 1999 on Election; (3) Law No. 22 of 1999 on Local Government; (4) Law No. 25 of 1999 on Balance between Central and Local Finance; (5) Law No. 28 of 1999 on the Implementation of Clean and Free from

Corruption, Collusion and Nepotism State; (6) Law No. 40 of 1999 on Press Freedom; (7) Law No. 22 of 2003 on the Structure and Position of MPR, DPR, DPD and DPRD; (8) Law No. 23 of 2003 on President and Vice President Election; (9) Law No. 24 of 2003 on Constitutional Court; (10) Law No. 17 of 2003 on Public Finance; (11) Law No. 14 of 2008 on Freedom of Public Information; (12) Law No. 38 of 2008 on State Ministry; (13) Law No. 39 of 2008 on Ombudsman of the Republic of Indonesia, and Law No. 25 of 2009 on Public Service. All these laws and regulations directly and indirectly encourage and have become the foundation for public sector reform in Indonesia up to now. Public sector reform in Indonesia stressed not only in the achievement of efficiency and the effectiveness of the government, but also strengthens accountability and democracy.

Under the President, Susilo Bambang Yudhoyono (SBY), public sector reform has become part of national policies, beginning with a pilot project in the Ministry of Finance through the policy of bureaucracy reform that stressed remuneration reform. Since 2004 several agendas of reforms have been taken up by President SBY aimed at reinforcing the role of the community in the public's service, through the establishment of the Public Service Law, the Ombudsman Law, the Law of Ministries, and the law of Freedom of Public Information. Since 2010, President SBY formed the Team of National Bureaucracy Reform led directly by the Vice President and the Minister of Administrative Reform. The team has proposed and designed the reform plan from 2010-2025, that includes the structural reform, managerial reform, cultural reform, financial reform, civil service reform and procedural reform. The reform should be implemented gradually in the ministries chosen, based on the agreement between the Ministry of Administrative Reform and the Ministry of Finance.

Reorganization of Local Government

After Soeharto's collapse, decentralization politics in Indonesia have undergone significant change. Decentralization is marked as part of a larger agenda to reorganize local government. This also marks the change in the power relationship between central and local government. A radical decentralization policy was stipulated in Law No. 22 of 1999, which later was revised with Law No. 32 of 2004 on Local Government. The tendency of the strengthening of political decentralization, as was mentioned in Law No. 22 of 1999, is a reflection of the centrifugal movement that happened in Indonesia after Soeharto's collapse, i.e. a movement that demands the widest local autonomy. From a political perspective, Law No. 22 of 1999 can be viewed as successful in stifling the centrifugal movement that happened in regions in the post-Soeharto regime era.

From a theoretical perspective, giving autonomy to the regions could make the provisions of service to the public become more efficient and effective. This could happen because of several matters, that is: (1) through autonomy, hierarchical optimization is made in service delivery resulting from the provision of services to the public that are done by the institution with a closer position to the community, so that strategic decisions could be made more easily; (2) the possibility of adjusting the service to the requirement and the available condition at the local level; (3) the increase in the maintenance ofthe available infrastructure through the allocation of the budget in accordance with the requirement and the available condition in its territory; (4) the possibility to transfer of the routine functions from the Central to the Region, so that the Central could concentrate in the policy functions; (5) the possibility of an increase in the competition to provide services around government units, and between the public and the private sectors, that are directed by the Regional Government; as well as (6) the possibility to make the bureaucracy become more oriented to the community.

Law No. 22 of 1999 abolished the deconcentration principle implementation on regency and city, in which this principle is only implemented at province level. Thus, all the regency and city government's authorities are, in principle, the authorities to support decentralization and also, to some extent, for assisting with tasks. Similarly, the meaning of decentralization is no longer regarded in the administrative perspective, but in the political context, where the regency and city local governments have the right to regulate and manage their own households upon their own initiative and capability. Law No. 22 of 1999 also abolished the hierarchy between regency/city governments with provincial government. The construction of relationship between central and local governments as regulated in Law No. 22 of 1999 has caused the shifting of power from provincial government to regency/city government. Law No. 22 of 1999 has even laid down the foundation for radical change in the relationship between central and local, and also in the overall Indonesian Public Administration System (Rohdewohld, 2003).

One of the major changes in the relationship construction between central and local governments according to Law No. 22 of 1999 and Law No. 32 of 2004, as compared to the previous local government law is the adoption of the residual power principle in the distribution of authority between each government levels. The authority of regency and city comprises all government authority, except those in politics, foreign affairs, defense, judicial, monetary and fiscal, religion, and others, which are set as the central authority. Thus, in principle, all other authority has been delegated to regency and city, so that an active delegation by the central government is unnecessary. In the explanation of article 11 subsection 1 of the Law No. 22 of

1999, it is stipulated that, in principle, all relevant authority has been distributed to the regency and city. Meanwhile, those that are not distributed to them are interpreted as authority that is too taboo to be decentralized (Hoessein, 2001: 18). Therefore, the delegation of authority is not necessary to be done through recognition by government. In terms of content, the form of authority distribution in the Law No. 22 of 1999 has similar meaning and spirit as the constitutions in many federal states.

Provincial authority as an autonomous region comprises authority in trans-regency and city government, and authority that is not, or yet to be, carried out by regency and city. Meanwhile as an administrative region, a province also has authority in government, which is delegated to a governor as the government representative. With this sort of form and content of the authority, provinces possess only limited authority.

The practice of radical decentralization from 2001-2003 has caused difficulty in coordination between the central and local government sectors. Therefore, the central government revised the Law No. 22 of 1999 by issuing a new policy that was stipulated in Law No. 32 of 2004, which attempted to find a new balance in the government. According to the law, local government shall exercise the widest autonomy to regulate and manage its own government affairs upon the autonomous and assisting task principles. The distribution of authority is conducted in enumerated manner in article 13 and 14 of the Law No. 32 of 2004, which stipulated that the obligatory affairs become the authority of provincial and regency/city governments. In Law No. 32 of 2004, a province is given back a number of areas of decentralized authority other than deconcentration ones.

The change in decentralized policy has caused the abolition of a central institution at local level. The Regional Office (Kantor

Wilayah) in a province and the Department Office in the regency/city are abolished. At provincial level, there is only a Regional Office with the authority that is retained by the central government, that is, the Regional Office of the Ministry of Finance, The Regional Office of the Ministry of Religious Affairs, Court, Police, and Indonesian Armed Forces. Meanwhile in regency/city, the department office is no longer present. The abolition of central institutions at local level caused yet another problem, i.e. the rationalization of employees who had previously worked at the Regional Office and Department Office. Some of the former employees of those institutions were transferred to the province/regency/city, while the others were transferred to the central government. The problem which then occurred, however, was the resistance of the local government for some reasons: (1) the strong local egoism in not accepting employees who are not originally from that region; (2) the huge number of employees, which made it impossible to absorb all into available positions in that local government; (3) unsuitable competence relative tothe region's need; and (4) rejection as a revenge to the "central government people," who were so powerful during the Soeharto regime.

With a total number of more than 2.5 million employees, the personnel transfer issue became a problem during the initial period of the 2001 decentralization implementation. Up to now, local government in Indonesia is facing overstaffing and understaffing syndromes both in term of quantity and quality. Local government in Java is mostly overstaffed while government outside of Java is understaffed. On the other hand, those overstaffed regions also suffer from employees with low qualifications. In other words, the employee stock is abundant, yet the quality is still poor.

In line with the change in authority distribution, the decentralization policy also features the change of financial relationship between central and local governments. Altogether with the stipulation of Law No. 22 of 1999, in the same year Law No. 25 on the Financial Balance between Central and Local Government was also stipulated. Various fiscal decentralization policies were stipulated in the Law No. 25 of 1999, and those that have been revised with the Law No. 33 of 2004, are:

(1) Introduction of "tax sharing" and "revenues sharing" concepts between central and local governments. In this regard, a sharing of land and building tax (PBB) and income tax (PPh) for individuals, and sharing over natural resources exploitation such as oil and gas, mining, and forestry. According to Law No. 33 of 2004 on Financial Balance between Central and Local governments, local income from tax sharing includes Sharing Funds from Income Tax article 25 and article 29 on Domestic Individual Tax Payer and Income Tax Article 21, on region's part of 20 percent. The fund is distributed between Local Provincial and Regency/City Governments, where for Income Tax article 25 and 29 is distributed with 60 percent for Regency/City and 40 percent for Province.

(2) An introduction of financial transfer from central government to local government in form of General Allocation Fund (DAU) and Special Allocation Fund (DAK). DAU is a "block grant" given to all regency/city governments to fill in the gap between fiscal capacities with fiscal needs. Central government is obliged to allocate at least 25 percent of the net domestic income for DAU. Meanwhile DAK is designed for specific purpose, and allocated for local government in specific manner too.

(3) Law No. 22 and Law No. 25 of 1999 relates to local government in getting domestic and foreign loans. However, in this regard, several limitations are applied for the sake of prudent financial management.

(4) A number of local taxes are given to provincial and regency/city governments according to Law No. 34 of 2000,

which has been renewed with Law No. 28 of 2009 on Local Tax and Retribution. Each province has income source from taxes i.e. Vehicle Tax, Vehicle Transfer of Title Tax, Vehicle Fuel Tax, Surface Water Tax and Cigarette Tax. The kind of local, regency and city taxes are Hotel and Restaurant Tax, Entertainment Tax, Advertisement Board Tax, Street Lighting Tax, Non-Metal and Rock Tax, Parking Tax, Ground Water Tax, Swallow Bird's Nest Tax, Land and Building of Village and Urban Area Tax, and Land and Building Ownership Right Tax. Land and Building Tax, which originally was the Central Tax, according to Law No. 28 of 2009 on Local Tax and Retribution, has been transferred to regency/city, so that it is now one of the most potential taxes for local income. So is the case with Land and Building Ownership Right Tax, it is also given to the regency/city.

(5) Apart from those income sources, there are also other special income sources. For Aceh and Papua, due to the special autonomy status granted by the government, those provinces get the so-called Special Autonomy Fund. Apart from that, local government also gets funds from central government that is given in form of deconcentration and assisting task funds, which is basically a central government's authority which delegates implementation to local government.

Toward e-Government

One of most important reforms in public sector in Indonesia is the application of Information and Communication Technology (ICT) in the government and public service. There are several driving forces that pushed the application of e-Government in Indonesia, especially at the beginning of the 2000s. Those factors were: part of the demand of the reform wanted the existence of transparency and openness in the implementation of the State's Affairs; the implementation of regional autonomy in 2001 based on the Law No. 22/1999 that demanded public service delivery that was more effective, efficient, clean, and transparent, as well as the response to the demands of the globalization. The reform that was rolled out in 1998 was born as a result of disappointment from the community in the implementation of the authoritarian government that was full of corruption, collusion and nepotism (KKN), as well as the failure of the government in overcoming the impact of the economic crisis, social dissatisfaction and politics that took place after 1997. After the reform, there were several adjustments made to the structure of the implementation of the State's affairs, therefore, the government implementation became more balanced and could support the checks and balances mechanism.

Another demand for application of IT in the public sector is globalization that has cut the barriers between the nations. This has resulted in an increasingly open inter-state life. What was carried out by a country cannot be free from observation by the international community. Because of this, the government in each country must be able to give information that is comprehensive to the international community in order to avoid misunderstandings that could lead to a country being despised. (Kementerian Komunikasidan Informasi, 2002: 2).

The application of e-Government in Indonesia, in fact, began before the reform era. This could be seen, for example, by the existence of the National Management Information System document (Sistem Informasi Manajemen Nasional/SIMNAS) in 1987 as well as the launch of the Indonesian Archipelago-21 (Nusantara-21) Project at the end of 1990 that was an important part of the Information and Communication Technology framework to connect the archipelago of Indonesia (Salahuddin and Rusli, 2005: 3-4). The Indonesian Archipelago-21 was one of the first integrated national Information System/Information Technology plans, which was a capital intensive plan which focused mostly on the Information Technology component.

However, this plan was discarded when the 1998 Asian financial crisis hit Indonesia and the government changed (Salahuddin and Rusli, 2005: 4). The Indonesian Archipelago-21 Project also touches on the topic of e-Government (Rahardjo, 2001: 2).

The next development of initiatives of e-Government happened in the reform period that was marked by the issuing of several regulations relating to the application of Information and Communication Technology, including the application of e-Government. These regulations were as follows (see in Salahuddin and Rusli, 2005; Gunadi, 2004; www.aoema.org):

- The Presidential Decree No. 20/1999 on The National Telematics Coordination Team (Team Koordinasi Telematika Indonesia/TKTI) that was replaced by the Presidential Decree No. 50/2000, and then the Presidential Decree No. 9/2003. The TKTI is a team consisting of the government departments, the private sector, the education and civil society whose objective is to coordinate the ICT-related activities nationally.
- The Presidential Instruction No. 2/2001 on the Utilization of Indonesian Language for Computer Applications
- The Presidential Instruction No. 6/2001 on Developing and Usability of the ICT in Indonesia. Through this Presidential Decree, the Government endorses the development and utilization of ICT in Indonesia. These are implemented through Five Year Action Plans
- The Presidential Instruction No. 3/2003 on National Policy on e-Government Development. This policy has been instrumental for the development of e-Government applications and other related initiatives by the regional governments.

Based on the above information, the approach that tended to be used in the application of e-Government in Indonesia was through a normative approach. Nevertheless, it is to be regretted that the regulation was made in the form of a President's Decree, and the President's Instruction could not be mounted legally in practice. There were so many obstacles that emerged in the process of the production of the rules, in the form of the laws, about ICT and e-Government, so that until now the Law on Electronic Information and Transaction has yet to be realized. In fact, the Bill was put forward as long ago as 2004. This shows there was still a lack of commitment by the elites in this country towards the progress of e-Government.

Nevertheless, to fill up the absence of policy and strategy relating to the development of e-Government, the government then made the several regulations above, especially the President's Instruction No. 3/2003. It could be said that before the directive of the President's Instruction No. 3/2003, there was no clear strategy from the government in developing e-Government. This began to change with the issuing of the President's Instruction No. 3/2003, which was issued with consideration to increase: (1) the progress of information and communication technology, both in speed and potential for wide use. This opened the opportunity for the access, management and efficient use of information in large volumes quickly and accurately; (2) the utilization of information and communication technology in the process, e-Government will increase the efficiency, the effectiveness, the transparency and the accountability in the implementation of the government; (3) good governance, effectiveness and efficiency as part of the policies and development strategy of e-Government; and (4) need of uniformity in the implementation of the development of e-Government and the integrity of each step by every institution within the government,

The President's Instruction No. 3/2003 was directed to Ministers, Heads of Non Departmental Institutions, Heads of

Secretariat in Higher State Institution; the Commander of the Indonesian National Army; the Head of Indonesian State of Police; the Attorney General of the Republic of Indonesia; the Governor; and the Regents/Mayors totake steps that were needed in accordance with the task, the function and their respective authority for the implementation of the development of e-Government nationally. In accordance with the policy and the Strategy of National Development of e-Government that was attached to the President's Instruction, they were to formulate and carry out the plan in each of the agencies by coordinating with the State Minister of Communication and Information.

Based on the President's Instruction No. 3/2003 it was hoped that efforts in development and implementation of ICT for e-Government would increase the quality of the public's service effectively and efficiently. The development of e-Government allowed the optimization and utilization of information technology in the arrangement of the management system and the process of the work in government institutions. The utilization of this information technology included: (1) electronic data processing, information management, management system and the process of the work; and (2) allowing the public service to be accessed easily and cheaply by the community all over the country's territory.

Nowadays, most of the ministries/agencies and local government in Indonesia use the ICT in delivery services (one-stop services) and provide that information to the citizen electronically. Some of the ministries and local governments have introduced and used ICT for electronic procurement. In some local governments, ICT has been applied to the daily financial reports, e-conference meetings and e-elections.

Civil Service Reform

Public sector reform in Indonesia has usually referred to the problem of how to develop capable, efficient and effective civil service. Civil service reform has become the most popular element of public sector reform in Indonesia. As many scholars have noted, civil service in Indonesia has been described as unresponsive, oversized, with low incentive and low morale, and driven by corruption. Since 2006, the government has focused serious attention to reforming civil service in Indonesia as explained below.

Establishment of Performance Measurement

The government has made and is making several reforms in relation to the Civil Service System, for instance: performance-based budgeting, where a government institution's budget has to be based on its targeted performance. The reform on performance-based budgeting has been declared in Law No. 17/2003 on State Finance. According to the law, every institution is obliged to establish a performance measurement during the allocation of their budget. Additionally, every individual in the institution is obliged to have an individual performance contract. Every year, each government institution is obliged to submit a Government Institution Performance Accountability Report (LAKIP) describing its accomplishments in the current year. The National Agency for Administration (LAN) has also issued the fundamental guide on Performance Management, both for state organizations and for civil servants. The performance management rules do not seem to have provided maximum results for either state institutions or PNS. This is due to the fact that this performance indicator is not used as the basis for individual performance evaluation, which will be used to determine position advancement and salary settlement. The individual performance evaluation is still based on the

Assessment List of Employee Achievements (DP3), which cannot be used as a performance indicator. DP3 cannot be used to measure the employees' performance for two reasons. First, the indicators are very abstract in nature, for instance, loyalty and leadership, and in an evaluation these cannot be transformed into concrete indicators. Second, the evaluation process is very subjective, as it is conducted by the head of the institution on the employees.

Reform to the civil servant and official performance has been implemented through the pilot project in the Ministry of Finance by using a Balance Score Card (BSC), which is applied step by step starting from an individual score card up to an institutional score card. Each civil servant and official in the Ministry of Finance signed an individual contract which functions as the performance measurement standard. The performance measurement has, in stages, produced a new culture of giving public service, though it still causes resistance from certain groups. The success of the performance measurement application in the Ministry of Finance is due to their willingness to commit to change.

Development of New Incentive System

Another reform in the civil service system is actualized through the pilot project for the reform of performance benefits. This project is also in operation in several other ministries and government institutions. The reform started in the Ministry of Finance in 2006, due to the remarkably high political commitment from Sri Mulyani as the Minister of Finance. Several changes have been implemented, such as competency-based personnel placement, opening new offices for public service, the trimming of several unnecessary internal structures, performance measurement and the provision of performance benefits. The remuneration reform has born positive results but it has not been easy since it requires the civil employees to change their thinking patterns and work culture. Furthermore, the reform has caused a decrease in the additional income or "take home pay" usually received by officials in the Ministry of Finance, since the system is more transparent and accountable. The reform sin performance benefits in the Ministry of Finance have been going for three years and are considered successful by the government. This reform thus extends to other ministries and institutions, such as the Attorney General, the Indonesian Police, the Supreme Court, the Audit Board and the State Secretary. This year (2010), the reform in performance benefits will be applied in more ministries and institutions. It should be noted, however, that officials and PNS have not improved their performance due to this spirit of reform; rather, it is because of the increase of income called performance incentives.

Development of an Assessment Centre and Integrated Information System

In order to map the civil servant competence profile, the pilot project in the Ministry of Finance also built an assessment center aimed as the basis of planning for the employees' career, rotation, and improvement. The establishment of the assessment center basically includes four main components, i.e. composing the dictionary of competence, consisting of details of competence terms competence standards consisting of the list of competences that should be possessed by an official in order to sit in a certain position; the methods and instruments of competence measurement needed; and a competence profile of each civil servant and official. The competence profile is data based and is used as the basis for the Ministry of Finance to plan and improve an employee's career. The kind of workshops and training that should be taken by the employees and officials are based on the analysis of the competence needed, which is carried out by the assessment center.

In addition, to strengthen the employees' database, the Ministry of Finance also recently built an integrated employees information system (SIMPEG). Through the integrated system, each of the employees in the Ministry of Finance is listed; all the necessary data is collected, including the employee's competence, education, official career, and other information needed. So far SIMPEG has included all employees in the Ministry of Finance both in the center and in the regions. The system is especially helpful to determine the planning and the career improvement of the employees, since Indonesia, up to now, has not developed such a system nationally. The Assessment Center and SIMPEG sampling projects in the Ministry of Finance are a prototype of the planning and career improvement system for all civil servants in Indonesia.

At the national level, so far the system of a single employee number in a national scale has been developed. The reform of the employee number system has arisen to overcome the employees data base problem which was not transparent, thus causing inefficiency in the state budget, since there were some employees who owned double numbers, received double salaries, or were even not recorded at all.

Open Bidding for Promotion

One of the reforms from the sampling project since 2006 in the Ministry of Finance is the official promotion through open bidding. The process of fulfilling an official position through open bidding is done by giving an open chance for each civil servant and official in the Ministry of Finance to apply for selection to a certain position. Through this system, it is hoped to select the best candidate to fulfill a vacant position. The open bidding system gives an open opportunity for all employees to apply to the selection committee for the vacant position themselves.

The aspects regarded for fulfilling a vacant position are the employee's competence, career achievement, work performance, work period, work location, career rank, record of discipline, and special requirements needed. To emphasize these aspects, the fulfillment of a vacant position through open bidding is not done in a closed room, unlike what commonly happens in most position fulfillments in Indonesia.

New Laws on Civil Service Reform

Civil service reform in Indonesia is truly a complex issue. The current system is the legacy from decades of corrupt system which is manifested in the corrupt culture, mentality, mindset, quality and service by the bureaucrats. Therefore, the reform should be carried out in radical manner which comprises several important aspects. The House of Representatives has launched an initiative to make State Civil Apparatus Law, which is currently still at the drafting level. This draft is based upon professionalism in management of the apparatus resources. Several reform ideas that are stipulated in the draft are as follow.

New Strategic Resource Management

The forthcoming law will replace outdated bureaucratic personnel administration with Strategic Human Resource Management (SHRM) to spearhead vertical and horizontal adjustments of the government agency workforce with a new strategic mission from the government. The State Civil Service Reform is based on the vision to change human resource management strategy, from the bureaucratic and personnel-based one toward a modern human resource system that puts forth competence, competition and performance development. In Indonesia's bureaucracy, the arrangement and implementation of the civil service so far is based on a very bureaucratic and clerical personnel administration. As a consequence, there is no vision and mission to develop the resources that the apparatus possesses. Apart from that, the approach used also puts so much emphasis on politics, affiliation, patronage, nepotism, and collusion. Political loyalty has been a dominant factor in bureaucracy, which has also been the main consideration for one's appointment to certain posts/positions, rather than competence and work performance.

The reform on the system and strategy of resource development that sets individual potential development as a priority is expected to create adjustment of functions held by every government agency. The new system will make competence, experience, and performance of the employees the main consideration in selecting people to hold positions in the government. This new system will use a bureaucratic merit (meritocracy) system and replace the political merit system currently in charge in Indonesian bureaucracy.

Civil Service as a Profession

The Indonesian Civil Service is defined by legislation as a profession which is apolitical, clean from corruption, and endowed with institutional capacity to deliver equitable public service, and to effectively implement policy management. The Basic Values and Code of Conduct of the profession is sanctioned by law. These days, one of the main problems in the Indonesian civil service is that state apparatus is not considered as a profession, but rather as a partial political vehicle. That is the reason why the present state civil apparatus is not professional. It is not considered as a profession; the civil apparatus does not have any basic professional value, nor do they have sufficient competence or code of conduct. They work as they wish. For politicians, this is very lucrative for advancing their self-interest and that of their party. As a consequence, what happens is co-optation committed by political interest in government function and services, and this, in turn leads to the creation of a highly political, unclean, corrupt bureaucracy that lacks capacity.

This law draft will make state civil apparatus a profession, where the profession should have basic values of professionalism, competitiveness, be apolitical, have a good service culture and high work performance. As a profession, state civil apparatus should have the competence required in a position/work. These competences should become the fixed requirements in recruitment and promotion. As a profession, a code of ethics and a code of conduct should also be developed and made the basis for carrying out tasks. Any violation of the code of ethics would be punished by sanction. Thus, this law will provide protection for the state civil apparatus profession from the intervention of partial political interest and also to prevent any collusion, corruption and nepotism within Indonesian bureaucracy.

Position-based System

A position-based personnel management system is applied in recruitment, appointment, placement, promotion, and termination of employees of Indonesian public service. In Indonesian bureaucratic practice, the recruitment, position, and rank filling still remains very closed and based more on proximity. This is actually the legacy of Soeharto's regime, during which every civil servant should be cadre of Golkar party (the regime's ruling party at that time). This system resulted in many incompetent people being placed on official positions, and some argue it is also the root of bribery in bureaucracy; positions can be sold or exchanged with specific economic and political interests. This practice has caused a savage bureaucratic disease in Indonesia (corruption, collusion, nepotism). The holder of a position must have loyalty and must submit tribute to his supervisor or political official.

By changing the career system into an open position system, it is hoped that the corruption, collusion, and nepotism practice (KKN) can be reduced. The recruitment and positioning of civil servants will be made in open manner, as should promotion. Promotion should be done through afit and proper test administered by the State Civil Apparatus Commission. As for the highest position in bureaucracy (Echelon 1), it should be made in an open manner for every state civil apparatus in Indonesia. This system will strengthen the profession of the state civil apparatus, and also the concept of the Unified State of the Republic of Indonesia, in which the apparatus can be transferred horizontally between ministries, as well as vertically between central and regional/local level. In this law draft, 10 percent of the state positions can be also filled from private sectors. Such a policy will push forward professionalism and competition in Indonesian bureaucracy.

Merit System

A merit system is operated as objective comparison between qualifications and competence required for jobs or positions with those of the applicants. The legal draft also stresses the importance of a merit system for Indonesian state civil apparatus. This is aimed to ensure that the filling of positions in bureaucracy is carried out by considering the qualifications required for a position with the qualification of an applicant. By applying an open promotion system, the qualification of every applicant can be seen and compared with the others, so that the best candidate is chosen. This system will replace that of filling a position which is based only on proximity between an official with his subordinate. The recording of the qualifications for a state civil apparatus will be done by the State Civil Apparatus Commission and is applicable in all parts of Indonesia.

Senior Executive Service (SES)

A Senior Executive Service as special cadre of bureaucracy reform will be established and it will apply to all strategic public agencies beyond the General Scale of IV/d (on top of the PGPS Scale IV/e). To complete the position-based promotion system, the drafted law also attempts to develop special competence for the highest positions in bureaucracy, through the creation of Senior Executive Service (SES). The introduction of SES is conducted to overcome various problems occurring in the current Indonesian bureaucracy: (1) the gap of competence, knowledge, and capacity of the officials between ministries and agencies at central and local levels; (2) exclusivity that happens in several ministries and local governments, which does not allow mobilization of state apparatus between ministries or between regions; (3) co-optation of bureaucracy by politicians in filling some positions, because until now the position assessing team is composed of political officials (both elected officials and political appointees); and (4) the weakening of the concept of the Unified State of the Republic of Indonesia, due to the growing egocentrism in each region, upon ethnic and tribal base.

The Senior Executive Service is a special cadre in bureaucracy for the highest state positions; in this regard the Echelon 1 official is the General Director. The filling of the position, both at national and regional levels, is done in an open manner by the State Civil Apparatus Commission in an independent manner. The available position is announced by the State Commission, while the candidates who have met the administrative requirements have to apply actively for the position. The available position can be filled by any official both at national and local levels, horizontally as well as diagonally. Meanwhile the remuneration system is done specifically by considering the work load, competence and performance. Once in five years, officials who want to continue their service period in that position should reapply, and may be reselected by the State Civil Apparatus Commission. This drafted law also gives a 10 percent quota for personnel from the private sector to fill certain available positions. Performance assessment is done to measure the amount of bonus and penalty given to an SES official. In the initial draft of the law, it was also recommended that an SES official should be drawn from officials from Echelons I and II, yet later the parliamentarians decided it should be only for Echelon I officials.

National Selection System

The application of the National Selection System for Indonesian Civil Service is administered by the National Personnel Agency. The practice of the State Civil Apparatus recruitment in Indonesia since 2001 has featureda decentralized system, in which every region should conduct the recruitment process of the civil servants onits own. This system, however, has faced distortion and bad governance, as the recruited civil servants usually come from the relatives/families of officials, politicians and public leaders. The decentralized recruitment system has also resulted in very corrupt transaction formation (buying and selling). The price of a formation can reach up to 100 million rupiahs (US$ 10,000). This transaction may take place because the large authority of the local government does not have the monitoring capacity of the central government. On the other hand, politicians need to acquire/reimburse the huge fund they used in direct election of local head. This formation transaction has created a very corrupt and poor bureaucracy.

The State Civil Apparatus Legal Draft is made to eradicate such a corrupt formation transaction within the civil servant recruitment. If the law is enacted, then the recruitment process of the civil servants will be done in decentralized manner by the

State Civil Service Agency, under the supervision of the State Civil Apparatus Commission. All kinds of examinations and recruitment examination processes will be carried out in a centralized manner by the State Civil Service Agency, and civil servants can be distributed to all agencies that need them both at national and regional/local levels.

Differentiation of Status

The Indonesian Civil Service will be comprised of: (1) Civil Servants, (2) Contract Government Employees. Currently, the Indonesian civil service system only acknowledges the State Civil Servant as the only kind of civil service. This has caused a huge financial burden for the state, because the state has to finance all those civil servants, including their pensions. On the other hand, by using a recruitment and promotion system that is not performance-based, the competence of the civil servants often disappeared. Highly-performing civil servants do not get any reward, and are treated similarly with those who do not perform at all. Civil servants cannot be fired for their poor performance. On the other hand, from the society's perspective, the position of civil servant has been considered as having distinguished and proud social status. Their purpose in becoming a civil servant, in the end, is distorted. Instead of aiming to give the best service to the public, they seek good social status. Even for carrying out a very modest job, every employee holds status as civil servant.

Upon that fact, state civil service reform in Indonesia is conducted through the State Civil Apparatus drafted law, which is directed to create competition amongst civil servants. Certain technical and functional works do not necessarily have to be filled by employees holding status as civil servants, but rather by employees contracted for a certain period of time. This contract employee is referred to as a Contract Government

Employee, i.e. an employee appointed by a bureaucratic official to fill certain positions with a minimum contract of 12 months. Government employees may join a worker union and are given pension rights in accordance with the accumulation of worked time. Further details on the Government Employee matters will be covered by Government Regulations.

Distribution of Civil Service Authorities and Management

Clear delineation of functions between authorities in the civil service management of Indonesia will be regulated. To draw a clear line on the authority of the agencies in the state civil service management, this law also regulates the distribution of authority between those agencies: (1) the President as head of the state holds the authority to select and appoint CSC commissioners; and as head of the government appoints ministers, heads of NPA and NIPA, and approximately 6,000 senior officials of public bureaucracy; (2) the Minister of State Administration and Bureaucracy Reform formulates general policies for administrative and personnel management of the Indonesian Public Service; (3) the Indonesian Civil Service Commission formulate directives to maintain practices of professional, apolitical, and high integrity civil service, investigate application of these practices by national and local governments' agencies, and manage the Senior Civil Service; (4) INPA (Indonesian National Personnel Agency) administers the National Selection of the Indonesian Civil Service, carries the Personnel Assessment Center, and provide assistance in the development of civil service personnel management; and (5) NIPA (National Institute of Public Administration) administers the Indonesian Civil Service Academy, provide career development training for the Indonesian Civil Service, and carry out research and studies on organization and administration.

Reform of Public Finance Management

One of the reforms being undergone in public sector in Indonesia is that of public finance management, which materialized through the issuance of Law No.17/2003 on Public Finance. The purpose of this law is to create a well-organized, efficient, effective, transparent and accountable state finance management which complies with the law. The most important reform in Public Finance which is conducted through this law is the shift of approach in financial management which is based upon: (1) integrated budgeting; (2) performance-based budgeting; and (3) mid-term expenditure framework. Integrated budgeting aims to integrate all kinds of state expenditure, integrate all budget documents, which were previously separated, into Activity Checklist (DaftarIsian Kegiatan/DIK), Project Checklist (Daftar Isian Proyek/DIP), and Authorization Decision Letter (Surat Keputusan Otorisasi/SKO) into one single budget document called the Budget Implementation Checklist (DaftarIsian Pelaksanaan Anggaran/DIPA). Performance-based budgeting aims to integrate the process of planning with that of budgeting, so as to attain the description of output, outcome and impact of each state's expenditure. Furthermore, performance- based budgeting is also meant to serve as the changing factor in employee performance measurement, which currently still has to be implemented due to the obstacles faced in bureaucratic reform. The implementation of State Finance Law, as it is mandated, is undertaken within three periods, respectively period of 2005-2009 (as the socialization and preliminary implementation phase), period of 2010-2014 (as the sequel implementation phase), and period of 2015 as the full implementation phase of the law.

Public Finance Management Reform has brought about substantial change in finance management. As a consequence of the reform, there have been task forces established within every agency as the unit responsible to implement and be accountable for the activity. For the first time in Indonesian government history, the Presidential Regulation on State Budget, Income and Expenditure 2006 could be implemented in compliance with its deadline (30 November 2005), while the DIPA of 2006 was successfully issued prior to the budgeting year, so that it was capable of being implemented at the beginning of the year.

Some progress has also been made thanks to the public finance reform, i.e. the introduction of cost standard in budget allocation, including the minimum and special cost standards, synchronization of function/sub-function/program/activity implementation from the planning process toward the budgeting, IT support enhancement in budgeting process, and introduction and implementation of the Mid-Term Expenditure Framework Implementation in the discussion process with the parliament (DPR). In the next phase, state financial reform will be comprised of the completion of program restructuring and ministerial and agency activities, including the formulation of outcome, output and indicator of performance by applying organizational structure and respective organization's specific task approaches. Then in the subsequent period, there will also be a reward and punishment system in implementing the performance-based budget.

Reform of Public Procurement

One of the reforms to thepublic sector being undergone in Indonesia is the reform of public good and services procurement, through the issuance of Presidential Decree No. 80/2003, which have since been modified several times. In Indonesian government, public procurement is a spot which is very prone to corruption. This is mainly caused by politicians co-opting bureaucracy to interfere in the procurement process. Some major changes in public procurement in Indonesia, however, can be observed: a more detailed regulation on procurement process, classification of types of goods and services procurement and related procedures, prohibition for any parties having connection with the committee and public involved in the process, the use of IT technology in procurement (e-procurement), integrity pact signing, and information openness for the public which enables them to be aware of the procurement process. Apart from that, currently every commitment maker official must be accountable in implementing public procurement, in order to prevent any chance for collusion and corruption.

Indonesia has established the Government Procurement Policy Agency (LKPP), an agency in charge of making regulation and monitoring the implementation of procurement which is conducted by a ministry/agency and regional government. LKPP also conducts a certification process for any party involved in government procurement, in order to assure those parties are qualified for the task. Furthermore, LKPP also gives testimony at trials concerning cases related to corruption in procurement. In some ministries/agencies and regional government, procurements has been done by using the e-procurement method (utilizing information and communication technology/ ICT).

The strong push for eradicating corruption and the tighter regulation in procurement have led to the revealing of a lot of corruption in procurement to the public, which brought several public officials to trial, including ministers and a regional chief, and some of them were sentenced to jail. Therefore, in the beginning, reform in the procurement system caused many public officials in charge with procurement related tasks to become worried as they might be easy prey for being accused of corruption. However, currently such an anxiety has declined but on the other hand it has proven to have enhanced the quality of public procurement itself.

Transparency and Accountability Reform

Public sector reform in Indonesia is marked with growing public sector openness and accountability to the public. In fact, this is just one of the demands made during the beginning of reform era. In 1999, the public demanded the strengthening of the public role in government, service and development. At the national level, this reform is marked with the stipulation of three laws, namely the Law on Public Procurement, the Law on the Ombudsman, and the Law on Public Information Openness. All those laws were aimed to strengthen the public position before the government. In the Public Service Law, public rights and duties and those of service providers are regulated. This law also obliges the service provider to provide acomplaint mechanism and follow up the complaints properly. In the Public Information Openness Law, the public is guaranteed by law to be able to learn and obtain information from officials and government administrators insofar as it is not in matters prohibited by law. Accordingly, government must give access to the public, provide information as well as announce it to the public.

To strengthen the public position, the Ombudsman Law regulates mechanisms of complaint-handling directly, itself. The Ombudsman is given the authority to call on concerned parties, and to handle complaint in a non-judicial manner. At its highest authority, the Ombudsman can inform the President and DPR if an agreed settlement were not well implemented by the service provider in the field. Currently there is also ongoing discussion on the Draft Administrative Procedure Law as the basis for changing the procedures fora public official in making decision. It is expected that this law will help to enhance the quality of decisions made by public officials.

Public Sector Reform in Local Government

In a very decentralized state like Indonesia, public sector reform occurred not only in national level but also in local government level. Decentralization in Indonesia is marked with a number of public sector reforms and innovations initiated by some local governments in the country. The success of decentralization in local innovation usually is very much affected by a local chief with a strong commitment to reform administration at local level. Some of the administrative reforms include program reform, procedural reform and government management reform. Some of the best practices in the public service are the result of decentralization, and they can be categorized as follow: (1) Integrated Service on Permits and Non-Permits (e.g. Sragen regency, Jembrana regency, Pare-pare regency, City of Jogjakarta); (2) Local Financial Management Reform (e.g. Gorontalo province, or clearing account system/ Giro to Giro in Solok Regency); (3) Reform in goods and services procurement (Ex: e-Procurement in the City of Surabaya); (4) Performance Agreement (Solok regency); (5) Local Performance Incentive (Gorontalo province and Riau Islands province); (6) Pact of Integrity (Solok regency); (7) Free education and health (Jembrana regency, South Sumatera province); and (8) other Service Reforms (e.g. drive thru of motor vehicle document service in Surabaya).

There are several factors influencing the public sector reform and innovations carried out by local governments in Indonesia. First, there is the political will and commitment of the Local Chief as the highest bureaucracy leader at local level to carry out the program. Second, the capability of the Local Chief along with the apparatus to involve local organizations, such as some particular institutions, and public leaders, NGOs, and other relevant parties to participate in listing the priorities in the implementation, monitoring and evaluation of the program. Third, there is an efficiency program on development in all sectors, as well as the attempt to change the bureaucratic paradigm and culture. Initially, the program implementation will be the cost center as it requires a relatively huge budget. For that purpose, it needs efficiency in all sectors. Fourth, there needs to be prioritizing in selecting the programs. The success of this program is also determined by the extent that the programs are in favor of the community's need. A thorough investigation, on how close and needed the program is for the community, should be undertaken when developing a program.

Public Sector Implementation: Status and Achievement

Public sector reform is not an easy task in Indonesia. Numerous challenges and resistance are hampering the implementation. The President has issued a grand design and roadmap for public sector reform, which will be referred to as the guideline in implementing the reform. In principal, public sector reform is carried out gradually using the agency level approach, in which every ministry and other government agencies would propose their respective reform program to the President, who still refers to the grand design and roadmap. However, this agency level approach faces a lot of barriers, including: (1) Every ministry and non-ministerial agency will determine by themselves the path of reform they will undergo, hence causing differences in the reform agenda between ministries and non-ministerial agencies at national level; (2) The spirit to run reform amongst the ministries' officials is generally motivated by the desire to get additional remuneration. Thus, the reform process is not moved by a good spirit and philosophy; (3) There are too many reform agenda which have to be done for every ministry and non-ministerial agencies in such a short time, making it difficult to measure the success of a reform conducted in the ministries and non-ministerial agencies; and (4) Various reform agenda run by the ministries and non-ministerial agencies do not necessarily correlate with the national purpose of the public sector reform.

The implementation of public sector reform in Indonesia is carried out by several teams formed by the President. The Vice President is acting as Director of the National Bureaucratic Reform, and is in charge of issuing various reform policies and strategies. In running his task, the Vice President is assisted by the National Bureaucratic Reform Independent Commission consisting of 7 members from different backgrounds. The Bureaucratic Reform Independent Team is assigned to give policy advice to the Vice President, conduct monitoring over the implementation of reform agenda, and submits the report to the Vice President. Bureaucratic Reform Implementation is carried out by the Minister of State Apparatus Empowerment and Bureaucratic Reform, who serves also as the responsible person for the success of various agenda set in the Bureaucratic Reform Grand Design and Road Map. To assure the implementation of the bureaucratic reform agenda, the President has also formed a Quality Assurance Team assigned to monitor and evaluate the bureaucratic reforms being run.

Public sector reform in Indonesia is a difficult task. There are various fundamental problems for the success of the reform. First, the bureaucratic reform machine, in this case, led by the Minister of State Apparatus Empowerment and Bureaucratic Reform, is facing difficulty to boost the implementation of bureaucratic reform. The lack of awareness, commitment and capacity to run the reform is among the fundamental problems that should be addressed through "reform the reformers" program. Secondly, there is intense resistance from politicians and bureaucrats alike against the bureaucratic reform. This is because the already deeply-rooted political cooptation over bureaucracy, where political party elements penetrate bureaucracy to gain income for funding the parties and their elites. On the other hand, bureaucrats have also indulged in the comfort zone created from the condition, hence perceiving any change as a threat. This condition is exacerbated by the multiparty system as applied in Indonesia. Thirdly, currently bureaucratic reformis only perceived as political discourse and most of bureaucrats see it solely as a means to add more incentive without being followed by a change of mindset and cultural set. This causes a bubbling of civil servant expenditure budget as the consequence of additional incentive to support bureaucratic reform. In 2011, civil servant expenditure for salary only amounted to 49 percent of the total national expenditure. This amount is estimated to rise because of the number of the Ministries and Ministerial Agencies which are to be the targets for bureaucratic reform. In 2011, nine ministries and non-ministerial agencies will be included in the bureaucratic reform project, following five ministries and non-ministerial agencies which had been included in bureaucratic reform project since 2007.

Table 1. Ranking of Global Competitiveness Index

Year	Ranking	Number of Country
2005	54	114
2006	54	122
2007	54	131
2008	55	133
2009	54	134
2010	44	139

Source: http://www3.weforum.org/docs/WEF_GCR_Indonesia_Report_2011.pdf

It is to be expected that various bureaucratic reforms being carried out would take time until the result can be felt by the public as consequence of a more effective and clean government. Up until now, the Indonesian government had yet to conduct any comprehensive evaluation upon bureaucratic reform success which had been intensively carried out since 2006 through pilot project in the Finance Ministry. Nevertheless, surveys conducted by several international institutions showed significant change in the Indonesian bureaucratic condition. Indonesia's Global Competitiveness Index Rank moved up from 54 out of 114 countries in 2005, to 44 from 139 in 2010. So has the country's Doing Business Rank, which improved from 131 out of 135 countries in 2006, to 121 out of 183 countries in 2011. Moreover, Indonesia's rating on the corruption perception index also reported a positive change, from 2.4 in 2006, to 2.8 in 2010. This data may not be directly correlated with or reflect only the condition in bureaucratic reform, yet it shows at least a form of success in the country's attempt to move toward good governance.

Table 2. Ranking of Doing Business

Year	Ranking	Number of Country
2006	131	155
2007	135	175
2008	127	178
2009	129	181
2010	122	183
2011	121	183

Source: http://www.doingbusiness.org/rankings

Table 3. Corruption Perception Index (CPI)

Year	Ranking	Number of Country
2006	130 (index: 2,4)	163
2007	145 (index: 2,3)	180
2008	126 (index: 2,6)	180
2009	111 (index: 2,8)	180
2010	110 (index: 2,8)	178

Source: www.transparency.org/policy_research/surveys_indices

Table 4. Human Development Index

Year	HDI	Ranking	Number of Country
2004	0,711	111	177
2005	0,719	110	177
2006	0,726	108	179
2007	0,734	108	177
2008	0,726	109	179
2009	0,734	111	182
2010	0,600	108	169

Source: data.menkokesra.go.id/hdi-indonesia-2010

Challenges, Opportunity and Lesson Learned

Successful public sector reform and transitions in Indonesia have shown the importance of state capacity and ability. This is reflected in the questions regarding: (1) the capacity of political leadership to set and maintain strategic priorities and reform of development; (2) the effectiveness of implementation of reform policy; (3) the flexibility of political leadership and capability of leaders to learn and to replace failing measures with innovative policy. Leadership capabilities are required to initiate public sector reforms in Indonesia, to overcome the resistance of status quo oriented groups that impose social burdens on the population, and to sustain an economic catch-up process.

The first core practice that is seen to be crucial for successfully steering capability and leadership is visioning. A leader without a vision provides little comfort to his followers. Yet, visioning is merely part of the process. A more important component is to provide the inspiration for followers to partake in such vision and experience it as something that is shared. To be effective, leaders need to look beyond the horizon of their own organization and envision a future characterized by hopeful positivism. They must be expressive and sufficiently passionate about the direction and goals they set forth after careful thought. Only then can they evoke genuine support and excitement amongst followers in achieving the vision they have set. Many leaders in Indonesia failed to communicate their vision effectively to their followers (Karim, 1999; 41). This factor is the most challenging in Indonesian public sector reform.

The second key of steering capability is the capacity and ability to challenge the process. Nothing is more perilous than to introduce a new order or change process. Yet successful leaders should be able to manage change whenever the situations demand it. They must ensure that the entities they lead and the systems they manage produce results. In rallying against the colonial masters Sukarno challenged the status quo, while Soeharto has changed the old order, it was during the Sukarno era there emerged the new structural efficiency model. Habibie, Abdurrahman Wahid, and Megawati have introduced new priorities on democracy and liberalization such as freedom of press and the decentralization process. Some mayors of local government in Indonesia have introduced, after the decentralization process in 2001, policies and action that display their aspiration to make significant changes and improvements (see Prasojo et al., 2004). Steering capability needs leaders who consistently challenge the status quo and old process. It is not the intention to transform every public sector leader into a Sukarno, but it is imperative that when systems do not work, policies fail to provide the desired impact or process are ineffective, public sector leaders tackle these in a forthright manner.

Apart from visioning and challenging the process of public sector reform in Indonesia, another practice attributed to successful steering capability is that of enlisting support and shaping the actions of the followership as a team. Leaders need to be able to create an environment for their followers to act. It would be difficult to fathom how leaders can be effective if they are not able to influence others to act in tandem with their vision, encourage collaborative modes of behavior, actively involve people at different levels and allow followers to take decisions on their own. Leaders have to be quite clear themselves about the beliefs and values that they are trying to propagate. This is characterized by "Leadership by example," we call it in Indonesia "*Ingngarso sung tulodo, ingmadya-bangunkarso, tut wurihandayani,*" In order for leaders to win the respect of followers, they need to model the way for others to achieve their vision.

In Indonesia, public sector reform needs a larger consensus among the political parties. The political leadership needs support from the party and society to be able to initiate and maintain reforms. The government should establish a broad consensus on reform with other actors in society, without sacrificing its reform goals and agenda. It means that the government includes on their policy not only the supporter power, but also the anti democratic veto (opposition) powers, as well as minority groups in the country. The government should be able to manage political cleavages so that they do not escalate into irreconcilable conflicts. It is also the obligation of the state to encourage the development of social capital among citizens and social groups and involve society actors in the political process. The government's incompetence to do so usually results in a drawn out conflict for reform between state and society and also among society itself.

Consultation, compromise and consensus can also be explained by the interaction of social capital, government policies and policy outcome. Negotiated agreements among political actors are the key to successful reform. In the scope of the bureaucracy, the consultation and consensus between overseers and subordinates, as well as among the overseers in the reform policy, is needed to avoid resistance to changes. Consensus building in transformation and development is a kind of participative governance, in which the citizens, groups, actors, and public servant are parts of the nation, and not as objects, but they are really subjects of this process. Good public management needs support from the whole of the nation and cannot stand alone without them.

Concluding Remarks

The government of Indonesia has taken public sector reform as a priority of national policy, systematically planned under President SBY. The reforms taken by the government before the SBY government have been described partially. But unfortunately, public sector reform in Indonesia has not shown significant improvement in the quality of the government management process and civil servants (PNS). The most favorable reforms in Indonesia are the reorganization of local government through the decentralization reform and civil service reform. Many agendas to be carried out remain, yet they are hindered due to a lack of political commitment and resources. For these reasons, Indonesian administration reform has remained on the agenda as a national priority for many years without any materialization. Public sector reformis not an easy task in Indonesia, for a change in the system must be accompanied by a change in the national elites and leaders' mindset and culture which have not been grounded in the spirit of reform. With strong political commitment, public sector reform in Indonesia will improve in the areas of government and public service delivery.

References

Boston, J., Martin, J., Pallot, J., and Walsh, P. (1996). *Public Management: The New Zealand Model.* Auckland: Oxford University Press.

Brandsen, T. and Kim, S. (2010). Contextualizing the meaning of public management reforms: a comparison of the Netherlands and South Korea, *International Review of Administrative Sciences,* 76: 367.

Caiden, Gerald (1969). *Administrative Reform.* Chicago.

Dror, Yehezkel (1976). Strategies for Administrative Reform, In Leemans, A.F.(ed.). *The Management Change in Government*, The Hague.

Hood, C. C. (1991). A Public Management For All Seasons?, *Public Administration,* 69: 3-19.

Gunadi (2004). E-Government Development in Indonesia, presentation in E-Government Workshop in APEC Telecommunications and Information Working Group 29th Meeting, Hongkong.

Karim, M.R.A. (1999). *Reengineering the Public Service: Leadership and Change in an Electronic Age*, Subang Jaya.

Kementerian, Komunikasidan Informasi (2002). *Kebijakandan Strategi Pengembangan E-Government*, Jakarta.

Kim, Pan Suk (2010). Korean Civil Service System and Civil Service Reform. In Kim, Pan Suk (eds.). *Civil Service System and Civil Service Reform in Asean Member Countries and Korea* (pp. 357-388). Daeyoung Moonhwasa Publishing Company, Seoul, Republic of Korea.

Laking, R. and Norman, R. (2007). Imitation and inspiration in public sector reform: lessons from Commonwealth experiences,

International Review of Administrative Sciences, 73: 517.

Lee, Hanh Been (1976). Bureaucratic Models and Administrative Reform, in Leemans, A. F.(ed.). *The Management Change in Government*, The Hague.

Osborne, D. and Gaebler, T. (1992). *Reinventing Government*. Reading, MA: Addison-Wesley.

OECD (1998). *Public Management Reform and Economic and Social Development*. Paris: PUMA.

Pennings, P. (2010). Exploring Variations in the Political Discourse on Public Sector Reforms 1981-2005, *Public Management Review*, Vol. 12, Issue 2: 173-190.

Pillay, S (2008). Cultural Ecology of New Public Management, *International Review of Administrative Sciences*, 74: 373.

Pollitt, C. and Bouckaert, G. (2000). *Public Management Reform: A Comparative Analysis*. Oxford: Oxford Press University.

Prasojo, E, Kurniawan, T., and Hasan, A. (2004). *Reformasi Birokrasidalam Praktek: Kasus di Kabupaten Jembrana (Bureaucratic reform in Practice: The Case of District Jembrana)*, Jakarta.

Rahardjo, B. (2001). Membangune-Government, paper presented at Seminar Nasional Jaringan Komputer II, Makassar.

Rohdewohld, R. (2003). Decentralization and The Indonesian Bureaucracy: Major Changes, Minor Impact?. In Edward Aspinal and Greg Fealy, *Local Power and Politics in Indonesia: Decentralization and Democratization*, Institute of Southeast Asian Studies, Singapore.

Salahuddin, M. R. and Rusli, A. (2005). Information Systems Planning for E-Government in Indonesia, paper presented in The Second International Conference on Innovations in Information Technology.

Samaratunge, R., Alam, Q and Teicher, J. (2008). The New Public Management reforms in Asia: a comparison of South and Southeast Asian countries, *International Review of Administrative Sciences*, 74: 25.

Appendix

Homepages of major agencies in public sector reform:
www.bkn.go.id

www.menpan.go.id
www.depkeu.go.id
www.lan.go.id
www.bappenas.go.id

Chapter 5 Public Sector Reform in Lao People's Democratic Republic

Suresh Balakrishnan and Khammoune Viphongxay

Introduction

The Lao People's Democratic Republic (Lao PDR) is making the transition from a centrally planned system towards a market-oriented economy, achieving an average economic growth rate of more than 7 percent per annum between 2001 and 2010. Although the Lao PDR is ranked as 122nd out of 182 countries according to the Human Development Index, it has made significant progress in improving human development, and is cited as one of the 10 Top Movers in the UNDP Human Development Report 2010. This impressive development has, in no small measure, been a result of significant strengthening of the public sector, which plays the main role in accelerating the country's development, through the use of a strategic mix of policy reforms and programme implementation. Such an achievement by a nation, ranked among the least developed countries in the world, offers an interesting case study of how public sector reform makes a difference in extremely challenging situations.

The rapid development of the Lao PDR has also brought in

its wake several new challenges that the country has to address. At the 9th Congress of the Lao People's Revolutionary Party, the political leadership of the country clarified the key issues that the nation will address in the next ten years. The underpinnings of the approach were outlined in the Break through Strategy that will also guide public sector reform in the immediate future.

No.	Issue	Strategic Response
1	Work style that has led to inadequacies in promoting commercial production and simultaneously generating real income for poor families	Opening up and addressing the characteristics of dogmatism, conservatism, irresponsibility, left and right extremism
2	The pace of social development that has not kept pace with the economy's growth rate, accentuating the income gap among social strata and between towns and remote areas, and the lack of discipline in planning and financial matters, as well as the lack of clearly defined policies	Improving management and governance regulations and systems in order to address obstacles that still hinder business and service operations
3	Delivery of services by state bodies at all levels has tended to be bureaucratic and non-transparent, sometimes creating loopholes conducive to corruption	Developing human resources, particularly the upgrading and nurturing of knowledge and competence of officials in all aspects to meet the growing development requirements.
4	Dependence on exploitation and export of natural resources for economic growth while agricultural productivity, agro-processing and light industry remain at a low level of development	Moving towards poverty eradication by mobilizing all possible financial sources associated with devising special incentive policies and the development of socio-economic infrastructure to promote growth in other areas.

The Lao PDR is a landlocked country surrounded by Thailand, Myanmar, China, Vietnam and Cambodia. The country is divided into sixteen provinces, plus Vientiane, the Capital City. It has a land area of 236,800 square kilometres and the population of 5.62 million inhabitants - hence the Lao PDR has one of the lowest population densities in the region (24 people per square kilometre). Around 27 percent of the population lives in urban areas, with the remaining population scattered widely in villages and small townships. The population demographic is fairly young, with 35 percent below the age of 15 years in 2005 and more than 58 percent below 25 (UN Population Division's World Population Prospects: 2010). The country has a diverse population made up of at least 49 main ethnic groups that can be classified into four ethno-linguistic families: Tai-Kadai, Mon-Khmer, Hmong-Mien, and Tibeto-Burman.

The Lao PDR is among the Least Developed Countries (LDC) in South-East Asia. The country is characterized by low levels of per capita income, low levels of human resource development, and the lack of economic diversification. It is ranked as 130th out of 177 countries in the global Human Development Index 2007-08; its rank is however higher than some of the other countries in the region such as Timor Leste, Myanmar and Cambodia. Estimates indicate that the poverty level has declined from 46 percent in 1992-93 to about 33 percent by 2002, and further to about 27 percent by 2008 (GoL and UN, 2009). Educational achievement levels have also significantly improved. Among persons of age 6 years and above, only 26 percent have no education, which is a major improvement from 43 percent in 1995. Over the same period, the Human Development Index for the Lao PDR improved steadily from 0.240 to 0.497.

These developments need to be viewed in the context of the challenges that the Lao PDR is facing. Living conditions have improved, markedly reducing poverty in urban areas, while poverty and near poverty still remain widespread, especially in rural areas where the vast majority of Lao people still live and work largely at a subsistence level. Income disparities have increased significantly in recent years as reflected by a significant rise in the country's GINI coefficient from 28.6 to 35.7 between 1992 and 1997. Malnutrition remains a significant concern with 37 percent of children below five years of age being underweight and chronic malnutrition affecting children in that age group (GoL and UN, 2008).

Political Development

The character of the state and the public sector is intrinsically linked to the long and complex history of the Lao PDR. As the Kingdom of Lan Xang Hom Khao around Luang Prabang, it played a major role in the region from the 12th century as the key point for trade that passed through this region. After its decline from the 16th century onwards, it came to consist of four kingdoms, Xieng Dong Xieng Thong (Luang Prabang), Xieng Khoang, Vientiane (Sikhottabong) and Champasak (Chamberlain, 2007). From the 19th century, these Lao kingdoms came under the sphere of influence of the French, who united three Lao kingdoms under the rule of the royal house of Luang Prabang, and managed these territories as part of French Indochina until the middle of the 20th century.

The country's first monarchical constitution, written in French, was promulgated on May 11, 1947 declaring it to be an independent state within the French Union. The military defeat of the French at Dien Bien Phu in 1954 led to the withdrawal of the French from the region, which was followed by elections under the Lao monarchy. The revised constitution of 1957 was very much the same as the first constitution, but the references to the French Union were removed, although the country continued its close educational, health and technological ties with the former colonial power. In the following years, there was much flux, and a series of nationalist and right-wing governments controlled most of the country with US backing, while the revolutionary Pathet Lao gathered strength in the northeastern and eastern regions. The victory of the communist forces in Vietnam and Cambodia was followed by the victory of the Lao People's Revolutionary Party (LPRP) that removed the Lao monarchy and its allies from power and established the Lao People's Democratic Republic in 1975.

The 1957 Constitution was abrogated on 3 December 1975, following the proclamation of the People's Republic. During the next decade the country was managed on the basis of revolutionary socialist principles - collectivization, nationalization, reeducation, and the like. The first legislature of the Supreme People's Assembly adopted the first Five Year Plan of Socio-Economic Development (1980-1985) and passed a number of new laws, such as the Law on the Council of Ministers, the Law on Local Administration Authority and the Law on Foreign Investment. In the decade that followed, the national leadership recognized that such orthodox policies were not delivering the required results. The high degree of decentralization at the administrative level, led to substantial divergences in applied procedures and standards, and the recruitment of large numbers of civil servants (Keuleers and Sibounheuang, 1999). The political leadership adopted the New Economic Mechanism at the 4th Party Congress in 1986. The prime feature of this new mechanism was the shift from a command and centrally planned economy to a market economy.

The new Constitution of the Lao Republic, adopted on 14th August 1991, marked the transition from direct administration by the Party towards a modern state governed by the rule of law. The Constitution established the legislature, the judiciary and the executive as the main institutions of the state under the guidance of a single political Party, the Lao People's Revolutionary Party (LPRP). Party committees at each level support the local authorities in the implementation of the country's socio-economic development plan. After the Third Legislature was elected in 1992, the Supreme People's Assembly changed its name to the National Assembly, and regional assemblies ceased to exist.

Economic Development

When the Lao PDR was proclaimed in 1975, the economy of the country was in ruins after more than 20 years of political struggle and war (1953-1975). The new government sought to accelerate development through advancements in the agricultural sector. Attempts to collectivize agriculture, which was designed to gain state control, but did not achieve the required results, and agricultural production stagnated. In 1979, the LPRP took its first steps towards market-oriented reform by easing restrictions on private trade and encouraging joint ventures between the State and the private sector. An interim three-year economic development plan began in 1979. The Government reduced agricultural taxes and increased state procurement prices for most crops, but it retained central planning.

More far-reaching reforms began with the introduction of the New Economic Mechanism (NEM) in 1986, coinciding with the commencement of the second five-year development plan. The New Economic Mechanism required corresponding reforms in the public sector to support the economic transition, which was high on the reform agenda. Several fiscal reforms were introduced in the late 1980's along with major political initiatives in the 1990's. The NEM recognized the dominant role of agriculture and sought to address shortcomings in this sector through reform measures to move toward a market economy. The Government abandoned the collectivization of agriculture, eased restrictions on private sector activities, and allowed state enterprises to have more decision-making authority. Lao PDR has joined the Association of South East Asian countries and is currently in negotiations regarding its membership of the World Trade Organization.

The Lao PDR economy continues its rapid expansion. Real economic growth, which reached 8.4 percent in 2006, was at 7.5 percent in 2007 and 7.2 percent in 2008, slowing down to 6.7 percent in 2009 during the global financial crisis, but it moved up to 7.8 percent in 2009-10 (GoL, 2010). It was estimated that GDP per capita in FY 2009-2010 was US$ 986, compared to the Five-Year Plan target of US$ 800 in 2010.

Robust growth in recent years occurred across all major sectors, led by mining and power [energy or power-generation, followed closely by manufacturing, and then by services and agriculture. Agriculture remains the backbone of the economy and accounts for 43 percent of GDP and 80 percent of the total workforce. A significant majority of the agricultural workforce consists of subsistence farmers growing rice and vegetables, and raising livestock. There are around 34 fully state-owned enterprises as well as 8 joint ventures and 59 provincial State Owned Enterprise operations. The Lao PDR also has a large micro enterprise sector, which accounts for a significant share of employment and businesses in the country. However micro enterprises have limited access to finance, which is a serious constraint for expansion. The remaining part of the economy is formed by heavy industry and services mainly hydropower, cement, beer, mining, and telecommunications. Thai Baht and US dollar are widely used as mediums of exchange.

In recent years, a high GDP growth rate has been driven by

high commodity prices in global markets and large inflows of foreign direct investment (FDI) attracted by the country's rich natural resource sectors (hydro, mining, forestry, and increasingly mechanized crop plantations). Public investment in the last five years amounted to about US$ 3 billion, with the government-funding portion of US$ 0.5 billion and the balance provided by the Overseas Development Assistance (ODA) funds. While 58 percent of the ODA was provided in the form of grants, the remaining 42 percent was received in loans. The Lao government approved private domestic and foreign direct investments of about US$ 9.7 billion in the period 2006-2010, in which private domestic investments were US$ 1.7 billion. The largest proportion of approved funds, US$ 2.9 billion, went to the electricity generation sector, followed by mining at US$ 2.7 billion, and services US$ 1.2 billion. During 2008-2009 alone, investment proposals worth US$ 4.3 billion were approved. The largest investments were from China, Thailand and Viet Nam.

Confidence in the Lao national currency, the Lao Kip (LAK), is reflected in an increasing percentage of LAK-denominated deposits and improved exchange rates as measured against major currencies such as the USD and the EURO. A key role played by the state in rapidly developing economies, which directly impacts people's lives, is a check on inflation. Keeping the inflation rate under 10 percent has been a major challenge for the Lao PDR authorities, and this goal has been reached. Like many Asian countries, the Lao PDR experienced hyperinflation during the Asian financial crisis and its aftermath, most profoundly in the years 1998 and 1999 when prices rose by more than 200 percent. The authorities tightened the money supply, slowing inflation to 23 percent in 2000. Since then, inflation has been kept below 10 percent, except for the 12.6 percent price level increase in 2003 when a drought drove up food prices. For the first time in the history of the Lao PDR, the annual average inflation was nil (0 percent) in 2009. The Consumer Price Index-based inflation (year-on-year) increased to about 7.7 percent in March 2011 from 5.8 percent in December 2010, which was driven largely by the rise in fuel costs. By contrast, food inflation declined to 7.2 percent in March 2011 from 14.2 percent in September 2010, which is attributed to the government's inflation control measures (Lao PDR Economic Monitor - May 2011 Update).

At the same time, the quality of growth (including equity and sustainability) and the underlying quality of FDI, natural resource management and environmental sustainability are critical emerging issues. Public assets, such as government-owned land and water resources, are also important areas for systematic public intervention due to the rapid growth of foreign investment approvals in land-related investments. This issue is more complex because legally enforceablel and titling for most Lao families and communities, especially in rural areas, is at a nascent stage. As a result, FDI will need to be more strategically mobilized to effectively contribute to the achievement of the goals outlined in the country's National Socio-Economic Development Plan (NSEDP) 2011-15, including the MDGs, and a further push towards the abandonment of the LDC status.

Public Sector Reform

Platform for Public Sector Reforms

Following the broad directions for market-oriented reforms based on the directions provided by the Party Congress in 1986, the Government of the Lao PDR launched its first public sector reform initiative in 1993. While economic transition was high on the reform agenda, the New Economic Mechanism required corresponding reforms in the public sector. A major personnel downsizing policy was implemented in the early 1990's, and some key institutions were created to support the process of building a more professional bureaucracy. The systematic efforts to improve public administration commenced soon thereafter through a small Public Administration Reform (PAR) project in 1994.

The PAR initiatives launched in 1994 were learning opportunities for the government and its development partners to arrive at a meaningful strategy to bring development assistance into this sensitive sector. The scope of these initiatives was limited, and the focus was on building awareness and capacity. Although only limited progress was made during these initial PAR experiences, by 1996, the Lao government had a better understanding of the complexity and long-term nature of public sector reforms. Building on the initial experience, the Party and the Government approved a broader Governance and Public Administration Reform Program Concept in 1997.

The focus of this reform effort was on high-level leadership. When the GPAR Programme was first established, a high-level Leading Committee was established, led by the current Prime Minister of the Lao PDR, Mr. Thongsing Thammavong, who was then President of the Central Committee of Organisation and Personnel. This measure was further supported by the establishment of the Committee for Government Organization Improvement, which was charged with coordinating and restructuring the central and local administration. The reform Programme was envisaged to be a broad platform driving a wide range of reforms. The initial vision of the reform programme had six main components: (1) financial management reforms; (2) personnel management reforms; (3) central government reforms; (4) local government reforms; (5) public sector legal reforms; and (6) other reforms related to the role of the state. Human Resource Development was the additional component that cut across all other reform components. This broad mandate reflected the deep understanding of the interrelated nature of steps required to build a modern state.

A simplified formulation of the public sector reform programme was intensely reviewed in the following years. A much deeper understanding of how better governance could contribute to development evolved from these discussions. Better governance was defined as "the broad policy framework in which state institutional and structural arrangements, decision-making, policy formulation and implementation and information flows are incrementally improved, based on internal and external conditions, to ensure optimal relationships and interaction between state and society." It envisaged steps to restructure the machinery of the state to become responsive and efficient, while addressing the priorities of equity. In doing so, it sought to make use of suitable financial management and monetary policies in order to leverage the private sector as a partner and complement to the public sector. The third critical element was capacity development, through strategic investments of scarce resources, in carefully selected infrastructure and human resources.

The government's proposed framework for governance reform is reflected in the National Socio-Economic Development Plan for the period 2006-2010. The strategic plan on governance emphasizes the government's commitment to building "an effective, efficient, well-trained, honest and ethical public service that is able to meet the needs of the multi-ethnic Lao people" (GoL, 2006). It highlights the need for greater accountability, transparency and public participation in planning and decision-making, as well as more accessible and efficient legal enforcement institutions. Given the projected increases in public revenues over the life of the current NSEDP period as a result of investments in the energy and mining sectors, there is an immediate requirement to strengthen governance for more accountable and transparent service delivery. The government's framework identifies four major governance themes; "Public Service Improvement, People's Participation, Rule of Law and Sound Financial Management." Each of these areas was seen as playing a critical role in ensuring the balanced and sustainable development of Lao society and administration.

Public Service Improvement

The Government has addressed the goal of Public Service Improvement, through several activities related in four strategic areas: improving the state management regulations and administrative framework, reforming organizational machinery and administrative framework of state agencies, improving civil service management and strengthening central-local relationships.

The Government of the Lao PDR put in place several regulations and framework to support substantive and sustainable change, concentrating on improving the roles, functions, duties and organizational structure, and appropriately modifying deployment and appointment of staff. The central-level focus was on enabling Ministries to address their macro management roles, while enabling decentralization of work, authority and responsibilities to the local authorities and technical units. The government issued a significant number of resolutions, decrees, decisions and instructions for this purpose. It established and simplified the administrative regulations making them more specific in order to facilitate the delivery of public services. The Prime Minister's instructions regarding expansion of One-Door-Service to all provinces (Ordinance 86) provided an impetus for an effective decentralization of services used by large numbers of people. Peer-to-peer learning of these simple innovations has followed, with several provinces replicating the successful pilot employed by the Xaysetha district in Vientiane

Capital.

The process of reorganizing ministries and agencies of the government is an on-going activity; in accordance with the priority of supporting internal efforts for improvement, manuals and tools to enable analysis and restructuring are seen as a key step forward. The roles, functions and rights of several-Ministries were reviewed. In recent years, the Prime Minister's Office has issued several decrees on the role and structure of several ministries and agencies. Some specific tasks were transferred to ministries and equivalent agencies to ensure more efficient management. A number of new organizations were established with the specific aim to respond to the changing situation during the new period. In an effort to streamline this strategic effort, the Government reorganized the established Ministry of Public Works and Transport to deal with the core functions of infrastructure development, and set up separate agencies to handle other tasks. On a similar note, a Ministry of Planning & Investment was established to help the Government provide direction and technical support to all ministries and agencies. More recently, the Government announced steps to restructure the various agencies under the Prime Minister's Office by setting up four new ministries.

Civil Service Management

The strong support of the government for implementing the NSEDP has led to strengthening of Civil Service Management on a continuing basis. The policy framework is provided by the Civil Service Statute of the Lao PDR based on Decree No. 82/PM issued on 19 May 2003 (GoL, 2003a), which amends Decree No. 171/PM of 11 November 1993. Several regulatory documents were provided to help discharge key civil service management functions such as selection, recruitment and deployment, grade and step determination, training and development, award granting and disciplinary measures, resignation and retirement.

Job descriptions have been employed in organizations at the central and local levels throughout the country. Actions were taken to separate administrative personnel from technical personnel in the education and health sectors in order to facilitate the employment of new civil servants and the application of policies in an appropriate manner. The government concentrated on the transfer of civil servants from the central level to local level. Efforts were made to increase the number of civil servants at the district level by increasing the recruitment quota of new personnel at this level.

An assessment of the capacity building initiatives for the civil service took place (GoL, 2008), and the lessons provide important insights for the detailing of the National Civil Service Training and Development Framework, which includes elements, such as a National Training and Development Policy and Procedures and Training Curriculum. The government has also set up a Civil Service Training Centre. The Training Centre develops and delivers training programs for public servants in high priority areas of governance, such as human resource management and e-Governance, provides a platform for leadership development, including result-oriented management, and establishes core values for quality service delivery and citizen oriented administration.

The Draft Code of Conduct for civil servants was developed, and it will soon be rolled out with implementation mechanisms. This Code will provide civil servants with clear guidance on matters that have a significant bearing on performance and effectiveness visavis the civil service as well as the people they serve. The systematic management of civil servants is being supported by leveraging information technology. The Information Technology-enabled Personnel Information Management System provides an Internet based platform to facilitate updates of the data base. This system will be expanded to support payroll operations with close support of all Ministries. The government has initiated systematic efforts to improve the salaries and benefits of civil servants, which are currently at a very low level.

Sub-National Administration

The government took important steps towards creating stronger local administration in urban areas. The decisions regarding the scope of functions and delegated authority for municipalities are being made, with the pilot program to be implemented in the World Heritage City of Luang Prabang. The lessons from Luang Prabang will be reviewed in the process of drawing up plans to establish the Municipality for Vientiane Capital. Local administrations in select districts are now being provided with authority and financial resources to plan and implement small investments for strengthening local service delivery -these include renovation of rural schools, construction of small water supply systems and foot bridges, etc. While the transferred funds are not very large, the big achievement is the capacity being created at the district level in order to take on greater responsibilities in local development.

The government closely looked at the need for capacity development and improvement of machinery for district administration. The Prime Minister's Instruction on this matter was been followed with pilot efforts in some districts. Given the capacity constraints in the districts, framework was developed to assist the district administrations. The government has also initiated steps to strengthen the performance of the lowest levels of administration at the village and village clusters. Mechanisms were also developed to oversee performance and support capacity building for the village and village clusters level.

Rule of Law

The institutions working on strengthening the rule of law are the Ministry of Justice, the People's Supreme Court and the Office of the Prosecutor General. Effective "rule of law" is a vital part of the development of governance systems in the Lao PDR. The Legal Sector Master Plan has been drafted, and a major national programme will implement the Plan in a systematic manner. While there is a need for several laws and legal instruments, the Government has systematically identified the priorities in law making, keeping in mind the social and economic development goals of the country. Laws on several critical functions are being formulated so that social and economic activities can be effectively carried out. The development of around 20 laws has taken place recently, such as the Law on Accounting, Law on Education, Law on Commercial Banks, Law on Value Added Tax, Law on the Protection of Children's Rights, Law on Audit, Law on Inspection, and Law on Public Security.

The Government of the Lao PDR attaches great importance on having an informed citizenry, who can contribute to the development of the nation. Mass media plays a major role in this endeavor. The Law on Mass Media was an important step towards providing the media with a clear mandate to carry out its work. This law enables journalists and mass media to expand their activities. The Government continues to provide leadership for the industrial and economic development of the country. While private enterprise plays an increasingly greater role, State Enterprises and Joint Ventures continue to play a major role in the national economy. The Law on Management of State Investment ensures that State Enterprises perform their mandated role and are managed effectively. In line with the strong role played by the Government in supporting the country's development, there was need to actively manage the country's financial resources. The Law on Treasury enables the government to manage treasury operations, which leverages the availability and use of Information Technology within the government. A Department of Enforcement of Judgment of the Ministry of Justice has been established to deal with and improve the situation in relation to the low level of judgment enforcement.

The Government of the Lao PDR is committed to its role in the global community, and is signatory to several international treaties and covenants. The Government signed the International Covenant on Civil and Political Rights in 2003, which is yet to be ratified. A framework for the Government's response to requirements of the international commitments has been provided through the Presidential Ordinance on Conclusion and Implementation of Treaties once passed, it will be a major step to a speedy implementation of several measures by the Government.

Providing access to relevant information is another key priority in the legal sector. Given the limited reach of mass media, radio has been the preferred medium for awareness building efforts. Radio has the potential to reach all parts of the country, and it is widely used by rural communities for receiving information and entertainment. While the materials are developed in Lao language, used by the largest segment of the population, the needs of members of ethnic communities who are not fully conversant with the Lao language has also been addressed. Radio programmes are specially translated and broadcasted in local languages. Other mass media, such as newspapers and television, are used to promote legal awareness. Information about several programmes and events are being shared with the citizens through these media.

The People's Supreme Court, District Courts and Courts of Appeal are growing gradually. Capacity building for judicial personnel is an important priority. The judicial system has also addressed the needs of specific segments of society. Emphasis has been placed on establishing women's and juvenile's units in courts. A Women's Advancement Unit is being set up in the Supreme Court. The Prosecutor's Office has also been expanding and The Appeal Prosecutor's Offices have been established in the North, Central and South of the country.

Citizen Participation

People's participation is a cross-cutting priority, which is addressed by different institutions ranging from the representation in the National Assembly to participatory planning in the villages. The National Assembly plays a vital role in promoting people's participation in governance as it is an elected body, with members chosen by the Lao people. As an institution, it enables people's participation through re-presentation, oversight and legislative appraisal.

Press coverage of National Assembly's activities has also increased. Every day, during the National Assembly's sessions, the National Assembly's activities are published in the newspapers and broadcasted live on TV and radio. The National Assembly performs oversight through a variety of means: by scrutinizing the performance of line ministries, through question-time and through debates during plenary sessions. In general, public participation in these processes is indirect. By contrast, the petitions system provides a more direct form of participation by giving the public a way to address grievances relating to judicial and administrative cases. To further strengthen the petitions system, several consultations have been held to clarify the respective responsibilities of the judiciary, executive and legislature in handling petitions. Consultations have also been held on upgrading the existing Department for Public Petitions to a Committee, possibly with ombudsman-like functions. Internally, capacity has been built by the training of provincial parliamentary staff on petitions processing.

The National Assembly hotline is another important channel for direct participation by the people. Since 2006, the hotline operates during each ordinary session of the National assembly. It receives anonymous comments, suggestions and concerns from the general public by telephone, fax, letter and email. At the end of each day, a summary report together with full transcripts is sent to each Member, as well as relevant line ministries. Many issues have fed into parliamentary debates, thereby increasing the quality of legislative scrutiny, oversight and debate. The hotline reports are also passed on to the local media, thereby increasing the quality of press coverage and analysis of important social issues.

Parliamentary inquiries have also commenced in the Lao PDR, with the first inquiry conducted by the Committee for Social-Cultural Affairs with respect to the education sector. The inquiry collected inputs from the Ministry of Education at the central level and from education officials, teachers and parents in the northern (at the local levels). Consultations are beginning on the feasibility of establishing an official gazette, which will be an important step in promoting awareness of new legislation.

Mechanisms were initiated, whereby communities have been asked to benchmark the quality of services, provide insights into key areas where improvements are of high priority, and provide assessments of how services have improved. The Decree on Civil Society Organizations is in place, and provides strong support for expanding the scope of civil society support for development activities in the country. Initial steps were taken to set up Local Councils in order to strengthen people's participation at the sub national level.

Financial Management

Public finance management reforms have evolved over this period on both the revenue and expenditure sides. There has been progress in the development of a new fiscal transfer system, establishment of greater control of public finance resources, alignment of policies with the budgetary constraints, and strengthening of external oversight and audit functions.

The Public Expenditure Management Support Programme (PEMSP) was adopted in 2005 through the approval of the Ministry of Finance (MOF) and the Prime Minister's Office (PMO). It helps mobilize and coordinate external assistance in support of GOL-led PEM strengthening initiatives, while ensuring technical consistency and appropriate sequencing and avoiding duplication of efforts. The PEMSP is structured in five components: (1) fiscal planning and budgeting; (2) budget execution, accounting, and reporting; (3) local government; (4) legislative framework; and (5) capacity building.

The centralization of the Treasury, Customs, and Tax functions mandated by the Amended State Budget Law (2006) has been a major step towards strengthened financial management. The Government Financial Information System was developed to facilitate budget execution and reporting, and has been progressively rolled out to central ministries/agencies and provinces. Efforts were made to improve the budget by incorporating off-budget funds and service delivery agencies' technical revenue into the budget. The single treasury account framework was implemented in a phased manner. Value Added Tax (VAT) was implemented in January 2010. The new Audit Law has been promulgated allowing the State Audit Organization (SAO) to directly report to the National Assembly instead of the Executive branch of Government.

The Lao PDR's Constitution of 1991 protects state, collective, and private forms of ownership. During the 1990s an active legislative program laid the foundations for developing market based rules and institutions to support private sector development. Today, agricultural production, and most manufacturing production, is in private hands, and SOEs only cover around one percent of employment. Nearly 97 percent of manufacturing units are small (less than 10 employees). Among the medium and large units, around one third are privately owned by Lao PDR citizens and just over half are joint ventures with foreigners. The remainder is government-owned. For investment inflows increased rapidly, spreading beyond the natural resource extraction sector (mainly hydropower, mining, agriculture, processing industries, and tourism). Between 2003 and 2010, actual investments increased from $110 million to almost $800 million, with hydropower and mining accounting for 80 percent of inflows. The main foreign investors are from Thailand, China and Vietnam, with other countries such as France, Australia and South Korea registering with significant investments. Laos has an increasingly strong higher-level regulatory business environment, but significant gaps remain with regard to inconsistent implementation of key laws, and the remaining gaps in subsidiary legislation.

In May 2002, steps were taken to enhance transparency of information about state-owned enterprises (SOEs) and the accountability of management. Decree No. 54/PM on the Management of State-invested Enterprises and Implementing Regulations (December 2002) clarified the roles and responsibilities of directors and managers of SOEs and their financial reporting requirements. The decree provided guidance on capital investments, procurement/transfer/replacement of assets, and treatment of dividends, as well as sanctions. In early 2004, the State Asset Management Board (SAMB) developed its data base and classification of all SOEs by performance.

Challenges of Public Sector Reform

The challenges that public sector reform as encountered are

both a function of the urgency with which the Lao PDR has sought to progress, as well as the serious capacity limitation that had to be tackled in this effort. However, the most serious limitation came from the basic weakness of the economy, which until recently left the Lao PDR almost completely dependent on development assistance.

Equity in Development

While the thrust of development succeeded in opening up several windows to strengthen economic growth, it was unable to simultaneously address the key priority of the government, which was to ensure equitable development. As mentioned earlier, GDP has increased significantly, but this process was accompanied by significant shortfalls in ensuring balances and equitable growth across the country. Poverty has been reduced considerably, but inequality persists. While raw materials exports have expanded rapidly, value addition and processing have lagged behind, resulting in lost opportunities to share the benefits of growth with the population. This basic limitation of a growth-led development policy has posed several other challenges to public sector reform.

With a large population living in poverty or near poverty, the government is required to step in and provide subsidized public services (health, education and infrastructure) that will improve the human capital. While the size of the budget and revenue generation has improved, the increase of domestic revenue has been unpredictable and limited, thereby constraining public spending and making this critical intervention dependent on foreign capital. The second major challenge has been the inability to transform labour available in the Lao PDR to make use of the employment and service sector opportunities emerging from economic growth. Skilled labour that is in high demand is not available, and this gap has to be met through short term labour imports from neighbouring countries, which strains the social and economic fabric of local communities. A large number of agricultural workers from rural areas have moved to urban areas to take low skilled jobs in the industrial sector, leaving some rural areas with a shortage of agricultural labour.

Gaps in Administrative Responses to Requirements of Growth

The government sought to progress, with as much speed as possible, to develop the administrative framework to support the pace of development and change in the country. In the quest for speed, there were instances of inadequate preparation of laws that affected implementation. On the other hand, there were instances when the preparation of laws and regulations on state administration were not appropriate or timely. However, the most critical issue concerns the gaps in ensuring awareness and enforcement of laws. There have also been issues of implementation because the structure of the administrative machinery, particularly at the sub national level, was not able to allow for situation-specific adjustments. For example, the implementation of One Door Service Centres, which have been very successful in some areas, have often encountered this constraint when expanded to other services. Another area presenting such challenges relates to the establishment of Municipalities, where the lack of clarity on scale and assignment of functions, have led to long delays in commencing implementation.

Deployment of Civil Servants

A critical part of the public sector reform effort was to ensure the adequate availability of civil servants on both central and local levels. The Lao PDR has encountered significant challenges in this area. This issue is rooted in the current design of the civil service, which allows little flexibility in moving appropriate personnel to positions and locations where they are most required. This problem is compounded by the fact that incentive and compensation systems are low, and totally inadequate to boost performance or deployment to remote areas. Both these issues have contributed to inadequate implementation of the mandate for deconcentration.

Quality of People's Representation

The Constitution places high importance on reflecting the aspirations and power of the people in the governance of the country. Notwithstanding the many steps taken in this direction, the major role for people's representatives has not yet been fully operationalized, particularly in terms of their interface in their constituencies. While the ministries and administrations have made significant progress in their structures and systems, the community organizations and civil society have not able to discharge all their assigned roles. These challenges reflect some basic limitations in the systems for people's participation. Participation depends very much on the clarity of the legal framework - the existing inadequate clarity has led to weak implementation. The lack of clarity is also related to limitations in transparency, which constrain many segments of society from having easy access to information. Complex and time consuming processes involved in providing people with official documents have also affected the involvement and participation of people in matters connected with governance.

Inadequate Adherence to the Rule of Law

As mentioned earlier, the rapid development of the legal framework has seriously challenged the consistency and comprehensiveness of laws being enacted. Frequent and significant revisions are being called for, which constrains the effectiveness of the administration and legal systems. This issue becomes even more complex when some laws are enacted without a competent enforcement authority being set up. The effectiveness of implementation is not just a matter of the legal system, since it also calls for strong coordination across all parts of the state. Unfortunately, this coordination is yet to reach the desired levels. Capacity building would be a key intervention to address some of these challenges, but this critical intervention is hampered by insufficient infrastructure, weak curriculum and inadequate qualified teachers for legal education.

The lack of capacity has seriously constrained the transition of the Lao PDR into a state consistently governed by the rule of law. Limitations in capacity have led to delays in case resolution. The capacity issue has also been heightened by the absence of clear criteria and use of standardized examinations for recruitment and promotion of legal and judicial officials. In the absence of a formal Code of Conduct in the sector, insufficient inspection, and a weak framework for disciplinary measures, there is little that can be done to address instances of the abuse of power.

Limited Internal Resources

Many of the efforts that have been outlined so far, particularly in capacity building, involves significant resources. The Lao PDR faces many constraints and challenges. Revenue collection in recent years failed to meet the ambitious but highly necessary targets. The issue was compounded by instances when collected revenue did not come into the treasury. One underlying issue is the overlap in tasks related to revenue collection and expenditure across central and local levels. The increasing pace of development activity has therefore been accompanied by a greater reliance on external loans and grants. Other issues are largely related to gaps in implementation. It has been pointed out that legal enactments related to financial management of state enterprises have not been effectively implemented. As a result, state enterprises continue to have large debt. Compliance with financial regulations is not being monitored strictly and regularly, leading to weak enforcement.

Lessons Learned and Conclusions

The Breakthrough Strategy announced by the 9th Party Congress of the LPRP, earlier in 2011, outlines political responses based on the significant lessons from the public administration reform experiences. Policy directions in terms of the second Strategic Plan on Governance and the 7th NSEDP are being aligned with the political directions.

Clear directions for reforms have been provided by the 9th Party Congress. The four elements of the breakthrough strategy approved by the 9th Congress affirm the move from conservative ideology to pragmatic modernization, critical investment in developing human resources, the improvement of management and governance systems, and the mobilization of resources for infrastructure and programmes that will eradicate poverty.

The first element of this strategy is termed the "imagination breakthrough," which refers to unlocking and addressing dogmatism, conservatism, irresponsibility, left and right extremism. The second element is the "breakthrough in human resources development," particularly the process of upgrading and nurturing the knowledge and competence of officials in all aspects, in order to meet the growing development requirements. The third element is the "breakthrough in improving management and governance," which includes development of regulations and systems addressing obstacles that still hinder business and service operations. The fourth element is the "breakthrough in poverty eradication" by mobilizing all possible financial sources associated with the special incentive policy, and developing socio-economic infrastructure to push development in other areas. The breakthrough strategy has important implications for the direction of governance reform and capacity development of the institutions that have to implement the next 7th NSEDP.

Responses to these issues are reflected in the 7th NSEDP "Growth with Equity" for 2011-2015, which has stressed the need for the public administration to be accountable, effective, transparent and responsive in order to guide the development of the country in a unified manner and to implement the State's duties in all fields, a capable and transparent public administration is needed at the national and sub-national levels. The 7th NSEDP aims to address these disparities by simultaneously promoting growth and (re)distributing its benefits for all. This requires a robust organizational coverage of the territory, which explains the Lao government's policy to improve the public administration from the central level down to the village level. Indeed, improving the capacity of the provincial, district and village authorities is vital as they play a key role in local service delivery, local development, social cohesion, just as ensuring the achievement of MDGs leads to tangible progress at the grass-roots. The 7th National Socio-Economic Development Plan (2011-2015) recognizes good governance as a cross-cutting objective of critical importance, calls for an expansion of people's participation, and points to the key role of civil society. Hence, the plan stresses the role of public administration in building the nation, the need to simplify administrative rules and procedures, improve and unify human resource management, and upgrade the skills of civil servants to improve their effectiveness, efficiency and ethical behavior.

It is evident that the further success of the public sector reform effort will need to address all aspects of reforms, which includes development or revision of required legislation, steps to establish or reorganize Ministries and other offices of the Government and clarify their mandate, procedures and regulations to manage the civil service as well as mechanisms for financing some of the initiatives described above. It is the synergy generated by employing these different elements that needs to underlie the Sector Wide Approach that is required in the Lao PDR in order to support the Government's Strategic Plan on Governance. While the separate reform initiatives have made good contributions, the efficiency and effectiveness is improved when the framework is planned well and respective responsibilities are assigned to different ministries, departments and sub-national authorities through a programmed approach. These measures will ensure that improved institutional framework and policies will be matched with better capacities to produce results and benefits.

In addressing the challenge of making major transformations in the public sector happen, the government has taken a step by step approach, often utilising pilot projects. Unfortunately, on reflection, it has become evident that many important policies and procedures that were piloted successfully have not yet been widely implemented. There is wide demand for implementing good practices. In the interfaces with sub-national stakeholders in particular, the question comes up as to when new policies and good practices will be implemented. The underlying reason for the slow scale up has been the excessive reliance on development assistance projects to support pilots and expansion. The lesson is that continuous reflection on policies and procedures is useful, but the priority with a good practice or successful pilot is to quickly take up wider implementation, preferably nationwide. Experiences also make it clear that there is no need for separate projects to implement these successful pilots. Once the framework, manuals and basic capacity, are in place, the government and its various offices can take the next steps. With the government slowly and steadily providing more resources to support the implementation of new mechanisms, it is timely to use the government machinery, primarily for implementing reforms, and also to supplement the government's support with development assistance.

In the effort to develop policies that are comprehensive and in line with global best practices, several important policy initiatives, that have taken several years and a lot of effort, are not yet complete. While policy development takes time, policy-making institutions and teams have the wider responsibility to external stakeholders to meet their commitments in the promised timeframe. The need is not about in-depth expertise or complicated management systems that take many years to develop. The real need is to develop the basic knowledge and competencies that civil servants require to carry out their basic functions in an effective and efficient manner. This also holds true with respect to capacity building in a country like the Lao PDR. The need is for skilled personnel in the civil service, who are able to read and understand simple manuals and guidelines, to make informed decisions and report to higher levels in a timely manner. The lesson from the efforts so far at training civil servants is that a few thousand well trained civil servants in the capital are not enough. For the reform effort to make a difference, basic competencies are needed even more, and among several thousands of civil servants in the provinces and districts. Hence, the two key points that need to be addressed, when preparing reform implementation plans, are urgency and scale.

The experience with public administration reform offers-several interesting insights and lessons in trying to facilitate major public sector transformations in least developed countries. While Foreign Direct Investment and exports of natural resources can be leveraged to speed up economic growth, the development of sound public institutions and facilitating equitable development call for an approach which may require more time and ensures capacity for all the key stakeholders involved in nation building. An imperative requirement is to ensure the clarity of mandates relative to different parts of the government and to establish sound coordinating mechanisms. At the same time, the leadership in developing countries needs to emphasize the importance of translating new and good policies into concrete development results, which benefit communities across the country.

References

Chamberlain, J. (2007). *Participatory Poverty Assessment - II.* Vientiane: National Statistics Centre and Asian Development Bank.

Government of the Lao PDR and United Nations (2009). *Employment and livelihoods: The Human Development Report of Lao PDR, 2008.* Vientiane (draft).

Government of the Lao PDR (2003a). *Decree 82/PM dated 19 May 2003: Decree on Civil Service of the Lao PDR.* Vientiane.

Government of the Lao PDR (2003b). *Decree 32/PO dated 28 May 2003 of the President:Amended Constitution of the Lao PDR.* Vientiane.

Government of the Lao PDR (2003c). *Law No. 02/NA dated 28 May 2003: Law on the Government of the Lao PDR.* Vientiane.

Government of the Lao PDR (2003d). *Law No. 03/NA dated 21 October 2003: Law on Local Administration of the Lao PDR.* Vientiane.

Government of the Lao PDR (2003e). *Public Service Reform, People's Participation, Rule of Law and Sound Financial Management: A Policy Paper of the Government of Lao PDR on Governance Issues.* Vientiane.

Government of the Lao PDR (2006). *Amended Law on the State Budget.* Vientiane.

Government of the Lao PDR (2008). *Decree 99/PM dated 23 June 2008: Decree on Administrative Positions of Lao Civil Service.* Vientiane.

Government of the Lao PDR and United Nations (2008). *Millennium Development Goals: Progress Report of Lao PDR.* Vientiane.

Government of the Lao PDR (2010). *Draft 7th National Socio Economic Development Plan: 2011-2015.* Vientiane.

Keuleers, P. and Sibounheuang, L. (1999). Central-Local Relations in the Lao People's Democratic Republic. In Turner, M. (ed.), *Central-Local Relations in Asia-Pacific: Convergence of Divergence*. NY: St. Martin's Press.

Stuart-Fox, M. (2004). Politics and Reform in the Lao People's Democratic Republic, *Working Paper No. 1, Program on Civil Society and Governance*. Williamsburg, VA: The College of William & Mary.

Winter, M. (2002). *Lao PDR: Fact Finding Mission Report*. Unpublished report prepared for UNCDF, Bangkok.

World Bank, Lao PDR (2007). *LAO PDR Public Expenditure Review: Integrated Fiduciary Assessment*. Vientiane.

World Bank, Lao PDR (2011). *Lao PDR Economic Monitor - May 2011 Update*. Vientiane.

World Food Programme (2007). *Lao PDR: Comprehensive Food Security and Vulnerability Analysis*. Rome.

Key Government of Lao PDR websites:

Ministry of Foreign Affairs: http://www.mofa.gov.la

Ministry of Finance: http://www.mof.gov.la

Public Administration & Civil Service Authority: http://www.pacsa.gov.la

Chapter 6 Public Sector Reform in Malaysia

Nik Rosnah Wan Abdullah

Introduction

Since the 1980s with increased globalization, curtailing of spending, and demands from the population, many governments are pressured into embarking on major public sector reform agenda aimed at achieving greater economy, efficiency and effectiveness. Following the lead, over the past two decades, many governments of ASEAN member countries have taken a series of initiatives to reform government processes, in an attempt to address the perceived shortcomings and generally to make government "work better." As pointed out by Peters (2001), "… if government is to be able to overcome the discontent and distrust of its citizens, it must find ways to become more efficient and effective in the processes of making and implementing policy."

For the Malaysian government, In the light of changed situations and changing policy priorities in the mid 1980s, there emerged a "paradigm shift" with the adoption of the market ideology and privatization policy undertaken as part of public sector reform. Since then, the Malaysian public sector underwent a major restructuring that brought about enormous change (Milne, 1986).

This chapter takes a close look at Malaysia's effort at public sector reforms. The reforms discussed are in specific examples and not intended to be a comprehensive examination. The aim is to share experience and inform government efforts in developing countries that are undertaking public sector reform initiatives in improving the content and approach to public sector reforms.

Literature Review

Public sector reform has been around for some thirty years since the late 1970s. Over the recent years, there have been general shifts in focus, moving away from the traditional concerns of public administration and public management, to an emphasis on decentralized forms of governance, extensive participation of the citizens (now viewed as clients and partners), accountability, and transparency in public management concerns (Farazmand, 1999).

To put it briefly, one of the general models of public sector reform in the early stage was decentralization of functions to government at lower tiers. It was thought that to handle the expansion of government tasks, was to give local and regional governments new competencies and resources. The other model is deregulation, accompanied by privatization. Privatization can be used to refer to any measure of public sector reform which has the effect of increasing the influence of the market mechanism on the allocation and utilization of resources (Batley, 1996). The thinking along these lines is that in a more open and competitive environment the delivery of public goods and services can only be run effectively if managed on the same or similar principles as the private sector. Privatizationis also advocated to modify administrative behavior (Walsh, 1995). Measures such as outsourcing, through an external supplier, or internal contracting arrangements, to create accountability are recommended (Walsh, 1995; Vickers and Yarrow, 1991).

Many of the reforms are influenced by the major shift in economic management policy in the UK and US (Vickers and Yarrow, 1991). Starting in the 1980s, the role and institutional character of the State has been questioned, and the public sector has been under pressure to adopt private sector orientations. The core paradigm which can be discerned as influential in the development of public sector reforms in the 1980s and 1990s was that public sector provision was inefficient and often ineffective; that it led neither to cost containment nor to quality improvement. With the problems so defined, the paradigm extended to a belief that the public and private sectors did not have to be organized and managed in fundamentally different ways.

More recently, the World Bank and other international governing institutions have been concerned with finding alternative ways of organizing and managing the public services and redefining the role of the state to give more prominence to markets and competition, and to the private and voluntary sectors. The alternative vision, based on issues of efficiency, representation, participation and accountability, has sought to create a market-friendly, liberalized, lean, decentralized, customer-oriented, managerial and democratic state. The focus was on creating institutional and organizational contexts which are to mirror what is seen as critical aspects of private sector modes of organizing and managing.

Mechanisms for Public Sector Reforms

The major mechanisms that promote public sector efficiency

and good governance according to the World Bank (1992, 2000) include: (1) public sector management emphasizing the need for effective financial and human resource management through improved budgeting, accounting and reporting, and rooting out inefficiency; (2) accountability in public services, and generally making public officials responsible for their actions and responsive to consumers; (3) a predictable legal framework with rules known in advance; a reliable and independent judiciary and law enforcement mechanisms; and (4) availability of information and transparency in order to enhance policy analysis, promote public debate and reduce the risk of corruption.

Besides these mechanisms, public sector reforms are usually associated with comprehensive changes in the institutions, organization and processes in the bureaucratic machinery of the state. These changes may be brought about through comprehensive reorganization plans (such as "reinventing" and re-engineering government, new managerialism) that may include streamlining the bureaucracy, improving coordination among agencies with overlapping functions, rightsizing, deregulation, privatization and decentralization. The reforms may be implemented in three areas: at the national level, specifically in the bureaucracy; at the local level, specifically among local institutions and local governments; and at the level of civil society, specifically in terms of encouraging people-participation in the processes of governance.

The prescriptions point towards market and private sector approaches to public sector management, under the guise of New Public Management (NPM). The profounder of the NPMs-fundamentally believe in market-orientation and the responsibility of self-aware citizens. The concept of NPM is particularly in line with established liberal values like: lean state, self-responsibility, free market, competition, performance orientation and transparency. The main targets of NPM are more transparency, more efficiency and more quality as well as cost reduction. It involves links to the political level (parliament), i.e., the strategic level. It is also connected to the general public, the citizens, i.e., to the market or customers. The goal is the transfer of private sector management practices, introduction of market forces to government, and establishment of liberal democratic principles (Hood and Peters, 2004).

It has been argued, however, that public sector reform along those models leads to the hollowing out of the state. Externalizing the provision of public services onto too many hands, including the market, tend to weaken the state. Literature also shows that operating with a business like manner in the public sphere can violate values of openness, fairness, equity and accountability (Box, 1999; Kim, 2000).

Malaysia's Political and Socio-economic Context

The Federation of Malaya (as Malaysia[1] was then known) was granted independence from Britain in 1957 with a relatively peaceful period of transition that was largely achieved by the granting of concessions to the main ethnic groups in Malaya (Means, 1998: 96). Its current population is 27 million and is essentially a plural society, with three major ethnic groups, Malays (66 percent), Chinese (25 percent), Indians (8 percent) and other minor ethnic groups (1 percent) (Malaysia, 2006: 238). Malaysia's racial divisions are parallel with a complex pattern of linguistic, cultural, religious, economic and political spheres. With the inter-ethnic "bargain" struck at independence on 31 August 1957, the British recognized the social contract that Malays are the *Bumiputera* (lit. "sons of soil"), and accorded special rights, in return for citizenship rights for the Immigrants who were mainly Chinese and the Indians. The structure of the Malaysian government is based on this social contract.

Since independence, the tension between races remains due to economic and specialization by race. The culmination of it was the racial riot on May 13, 1969, which represents a watershed in Malaysia's history. In response to the 1969 race riots, the government launched the New Economic Policy (NEP) in 1971, with a two-prong objective: "restructuring society to eliminate the identification of race with economic function" and "poverty eradication regardless of race." One part of this policy was the stated goal to reach corporate equity ownership levels of a minimum 30 percent *Bumiputera* and 40 percent other Malaysian and a maximum 30 percent foreign ownership, a goal which remains to this day. Another major part of this policy was to eradicate poverty by improving the economic competitiveness of the poor who are mainly *Bumiputera*. The NEP was the reflection of the leadership that was committed to achieving national unity by reducing poverty and achieving inter-ethnic economic parity, especially between the politically dominant Malays and economically ubiquitous Chinese. The subsequent policy decisions were the National Development Policy (NDP) and Vision 2020 (the 30-year perspective plan that seeks to transform Malaysia into a developed country by 2020) which marked the new beginning of reforms. These two documents have recognized the pivotal role of the private sector as the main engine for economic growth and development with the public sector playing only a facilitative and supportive role in the process.

The Malaysian Public Sector Reform Programmes

Since independence in 1957, the Malaysian public service has been entrusted with the twin task of socio-economic development and transformation as well as nation building. The reform revolved around the need to improve the quality of public sector management and shift the responsibility for economic development to the private sector. Each of the reform efforts can be seen as a product of environmental factors (particularly economic conditions and societal demands) and the developmental policies and objectives of the government (Muhammad Rais, 1995; 1997; Muhammad Rais et al., 2003).

Upon independence, the primary orientation was towards the maintenance of law and order and a limited developmental role. The early reform attempts until the 1970s were geared towards institution building and strengthening the administrative capacity to promote state-led socio-economic development. Following the introduction of the NEP in 1971, a renewed sense of purpose and urgency followed. Many new institutions, mainly the public enterprises, were established, and along with these, an expanded role for the government in development. Although the government reform began in the 1970s, the effort was stepped up in the 1980s at the time when Malaysia was beset by economic recession, and public enterprises generally reported disappointing performances, with inefficiency and ineffectiveness at the very peak, costing the tax payers significantly. In the face of these challenges, the government, at the macro level, thought that it needed to respond to economic challenges and global uncertainties, and formulated a strategic approach that linked reform of the public sector with its effectiveness and efficiency in promoting economic development and that the reform would fundamentally suit the needs of the management of the market economy. As evidenced in the Mid-Term Review of the Fourth Malaysia Plan (1981-1985) (Malaysia, 1984), and the subsequent Malaysia Plans, the government decided to reduce its role and involvement in the economy, and instead foster development through greater reliance on market forces. In essence, the government reformed the public sector to enhance private sector development and promote productivity and competitiveness whilst at the same time ensuring equity and social justice.

In 1991, the government launched the Second Outline Perspective Plan (1991-2000) which was more commonly known as the National Development Policy (NDP) (Malaysia, 1991). The OPP2 has specified the targets: economic growth, public-private partnership, greater investment and competence of the public service; and the strategies to be pursued to achieve those developmental goals. In the same year, the Vision 2020, a 30-year strategic plan that Malaysia should become a fully industrialized country by the year 2020 (Mahathir, 1991), was introduced by the then Prime Minister Dr. Mahathir which outlined Malaysia's aspirations and policy implications to achieve the goal of a fully developed nation status. It is important to note that both documents are complementary in nature. The focus was on industrialization as the country's development base and the private sector as the engine of growth, with the government as the enablers. They also emphasized public-private co-operation as a means to promote investment and hasten the process of economic growth. In order to enable the public service to play its new and emerging roles, the public service was expected to play a vital role in achieving national developmental goals.

The linkage between public sector reform and economic development can be clearly discerned in Vision 2020 which charted the future course of the country and how it should go about attaining the developed Malaysia in its own mould. It envisioned a nation that must be fully developed along all dimensions economically, politically, socially, spiritually, psychologically and culturally. As Malaysia is a multi-ethnic society, it must be fully developed in terms of national unity and social cohesion, infused by strong moral and ethical values, living in a society that is democratic, liberal and tolerant, caring, economically just and equitable, progressive and prosperous, and an economy that is competitive and resilient.

Abdullah Badawi's administration from 2003-2008 made several reforms, most notably, the transparency and accountability in the public sector. He declared outright war on corruption, patronage and abuse of trust. The framework mapped out was to clean up the private sector and smarten up the public sector. The public service was galvanized out of its inertia and KPIs, key performance indicators emulating the appraisal systems and accountability of the civil service, were introduced. All the while, however, the consistent Vision 2020 for the country as charted by Mahathir, remained.

When Najib Tun Razak took office in April 2009, the focus was on making Vision 2020 a reality within the timeline. In line with it, the One Malaysia (1 Malaysia) concept tagged with a slogan People First Performance Now was announced. The Cabinet, government agencies and civil servants were called on to strongly emphasize ethnic harmony, national unity and efficient governance, and attached with it the values of perseverance, a culture of excellence, acceptance, loyalty, education, humility, integrity and meritocracy. The 1 Malaysia concept aspires to strengthen relationships among the various ethnic groups to develop the country as a united developed nation in 2020 and beyond.

Since the 1980s, the Malaysian government has initiated urgent reforms to reshape the government's role and improve the efficiency of the public sector, in moving towards the goal of a developed nation by the year 2020. To achieve these objectives, various mechanisms were introduced in promoting openness and flexibility in the public sector, and this remains until the present with improvements made along the way. The paper focuses on four major reforms: (1) The Look East Policy; (2) ICT and e-Government; (3) Transparency and Accountability; and (4) the Government Transformation Programme (GTP) under the New Economic Model.

The Look East Policy-Privatization and the Malaysia Incorporated Policy

The policy atmosphere changed during 1983 when the government adopted the major public sector reform, the privatization programme under the "Look East Policy." The Look East Policy was essentially an attempt to encourage Malaysians to change their traditional perspectives of Western countries as role models and instead look towards the East. The underlying assumption was that Malaysia had much to learn from countries like Japan and South Korea, in terms of the high productivity, strong ethical standards and management philosophy and practices, which have helped those nations succeed in achieving remarkable economic progress (Mahmood and Johari, 1992).

A direct outcome of the Look East Policy was the introduction of the Malaysia Incorporated Policy in 1983 which was an attempt to emulate the Japanese and the Korean models of economic development by forging a new relationship between the public and private sectors. The concept sees the government as the provider of an enabling environment and that the private sector is to be the engine of growth for the nation. The central thrust of this approach is that cooperation and collaboration between the government and private sector is essential for accelerated economic development. Hence, the Malaysia Inc. policy not only called for an end to the traditional antagonistic relationship between the public and private sectors but also underscored the need for establishing a symbiotic relationship between them for realizing national developmental goals. In view of this, consultative panels were set up at each agency at federal and state levels; all public sector agencies began to hold regular dialogues with private sector partners to identify the problems of service delivery and decide on policy implications.

The Malaysian government, in its Guidelines on Privatization (EPU, 1985) has identified five different objectives for the privatization policy: (1) to reduce the "financial and administrative burden of the government"; (2) to "promote competition, improve efficiency and increase productivity" in the delivery of services; (3) to promote private sector participation in economic development and stimulate private investment, to accelerate economic growth; (4) to help reduce "the presence and size of the public sector"; and (5) the most important objective, the policy was to contribute towards meeting the objectives of the New Economic Policy (NEP) especially those regarding *Bumiputera* entre-preneurship and participation in the privatized service (EPU 1985). Under the policy, many public assets were privatized or contracted out under government leasing arrangements.

In line with the NEP and the NDP, the Government stipulated that *Bumiputera* should hold a minimum of 30 percent equity in all privatized projects. In other words, privatization was supposed to accelerate growth, improve efficiency and productivity, trim the public sector, reduce the government's financial and administrative role, and redistribute wealth to the *Bumiputeras*. Under the privatization policy a large number of services and projects that were previously in the public domain were privatized and corporatized. Over a period from 1983-1995 privatization grew rapidly with 204 projects privatized, of which 56.4 percent were from Federal government projects and 43.6 percent State Government (Malaysia, 1996: 2000). The privatized projects were in the construction sector, in utilities such as electricity, gas and water, highways and in the health sector (Malaysia, 1996; 2000).

ICT and E-Government

With the advent of globalization in the early 1990s, and the emergence of the new information and communication technologies (ICTs) that herald new opportunities for growth and development in countries around the world, governments worldwide sought to harness the potential offered by these new technologies to create new dimensions of economic and social progress. It became apparent then to the Malaysian government that a fundamental rethink and redesign of the governmental processes was essential in order to achieve dramatic improvements in the public service delivery. Therefore, the government proceeded to lay the foundations for the transition to the knowledge-based economy, promoting the information and communication technology (ICT) as its important agenda. The Government took a bold initiative increasing the Malaysian Multimedia Super Corridor (MSC) to turn Malaysia into a knowledge economy. The MSC attempts to create an ideal environment for ICT-related production as well as provide the backbone for an information super highway. It hoped that the MSC would become a new engine for economic growth. The vision behind Malaysia's MSC is to create an oasis for ICT and ICT-related companies that will make Malaysia a multimedia hub and create spillover effects into the rest of the Malaysian economy. To provide the enabling environment, the government was set to a major reform in the public sector and introduced a major revision in its procedural matters. The public agencies in general have been asked to review the existing ways of doing things in order to reduce red-tape and expedite the delivery of services and to take appropriate actions to ease regulations and procedures for the benefit of their clients (Sarji, 1994; 1996).

The emphasis was on efforts to rid administration of bureaucratic practices and speed up the approval process for applications related to issuance of permits, licenses, and land administration as well as economic, investment and other matters, which eventually has led to the introduction of new application forms, merger of several forms into a composite application form, reduction of time taken for processing of applications, extension of validity of licenses, and the establishment of licensing centers especially at the local level. Some of the prevailing systems have been abolished and the corresponding procedure has been streamlined. With the latest advancements in the field of information technology (IT) and the enabling effects of its numerous systems and applications, the public service has incorporated the extensive use of IT in further strengthening these strategies.

Since then, as elsewhere, ICT and e-Government have become a leading component of the current administrative reform and governance innovations in Malaysia. The government invested huge amount of resources under successive five year plans to develop necessary IT infrastructure and facilities throughout the country and undertook a variety of programmes seeking to enhance the performance and quality of services by harnessing IT and multimedia. The establishment of the Multimedia Super Corridor (MSC) in 1996 is seen as a milestone as it has contributed to acceleration of the IT application in the public sector. E-Government is among the leading MSC flagships and it aims at achieving public service excellence by reducing paper work and streamlining the service provisions so that the citizens can access services at anytime and from anywhere.

Transparency and Accountability

The Malaysian government acknowledged the prevalence of corruption and recognized the dangers of corruption to economic growth, and has set itself the task of fighting corruption in the public sector since the early 1960s. The legal framework was the Prevention of Corruption Act (PCA) of 1961, and the implementing body is the Anti-Corruption Agency whose major functions were: (1) to investigate and prosecute offences under the act; (2) to introduce preventive measures against corruption in the civil service and statutory boards; and (3) to investigate disciplinary complaints against civil servants (Marican, 1979). The PCA of 1961 was revised, and subsequently repealed and replaced with the Anti-Corruption Act 1997.

Other institutions include the Public Accounts Committee (PAC), which mandates that the accounts of the Federation and the States be examined by the Auditor-General which then has to be submitted to the King and, finally, to the House of Representatives. The PAC acts to ensure financial accountability on the part of government agencies and departments. It initiates action on concerns expressed in the Auditor-General's report.[2] It has the power to summon people, or request the issuing of letters, papers and records, and to issue statements to Parliament. The PAC will identify areas in the report which warrant explanation and may request relevant agencies or ministries to respond to queries of non-conformity raised in the Auditor-General's report.

The Public Complaints Bureau (PCB), established in 1971, serves as a channel for the public to lodge official complaints against government departments, agencies and public servants. The PCB provides a non-judicial, informal and inexpensive remedy to those with grievances against the public administration. Among the complaints received from the public are: delays in taking action, lack of public facilities, amenities and services, failure of enforcement, failure to adhere to procedures, and abuse of power and misconduct by civil servants, and unfair action. Complaints relating to corruption were referred to the ACA for investigation and further action. The PCB comes under the Prime Minister's Department and is supervised by the Chief Secretary to the government.

The effort of fighting corruption was stepped up when Abdullah Badawi assumed office in 2003. He pledged to eradicate corruption and promote good governance and good values in the public sector (Badawi, 2005). To promote transparency and integrity and combat corruption in the public sector, an integrity agenda was developed that targeted not only the public sector, which is perceived as the main perpetrators of corruption, but also aims to involve all sectors of society. The National Integrity Plan (NIP) was launched in April 2004, whose purpose was "… to develop a society which is morally and ethically strong with its members possessing religious and spiritual values that are steadfast and is supported by good values" (Malaysia, 2004: vii, 18). The National Integrity Plan (NIP) is a comprehensive plan that aims to bring about societal change in all sectors of the society. It is in line with the fourth challenge of Vision 2020 which is to establish "a fully moral and ethical society, whose citizens are strong in religious and spiritual values and imbued with highest ethical standards." The Plan details the strategies, programmes and activities to be implemented by all sectors of the society.

Simultaneously, the Malaysian Institute of Integrity (*Institut Integriti Malaysia* - IIM) was also launched to ensure that all planning, implementation, coordination, monitoring and evaluation related to the implementation of the NIP would be carried out.

Government Transformation Programme (GTP) under the New Economic Model

Currently, the buzz word in Malaysia is the Government Transformation Programme (GTP) that was introduced alongside the 1 Malaysia concept with the tagline "People First and Performance Now." The GTP aimed at radically transforming the way the government worked so it could quickly deliver real solutions to real issues and tangible outcomes that can be felt and experienced by the people. The objective is two-fold: (1) to transform the government to be more effective in its delivery of service; and (2) to move Malaysia forward to become anadvanced, united and just society with high standards of living for all. The GTP is led by the Performance Management and Delivery Unit (PEMANDU) within the Prime Minister's Department.

A series of Key Performance Indicators (KPI) was introduced in order to measure and improve efficiency and quality of the public sector as well as realizing the 1 Malaysia concept. The KPI provides a mechanism for evaluation of ministers and other government agencies including performance reviews carried out every six months. Six major identified policy areas, known as National Key Result Areas (NKRAs), were identified in which the KPIs were set to improve the effectiveness of the public sector. These include crime prevention, reducing government corruption, increased access to quality education, improvements in the standard of living for low income groups, upgrades to rural infrastructure and improvements in public transportation.

At the same time, the Economic Transformation Programme (ETP) was also introduced to propel Malaysia towards becoming a high-income developed nation. It is focused on key growth areas know as the 12 National Key Economic Areas (NKEAs) namely oil, gas and energy; palm oil, financial services; tourism; business services; electronic and electrical, wholesale and retail, education, healthcare, communications content and infrastructure, agriculture and greater Kuala Lumpur/Klang Valley. It aspires to achieve a Gross National Income (GNI) growth of 6 percent per annum that will allow Malaysia to achieve the targets set under Vision 2020. Malaysia is targeting a GNI per capita from $6,700 USD or RM 23,700 in 2009 to more than $15,000 USD or RM 48,000 in 2020 in accordance with the current World Bank's definition of high income.

Outcome of Reforms

A review of the nature and directions of public sector reforms in many ASEAN member countries attempted so far shows that they are not only in tune with the contemporary political and business environment, they also demonstrate the government's willingness to learn and adopt from other contexts in its quest for enhanced public service performance. For Malaysia, the success of its public sector reform in promoting economic growth and poverty reduction is well documented.

The Look East Policy, Privatization and the Malaysia Incorporated Policy

These policies have had a major impact of Malaysia's economic growth. The consultative mechanisms and dialogue sessions being held under Malaysia Inc. are seen positively as they provide two-way communication channels between the public and private sectors, and serve as platforms to agree on policy implications, to address the needs of both parties involved which have led to considerable administrative improvements and procedural changes, that later paved the way for administrative improvements in different areas (Bahari and Balan, 1999; Cheung and Scott, 2003).

As Megginson and Netter (2001) put it, studies have collectively shown a consistent result: privatization induces output, efficiency, and profitability improvements. Despite various criticisms, the privatization programme has made good progress and has led to significant gains to the government, at least in terms of trimming the public service and reducing governmental expenses, as reported in the government's documents (Malaysia, 2001; 2006). From 1985-2005, a total of 471 projects have been privatized which has led to the reduction of 113,220 employees in the public sector workforce, and has also helped the government to save a massive RM 153.9 billion in capital expenditure and RM 7.7 billion in operating expenditure annually (Malaysia, 2006). In terms of the ethnic implications and equity, it has widened *Bumiputera* participation in commercial and industrial activities, by participation through the management-buy-out (MBO) exercises, contracting works and vendor programmes, collaborations and joint ventures. In terms of efficiency and productivity, the services and management of the privatized entities was said to be significantly improved due to the upgrading of facilities which were able to acquire new and modern technology, expanded capacity and network, and fostered changes in management, and also led to faster implementation of projects.

Aside from the "official views," a study by Qian Sun and Tong (2002) on a sample of 24 state-owned enterprises that were privatized via public listing on the Malaysian exchange, compares financial and operating performance of the firms before and after privatization. Measures that improve following privatization include profitability, output level, and dividend payout; leverage declines. After privatization, the firms were found to have their absolute levels of total profits increased three-fold, more than double their real sales, increase their dividend payout, and significantly reduce their leverage. The study observed increased linkages between ownership and corporate governance with such performance changes. The results are said to be similar to that of other comparative multi-country studies.

Though comprehensive assessment on the overall impacts of privatization is lacking, evidence shows that it has been effective in trimming Malaysia's bloated bureaucracy significantly. It has had major impact on the public payroll as a total of 105,000 public sector employees have been transferred to the private sector (Muhammad Rais, 1995). The public sector as a source of employment became more limited. By 2003, a total of 471 projects have been privatized which has led to the reduction of 110,759 employees in the public sector workforce. It has also helped the government to save a massive RM 125.2 billion in capital expenditure and RM 7.7 billion in operating expenditure annually (Commonwealth Secretariat, 2004).

On the downside, as argued by Jomo (2003) and Jomo and Gomez (1999), despite its contributions to economic growth, privatization in Malaysia, has remained a contentious issue. There is a widespread view that the privatization policy in Malaysia has favored vested interests involving extra-legal tactics and widened opportunities for kickbacks and graft. Since often no such formalities as a tender system were involved, many beneficiaries were chosen based on political and personal connections (see Gomez and Jomo, 1999).

ICT and E-Government

The ICT and e-Government policy reform has helped reduced the distance between the government and the citizens. The public is able to obtain services conveniently without any loss of time. The old relationship characterized by rigidity, long delays, unnecessary complexity, and public distress is being replaced by a new relationship, which is characterized by speed, better public access, reduced cost, and public ease and convenience. The public service delivery system has been raised to a new level. Most public procurement procedures are handled online with stages of procurement such as bidding, awarding contracts, delivery and payments are handled online; taxpayers can handle their tax matters online in the convenience of their home, as all tax procedures including filing, billing and payment are processed online and information can be retrieved 24/7. Issuance and renewal of passports can now be made within a day as compared to two weeks previously. A wide range of information and services to support business activities such as the civil service information are also provided. Various services essential for corporate activities are provided. In sum, there is a vast impact: improvement of efficiency and transparency of public management. IT strengthened communications with the public about government administration and policies and increased efficiency of information resource management (Nik Azmin, 2006).

Nevertheless there are still some hitches. A 2008 study on usage of E-Perolehan (E-Procurement) initiative show that out of 120,000 government-linked suppliers (registered with Ministry of Finance), only 41.6 percent or approximately 50,000 suppliers were *E-Perolehan* enabled, and only 5 percent or 6,000 suppliers are active users of the system. The rest are classified as inactive or casual participants. The reasons cited were: (1) costs involved before a supplier becomes *E-Perolehan* enabled; suppliers have to bear cost of purchasing a smartcard for transactions, pay for training, and software renewal; (2) the majority of the supplier community falls within small-medium size industry grouping that has not been well-versed with the use of state-of-the-art information systems; and (3) although the government encourages suppliers to become e-Perolehan enabled, the practice is not made mandatory. The public sector users still prefer to conduct business through the traditional/manual system, as they were not fully equipped to handle the new system, particularly in state and local governments (Maniam, 2008).

Looking at the macro level on the progress of Malaysia in e-Government implementation, from a UN e-Government Survey 2010, among the 192 member states, Malaysia was placed at 32nd globally, whilst it was at 6th place among Asian countries, besides the Republic of Korea, Singapore and Japan, thus reflecting a significant progress towards e-Government implementation (Table 1).

Table 1. E-Government Development: Top Ranked Countries in Asia, 2010

Rank	Country	World E-Govt Development Ranking	
		2010	2008
1	Republic of Korea	1	6
2	Singapore	11	23
3	Bahrain	13	42
4	Japan	17	11
5	Israel	26	17
6	Malaysia	32	34
7	Cyprus	42	35
8	Kazakstan	46	81
9	United Arab Emirates	49	31
10	Kuwait	50	57

Source: United Nations e-Government Survey 2010.

However, Malaysia does not score particularly high when compared to regional and world leaders in e-Government. Based on the e-Governance readiness index, in terms of vital infrastructure like ownership of a personal computer and access to internet, Malaysia does not do well. Internet access is low, and the proportion of people receiving e-Government benefits is low. The challenge for Malaysia is not to increase the range of services available online but to increase access of the people through substantially expanding the coverage of computer ownership, telephones, and high speed internet connection, and also training for public sector users.

Transparency and Accountability

Despite various reforms implemented with the aim of fostering administrative accountability and responsiveness, the public sector has not been able to extricate itself from increasing graft and corruption charges (Siddiquee, 2006; 2008; Leong, 2006).

Political corruption and financial dealings between businesses seeking government approval or contracts and senior officials are open secrets and have long been a key concern among international investors. Locally, it has become an important issue in both political and administrative circles. It is also reflected in Transparency International's (TI) corruption perceptions index (CPI) through the years from 1995 to present. CPI shows that Malaysia's ranking has slipped further to 56th position out of 178 countries in 2010, and the CPI score has slipped to 4.0, as compared to score of 9.3 by countries like Singapore, New Zealand and Denmark, which are tied at the top, followed closely by Finland at 9.2 score. Malaysia remains well behind other countries such as Hong Kong, Taiwan, and Australia.

Accountability and transparency are two key requirements for good governance. Other major characteristics often cited include participatory, consensus oriented, responsive to present and future need of society, effective and efficient, equitable and inclusive and follows the rule of law (World Bank, 1992). In a survey made on 16 major Asia Pacific investment destinations, by a Hong Kong based Political and Economic Risk Consultancy (PERC), Malaysia scored 6.70 out of 10 in the 2010 survey on corrupt nations.[3] Top on the list is Singapore with 1.07 score, followed by Hong Kong with 1.89.[4] The issue of corruption seems to hamper Malaysia's development in terms of its economic progress.

For Malaysia, the primary goal during the 1970 to the present day is to address ethnic imbalances in the economy, and to achieve that endits main goal was to promote the growth of industrial and commercial enterprises owned by the *Bumiputera* majority. All other goals including that of international competitiveness and industrial efficiency were subordinated to that (Jomo, 2000; Gomez and Jomo, 1999). Hence, it is worthy to highlight that, Malaysia is ranked 19th place out of 153 countries

Table 2. Country Ranking in Global Peace Index 2011

Rank	Country	Rank	Country
1	Iceland	11	Ireland
2	New Zealand	12	Qatar
3	Japan	13	Sweden
4	Denmark	14	Belgium
5	Czech Republic	15	Germany
6	Austria	16	Switzerland
7	Finland	17	Portugal
8	Canada	18	Australia
9	Norway	19	Malaysia
10	Slovenia	20	Hungary

Source: Global Peace Index 2011

in the Global Peace Index (Table 2). It is ranked 2nd place among Asian countries, besides Japan (ranked 3rd in the world), and 1st among Southeast Asian countries. The indexis composed of 23 indicators, ranging from the country's level of military expenditure to its relations with the neighboring countries as well as the level of respect for human rights. The index was said to be tested against a range of determinants of peace, including levels of democracy and transparency, education and national well-being.[5]

Government Transformation Programme (GTP) under the New Economic Model

In its entirety the GTP is designed to provide all Malaysians access to improved public services irrespective of race, religions and regions. The six areas under the NKRAs are the most basic of requirements that the public wants to be improved in order to move into a high income and developed country status. It is early days to evaluate the GTP. However, while many of the targets set under the GTP are ambitious, its inaugural annual report, Year 1 of Horizon 1 (2010-2012) (JPM, 2010) of the GTP shows the government's commitment to deliver positive outcomes. The report highlights its successes as well as its shortcomings. It was reported that the feedback received about the GTP showed that the community felt that the programme took into account all aspects of their needs.

Conclusion

What is notable is that the Malaysian government met the challenges of globalization and economic crisis, through the public sector reform effort that was driven by the need to create good governance, to provide a strong foundation for economic recovery, and sustainable growth. What is currently needed is for the public sector to review the role of all government agencies in beefing up its service delivery and procedures to achieve the Government Transformation Programme (GTP).

Notes

1) In 1963 Singapore briefly joined the Federation, which then became known as Malaysia and also include the states of Sabah and Sarawak in North Borneo. Singapore was expelled from the Federation in August 1965.
2) The Auditor General's report relates to the accounts of the federation and the States (a) the accounts of the Federation and the appropriation of the sums granted by Parliament to meet the public expenditure; (b) accounts of public authorities and other bodies administrating public funds as may be laid before the House; (c) reports of the Auditor-General laid before the House in accordance with Article 107 of the Constitution; (d) other matters as the Committee may think fit, or which may be referred to the Committee by the House.
3) The survey looked at how corruption affected different levels of political leadership and the public service, and how major institutions fared in terms of corruption. It examined how corruption is perceived to affect the overall business environment.
4) The survey polled 2,174 middle and senior business executives in Asia, Australia, and the US.
5) The details are said to be obtained from wide sources including the International Institute of Strategic Studies, the World Bank, UN office and Peace Institutes and the Economic Intelligence Unit.

References

Ali, A. H. (2001). Serving in the knowledge age: Realigning the public service for the knowledge advantage, *International Review of Administrative Sciences*, Vol. 67, No. 2, pp. 273-285.

Awang, Z. H. (1995). Response of Public Administration System of Malaysia to Global Challenges. In Salleh, S and Carino, L.V.(eds.). *Globalization and the Asian Public Sector*, Asia Pacific Development Centre, KL

Badawi, Abdullah (2005). Charting the Course for Asian Economic Integration, speech delivered at the Future of Asia Conference.

Bahari, M. and Balan, S. (1999). "Malaysia incorporated," in Karim, MRA (eds.), *Re-engineering the Public Service: Leadership and Change in an Electronic Age*, Pelanduk Publications, Selangor, Malaysia, pp. 273-92.

Batley, R. (1996). Public-Private Relationships and Performance in Service Provisions, *Urban Studies*, Vol. 33, No. 4-5, pp. 723-751.

Box, R. C. (1999). Running Government likea Business: Implications for Public Administration Theory and Practice, *The American Review of Public Administration.* March 1999, Vol. 29, No. 1, pp. 19-43.

Cheung, A. B-L and Scott, I. (eds.) (2003). *Governance and Public Sector Reform in Asia*, Routledge/Curzon.

Commonwealth Secretariat (2004). *A Profile of the Public Service of Malaysia*, London.

EPU (1985). *Guidelines on Privatization*, Kuala Lumpur: Government of Malaysia.

Farazmand, A. (1998). Globalization and PublicAdministration, *Public Administration Review*, http://www.accessmylibrary.com/article-1G1-58038531/globalization-and-public-administration.html

Gomez, E. T. and Jomo, S. K. (1999). *Malaysia's Political Economy: Politics, Patronage and Profits*, Cambridge University Press.

Hood, C. and Peters, G. (2004). The Middle Aging of New Public Management: Into the Age of Paradox? *Journal of Public Administration Research and Theory*, 14 (3): 267-282.

Jomo, K. S. (2000). Malaysia's Privatization Experience. In Ash, R. and

Booth. A. (eds.). *The Economies of Asia 1950-1998*, London: Rutledge.

Jomo, K. S. (2003). Mahathir's Economic Legacy: A Chequered Record of Experiments Crises and Escapes, *Aliran Monthly*, 8.

Kettl, D. F. (1998). *Reinventing government: A Fifth Year Report Card*, Washington D.C: Brookings Institution.

Kim, P. S. (2000). Administrative Reform in the Korean Central Government: A Case Study of the Dae Jung Kim Administration, *Public Performance & Management Review*, 24 (2): 145-160.

Lieberman, I. W. (1993). Privatization: The Theme of the 1990s: An Overview, *Columbia Journal of World Business*, 28(2): 8-17.

Mahathir, M. (1991). *Malaysia: The Way Forward, Petaling Jaya: Centre for Economic Research & Services*.

Mahmood, Taib and Johari, Mat (1992). Administrative Reforms in Malaysia Toward Enhancing Public Service Performance, *Governance*, Vol. 5, Issue 4, pp. 423-437.

Malaysia (1984). *Mid-Term Review of the Fourth Malaysia Plan, 1981-1985*, Kuala Lumpur: Government Printer.

Malaysia (1991). *The Second Outline Perspective Plan, 1991-2000*, Kuala Lumpur: Government Printers Malaysia.

Malaysia (1996). *Seventh Malaysia Plan (1996-2000)*, Kuala Lumpur: Government Printers Malaysia.

Malaysia (2001). *Eighth Malaysia Plan (2001-2005)*, Kuala Lumpur: Government Printers Malaysia.

Malaysia (2006). *Ninth Malaysia Plan 2006-2010*, Putrajaya: EPU.

Maniam, K. (2008). *Technology Acceptance for Government E-Procurement: A Study on e-Procurement in Malaysia*, Ph. D. Thesis, Faculty of Economics and Administration, University of Malaya.

Marican, M. Y. (1979). Combating Corruption: The Malaysian Experience *Asian Survey*, Vol. 19, No. 6, pp. 597-610.

Means (1991). *Malaysian Politics: The Second Generation*, Singapore: Oxford University Press.

Megginson, W. L and Netter, J. M. (2001). From State to Market: A Survey of Empirical Studies on privatization, *Journal of Economic Literature*, Vol. 39, No. 2, pp. 321-389.

Menteri, Jabatan Perdana (2010). Government Transformation Programme, Annual Report.

Milne, R. S. (1986). Malaysia-Beyond the New Economic Policy, *Asian Survey*, Vol. 26, No. 12.

Molz, R. (1990). Privatization in Developing Countries, *Columbia Journal of World Business*, 25(1&2): 17-24.

Muhammad Rais, A. K. (1995). *Improving the efficiency of the public Sector: A Case Study of Malaysia*, Report for the Twelfth Meeting of Experts on the United Nations Programme in Public Administration and Finance, New York 31 July-11 August, 1995.

Muhammad Rais, A. K. (1997). Reengineering the Malaysian Public Service and the use of Information Technology in Promoting Efficiency and Quality, *Asian Review of Public Administration*, Vol. xix, No. 1.

Muhammad Rais, Bin Abdul Karim, and Nazariah, Mohd Khalid (2003). *E-Government in Malaysia*, Subang Jaya, Selangor: Pelandok.

Nik Azmin and Nik Hussain (2006). *General Overview of Networking the Government Electronic Government*. Paper presented at MAMPU MyICMS 886 Goals Workshop, Prime Minister's Department, Putrajaya (August).

Peters, B. G. (2001). Politicians and Bureaucrats in the Politics of Policy Making. In Osborne, Stephen (ed.). *Public Management: Critical Perspectives on Business and Management*, Routledge.

Qian Sun and Tong, Wilson H. S. (2002). Malaysia Privatization: A Comprehensive Study, *Financial Management*, Vol. 31, No. 4 (Winter, 2002), pp. 79-105.

Sarji, A. (1993). *The Changing Civil Service - Malaysia's Competitive Edge*, Kuala Lumpur: Pelanduk Publications.

Sarji, A. (1994). *The Civil Service of Malaysia: A Paradigm Shift*, Kuala Lumpur: Percetakan Nasional.

Sarji, A. (1996). *The Civil Service of Malaysia: Towards Efficiency and Effectiveness*, Government of Malaysia, Kuala Lumpur.

Siddiquee, N. A. (2006). Public Management Reform in Malaysia, *International Journal of Public Sector Management*, Vol. 19, No. 4.

Siddiquee, N. A. (2008). Service delivery innovations and governance: the Malaysian experience, *Transforming Government: People,*

Process and Policy, Vol. 2, Issue 3, pp.194-213.

The Star, 24 January 2008.

The Star, June 20, 2009: Najib: KPI for all government matters.

Transparency International (2009). *Corruption Perception Index 2009*, Berlin: Transparency International.

United Nations (2008). *UN e-Government Survey 2008: From e-Government to Connected Government*, New York: United Nations.

Vickers, J. and Yarrow, G. (1991). Economic Perspectives on Privatization *Journal of Economic Perspectives*, Vol. 5, No. 2, pp. 111-132.

Walsh, K. (1995). *Public Services and Market Mechanisms: Competition, Contracting and the New Public Management*, New York: St. Martin's Press.

World Bank (1992). *Governance and Development.*

World Bank (2008). Accessed 10/10/10, http://siteresources. world-bank.org/DATASTATISTICS/Resources/GDP_PPP.pdf

Yusoff, M. and Radzi, M. (2002). E-Government Opportunities and Challenges: Malaysia's Experience, http://egovaspac.apdip.net/topic/country/my/radzi-yusoff, accessed on 1/3/2010

Chapter 7 Public Sector Reform in Myanmar

Htay Htay Lwin

Introduction

Myanmar is a country prospering in different national races, cultures, natural resources, political ideologies and so on. Recently, Myanmar has moved towards transformation through a new administrative system. The change has been effected by transferring of hegemony from the State Peace and Development Council (SPDC) Government to the new Union Government, with its great emphasis on poverty alleviation, rural development, reducing unemployment, the maintenance of law and justice and achieving the socio-economic development of the citizens. Accordingly, the newly elected government is initiating efforts towards achieving good and clean governance, development of democracy practices, improving efficiency and effectiveness of the public sector and enhancing greater co-operation with inside and outside sources.

Throughout its history, Myanmar has made changes to its administrative system that have resulted in problems, conflicts and international percussions. The administrative system in Myanmar changed from monarchism to imperialism, then to a socialist democratic system, followed by a centralized system and finally to the adoption of a market oriented system by the recent government. Successive governments have tried their best to solve the problems that obstruct the achievement of a modern developed nation, but still so many remain.

Historical Background

Period of Absolute Monarchism

Transition to an urban civilization in Myanmar can be observed since 2nd century BC with the establishment of Wethali by Rakhines, Beikthanoe, Hanlin, Tagaung and Tharekhittaya by Pyus, and Thaton or Suvanabonmi by Mons. During this period, King Anawrahta unified the Bagan Empire and it was known as the first Myanmar Naing Ngan in that era. The Bagan administrative structure was systematic; hierarchical establishments of cities and towns, building of forts to protect from internal and external invasions and appointment of Governors to administer the capital city and the local levels through the king's power.

After Bagan, Pinya and Sagaing eras lasted through 13 dynasties, and from 1552 to 1581, King Bayintnaung founded the vast Hanthawady Empire (Taungoo era). This empire was ruled by 34 successive kings. In late 16th century, King Nyaungyan established Inwa Kingdom. The most famous among the Inwa Kings was King Tharlun, who ruled from 1629 to 1648, and undertook various reform measures. In 1752, King Alaungpaya reunited Myanmar and established the Konbaung Dynasty (1752 to 1885). To guide the King to use the administrative, legislative and executive powers fairly, offices such as Byedike, A Nauk Yone Taw, Hluttaw, A Shay Yone Taw, Tayar Yone of the council of ministers were formed to monitor this situation (Appendix 1).

During the Konbaung period, the administrative structure was a Dual Government System, comprised of a Central Administration (Nay Pyi Daw) and a Local Administration. The King was the national leader as well as head of government. King Mindon, the founder of Mandalay City, performed reform measures in various sectors such as administration, finance, industry and defense, etc. during his rule from 1852 to 1878. Under the administration of his successor, King Thibaw, the whole of Myanmar fell to British Rule on January 1, 1886.

The British had already controlled part of Myanmar from 1826 after the breaking out of First Anglo-Myanmar War. The Second Anglo-Myanmar War broke out in 1852 and lower Myanmar was placed under an Indian Chief Governor. The British ruled Myanmar as part of British-India until 1937. The Myanmar nationalist movements were led by the Young Men's Buddhist Association (YMBA) in 1906, and the General Council of Burmese Associations (GCBA), followed by other movements throughout the early decades of the 20th Century. 1923 to 1937 was regarded as the period of the Diarchy Administration (Appendix 2). Post Diarchy Administration was the 91 Departments Administration, practiced in Myanmar from April 1937 till December 1942. The territory of Myanmar during the British rule excluded the Shan State and Karenni areas (Appendix 3).

The Japanese took hold of the country in 1942 and in August 1943, it granted sham independence which was followed by an anti-fascist revolution on March 27, 1945. During the Japanese Military Administration, the whole of Shan State, Karenni and Wa States were to be amalgamated. Between 1945 and 1947, White Paper Administration was practiced again by the British government. In 1947, Sorrento Villa Rehabilitation Programmes were introduced. National consolidation in Myanmar was built through the Panglong Agreement on February 12, 1947 and Myanmar regained its independence on January 4, 1948.

Post Independence Period (1948-1988)

Post independence, Myanmar was a parliamentary democratic administration by the Anti Fascist People's Freedom League (AFPFL) Government from 1948 to 1958. A new constitution was set up in 1947 which legitimized a government administrative system consisting of the cabinet that was responsible to a bicameral legislature; the Chamber of Deputies and Chamber of Nationalities. The first two year plan was set in April 1948 for the purpose of maximizing development during the next two years and laying the foundation of a planned economy. However, it failed due to internal insurgencies, skill shortages, low morale, and improper administration.

The Eight Year Plan, also known as the Pyidawtha Plan was set out in 1952 to improve the standard of living of the people. However, it was abandoned in 1955 because of insufficient preparation, organization and supervision, weak collaboration amongst various administrative levels and regions, internal insurgencies, the bust of the world rice market, low skills and productivity, corruption and a huge external-dependency. In 1955, a new first four year plan was launched but later discarded after an unstable political situation. In order to restore law and order, and to hold a free and fair election, a Caretaker Government (military administration) intervened in 1958 (Appendix 4).

The Caretaker Government abolished the feudal system in the Shan and Kayah States. The chieftains (Sawbwas and Saophalongs) of those regions retained their feudal rights and privileges after the Union of Myanmar came into being. However, achieving a welfare state, the Government introduced the popular style government in the Shan and Kayah States. The Caretaker Government tried to reduce commodity prices and to raise the standard of living for the people of the country through establishment of the Defence Service Institute and the Burma

Economic Development Corporation, and shifting the squatter quarters to new satellite towns near Yangon.

In February 1960, the Caretaker Government held a general election where U Nu won a massive victory. The elected Pa-Hta-Sa (Pyidaungsu Party) Government ruled until 1962. However, with the threat of intense national disintegration and a deviation from the socialist course, the Revolutionary Council Government (military administration) took over power in 1962 and stabilized the country. During 1948-62, Myanmar's economic structure had changed slightly, with a widening of the gap between the rich and the poor, greater regional disparities, a decline in the educational standard and a reduction in capacity building.

In 1962, the Revolutionary Council assumed power to set the country on the path to Socialism, suspended the 1947 Constitution and abolished the bicameral Parliament. The Revolutionary Council also abolished the *Supreme Court and the High Court, and the Chief Court* was established to act as a final court of appeal in the Union. On May 9, 1962, the Central Security and Administrative Committee was created, and Security and Administrative Committees for State, Divisional, District, Township and Village were simultaneously organized. The new Government practiced nationalization in almost all businesses except agriculture, small businesses and transportation. The organizational structure of the Government was divided into three levels - the Cabinet, the Secretariat and the different government departments.

The Revolutionary Council Government gave way to the establishment of the Socialist Republic of the Union of Myanmar in 1974. The state power was later handed over to the Burma Socialist Programme Party (BSPP) Government on March 1974. Between 1974 and 1987, unicameral Pyithu Hluttaw and various levels of People's Council were formed, and representatives of the people performed administrative and legislative duties. During the BSPP period, three new states (Chin, Mon, and Rakhine States) were recognized.

The BSPP was the leading role in the country, despite the Pyithu Hluttaw as the highest organ of the State power, and exercised the sovereign power of the state on behalf of the people. By the 1974 Constitution, the legislative power of the State was vested solely in the Pyithu Hluttaw. It may delegate executive and judicial powers of the State to central and local organs at different levels. The BSPP was the sole political party and responsible to lay down the policies and guidelines for the state and all organs of the state. According to the 1974 Constitution, 14 States and Divisions were equal in power and status, assuming that it achieved national unity and mutual understanding among the nationalities. During the BSPP period, efforts were made to enhance the public participation especially farmers and workers.

Myanmar had adopted the inward-looking development strategy with the self-reliance policy and State-owned Economic Enterprises (SEEs) played the foremost. Although the agriculture sector had been exempted from nationalization, all land was state-owned and control was put on output, pricing, marketing, input supply and cropping choice, etc. External trade was also under state control, but the inefficient domestic distribution system led to development of black market and illegal border trade. Accordingly, there was stagnation of real GDP, and a decline in the savings rate, investment and export earnings. Moreover, delay in decision making and implementation of reforms, a red-tape laden bureaucracy and influx of paperwork, a lack of transparency and information asymmetry, generated undesirable effects rather than achieving welfare of people.

The Revolutionary Council made arrangement to introduce a new administrative system that led a socialist way of democratic life among the people and decided to abolish the capitalist parliamentary system from 1964. Arrangements were made in which executive functions were to be carried out by means of collective performance. Although its main task was on replacing the bureaucratic machinery, the cumulative adverse affects of nationalization, mismanagement, inappropriate economic policies (e.g. frequent demonetization, etc.) soon began to show, and the performance of the economy began turning down between 1962 and 1977.

Accordingly, various reform measures were carried out but unable to sustain economic growth during the period. Also in early 1980s, sluggish, high inflationary pressures and other difficulties led to general discontent within the economy. Consequently, demonstrations broke out in mid-1988, leading to anarchy in the country. The rule of law and stability deteriorated and a wave of panic swept the country. The State Law and Order Restoration Council (SLORC) took control and established a new government in Myanmar in September 1988 to bring national unrest to an end.

The SLORC/SPDC Era
(Market Oriented Economic System, 1988-2011)

As the SLORC adopted a market oriented economic system in late 1988, various actions of reform were undertaken in economic and social sectors. During this period, multiparty general elections took place in May 1990 and convened the National Convention in 1993. The administrative structure of the public sector in Myanmar between 1988 and 1997 was modified with the addition of new ministries for the purpose of implementing particular reforms effectively. Initially, there were twenty ministries under the SLORC Government (Appendix 5). Later, they were increased to thirty ministries.

In 1996, the National Convention was adjourned temporarily.

The State Peace and Development Council (SPDC) was formed in 1997 and it laid down 12 political, economic and social objectives. During the period, efforts were made for the emergence of a peaceful, modern and developed nation. Some modification of reform measures was performed to streamline the development process. The administrative structure of the SPDC Government can be seen in Appendix 6.

In 2003, *the Seven Step Road Map* was announced and reconvening of the National Convention was undertaken in the following year. It was successfully concluded in 2007 with the formation of the Commission for the Drafting State Constitution (2008), comprised of 54 members. The Constitution of the Republic of the Union of Myanmar was successfully drafted in February 2008, and the ratification of the draft Constitution of the Republic of the Union of Myanmar was announced in May 2008, followed by the General Election being held on November 7, 2010. The election was held in all seven regions and seven ethnic states across the country in which thirty-seven political parties and eighty two independents participated. The New Union Government started convening the Regular Secession of Hluttaws in Naypyidaw in January 2011 and will carry out legislative duties to make laws.

Public Sector in Myanmar and Reform Measures

The public sector administers/works within government ministries, departments and agencies that are staffed by public servants. Usually, countries, which have relied on the market system, have grown fastest only with vigorous and consistent actions of the public sector. Public sector intervention is vital for efficient provision of public goods; maintenance of law and order, governing legal, regulatory and supervisory systems for the proper functioning of the market and the development and maintenance of infrastructure for the economy. Formulating and implementing an effective and efficient administrative system in a dynamic environment is not an easy or simple task for a country. Building an effective administrative system is of utmost importance in bringing about the political, social and economic conditions for the citizens to be able to participate and contribute to a better quality of life. Public Sector Reform (PSR) revitalizes the administration of the public sector in decision making, organizing, resource allocation, accomplishing and delivering public services. In order to achieve the policy objectives, not only is it vital to structure the administrative system, but also to learn through practice, is crucial in the implementation process.

In Myanmar, the adoption of the market-oriented system since 1988, led to a significant change in terms of overall policy framework. The ultimate goal of becoming a peaceful, modern and developed country calls for the shared commitment by citizens, under the concept of unity in diversity. The regional development in Myanmar can be accorded with the aspects of: (1) national unity; (2) territorial integrity; (3) special requirements and needs; (4) challenging potentials; (5) necessary reallocation/rehabilitation; and (6) special plan of actions.

The development programs, initiated in the post 1988 period, include provision of tertiary education facilities, health and other social development in building capacity and technical knowhow for facing the long term development of the region, aiming for balanced and proportionate development all over the country. Among the initiatives and endeavors planned for the development of Special Zones, achievement was made in the following projects: Model Village Development, Low Cost Housing for Rural Areas, Greening Project, Micro-Credit Programs and Community Development.

Economic Reforms

The role of the public sector is significant in socio-economic development and also in achieving the targeted socio-economic policies in any nation. During the late 20th Century and the early 21st Century, collaboration between the public and private sectors became an alternative form of public sector organizations. It is implicit that public and private partners share the responsibility in the decisions to provide services in a community. These comprise of outsourcing and subcontracting, provision of concession, seeking private sector financing, making use of service and management contracts, Public-Private Partnerships and Privatization.

The previous socialist regime, with SEEs in the economy, ran huge budget deficits and was unable to deliver the goods and services it would like to deliver. In order to achieve the economic objectives, the SLORC announced the economic reforms in post 1988 period to change the policy framework of the former socialist government with such aims as to liberalize the economy, to encourage private participation, and to promote integration into the world economy. The major objectives of the economic reforms are to adopt a market-oriented system for the allocation of resources and the distribution of goods and services, to encourage private investment and entrepreneurial activity at home and to open the economy to foreign direct investment and to promote export.

Agriculture

In Myanmar, agriculture contributes a significant share in GDP and total export earnings. As more than 70 percent of the total population lives in rural areas, agriculture, livestock and fishery play a vital role for their livelihood. Reforms in this sector had taken place before the assumption of state power by the SLORC government. These were comprised of the abolishment of government procurement of major crops, liberalization of domestic marketing, and controls on internal trade in industrial crops were also liberalized.

After 1988, the elimination of government controls on cropping patterns and reform measures in production, trade and marketing, pricing, and institutions were laid down in the agriculture sector. The introduction of summer paddy with pump irrigation technology, provision of research and extension activities, agricultural credit, supports for agricultural mechanization and development of new agricultural land were undertaken. According to the Myanmar Rice Policy of 2003, decontrolling in paddy, rice and rice product trade encourages the establishment of a market oriented system in the country.

The major functions of reforms include encouragement of basic crop research, the breeding of High-Yield Varieties (HYVs), upgrading the quality of crops, producing hybrid varieties/bilateral, commercial cooperation and introducing improved varieties of field crops, fruits and vegetables from abroad. Privatization measures were also made welcoming local and foreign investment, which was to develop new agricultural land through the utilization of cultivable, fallow, and wasteland for plantation, orchard, and seasonal crops. Contract farming was also made with the private sector to grow annual crops and plantation crops. Special privileges are granted to entrepreneurs who undertake large-scale cultivation of 5,000 acres or more. Within a twenty-one year period from 1988 to 2009, 366 dams were built and 27 dams are under construction. The reform had a positive effect on all these participants through the creation of employment opportunities and increased income. The driving force of this success was market forces, generating upright achievement in the transition economy.

Livestock and Fishery

Livestock production and fisheries are typically inter-dependent with agriculture, as well as crucial for rural development in Myanmar. Since 1988, major reforms in the livestock sector have been implemented to increase the production of draught animals, to expand dairy production, to increase meat production, and to increase the income of livestock farmers. The Ministry of Livestock and Fishery has laid down policy objectives in line with the government's economic objectives by increasing livestock production, undertaking conservation and effective utilization of livestock resources, promoting investments, and uplifting the socio-economic status of livestock communities.

The Fishery Sector has also become important for the economy because of its vast potential. Myanmar has a long coastline with 2,832 kilometers, which provides a very good base for the development of shrimp and prawn culture. Inland water bodies, natural lakes, reservoirs, river systems, ponds, etc., cover an area of about 8.2 million hectares. From 1988, the private sector has been allowed to take part in fishery culture, catching, processing and exporting businesses and the fisheries sector has been developing rapidly during a short period.

Major reforms in fisheries and aquaculture sector include granting of fishing rights to foreign fishing vessels, marine fisheries, fresh-water fisheries, etc. Increase of Foreign Direct Investment (FDI) is also one of the factors contributing to the development of this sector. To manage the vast potential for expansion, as well as coping with the increasing fishing activities, new regulatory frameworks were set out. The Myanmar Fisheries Federation was formed in December, 1999, and operated in conjunction with State, Divisional, and Township levels. In order to achieve long-run development of fishery production, conservation and rehabilitation of fishery resources, promotion of fisheries research and surveys, collection and compilation of fishery statistics and information, extension services, supervision of fishery sectors, and sustainability of fishery resources has been conducted.

Forestry Sector

The Forestry sector in Myanmar was crucial for the economy during the period of monarchism as well as the Colonial era, and is still important for the socio-economic development of Myanmar. The Forestry Sector became a major source of foreign exchange earnings especially in the 1990s. The export earnings of the forestry sector in the early 1990s accounted for about 30 percent of the total export earnings, with teak as the most important among forest products. Forest management in Myanmar became focused on sustainable management of natural teak-bearing forests. Emphasis has been placed on sustained production of forest products in the long run and conservation of environmental conditions and increased production of value added wood products. Myanmar is committed to sustainable development of forests and biological resources through accession to a number of international conventions and agreements.

In 1995, the Myanmar Forest Policy was formulated to be in line with the forest principles adopted at the United Nations Conference on Environment and Development (UNCED), which emphasized the future development process of the forestry sector and the sustainability of the forests. It also underlines sustainable forest management without impairing the production capacity, while meeting the social and community needs, and conserving the biological diversity and environmental stability.

Government has enacted other forest related laws, notified rules and regulations in order to supplement the implementation of the forest policy. The Community Forestry Instructions (CFI) issued in 1995 also aims to decentralize forest management addressing the basic needs of local people through a participatory approach and environmental restoration. Measures such as extension of reserved forest area, preservation, and conservation of nature and wildlife sanctuaries, establishment of teak and other hardwood plantations, greening of the dry zone, plantation of trees for industrial raw materials, village wood lots plantation and watershed plantations are carried out extensively. A special project for Greening of Nine Arid Areas in Central Myanmar commenced in 1994-95 and grew with new greening projects, so that in later years, this project was expanded to cover thirteen districts.

Mining Sector

With the endowment of numerous precious stones and minerals, Myanmar has a long history of mining. Gems from this area, including Jade, have been renowned since 2nd Century BC. Other minerals such as gold, silver, lead and zinc, etc., were extracted since 15th Century AD. In 1930s, Myanmar stood as one of the leading exporters of tin and tungsten in the world. During the post 1988 period, various reforms were conducted in the Mining Sector. These reforms include building a legal framework and allowing private sector participation in mining. The mining sector rebounded during 1991-93, after years of stagnation.

To exploit underutilized mineral resources, the Ministry of Mines invited interested foreign investors and also set up joint ventures with foreign companies. Foreign participation was welcomed in the production of copper, lead, gold, zinc, iron and steel. Much of the growth came from realization of copper and gold, reflecting agreements between the state sector and foreigners, and also onshore gas extraction.

The new Myanmar Mines Law was promulgated in 1994, with the main objective being to step up the production level, in order to fulfill the growing domestic need for minerals and metal products, and to promote exports. Investments can be undertaken through production sharing or profit sharing arrangements, both of which are consistent with international practice and the Ministry of Mines is flexible enough to negotiate on a case by case basis. These opportunities consist of participating in mineral exploration, the improvement and revamping of existing mines and plants, the expansion of production capacities using more profitable, efficient and appropriate technology, or new projects with already known or partly known deposits.

Energy Sector

The highest portion of foreign investment in Myanmar since the early 2000s has been contributed to the exploration of oil and gas in the energy sector. Myanmar has a very high potential in the development of oil and gas, with new discoveries of offshore gas fields developed by foreign investors, which are operating under the production sharing contracts. The public sector in Myanmar is mainly responsible for carrying out the fulfillment of domestic energy requirements as well as energy conservation measures.

A wide range of reforms were being undertaken such as carrying out exploration and extraction of crude oil and natural gas by the Ministry concerned, and with foreign oil companies on contractual basis in onshore and offshore areas, and also enhancing production from existing oil wells, reducing wastage and losses, and extraction and exploration to develop new oil fields in onshore areas. In accordance with the guidance of the government, the Ministry of Energy has laid down the energy policy and strategy to maintain the status of energy independence, to employ hydroelectric power as one of the vital sources of energy sufficiency, to generate and distribute more electricity for economic development, to save non-renewable energy for future energy sufficiency of the nation, to promote efficient utilization of energy and impress on energy conservation and to prevent deforestation caused by excessive use of wood and charcoal for fuel.

Between 1988 and 2010, the MOGE have drilled new test wells in oilfields and promoted production of oil from existing old oil wells onshore, and of gas in offshore areas. Natural gas output is increasing sharply year by year, making up an exportable surplus. Compressed natural gas also increased as the state had initiated a CNG programme concerning road transport. To increase the petroleum reserves and to boost the existing production level, the MOGE invited multinational oil companies and worked in joint venture on a production sharing basis, in both onshore and offshore areas. In addition, the energy sector in Myanmar has collaborated with BIMST-EC Energy Sector Cooperation, ASEAN Energy Sector Cooperation, Greater Mekong Sub-region Economic Cooperation, and Ayeyawaddy-Chao Phraya-Mekong Economic Cooperation Strategy.

Processing and Manufacturing Sector

Myanmar's manufacturing sector accounted for only 16.8 percent of GDP in the financial year 2008-2009. In accordance with the adoption of a market-oriented economic system, restrictions on private sector involvement in the industrial sector had been reduced. The Private Industrial Enterprise Law was enacted in 1990 to govern establishment and operation of private enterprises. Its provisions allows private firms to operate in all industrial sub-sectors except those reserved for the state as specified in the State-owned Economic Enterprises Law.

One of the key aspects of the government's policy for

industrial development was the enactment of Foreign Investment Law in late 1988 which allows foreign investors to establish wholly owned enterprises or enter into joint ventures with Myanmar citizens. Foreign investment is allowed in all sub-sectors except for those reserved for the state sector. A range of benefits and streamlined procedures are provided to foreign investors such as guarantees against nationalization, and for the repatriation of capital and a foreign exchange component of profits. Tax benefits also extended to local investors in Myanmar Citizens Investment Law (1994).

Changes were also made in pricing policies with the removal of former price controls. State enterprises were given more autonomy in pricing, input procurement and production. These enterprises could enter into agreements with private and foreign investors on production through consignment basis, leasing out facilities to these investors or enter into joint ventures. Privatization of state enterprises was also announced during this initial stage of policy changes.

Policies in promoting the development of the industrial sector are the transformation from agricultural economy into agro-based industrial economy, development of import substituting industries, promotion of SMEs towards large-scale industries, development of export-oriented industries, conducting research and development, encouraging the production of value-added manufactured products utilizing local natural resources as far as possible, standardization for manufacturing machinery and parts, and protecting environmental pollution. In order to implement Myanmar's industrial development strategy based on its long-term vision, the following Committees were formed: (1) the Central Industrial Development Committee (CIDC); (2) the Myanmar Industrial Development Committee (MIDC); and (3) the Myanmar Industrial Development Working Committee (MIDWC), which is responsible for coordinating and implementing industrial development activities as laid down by the CIDC and MIDC.

The development of industrial zones and industries for 2008-09 reached 28 industrial zones, 9,702 industries, 43,784 private industries, 10,438 cottage industries and 820 SOEs. A Zone Supervision Committee for each of the 28 industrial zone was also formed, in order to relocate small and medium-sized industries (SMIs) located in residential areas and for close coordination and promotion of industries in their respective areas.

The SPDC promulgated the Special Economic Zone Law in January 2011 to attract more foreign investment and thereby enhance the economy. Investment reached $31.957 billion (U.S.) as of October 2011. The foreign investment coming from 430 enterprises, of 31 countries and regions, were respectively injected into 12 economic sectors which are oil and gas, electric power generation, manufacturing, real estate, hotels and tourism, mining, transport and communications, livestock breeding and fisheries, industry, construction, agriculture and services sector.

Monetary Development

The structure of the Myanmar financial system in the early 1990s was comprised of banking and non-banking financial institutions, on the one hand, and government financial organizations, on the other. With the exception of the Myanmar Agricultural Development Bank (MADB), all the banking and non-banking financial institutions as well as government finance organizations were placed under the Ministry of Finance and Revenue. Government financial organizations include the Budget Department, Customs Department, Internal Revenue Department, Pension Department, and Revenue Appellate Tribunal.

Financial institutions in Myanmar are headed by the Central Bank of Myanmar (CBM). Traditionally, it is responsible for issuing currency, and formulating and implementing monetary policy. The Central Bank of Myanmar Law confers upon the CBM broad powers to operate with relative independence and to exercise supervisory and regulatory authority over a wide range of financial institutions, both state-owned and privately owned. Twenty-one private commercial banks and forty-seven representative offices of foreign banks have been established since 1992. The strategy of the government regarding financial development is to require domestic private banks to become more efficient and competitive before allowing foreign banks to upgrade their representative offices into fully fledged banks. Non-bank financial institutions include the Small Loans Department and Myanmar Insurance. New types of insurance such as oil and gas, travel and health were undertaken with the enactment of the Myanmar Insurance Law in 1993. The Insurance Business Law was promulgated in 1996 to promote and liberalize this industry.

Fiscal Development

Taxation reforms were also conducted by the government to ease out the former tax structure. There are fifteen categories of taxes and duties in the Myanmar government's tax structure, grouped under four major heads. From late 1988, three types of measures were carried out to reform the tax structure and administration. The first type was to broaden the tax base. Thus, the Commercial Tax which replaced the Commodity and Services Tax was designed to broaden the base of indirect taxation with lower tax rates on goods and services. The second type of measure was intended to improve tax administration. Thus, measures for improvement of administrative capabilities, such as recruitment of graduates through the Public Service Commission, on-the-job training, refresher courses, and high-level courses were carried out. The third category was concerned with streamlining and simplifying procedures in the collection of taxes.

Trade and Investment

Reforms in the trade sector were initiated, with the aim of supporting internal and external trade activities, upgrading the commercial efficiency, increasing the foreign exchange earnings of the country through export promotion and encouraging the trading activities of cooperatives and private entrepreneurs within the country. These reforms were regulated by four major pieces of legislation; the Union of Myanmar Foreign Investment Law was promulgated on 30 November 1988, formation of the Foreign Investment Commission (FIC), on 7 December 1988, Myanmar's Citizen's Investment Law on 31 March 1994, and the formation of Myanmar Investment Commission (MIC) on 4 May 1994.

Myanmar is currently trading normally with over 80 countries and regions, the majority of which are Asian countries. Formalization of border trade involved designating official points of entry, setting up customs and banking facilities etc. The Department of Border Trade was established, with branch offices providing one-stop service for border trade matters. At present, there are 12 official border trade points for dealing trade transactions with neighboring nations.

The post 1988 trade liberalization measures were introduced by allowing private individuals or enterprises to carry out export-import business which had previously been monopolized by the state, realigning export and import procedures, lowering technical barriers to trade, providing incentives to exporters by allowing 100 percent retention of export earnings for the importation of goods, and the exemption of commercial tax and customs duty on certain imported items. The Union of Myanmar Federation of Chamber of Commerce and Industry (UMFCCI) was reorganized for the promotion of private participation in trade and industry.

Infrastructure Development

As infrastructure is crucial for economic development, necessary infrastructural development works are being undertaken to promote development of every region of the country. Infrastructural development in Myanmar can be observed as construction of economic and social infrastructure in the respective sectors supporting the national economy. Thus, the government has accorded high priority to infrastructure development projects such as construction of dams and reservoirs in the agriculture sector, roads and bridges, port facilities, and airports in the transport sector, communication networks in the communication sector, power generation plants, both hydro and gas plants in the power sector, etc. Ministries of Construction, Rail Transport, and Defence are responsible for undertaking the implementation of such infrastructural projects.

In the Communications Sector, the government has been striving for the improvement of information technology in the country to be on a par with the advanced nations the world. Efforts have also been made to achieve regional development with a modern communication system. New digital microwave lines are being installed. The International Direct Dialing Channel was introduced after 1988 and also increases the number of telephone exchanges and network, allowing for better communication throughout the nation. By enhancing the development of ICT and the Internet access throughout the country, and establishing the Yadanarbon Teleport in 2007 and the Yadanarbon Cyber City, there is significant improvement in this area.

Social Sector Reform

Education Sector

Education is an important investment tool in improving the productivities of the population and creating, adapting and spreading knowledge. It can enhance the skills and attitudes of the human resources in both public and private sector. This can in turn produce greater efficiency and effectiveness in providing public goods and maximizing utility for the citizens.

Education in Myanmar enjoys a favorable environment as the people have traditionally given education the highest priority in their lives. In Myanmar, the formal education system is carried out by the Ministry of Education. In the education sector, the administration and education decision-making processes are centralized. Policy formulation, the coordination and funding of the Ministry is implemented through various councils formed under the Ministry. Since 1998, nationwide seminars have been held in both basic and higher education annually, to prepare education promotion programs and assess progress. Regarding higher education, measures have been taken in discussions, and cooperation on academic matters with foreign universities, so as to keep abreast with them, initiating the teaching of subjects within the country that were studied abroad before. Moreover, development of education research work and the utilization of ICT have also been carried out.

The Thirty-Year, Long-Term Education Development Plan was launched by the Ministry of Education in 2001 and covers the Fiscal Years 2001-2002 through to 2030-2031. The components of the plan for the higher education sub-sector were formulated in order to develop an open education system that would nurture a better qualified human resource, provided with lifelong learning opportunities, through teaching, learning and research enhanced by harnessing information and communication technology, and be responsive to community needs.

In order to facilitate educational promotion, the thirty-year long-term plan has been merged with the special four-year plan initiated a year earlier. It later became part of the long-term plan. The government has formulated 21 sector-wise work programs to be completed in the special four-year plan. The programs cover the extended opening of universities and colleges, establishment of ICT buildings that contribute towards e-education, increased production of teachers, and the establishment of degree courses and diploma courses under academic programs including the development of human resources. Apart from upgrading formal basic and higher education, upgrades in technical and vocational training, monastic education that helps boost literacy, post school education and job-oriented training have also been implemented.

Health Sector

According to the World Health Organization (WHO) “health” is defined as a state of complete physical, mental and social well being and not merely the absence of disease or infirmity. Health is considered to be the result of many interactions of various factors such as: heredity, environment, life-style, socio-economic conditions, family welfare services and other factors. Health is not only the well-being of an individual, but also the overall well-being of the whole communities and nations. Myanmar also adopted the aim of health for all people of the country by the year 2000 (HFA/2000).

The health sector includes health services, hospitals, social welfare institutions, education and training, pure medical research, medical social work, social work, formally trained medical practitioners and traditional medical practitioners. Myanmar has a population of over 58 million a growth rate of 2.02 percent. Like other developing countries, health is assigned priority in the national agenda. The National Health Plan 2001-06 was laid down to put into practice the national objective of uplifting of health, fitness and educational standards of the entire nation, to implement the National Health Policy, to strengthen rural health services, and to develop a new health system in keeping with the political, economic and social conditions.

The Government also laid down social objectives which included "uplifting health, fitness and educational standards for the entire nation" and this was to be fulfilled by the implementation of the National Health Policy. The Myanmar government formed a National Health Committee (NHC) which formulated a new National Health Policy in 1993. The policy aims to raise the level of physical and mental well-being of the people, follow the guidelines of the population policy, produce sufficient and efficient human resources for health locally, abide by the rules and regulations mentioned in the drug laws and by laws, enhance the role of the private sector and non-governmental organizations in delivering health care also in rural and border region, explore an alternative health care financing system, promulgate new rules and regulations, expand environmental health activities, encourage medical research including indigenous medicines, forecast emerging health problems and initiate preventive and curative measures and strengthen collaboration with other countries. In order to achieve increasing life expectancy and curb morbidity and mortality, basic health care activities have been implemented. Public health education programs, several disease control programs and mass national campaigns are being carried out.

The Ministry of Health collaborates with other related ministries and social welfare organizations such as the Maternal and Child Welfare Association, the Red Cross, the Myanmar Medical, Nurses Association, Non Government Organizations

(NGOs) and International Non Government Organizations (INGOs) to carry out national health care functions all over the country. Due to various types of support from the government, responsible personnel of the Ministry of Health, participation of the general public and cooperation of local and international social organizations, the development of national health care in Myanmar has been achieved.

New Administrative Structure (2011 Onwards)

There is impetus for achieving a modern developed and democratic nation comprised of Good Governance and Clean Government, and this can be attained through the transformation and restructuring of the public sector within the nation. Four pillars of Good Governance; accountability, transparency, predictability and participation are instrumental in achieving sound public administration. Public sector reform requires participation of stakeholders inside and outside of government, indicating a broader role of the people, with a compact, efficient and effective role of government.

The SPDC Government turned over the administrative authority to the new union government at the end of March 2011. At present, the public sector in the Republic of the Union of Myanmar comprises the government, local authorities, and State Economic Enterprises (SEEs). The government includes the Pyithu Hluttaw, Amyotha Hluttaws and Pyinae and Tine Daythagyi Hluttaws (Three-chamber parliament), other governmental councils and organizations, ministries and departments. The Pyithu Hluttaw and Amyotha Hluttaw are jointly regarded as Pyidaungsu Hluttaw. The local authorities consist of the districts, townships general administration departments and also of wards and village tract levels. The State Economic Enterprises (SEEs) are obliged to contribute to the budget and depend on the budget for financing the working capital and investment.

The Union Government is constituted with a president, two vice presidents, 34 ministries with 30 ministers, Union Supreme Court, Financial Commission, Union Constitutional Tribunal, Union Election Commission, Union Civil Service Board and Nay Pyi Taw Council. Among them, two new ministries, Ministry of Presidential Office and Ministry of Industrial Development, are included as two more ministries than the previous SPDC Government (Appendix 7, 8).

Out of 30 Union Level Ministers, four ministers are jointly responsible for eight Ministries, specifically the Ministry of National Planning and Economic Development and the Ministry of Livestock and Fisheries, the Ministry of Labour and the Ministry of Social Welfare Relief And Resettlement, the Ministry of Sports and the Ministry of Tourism, and the Ministry of Myanmar Industrial Development and the Ministry of Border Affairs.

According to the new constitution adopted in 2008, the administrative structure of the Republic of the Union of Myanmar comprises Nay Pyi Taw Union Territory, States (Pyinae), Regions (Tine Daythagyii) and Self Administered Zones or Divisions. The capital of the Union, the Nay Pyi Taw is prescribed as Union territory, under the direct administration of the President. The Nay Pyi Taw Council is led by a Chairperson with nine members. The Chairperson is responsible for carrying out functions on behalf of the President. A Regional (Tine Daythagyii) Government or a State (Pyinae) Government is made up of a Chief Minister and other Ministers, a Chief Justice of the High Court, a Chief Attorney General and a Chief Advocate General. Apart from appointing a Chief Minister for respective Regions or States, Regional or State Ministers for National Races' Affairs are appointed as well, except in Chin State and the Sagaing Region. The Six Self Administered Zones or Divisions established in Myanmar include: (1) Naga Self-Administered Zone; (2) Danu Self-Administered Zone; (3) Pa-O Self-Administered Zone; (4) Palaung Self-Administered Zone; (5) Kokang Self-Administered Zone; and (6) Wa Self-Administered Division.

In each Zone or Division, a Chairperson to the leading body is appointed. Myanmar territorial formation is based on 14 States and Regions (Divisions), where States are formed in accordance with the ethnic lines, a balanced and proportionate growth among States and Divisions is fundamental for the nation building.

The rationale for reforming the public sector is to ensure effective, competent and careful delivery of services to citizens and promote the welfare of the society. Lacking a competent public administration, thriving economic reform cannot take place. Strong political leadership is also required and the creation of a new mindset amongst politicians and public officials need to be established. Five future aspirations laid down by the New Union Government are to achieve good governance and clean government, development of democracy practices, maintenance of justice, improving the efficiency and effectiveness of the public sector, and enhancing integration among ministries, and the success of these processes depends on their implementation.

Challenges and Prospects

After twenty three years of rebuilding national peace and tranquility, the achievement of community welfare becomes an important role for Myanmar. The administration of the newly elected Union Government initiated in 2011 is based on the three types of might: political, economic and military. The accomplishment of the national causes of the non-disintegration of the Union, Non-disintegration of national solidarity, and Perpetuation of sovereignty, are the nation's duty; not only present generations, but also those of the future, to safeguard our continued prosperity. Reforms in the public sector during the past two decades highlight the long term process and have achieved significant progress in maintaining peace and tranquility, the development of the economy, upgrading international cooperation and initiating a new democratic administration. However there still are some challenges and impediments due to various sources including natural factors.

Unlike other countries, Myanmar is home to over 100 ethnic groups. Without national unity, political instability would hamper the achievement of other goals. In economic sectors, prudent measures are also a prerequisite for striving towards the market economic systems, the practicing of open door policy, mitigating market failure, attracting foreign investments and establishing special economic zones, with the provision of assistance to national entrepreneurs are also crucial. The distribution, down to the grass-roots level, of benefits achieved from economic growth, is of particular importance. According to the geographic situation, Myanmar is situated in the strategic location of the Southeast Asia and abundant with various natural resources. In order to achieve a modern democratic nation, development and maintenance of human resources is vital in each and every sector of the economy as well.

Based on sectoral reforms, there still remain limitations. Though agricultural trade was relaxed in post 1988, state sector plays a significant role. The major growth of agricultural output is due mainly to the extensive, rather than intensive, development. By the active and continual partaking of private and foreign sectors in provision of farm inputs, financial and technical assistance is an on-going requirement for agricultural development. Rather, maximization of farmers' income is also important together with increasing output and productivity. Major threats in the forestry sector include encroachment by farmers, shifting cultivation, forest fires, building of dams, urbanization and building of roads, lack of awareness of the importance of biodiversity.

Industrial development is a priority goal that is important to the whole development process. The industrial structure throughout the period was mainly based on resource-based type. Efforts towards achieving modernized version and innovation-intensive industries are the prerequisite. Hindrances in the industrial sector of Myanmar have comprised of insufficient electricity, inputs, capital, and the existence of multiple exchange rates, together with frequent policy changes and the lack of a level playing-field for SOEs vs. private enterprises. Hence, development of both export-oriented and import-substituting manufacturing industries, expansion of supporting industries, upgrading rural industries and cooperation with foreign investors are required.

Another challenge is in external sector lacking in profound changes for the pattern of trade, continuously unfavorable terms of trade and the existence of South-South regional trading due to economic sanctions. As a result, there was a burst in FDI and exports at the early post 1988, which dissipated later on. General problems in the implementation of fiscal strengthening include tax evasion, tax exemption, lack of transparency, and complexity in tax rates, drawbacks in the tax system, corruption and inefficient accounting systems. The setting of a stable and reasonable exchange rate, promotion of bank service facilities and the establishment of a capital market, have become the prospected challenges in monetary sector. Reforms of the legal framework also need modification, including modest action or some modification on corporate law, property law, bankruptcy law, anti-monopoly law, labor law and so on. These are some areas that remain due to a lack of major revision since post 1988 period.

One of the aims of the Union Government is the preparation of a favorable entrepreneurial business environment in the potential service industries of tourism, transportation, banking, health and education services. The implementation measures should take into account streamlining the operation of service providing agencies, improving organizational performance, provision of business-friendly governmental framework, and nurturing HRD, acculturation and proper incentive systems.

Conclusion

Although the market system is indispensible in achieving prosperity, government supports, consistent actions, provision of information and guidance, and regulating and controlling the use of natural resources are advantageous for the long-term well-being of the citizens. The open market economy can operate effectively only within a transparent, publicly accountable and consistent administrative system. It is essential for the government to set up the appropriate legal framework and establish an efficient, impartial and result oriented administrative system. The development of well-trained, efficient and dedicated public servants, who are appropriately compensated and motivated, will be one of the main requirements in the reform process.

In this globalized era, Myanmar is more or less experiencing costs and benefits affected by the world economy. From the experiences of Myanmar through the years, from the time of Myanmar Kings to the socialist period, some specific issues on design and process factors are worth considering for the development of effective administrative systems. Leadership, governance, participation and communication will be the required skills for Myanmar citizens in order to work in a cooperative and coordinated way. For this, a system of recruitment and advancement for civil and public service, that would always be updated, is essential.

Managing fundamental reforms in the public sector requires a long period of time, though step-by-step accomplishments can contribute, to a certain extent, for the best outcome. Major components of public sector reforms include institutional development, organizational development, human resource development and information development. Reforms in the public sector of Myanmar would depend on the various situations for the long run development of the nation based on justice, freedom and equality. In transition towards the emergence of modern democratic nation, the Union Government is committed to achieve and sustain national solidarity and national recon-solidation, to implement a proper market economy, to attain equal and efficient social development all over the country especially through poverty reduction and rural development. These goals are indispensable, and synchronized implementation is necessary through a new and open administrative system.

Major determinants of a successful public sector reform include: the unambiguous political support by the government over an extended period for introducing the reform, setting up visible goals and strategies for its achievement, constructing effective communication between all the actors and stake-holders, the contribution of the ministries or implementing agencies in the identification of issues to be focused on and encouraging feedback, the monitoring and evaluation process. Steps towards developing creative and responsive leadership and measuring policies outcomes and incentives are also fundamental during the reformation period. In general, uncertainty and unpredictability in the macroeconomic environment of Myanmar have so far hampered the achievement of widespread development with well-designed and rational policies. Clear identification of its policies, maintaining macroeconomic stability and assessment of the outcomes at various stages of the reform period are indispensible for the future accomplishment of desired goals.

References

Adamolekun, L. (2002). *Public Administration in Africa, Main Issues and Selected Country Studies,* lbadan: Spectrum Books Limited.

Berg, F., Jenei. G., and Leloup, L. T. et al. (2002). *East-West Co-operation in Public Sector Reform, Cases and Results in Central and Eastern Europe,* IIAS/EGPA, IOS Press, Amsterdam, The Netherlands.

Black, J. and Jacobzone, S. (2009), *Tools for Regulatory Quality and Financial Sector Regulation: A Cross-Country Perspective,* OECD Working Papers on Public Governance, OECD, Paris.

Caiden, G. E. (1969), *Administrative Reform.* London: The Penguin Press.

Campo, S. S and Pachampet, S. (2000). *To Serve and Preserve, Improving Public Administration in a Competitive World,* Vol. 1, Asian Development Bank.

Central Statistical Organization (CSO) (2009). *Statistical Yearbook 2009,* Ministry of National Planning and Economic Development, Myanmar.

Chittoo, H. B., Ramphul, N., and Nowbutsing, B. (2009). Globalization and Public Sector Reforms in a Developing Country *Culture Mandala: Bulletin of the Centre for East-West Cultural & Economic Studies,* Vol. 8, Issue 2, December.

Christensen, T., Lægreid, P., and Paul, G. et al. (2007). *Organization Theory and the Public Sector Instrument, Culture and Myth,* New York: Routledge.

Donahue, John D., and Nye, Joseph S., Jr. (2003), *For the People Can We Fix Public Service?.* Massachusetts: Cambridge.

FAO (1999), *State of the World's Forests 1999.* Food and Agriculture

Organization of the United Nations, Rome.

Halligan, J. and Turner, M. (1995). *Profiles of Government Administration in Asia,* Australian Government Publishing Service, Canberra.

Kjaer, A. M. (2004). *Governance,* Oxford: Polity Press.

Kooiman, J. (2003), *Governing as Governance*, London: Sage.

Lwin, Htay Htay (2010), Public Sector and Market-oriented Economic System, Workshop on Capacity Enhancement of Civil Service by CSSTB & SPF.

Meier, Gerald M. and Rauch, James E. (2002). *Leading Issues in Economic Development* (7th ed.), New York: Oxford University Press.

Myat, Thein (2004). *Economic Development of Myanmar*, ISEAS, Singapore.

OECD (1995). *Recommendation on Improving the Quality of Government Regulation*, Paris.

OECD (2004). *Reviews of Regulatory Reform, Mexico: Progress in Implementing Regulatory Reform*, Paris.

OECD (2005). *Guiding Principles for Regulatory Governance and Performance*, Paris.

Osborne, S. and Brown, K. (2005). *Managing Change and Innovation in Public Service Organizations*, London: Routledge.

Rabin, J. (ed.) (2005). *Encyclopedia of Public Administration and Public Policy*, New York: Taylor & Francis Group.

Stiglitz, J. (2000), *Economics of the Public Sector* (3rd ed.), New York: WW Norton & Company.

The New Light of Myanmar Newspaper, Various Issues, Yangon, Myanmar.

Veenswijk, M. (2005). *Organizing Innovation: New Approaches to Cultural Change and Intervention in Public Sector Organizations.* Amsterdam, The Netherlands.

Visentini, G. (2001). *Mixed and Market Oriented Economies, the Italian Situation*, The Netherlands.

World Bank (1996). *From Plan to Market, World Development Report 1997*, Oxford: Oxford University Press.

World Bank (1997). *The State in the Changing World, World Development Report 1997*, Oxford: Oxford University Press.

World Bank (2000). Higher Education in Developing Countries: Peril and Promise, The United States.

Appendix 1 Administrative System under Myanmar Kings

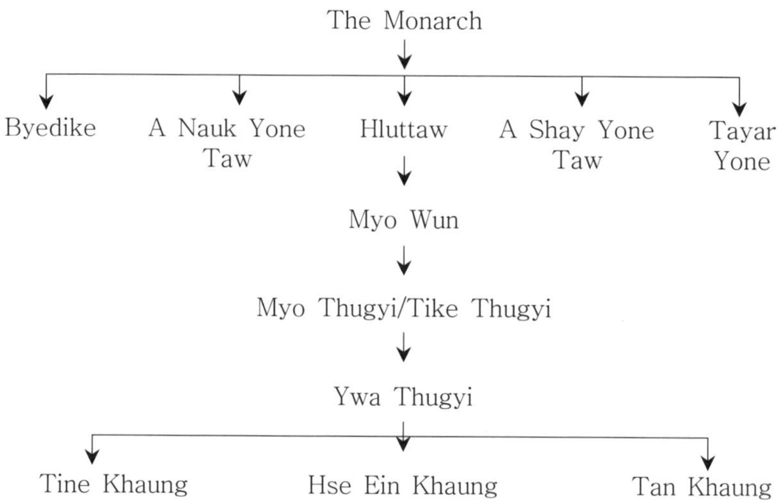

Source: Myanmar National Archive Department.

Appendix 2 Colonial Administrations in Myanmar (1897–1937)

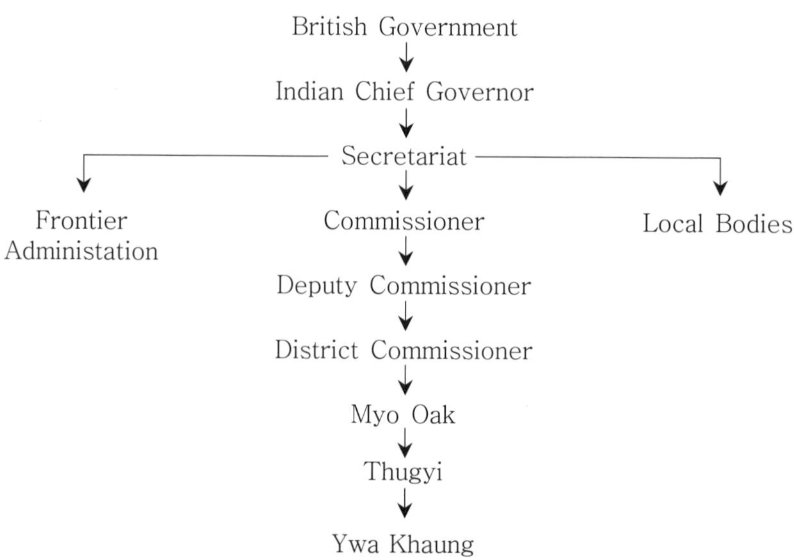

Source: Myanmar National Archive Department.

Appendix 3 Colonial Administration After 1937

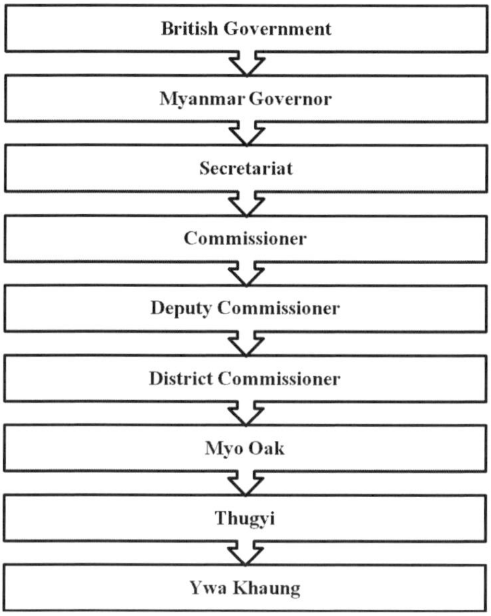

Source: Myanmar National Archive Department.

Appendix 4 Administrative Structure: Parliamentary Democracy Period (1948- 1962)

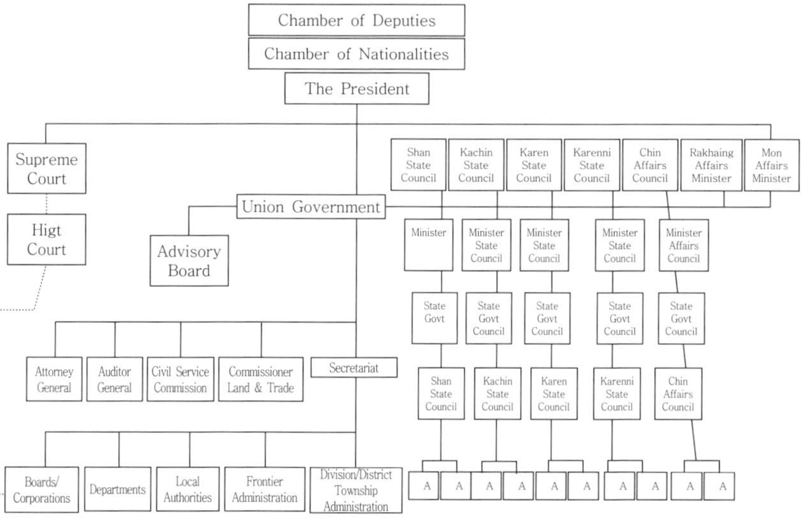

Appendix 5 The Structure of the State Law and Order Restoration Council Government Parliamentary Democracy Period (1988)

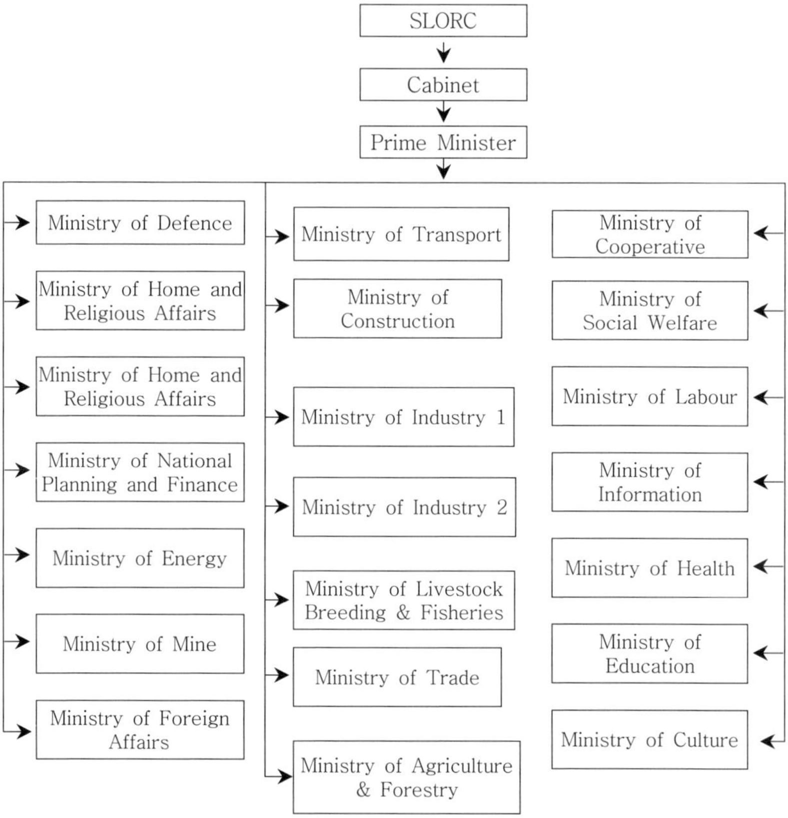

Source: Ministry of Information, 1991.

Appendix 6 The Structure of the State Peace and Development Council Governmant

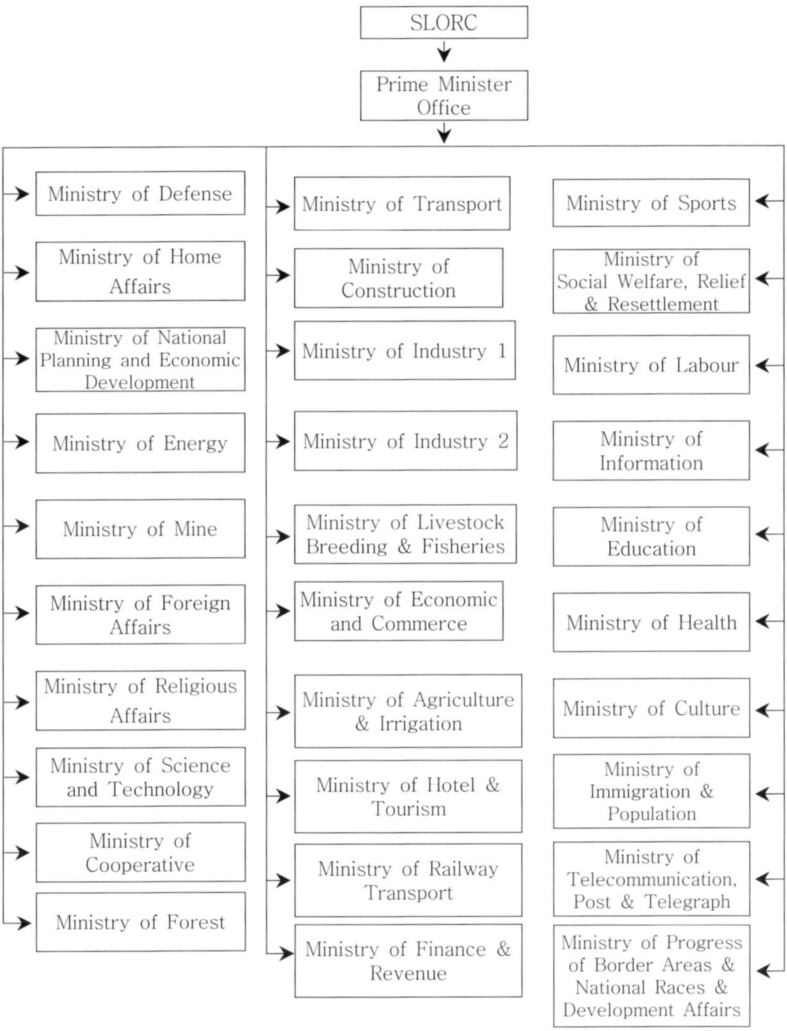

Source: Ministry of Information, 1997.

Appendix 7 Union Government Ministries of Myanmar (2011 Onwards)

1. Ministry of Defense
2. Ministry of Home Affairs
3. Ministry of Border Affairs
4. Ministry of Foreign Affairs
5. Ministry of Information
6. Ministry of Agriculture And Irrigation
7. Ministry of Finance And Revenue
8. Ministry of Construction
9. Ministry of National Planning And Economic Development
10. Ministry of Commerce
11. Ministry of Communications, Posts And Telegraphs
12. Ministry of Social Welfare Relief And Resettlement
13. Ministry of Forestry
14. Ministry of Livestock And Fisheries
15. Ministry of Mines
16. Ministry of Cooperatives
17. Ministry of Labor
18. Ministry of Transport
19. Ministry of Hotels And Tourism
20. Ministry of Industry-1
21. Ministry of Industry-2
22. Ministry of Rail Transportation
23. Ministry of Energy
24. Ministry of Electric Power-1
25. Ministry of Electric Power-2
26. Ministry of Education
27. Ministry of Health
28. Ministry of Culture
29. Ministry of Religious Affairs
30. Ministry of Science And Technology
31. Ministry of Immigration and Population
32. Ministry of Sports
33. Ministry of President's Office and
34. Ministry of Myanmar Industrial Development

Appendix 8 The Structure of New State Constitution

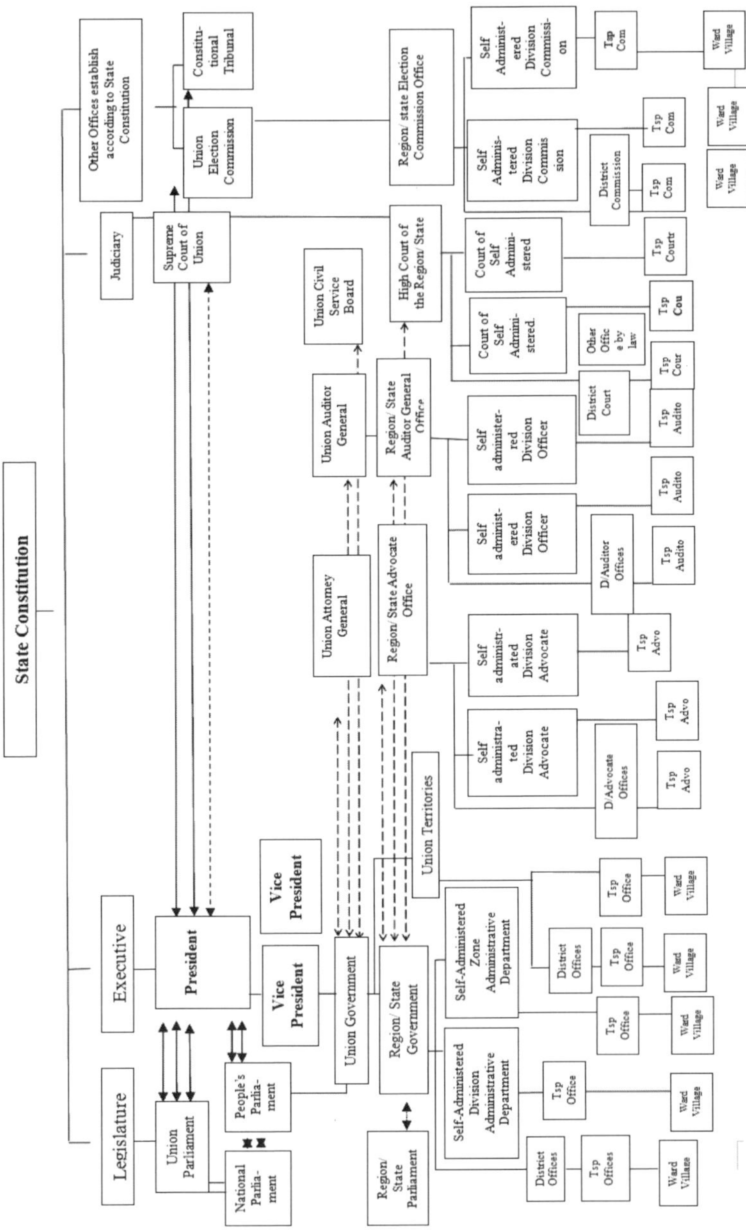

Note: A=Division/ District/ Township Administration

Source: Myanmar National Archive Department

Chapter 8 Public Sector Reform in the Philippines

Alex B. Brillantes, Jr. and Herisadel P. Flores

Introduction

The search for responsive and meaningful politico-administrative structures is one that has preoccupied scholars and practitioners of public administration and governance for years. This search has been reflected in the phases that marked the evolution of the discipline of public administration. More specifically, the evolution and development of modern and contemporary public administration have generally been marked by the following phases: Development Administration (1950s to 1960s); New Public Administration (1970s); New Public Management (1980s to 1990s); Reinventing Government (1990s); Public Administration as Governance (1990s to the present).[1] Responsive public administration and governance structures were a central issue during all of these phases. At the heart of this search is the imperative for reforms in the public sector. Reorganization and decentralization are among the major interventions and strategies for reforming the public sector. This paper focuses on decentralization as a public sector reform strategy focusing on the experience of the Philippines.

In 1991, the Philippines embarked on a massive decentralization program that involved the substantial transfer of power, authority, responsibility and accountability to the sub-national institution local government units. This was brought about by the enactment of the Local Government Code – Republic Act No. 7160 (RA 7160) – that significantly transformed the nature of relations between the national and local governments. This massive decentralization program was one of the numerous historical attempts made by the Philippines to reform public administration.

Public administration reform "can be very comprehensive and include process changes in areas such as organizational structures, decentralization, personnel management, public finance, results-based management, regulatory reforms, etc. It can also refer to targeted reforms such as the revision of the civil service statute."[2] Decentralization, therefore, can be an instrument to bring about reforms in public administration towards the much desired goal of good governance. We have argued elsewhere[3] that reforms in public administration, in order to be more successful, have to go beyond reforming structures and processes. They have to include reforms aimed at changing the mindsets and behaviour of the stakeholders, reforms aimed at bringing about transformational leadership within the context of strong political will to implement reforms, though sometimes painful and even costly, and finally reforms that will enable and encourage active citizen engagement to own the changes and hence ensure sustainability.

This paper will focus on one aspect of public administration reform: that of reforming structures and institutions. More specifically, it will zero in on the efforts to reform sub-national institutions and processes with decentralization and devolution as the instruments for said reforms. This includes laying down the enabling framework for active citizen engagement in the processes of governance, coupled with changing the mindsets and paradigms of local and national bureaucrats that are more sensitive to local and frontline issues and concerns, yet not losing sight of the bigger picture, within the context of the widely accepted, hackneyed and overused, but certainly still relevant slogan "think global act local."

This paper focuses on decentralization (through devolution) as a tool to bring about reforms in public administration and eventually good governance. It takes off from the Worldwide Governance Indicators (WGI) to measure the performance of public sector institutions developed by the World Bank. These include voice and accountability, political stability, government effectiveness, regulatory quality, the rule of law, and the control of graft and corruption. These essentially are operational indicators of the traditional and long accepted values of good governance that include transparency, accountability, participation and rule of law. The paper then zeroes in on the Philippine decentralization experience focusing on the Local Government Code of 1991 and suggests how the above indicators may be used as a framework to look at decentralization and local governance.

To still further evaluate how decentralization has promoted good governance - and indeed improved the quality of life of the people - the Philippine attainment (or non-attainment) of the Millennium Development Goals are used. The paper concludes that a mixed picture of reforms in the public sector at the local level emerges, when applying the governance indicators and the MDGs. However, there is still promise that with effective and meaningful implementation of decentralization, good governance may still be attained. The figure below presents a framework on how public sector reform through its various forms can lead to good governance (which also facilitates an effective public sector reform) and the attainment of societal goals, economic growth and human development.

Figure 1. Public Sector Reform and Governance Framework

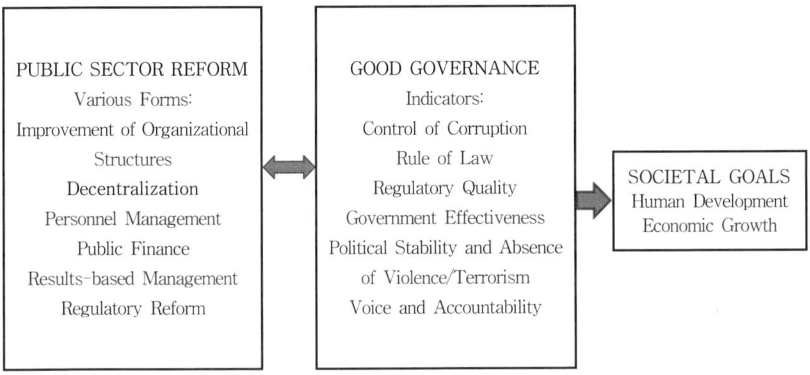

Using the Philippine experience as an empirical referent, this paper discusses how decentralization has been an instrument to bring about public sector reform in the country. More specifically, the paper tries to identify the achievements and shortcomings of decentralization in improving governance, particularly in terms of controlling corruption, ensuring the rule of law, improving regulatory quality, enhancing government effectiveness, maintaining political stability, and promoting voice and accountability in public processes.

In order to achieve this, the succeeding section discusses the objectives and elements of public sector reform. The third section will take a closer look at the six governance dimensions identified by the WGI and how the Philippines has performed in each dimension. This will be followed by a revisiting of RA 7160 provisions that are of particular relevance to governance. The fifth section will provide an assessment of the Philippines experience in adopting decentralization as a tool for improving governance. Governance outcomes with regard to promoting human development and economic growth will then be examined in the sixth section. The last part concludes and provides some recommendations on ways to move forward in the country's decentralization agenda.

The Objectives and Elements of Public Sector Reform

The objective of every public sector reform is to improve the quality of life for citizens. To put it differently, it aims to facilitate human development. This latter concept is now being espoused by many thinkers and policymakers as a rightful goal as well as a necessary condition to national development. The United Nations (UN) defines human development as "a process of enlarging people's choices and enhancing human capabilities (the range of things people can be and do) and freedoms, enabling them to: live a long and healthy life, have access to knowledge and a decent standard of living, and participate in the life of their community and decisions that affect their lives."[4]

Governments can facilitate human development by making quality goods and services more accessible to citizens. In order to develop their full potential, people should have access to basic needs such as food, potable water, clothing and shelter, as well as education, health, transportation, electricity, and communication services among others. This can be achieved either by direct government provision or by creating an enabling environment for both civil society and the market to provide these things.

Civil society and private sector participation in service delivery promotes democratization, which can also be an end in itself. Democratization is "a process which leads to a more open, more participatory, less authoritarian society."[5] While its impact on equality and efficiency is still being debated, it is widely accepted that democratization promotes quality and responsiveness in service delivery. In view of this, democratization is almost always considered as an essential component of any public sector reform.

Economic growth may no longer be considered as the sole precondition for national development, but its importance in attaining a country's development objectives remains widely recognized. The experience of many countries showed us that debt-driven growth, without concomitant investments on human development, is not sustainable. Nor does it automatically bring about better quality of life for citizens. In fact, public service delivery may even suffer in the long-term as the government eventually grapples with the high cost of debt servicing. Nonetheless, another kind of growth – one that is investment-driven – is necessary for job generation. Access to productive employment by working-age members is essential to a household's human development. A growing economy can also better support government projects that may bring about more growth such as infrastructure and research. It is because of these reasons that governments of most developing countries are instituting reforms that would encourage local and foreign investments within their boundaries.

Like any developing country, the Philippines has been aspiring for a better quality of life for its citizens. Even as early as the 1950s, the government emphasized the importance of achieving better living conditions for people in its medium-term development plans.[6] This goal has been elusive, however. At present, around one-third of Filipinos still live in poverty. While some have attributed this lack of success to fortuitous events in the country's history, some have pointed out to the failure of the nation's institutions as the main reason.

Interest in the impact of institutions in a country's development has been sparked (stoked may be a better term) by the works of the economist Douglass North. Institutions, according to North, are "humanly devised constraints that structure human interaction." They are made up of formal constraints (rules, laws, constitutions), informal constraints (norms of behaviour, conventions, self-imposed codes of conduct), and the enforcement characteristics of these two. Taken together, they "form the incentive structure of society."[7]

Public sector institutions as well as their enforcement fall under the realm of governance. Governance, as defined by the Asian Development Bank is the "institutionalization of a system through which citizens, institutions, organizations, and groups in a society articulate their interests, exercise their rights, and mediate their differences in pursuit of the collective good."[8]

As mentioned earlier, the WGI identifies six dimensions of governance: control of corruption, rule of law, regulatory quality, government effectiveness, political stability and absence of violence, voice, and accountability. These indicators will be discussed in more detail in the following section.

Governance Indicators Measuring the Strength of Public Sector Institutions

The Worldwide Governance Indicators were developed by Daniel Kaufmann of the Brookings Institution and Aart Kraay and Massimo Mastruzzi of the World Bank. They consist of six composite indicators of broad dimensions of governance and summarize 31 different data sources that capture governance perceptions as reported by survey respondents, non-governmental organizations, commercial business information providers, and public sector organizations worldwide.[9]

The WGI define governance as "the traditions and institutions by which authority in a country is exercised. This includes (1) the process by which governments are selected, monitored and replaced; (2) the capacity of the government to effectively formulate and implement sound policies; and (3) the respect of citizens and the state for the institutions that govern economic and social interactions among them." Two measures of governance corresponding to each of these three areas were constructed to come up with six dimensions of governance.[10]

With regard to the process by which governments are selected, monitored and replaced, the following indicators were developed: (1) voice and accountability (captures perceptions of the extent to which a country's citizens are able to participate in selecting their government, as well as freedom of expression, freedom of association and a free media); and (2) political stability and absence of violence/terrorism (captures perceptions of the likelihood that the government will be destabilized or overthrown by unconstitutional or violent means, including politically-motivated violence and terrorism).[11] Measuring the capacity of the government to effectively formulate and implement sound policies are the following: (1) government effectiveness (captures perceptions of the quality of public services, the quality of the civil service and the degree of its independence from political pressures, the quality of policy formulation and implementation, and the credibility of the government's commitment to such policies); and (2) regulatory quality (captures perceptions of the ability of the government to formulate and implement sound policies and regulations that permit and promote private sector development).[12] The respect of citizens and the state for the institutions that govern economic and social interactions among them is measured by the following dimensions: (1) rule of law (captures perceptions of the extent to which agents have confidence in and abide by the rules of society, and in particular the quality of contract enforcement, property rights, the police, and the courts, as well as the likelihood of crime and violence); and (2) control of corruption (captures perceptions of the extent to which public power is exercised for public gain, including both petty and grand forms of corruption, as well as "capture" of the state by elites and private interests).[13] The table below shows how the Philippines ranks among the nine[14] countries of the Association of Southeast Asian Nations (ASEAN) in each of the above mentioned dimensions for the year 2009:

Table 1. Governance Indicators of the Philippines

Governance Dimension	Philippine Ranking
Voice and Accountability	2nd
Political Stability and Absence of Violence/ Terrorism	9th
Government Effectiveness	5th
Regulatory Quality	5th
Rule of Law	6th
Control of Corruption	7th

Source of basic data: World Bank http://info.worldbank.org/governance/wgi/index.asp.

The Philippines' rankings show that its performance varies from one governance dimension to another. In terms of voice and accountability, the country is second only to Indonesia, while it is last in political stability and absence of violence/ terrorism. It ranked in the middle in terms of government effectiveness and regulatory quality. The Philippines ranked lower than most ASEAN countries with regard to rule of law and control of corruption. In terms of controlling corruption, the Philippines performed the worst among its fellow middle-income countries in the region, namely Indonesia, Malaysia, and Thailand. Within this same grouping, only Indonesia performed worse in terms of rule of law. Viet Nam, which has a lower per capita income than the Philippines, performed better in both rule of law and control of corruption.

A Governance Milestone: The Local Government Code of 1991

On October 10, 1991, the Philippines adopted a policy that – in terms of influence on how the country is presently governed – is arguably second only to the Constitution[15] that enabled its enactment. This is RA 7160 or the Local Government Code of 1991(the Code for brevity). The primary aim of this policy is to enable local governments to "attain their fullest development as self-reliant communities and make them more effective partners (of the national government) in the attainment of national goals." In view of this, the "territorial and political subdivisions of the State shall enjoy genuine and meaningful local autonomy" (RA 7160, Section 2).

Under RA 7160 the Philippines is territorially and politically subdivided into provinces, which are further subdivided into cities and municipalities. Generally, cities are more urbanized and enjoy a wider range of political powers than municipalities, which upon achieving certain criteria of urbanization,[16] may become cities through legislation. Highly urbanized cities such as those located in the national capital and other economic centers throughout the country are politically independent from provinces.[17] Cities and municipalities are composed of barangays (villages), which represent the lowest tier of local government in the country.

The local government structure is headed by the chief executive: a governor in the case of a province, a mayor in the case of a city or municipality, and a captain in the case of a barangay. The chief executive – elected at large – is backstopped by a corps of appointed local civil servants in the performance of his/her executive and administrative functions. The vice chief executive, also elected at large, presides over the local council (*sanggunian*). It should be noted that a village does not have a vice chief executive, and that the captain presides over the *sangguniang barangay*. The members of the *sanggunianare* elected at large in the case of a municipality or *barangay* and per district in the case of a province or city. It serves as the legislative arm of the local government and is held as coequal of the executive branch. The *sanggunian* secretariat provides legislative and administrative support to the provincial, city and municipal councils.

RA 7160 has delegated to local governments in general the responsibility to "ensure and support, among other things, the preservation and enrichment of culture, promote health and safety, enhance the right of the people to a balanced ecology, encourage and support the development of appropriate and self-reliant scientific and technological capabilities, improve public morals, enhance economic prosperity and social justice, promote full employment among their residents, maintain peace and order, and preserve the comfort and convenience of their inhabitants" (Sect. 16).

To capacitate the local governments in performing these tasks, RA 7160 has devolved to them the power to create their own sources of revenue and to levy taxes, fees and charges that shall accrue exclusively for their use and disposition (Sect. 18). The law also provides that local governments shall have a share in the national internal revenue taxes. Under this provision, 40 percent of the collection of the third fiscal year preceding the current one shall constitute the local governments' internal revenue allotment (Sect. 284). In addition to this, more than 70,000 employees were transferred from the national government to local governments, most of them from the Department of Health, Department of Agriculture, Department of Budget and Management, and Department of Environment and Natural Resources.[18] Also, relevant national government agencies (NGAs), with the Department of the Interior and Local

Government (DILG) taking the lead, continue to provide technical assistance to local governments.

In devolving powers and responsibilities to local governments, RA 7160 has several built-in provisions that, when properly enforced, may contribute to the improvement of governance in the country. For instance, implementing the various check and balance provisions of the Code may further control corruption. These include the provisions on the oversight function of the *sanggunian* over the local chief executive found in Sections 444 (for municipalities), 455 (for cities) and 465 (for provinces). In the case of the province, Section 465 states that the governor shall "be responsible to the *sangguniangpanlala wigan* (provincial board) for the program of government." The governor should also "present the program of government and propose policies and projects for the consideration of the *sang guniangpanlala-wigan*" and "as often as may be deemed necessary, provide such information and data needed or requested by said *sanggunian* in the performance of its legislative functions. Administrative complaints may also be filed against erring local elective officials with the higher *sanggunian* that has jurisdiction over them, e.g., an administrative complaint may be filed against a municipal mayor with the *sangguniangpanlalawigan* (Sect. 61).

With regard to promoting the rule of law, Section 30 provides that governors shall "review all executive orders promulgated by the component city or municipal mayor within his jurisdiction." Likewise, city and municipal mayors shall "review all executive orders promulgated by the *Punong Barangay* (village chief) within his jurisdiction." Sections 56 and 57, on the other hand, provide for the review of ordinances by the *sanggunian* of the higher LGU that has jurisdiction over the LGU that passed the ordinance. To illustrate, the *Sangguniang-Panlalawiganshall* review the ordinances passed by the component cities and municipalities under its jurisdiction. The

Sangguniang Panlungsod and *Sangguniang Bayan*, on the other hand, shall review the ordinances passed by the *barangays* under their jurisdiction. This is to ensure that ordinances are consistent with the law and within the power conferred upon the local councils that passed them.

A wide range of regulatory powers were also devolved to local governments, but perhaps the most important of these are the regulations of land use and business. Section 20(c) specifies that LGUs shall "…prepare their respective comprehensive land use plans enacted through zoning ordinances which shall be the primary and dominant bases for the future use of land resources …." Municipal councils are tasked to "regulate any business, occupation, or practice of profession or calling which does not require government examination" (Sect. 447.3.ii). City councils, on the other hand, are given the responsibility to "regulate or fix license fees for any business or practice of profession within the city" (Sect. 458.3.ii).

Local governments may also regulate various economic activities through the wide range of taxing powers devolved to them. Provinces, for instance, may impose taxes on printing and publication, businesses enjoying franchise, quarrying, professionals, amusement places, and delivery trucks (Sect. 134-141). Municipalities may impose taxes on the following businesses: manufacturers and the like, wholesalers, distributors, dealers, exporters, millers, retailers, banks and other financial institutions, and peddlers (Sect. 142-150). Cities may impose taxes that provinces and municipalities impose (Sect. 151). *Barangays*, on the other hand, may only impose taxes on stores and retailers with fixed business establishments and with gross annual sales of Php 50,000.00 or less, in case of *barangays* within cities, and Php 30,000.00 or less, in case of *barangays* located in municipalities (Sect. 152).

Various provisions of RA 7160 promote government effectiveness. One of the operative principles of decentralization espoused by the said law is the provision that local governments should have an accountable, efficient, and dynamic organizational structure and operating mechanism to meet the priority needs and service requirements of their communities (Sect. 3.b). Another operative principle is that local officials and employees should be appointed or removed according to merit and fitness (Sect. 3.c). To allow the local governments to effectively carry out their functions, they were given the power to create and broaden their own sources of revenue, the right to ajust share in national taxes, and an equitable share in the proceeds of the utilization and development of the national wealth within their respective areas (Sect. 3.d). Also, in order to address concerns transcending territorial boundaries effectively – and for other purposes commonly beneficial to them – local governments are allowed to group themselves and consolidate or coordinate their efforts, services and resources (Sect. 3.f).

A vibrant but orderly politics at the local level is also promoted by various provisions of the Code. Recall elections, for instance, provide a mechanism for the orderly transfer of power from local officials who have apparently lost the confidence of the citizens to duly elected successors.[19] On the other hand, in order to promote the contestability of local elections, Section 43(b) specifies that no elective local official should serve for more than three consecutive terms in the same position.

Direct citizen participation in local governance is also facilitated by the Code. Through the process of local initiative, for instance, registered voters of an LGU may directly propose, enact, or amend any ordinance (Sect. 120). On the other hand, the process of local referendum allows registered voters of the LGU to approve, amend, or reject any ordinance enacted by the *sanggunian* (Sect. 126). Also, Section 10 specifies that "no creation, division, merger, abolition, or substantial alteration of boundaries of local government units may take effect unless approved by amajority of the votes cast in a plebiscite called for the purpose in the political unit or units directly affected."

RA 7160 also provides a venue for the civil society to actively participate in local governance. The said law specifies that LGUs: (1) should promote the establishment and operation of people's and non-governmental organizations (POs and NGOs); (2) may enter into partnership with the said organizations in the delivery of certain services and implementation of various projects; and (3) may provide financial or other forms of assistance to POs and NGOs for various projects to be implemented within their territorial jurisdiction (Sect. 34-36). Also, under the Code, the local health boards and local development councils require the membership of representatives from NGOs (Sect. 102, 108). Local school boards, on the other hand, require the membership of the representatives of the federation of parents-teachers associations, teachers' organization and non-academic personnel of public schools in the concerned LGU (Sect. 98).

To enhance the accountability of local governments, RA 7160 provides that on or before March 31 of each year, every local chief executive shall submit an annual report to the *sanggunian* concerned on the socio-economic, political and peace and order conditions, as well as other matters concerning the LGU. A copy of the report should be forwarded to the DILG, in the case of provinces, and to the *Sangguniang Panlalawigan* in the case of component cities and municipalities (Sect. 97). In the case of *barangays*, the law specifies that a Barangay Assembly composed of all residents of the village 15 years old and above should meet at least twice a year to hear and discuss the semestral report of the *sangguniang barangay* concerning its activities and finances as well as problems affecting the community (Sect. 397).

The above mentioned provisions of RA 7160 promote good governance in a decentralized setting. Like all formal rules, however, they do not mean much if the quality and consistency of their enforcement is low. They do not mean anything if they are not enforced at all. The following section will look at the current the Philippines experience in decentralization and how this type of public sector reform has contributed to the improvement of governance in the country.

Decentralization as a Means of Improving Governance

This section will look at how decentralization, as one of the most extensive reforms ever undertaken by the Philippines public sector, has contributed to improving governance in the country. As in the previous section, the discussion will be guided by the framework of the WGI and will focus on its six governance dimensions. It should be noted however that the present study did not apply the WGI method in measuring the performance of LGUs. The authors were unable to do a study of such magnitude due to time and resource constraints. Instead, they made a survey of the results of existing empirical studies that approximate the indicators comprising the WGI. When no such study was available, the authors turned to the recent works of respected scholars who had made an appraisal of what decentralization had achieved so far since the enactment of RA 7160 almost two decades ago.

Control of Corruption

The Philippines holds the unenviable distinction of being one of the most corrupt countries. The WGI ranked the "Pearl of the Orient" as the seventh least corrupt out of nine countries of the ASEAN (Myanmar not included) in 2009 – besting only Cambodia and Laos. Transparency International's ranking of the island nation as the 134th least corrupt out of 178 countries included in its 2010 study[20] implies that no significant improvement in situation has been observed recently. Among its neighbours, the Philippines only did better than Cambodia, Laos and Myanmar, which ranked 154,th 154,th and 176th respectively. The Corruption Perception Index (CPI) score of the country also did not move from 2.4,[21] the mark that it had the previous year. These levels reflect a continuing deterioration since the country pulled off a CPI score of 3.6 in 1999. Given these dismal figures, one may ask how decentralization contributed to controlling corruption in the country. Did decentralization improve or worsen the Philippines' corruption situation?

The Transparency and Accountability Network (TAN) observed that devolution and decentralization paved the way for new opportunities for corruption and rent-seeking in the country, as well as for the emergence of new players in the persons of local chief executives.[22] Harris-White and White noted that in the Philippines, the process of democratization has increased the level of corruption aside from making it more decentralized and uncoordinated.[23]

Recent empirical studies of the Social Weather Stations(SWS)[24] however, showed that Filipinos think corruption is less likely to happen in the LGUs than in the national government. Municipal and city governments were also seen as more sincere in fighting corruption than most national government agencies. These LGUs were even seen as more sincere in fighting corruption than the government agencies especially mandated to do so such as the *Sandiganbayan,*[25] Commission on Audit, Office of the Ombudsman, Presidential Commission on Good Government, and Presidential Anti-Graft Commission. There has also been a significant improvement in the net sincerity[26] rating of city and municipal governments from 2007 to 2009, when they garnered ratings of plus 26 and plus 35, respectively.[27]

Local governments in general were perceived as less corrupt in 2009 than in 2004. However, 32 percent of enterprises reported that they were asked for a bribe when getting local government permits and licenses. The said percentage is no difference from the proportion of those who were asked for a bribe when getting national government permits and licenses. Still, this figure is a big improvement from the previous year (2008) when bribe-solicitations in getting local government permits and licenses reached a peak of 49 percent.[28]

Enterprises are also more likely to bring their complaints to LGUs than other government agencies if harassed by corrupt government officials. Only the Office of the Ombudsman and the National Bureau of Investigation (NBI) are trusted by more enterprises in this regard. It should be noted, however, that most enterprises would rather not bring their complaints to anyone, primarily because of the perception that nothing would be done to address them anyway. Also, it should be pointed out that the proportion of enterprises that trust LGUs dropped from 8 percent in 2005 to 5 percent in 2008.[29] These findings lend evidence to the claim that LGUs on their own generally contribute little, if anything, to solving corruption. It may even be true that decentralization has started to reap some dividends in terms of controlling corruption in the country.

Rule of Law

Under RA 7160, ordinances passed by a local government are subject to review by the *sanggunian* of the higher local government that has jurisdiction over it. In the case of ordinances by provinces and highly-urbanized cities, it is the DILG that does the review. This provision is included to ensure that local governments do not go beyond the powers delegated to them by making rules that are contrary to the law of the land. It is also necessary so that citizens would be protected against impositions by local authorities that may impinge upon their constitutionally-protected freedoms.

In the past, however, various ordinances have slipped through this system of check and balance until they were declared as unconstitutional by the Supreme Court. For instance, an ordinance prohibiting short-time admission and wash-up rate schemes in hotels, motels, and similar establishments in the city of Manila was invalidated by the High Tribunal on the ground that it arbitrarily and whimsically intrudes into the rights of the said establishments as well as their patrons.[30] Another ordinance prohibiting the establishment or operation of businesses providing certain forms of amusement, entertainment, services and facilities in the Ermita-Malate area (within Manila) was declared void for infringing the constitutional guarantees of due process and equal protection of laws.[31]

At present, the constitutionality of the following ordinances are being contested by concerned parties: (1) Barangay Ayala Alabang Ordinance No. 1 prohibiting sex education for children, requiring people buying condoms to present a doctor's prescription, and penalizing anyone who advertises, sells, offers for free, endorses, promotes, prescribes, or distributes abortifacients[32]; (2) Island Garden City of Samal Ordinance No. 156 revising the island city's revenue code; and (3) Manila City Ordinance No. 8229 exempting a telecommunications company from payment of real property taxes on all machinery and equipment, as well as from payment of local franchise tax.

The constitutionality of one of RA 7160's provisions was also the subject of question in the past. A trial court declared as unconstitutional Section 187, which lays down the procedure for approval and effectiveness of tax ordinances and revenue measures, arguing that its vesture in the Secretary of Justice of the power of control over local governments is in violation of the policy of local autonomy mandated in the Constitution. The

Supreme Court later reversed the trial court's decision declaring that implementing Section 187 was merely an act of supervision and not of control by the Secretary of Justice.

The continued passage of ordinances that have no legal and constitutional bases implies two things. One is that some local councils, or at least some local legislators, do not have enough capacity to determine what is contrary or not contrary to law. The other is that some local councils, or at least some local legislators, are willing to challenge the *status quo* in order to determine the full extent of local authority. The latter implication is acceptable, if not laudable, in as much as the intention is to promote the general welfare of citizens. The same, however, is deplorable if done to pursue selfish interests and/or without regard to the rights and freedoms of those who will be negatively affected.

Regulatory Quality

The quality of a country's regulations - especially those concerned with property and the pursuit of profitable activities - is very important in encouraging private investments. Private investments are, of course, important in generating productive employment. Productive employment is, in turn, a key component in attaining human development. How did decentralization affect the quality of regulations in the Philippines? This is the key question that we would like to answer in this subsection.

Globally, the Doing Business in the Philippines initiative of the World Bank (WB) and the International Finance Corporation (IFC) looks at domestic small and medium-size companies and measures the regulations applying to them through their life cycle. Started in 2002, its goal is to provide an objective basis for understanding and improving the regulatory environment for business.[33] In its latest report, Doing Business 2011, the Philippines ranked 148th out of 183 countries in terms of ease of doing business. Among ASEAN member-countries (Myanmar not included), only in Laos it is more difficult to do business than in the Philippines.[34] The country's current ranking is two rungs lower than its 2010 position, implying that the situation has not been improving - rather it could be deteriorating - in the recent period.

Locally, Doing Business in the Philippines, also published by the WB and the IFC, compares business regulation in 25 cities across the country. It provides a quantitative measure of the national and local regulations for starting a business, dealing with construction permits, and registering property imposed on domestic small and medium-size enterprises.[35] Two reports had been produced thus far, one in 2008 and another earlier this year (2011).

Despite the poor national showing in the global rankings, Doing Business in the Philippines 2011 study found that city governments have actively reformed their business regulations over the past two years. Most of the city governments included in the said study have simplified procedures and cut costs for local enterprises, mainly by reengineering business processes. Since 2008, 65 percent of the 21 cities benchmarked by the study made reforms in at least one of the areas measured.[36]

This is supported by the 2009 findings of the SWS that majority of enterprises said transaction procedures in city and municipal government offices are transparent. At least two-thirds of enterprises also said that the process of annual renewal of business permits and licenses became easier as compared to three years ago. The same proportion asserted that they don't use intermediaries in renewing local permits and licenses. The majority, or 63 percent of enterprises, also expressed satisfaction with their city or municipal government in promoting a good business climate. By contrast, only 42 percent said they were satisfied with the national government in terms of doing the same.[37]

Regardless, some NGAs have come up with projects in support of local initiatives aimed at providing a more conducive regulatory environment for business. One such agency is the Land Registration Authority (LRA), which embarked on a nationwide land-titling computerization project. This project will consolidate land records into a single national database and facilitate the registration and authentication of titles.[38]

A number of policies at the national level, however, run counter to the initiatives of local governments to improve business regulation. For instance, Republic Act No. 9514 amending the Fire Code of the Philippines mandates a Fire Safety Inspection Certificate (FSIC) to be issued by the Bureau of Fire Protection (BFP) as a prerequisite to any permits or licenses issued by local governments. The Implementing Rules and Regulations of this new Fire Code require any new business to secure an FSIC as a prerequisite to a business permit, even when the new business is leasing space in a building that has a certificate. Nonetheless, some national-level reforms can also promote better business regulations at the local level. Republic Act No. 9485 or the "Anti-Red Tape Act" requires all government agencies, including local governments, to draft their Citizen's Charter, an official document that describes the procedure for obtaining a particular service and the guaranteed performance level that the public may expect.[39]

Government Effectiveness

An effective government is one that is able to facilitate the access of its citizens to the services they need. To be able to do this, the government itself should have access to adequate resources. Does the Philippines brand of decentralization promote both? This subsection tries to answer this question.

After the enactment of RA 7160, a marked increase in local government spending occurred as more resources had been made available to LGUs. Manasan (2005) reported that total LGU spending rose from an average of 1.6 percent of the Gross National Product (GNP) in 1985 to 1991 to 3.3 percent of the GNP in 1992 to 2003. The LGU share in total government expenditure excluding debt service increased from an average of 11 percent before the implementation of RA 7160 to an average of 21.2 percent afterwards. Among all major sectors, social services posted the fastest rate of growth, increasing by an average of 21.7 percent annually from 1992 to 2003. The overall rate of growth in LGU spending for the same period was 8.2 percent. Health services were a priority in LGU spending between 1992 and 2003 followed by education, housing/community development, and social welfare in that order.[40]

Did this growth in spending translate to improvement in the effectiveness of local services delivery? Surveys to assess satisfaction with public services point to mixed results on local government performance. A 2005 study by WB and ADB showed that localities continue to experience various problems such as uncertain access to potable water and electricity, declining literacy rates, environmental degradation, rising unemployment rates, lack of low-cost housing, and unreliable police and fire department services. Public infrastructures are also lacking in most areas.[41] Capuno (2007) in response to a WB survey asserted that the low quality of decentralized primary health care services leads to high bypass rates of local health units. The WB survey indicated that 74 percent of people were bypassing rural health units while 68 percent were bypassing barangay health centers.[42] Nonetheless, the WB and ADB study also showed that there area growing number of excellent examples in local services delivery. These seem to be hinged on the local governments' ability to access resources more effectively, and manage them with more transparency and accountability.[43]

With empirical evidence going both ways, it is quite difficult to determine the direction of decentralization's impact in terms of government effectiveness. On the other hand, evidence also suggests that an improvement in local government's financial capacity, somehow translates to better services. With the historically poor showing of the majority of LGUs in raising revenues, however, it may still take quite sometime before the country fully realizes the benefits of decentralization under this governance dimension.

Political Stability and Absence of Violence/Terrorism

The impact of decentralization in political stability and violence/terrorism is also mixed. In 2010, the Independent Commission against Private Armies (ICAPA) identified 107 private armies existing in the country, as well as 123 personalities leading these illegal armed groups. The Political Democracy and Reforms (PODER) Program of the Ateneo School of Governance also found out that 73 percent of the identified private army leaders are local politicians belonging to traditional political dynasties. Provincial election hot spots, which regularly experience high frequency of election-related violence, were also found to be ruled by entrenched political clans identified as patrons of private armies. PODER's study identified private armies, warlike political clans, and loose firearms as enabling factors of election-related violence. More alarming is the finding that these factors operate not only during, before and after every election period, but that they are entrenched throughout the life cycle of a local political system. Equally disturbing is the observation that election-related violence seems to be a useful electoral tactic in provinces where political clans with private armies dominate.[44] These realities diminish the competitiveness of local elections in the country and serve as an affront to the people's right to suffrage.

Meanwhile, the process of recall election empowers the

people by allowing them to constitutionally remove and replace elected local officials who have lost their confidence. On its website, the Commission on Elections (COMELEC) records that the following recall elections have been conducted since the enactment of RA 7160.

Table 2. Recall Elections since the Enactment of RA 7160

Year	Local Government Unit	Official(s) Concerned
2002	City of Puerto Princesa, Palawan	Mayor
2000	City of Pasay, Metro Manila	Mayor
1997	City of Caloocan, Metro Manila	Mayor
1997	Municipality of Narvacan, Ilocos Sur	Vice-Mayor
1997	Municipality of Basilia, Surigao del Norte	Mayor, Vice-Mayor and Six Councilors
1993	Province of Bataan	Governor

Source: COMELEC.

Despite the provision for recall and the prohibition on local officials to hold the same position for more than three consecutive terms, the contestability of elective local positions has been somewhat low. This is due primarily to the prevalence of political dynasties in the country. The wider latitudes of power devolved to LGUs somehow made local political contests more bitterly fought. Once elected, there is every motivation for local officials to stay in power and get reelected. Even during their term breaks, they would want to place their relatives in power so that they can easily reclaim their former positions when they are legally eligible to run again. The control over private armies by traditional political clans discussed earlier further limits the participation in local political contests to just a few families.

A study by Balisacan and Fuwa (2004) showed that generally, the presence of a political dynasty has a significantly negative impact to the growth of a province's economy. This is primarily due to the reason that the lack of a competitive political system leads to suboptimal policy choices. That is why the last governance dimension to be discussed in the next subsection cannot be considered as the least in terms of importance.[45]

Voice and Accountability

Aside from the process of recall, RA 7160 provides for direct people participation in local governance through the processes of initiative, referendum and plebiscite. Unlike recall and plebiscite, which have been exercised by the people relatively more frequently, initiative and referendum are seldom used as avenues for participation in local governance. One instance when initiative was used by the people to enact an ordinance was on 14 May 2011. On the said date, the majority of the registered voters of Barangay Milagrosa in Quezon City who turned out to vote passed an ordinance for the prevention and control of the proliferation of illegal settlers, mendicants, and drug trafficking.[46]

On the other hand, the people of the Municipality of Sadanga, Mountain Province voted on 25 October 2010 to name the municipality's foundation day anniversary. The people chose between the names Fvegnash, which is the festival's original name, and Pagey asit was called during that time. The name Fvegnash was eventually adopted as it was voted by the majority during the referendum.[47]

Countless plebiscites have been held in the past to approve the creation and conversion of LGUs. However, there were several cases when the people rejected – through plebiscite – Acts of Congress mandating the creation and conversion of LGUs. COMELEC lists the following instances on its website.

Utilizing the democratic processes of initiative and referendum would allow citizens to directly participate in governing the affairs of their LGUs. As any student of local governance would

Table 3. Plebiscite Held and Their Results

Plebiscite Held	Result
13 December 2008	RA 9495 mandating the division of the Province of Quezon into Quezon del Norte and Quezon del Sur was rejected
30 March 2001	RA 9021 mandating conversion ofthe Municipality of Meycauayan, Bulacan into a city was rejected
23 October 1999	RA 8535 mandating the creation of the City of Novaliches out of 15 barangays of Quezon City was rejected
14 March 1999	RA 8474 mandating the conversion of the Municipality of Ilagan to a component city of Isabela was rejected
20 June 1995	RA 7891 mandating the division of the Province of Isabela into Isabela del Norte and Isabela del Sur was rejected

Source: COMELEC.

expect, people's initiative was first exercised in the Philippines to address concerns that directly affect the everyday lives of citizens. In Barangay Milagrosa, Quezon City, these are common neighbourhood concerns like illegal settling, mendicancy, abusive barangay officials, and drug-trafficking. Such concerns are of the utmost importance to residents of a community in danger of being destroyed by these societal problems, but are easily taken for granted by jaded local politicians.

In the future, the authors expect to see more citizens asserting their rights to better public services by compelling their local officials to act by virtue of ordinances that they themselves (the citizens) have crafted. The authors expect to see these in the areas of peace and order, public safety, solid waste management, public market management, traffic management, flood control, and ecological management among others. At present, however, an extensive information and education campaign may be needed to make citizens aware that processes like initiative and referendum are available for them to utilize in shaping the destiny of their respective communities.

Decentralization Outcomes on Economy and Human Development

The bottom line of all discussions on public sector reform and improving governance boils down to what has been the outcome for the people thus far? Did it bring about economic growth and ultimately, human development? Did it bring down unemployment and underemployment? How about higher wages? Did it lead to longer and happier lives for the citizens? Are the people enjoying more freedoms now than before? The desired outcomes can be expressed in myriad ways. This study, however, will assess the present state of the Philippines economy and human development in terms of more traditional measures of economic growth and human development. A snapshot of the country's achievements so far in going after the Millennium Development Goals will also be provided. It should be noted that these outcomes cannot be entirely attributed to decentralization, or to any singular public sector reform for that matter. It is even very possible that these outcomes were influenced by factors effectively beyond the scope of governance. Nonetheless, the authors believe that decentralization – with its scale and scope – has significantly influenced these outcomes, and should be partially credited or blamed for all the successes and failures of governance in the Philippines.

Economic Growth Outcomes

Data from the World Bank's website show that for the period 2005-2009, the Gross Domestic Product (GDP) of the Philippines is growing respectably at an average annual rate of 4.42 percent. This is slower than the 5.73 percent average annual growth rate of ASEAN member-countries (excluding Brunei and Myanmar), but faster than those of Malaysia (4.12 percent) and Thailand (2.98 percent). Indonesia's GDP is growing at a faster rate than that of the Philippines at 5.60 percent.

Also based on World Bank data, the Philippines' GDP per capita in 2009 is 1,215 in constant 2000 USD. This is comparable with that of Indonesia (1,124), but much lower than those of Malaysia (4,992) and Thailand (2,567). The country's GDP per capita is growing at an average annual rate of 2.4 percent for the years 2005-2009. This figure is lower than the regional (excluding Brunei and Myanmar) average of 3.9 percent, but comparable to those of Malaysia (2.4 percent) and Thailand (2.2 percent). Indonesia's GDP per capita is growing more rapidly at 4.2 percent.

Human Development Outcomes

The Philippines placed 97th out of 169 countries in the 2010 Human Development Rankings of the United Nations Development Programme. Among ASEAN member-countries, the country ranked 5th ahead of Indonesia, Vietnam, Laos, Cambodia, and Myanmar. With an HDI of 0.638, the Philippines is considered a country with a medium level of human development. For comparison purposes, Singapore has an HDI of 0.846 while Myanmar's is 0.451.[48]

Philippine Achievements in the Millennium Development Goals

The efforts of the Philippines government to fulfil the nation's commitment of attaining the MDGs by 2015, so far, have had mixed results. With the deadline fast approaching, the country has low likelihood of achieving three of the eight MDGs, three have medium chance, and two have high probability of being achieved. The following[49] gives a closer look at how the Philippinesis faring in each of the MDGs:

Goal 1: Eradicate Extreme Poverty and Hunger

Poverty incidence has dropped from 45.3 percent in 1991 to

32.9 percent in 2006. During the same period, subsistence incidence fell from 24.3 percent to 14.6 percent. In a disturbing development, however, both poverty and subsistence incidence increased from 2003 to 2006. More alarming is the fact that this happened in a period of significant economic growth. Inequality remains a serious problem as the country's Gini coefficient only improved slightly from 0.47 to 0.46 after a decade and a half. The country only has a medium probability of achieving this goal.

Goal 2: Achieve Universal Primary Education

After peaking at 97 percent in SY 1999-2000, the elementary education participation rate (EEPR) declined to 85.1 percent in SY 2008-2009. In a more positive light, school efficiency, as measured by cohort survival rate, has improved from 68.7 percent to 75.4 percent during the same period. The percentage of Grade 1 pupils who were able to complete the elementary level has also increased significantly from 66.5 percent to 73.3 percent. The country has low probability of achieving this goal.

Goal 3: Promote Gender Equality and Empower Women

By SY 1999-2000, the EEPR of girls has surpassed that of boys and has remained higher since then. Enrolment rates for secondary and tertiary educations have also been higher for female than male students. Women are becoming more visible as leaders and decision-makers in their chosen fields. Electoral positions, however, are still dominated by men. Incidence of physical injuries and/or wife battering reported to the Philippines National Police has been decreasing after peaking in 2001. Despite this, 2009 posted the highest number of recorded cases of violence against women over the past decade. The country has a high probability of achieving this goal.

Goal 4: Reduce Child Mortality

The target of reducing the infant mortality rate (IMR) to 19 deaths per 1,000 live births is almost achieved with the country's IMR pegged at 25 : 1,000 in 2008. Under-five mortality rate has also decreased significantly from 80 deaths per 1,000 live births in 1990 to 34 : 1,000 in 2008. However, infant deaths still constitute 74 percent of under-five mortality, while neonatal deaths make up 64 percent of infant fatalities. There is high probability that the country will achieve this goal.

Goal 5: Improve Maternal Health

Maternal mortality rate (MMR) decreased significantly from 209 per 100,000 live births in 1990 to 162 : 100,000 in 2008, but this is still far from the target of 52 : 100,000. More than a third (36.4 percent) of deliveries were still assisted by *hilots*[50] in 2008, practically the same as five years previously. With regard to the use of contraceptive methods, the country is still very far from the target of 80 percent prevalence rate by 2015. The government estimates that only 51 percent of married women are using contraceptive methods. There is low probability that the country will achieve this goal.

Goal 6: Combat HIV and AIDS, Malaria and Other Diseases

While the prevalence rate of human immunodeficiency virus (HIV) infection remains below one percent of the total population, the rapid increase in the number of persons infected over the past few years is alarming. An average of five new infections are reported daily. Deaths due to malaria decreased from 1.5 deaths per 100,000 to 0.02 : 100,000 over the same period. Tuberculosis, meanwhile, remains as a leading cause of morbidity and mortality in the country. The probability of achieving this goal is low.

Goal 7: Ensure Environmental Sustainability

The proportion of the country's population with access to clean and safe sources of water increased from 73.8 percent in 1991 to 81.4 percent in 2008. In the same period, the proportion of Filipinos using sanitary toilet facilities increased from 71.8 percent to 88.6 percent. In terms of protecting marine resources, however, the country's performance is dismal. Almost all of its coral reefs are put at risk because of human activities. More than 70 percent of the mangrove forests have been destroyed. All main fish species are severely being overfished. Philippine biodiversity, while one of the richest in the world, is also one of the most threatened. There is medium probability that thecountry will achieve this goal.

Goal 8: Develop a Global Partnership for Development

International trade volume has continuously declined in the past decade. The IT bubble burst in 2001 and the global financial crisis in 2008 brought about negative growth rates in both exports and imports. Net foreign direct investments (FDIs) peaked in 2006 and 2007 before falling to almost half in 2008. It experienced somewhat of a resurgence in 2009, but is still far from the levels attained in 2006 and 2007. The probability of achieving this goal is medium.

Conclusion and the Way Forward

The Philippines' decentralization law, RA 7160, is replete with provisions promoting governance. However, the extent to which these provisions are enforced or implemented vary. At present, several periodic empirical studies are conducted measuring the quality of governance in the country. Some of these studies – like WB and IFC's Doing Business in the Philippines and SWS's Surveys of Enterprises on Corruption – recognize the significance of the local governments' role and influence in the country's overall quality of governance. Based on the results of these studies, the authors found out that, to some extent, decentralization has contributed positively in some aspects of governance, particularly in the control of corruption and regulatory quality. With regard to the other governance dimensions, however, available information indicates that decentralization's influence is mixed and in some cases, nominal.

In view of the country's mediocre record in terms of economic and human development performance, a tool as powerful as the Local Government Code should be optimally used. Nonetheless, the authors admit that there are still areas for improvement in the law's implementation, as well as in some provisions of the law itself. Given the varying performance of local governments in the six governance dimensions, it is recommended that the national policymakers build upon the achievements of decentralization by reinforcing rather than stifling local efforts in improving governance. Coordinating and harmonizing national and local business regulations would be a good start, for example. Where performance is below the desired level, the course of action should be to capacitate local governments rather than renationalize the function. These recommendations rest on the observation that with sufficient resources and proper motivation, LGUs can be effective partners in pursuing the long-elusive goal of national development.

Only then can it be argued that decentralization has positively contributed to the overall goal of public administration reform. After all, as suggested at the outset, and as the evolution of public administration may show, decentralization – together with other strategies such as the reorganization of the bureaucracy – may be very important weapons in the arsenal for meaningful and sustainable public administration reform.

Notes

1) Alex B. Brillantes, Jr. and Maricel T. Fernandez. "Is There a Philippine Public Administration? Or Better Still, *For Whom Is* Philippine Public Administration?," *Philippine Journal of Public Administration,* 52, Nos. 2-4 (2008).
2) United Nations Development Programme (UNDP), *Public Administration Reform Practice Note* New York, NY: UNDP, 2004, 2.
3) Alex B. Brillantes, Jr. and Maricel T. Fernandez. "Toward a Reform Framework for Good Governance Focus on Anti-Corruption," *Philippine Journal of Public Administration,* 54, Nos. 1-2 (2010).
4) UNDP. "The Human Development Concept," UNDP, http://hdr.undp.orgen-humandev (accessed April 8, 2011).
5) Boutros, Boutros-Ghali. *An Agenda for Democratization* (New York, NY: United Nations, 1996), 1.
6) Gonzalo Jurado. "Growth Models, Development Planning, and Implementation in the Philippines," *Philippine Journal of Development,* 30, No. 1 (2003).
7) Douglass North (1993). "Prize Lecture: Economic Performance through Time". Nobelprize.org, http://www.nobelprize.org/nobel_prizes/economicslaureates/1993-north-lecture.html (accessed April 8, 2011).
8) Asian Development Bank (ADB). Governance: Sound Development Management (Manila, RP: ADB, 1995) quoted inBrillantes and Fernandez, *Is There a Philippine Public Administration? Or Better Still, For Whom Is Philippine Public Administration?*, 258.
9) Daniel Kaufmann, Aart Kraay and Massimo Mastruzzi. "The Worldwide Governance Indicators: Methodology and Analytical Issues," *Policy Research Working Paper,* No. 5430 (2010), 2.
10) Ibid., 4.
11) Ibid.
12) Ibid.
13) Ibid.
14) Comparator countries are Brunei, Cambodia, Indonesia, Laos, Malaysia, Singapore, Thailand, and Viet Nam. ASEAN's tenth member, Myanmar, is not included in the rankings.
15) The current Philippine Constitution was ratified by the Filipino people on February 2, 1987.
16) The criteria for becoming a city are population of at least 150,000, land area of 100 sq.km. and locally generated income of at least PHP 100 million based on 2000 constant prices.
17) To be considered highly urbanized, a city should have a minimum population of 200,000 and latest annual income of PHP 50 million based on 1991 constant prices. Some cities that do not pass these criteria are politically independent of their host province through the strength of their own charters. They fall under the classification of "independent component cities." One municipality, the Municipality of Pateros, is independent of any province by virtue of its being included in the

national capital region.

18) Proserpina D. Tapales, Perfecto L. Padilla and Ma.Ernita T. Joaquin. "Human Resources Development and Management in Local Government." In *Local Government in the Philippines: A Book of Readings Volume I*, eds. Proserpina D. Tapales, Jocelyn C. Cuaresma, and Wilhelmina Cabo (Quezon City, RP: Center for Local and Regional Governance and National College of Public Administration and Governance, University of the Philippines, 1998), 205.

19) The official who is the subject of recall is automatically considered as a candidate in the recall election. Should he/she win in the said election, the citizens'confidence on him/her will thereby be affirmed, and he/she shall continue in office. Book I, Title Two, Chapter 5 of RA 7160 describes the process of recall.

20) See http://www.transparency.org/policy_research/surveys_indices/cpi/2010/results.

21) A country's CPI rating may range from 0 to 10, where a grade of 10 means the country is perceived as very clean while a rating of 0 means the country is perceived as very corrupt.

22) Transparency and Accountability Network (TAN), "Corruption and Anti-Corruption in the Philippines," a paper prepared by TAN for GTZ Philippines (2011), 17.

23) B. Harris-White and G. White (eds.). "Liberalization and the new corruption," *IDS Bulletin*, 27, No. 2 (1996) quoted in Jens Chr. Andvig and others, Research on Corruption: a Policy Oriented Survey (Oslo, Norway: Norwegian Agency for Development Co-operation, 2000), 58.

24) The SWS Survey of Enterprises conducted in five areas in 2009 and the SWS National Surveys of Adults in 2009.

25) The *Sandiganbayan* is a special court, with rank equivalent to the Court of Appeals, that has jurisdiction over criminal and civil cases involving graft and corrupt practices andother such offenses committed by public officers and employees (with salary grade 27 or higher), including those in government-owned or controlled corporations, in relation to their office as may be determined by law.

26) The difference between the proportions of respondents who said the government agency is very/somewhat sincere in fighting corruption and those who said that it is somewhat/very insincere.

27) Mahar Mangahas, Mahar, "Transparent and Accountable Governance: The 2009 SWS Surveys on Corruption." A presentation for the "Forum on the SWS 2009 Surveys of Enterprises on Corruption and Anti-Corruption Strategies" held on 19 February 2010 at the AIM Conference Center, Makati City.

28) Ibid.

29) Ibid.

30) *White Light Corporation, Titanium Corporation, and Sta. Mesa Tourist and Development Corporation v. City of Manila, represented by De Castro, Mayor Alfredo S. Lim*, GR No. 122846 Republic of the Philippines (2009).

31) *City of Manila et al. v. Hon. Perfecto A.S. Laguio, Jr. et al.*, GR No. 118127 Republic of the Philippines (2005).

32) As of writing, this ordinance is suspended by the Muntinlupa City Council's Committee on Health and Sanitation.

33) World Bank (WB) and International Finance Corporation (IFC). *Doing Business 2011*: Making a Difference for Entrepreneurs (Washington, DC: The International Bank for Reconstruction and Development/The World Bank, 2010), 12.
34) Ibid, 4.
35) WB and IFC. *Doing Business in the Philippines 2011* (Washington, DC: The International Bank for Reconstruction and Development/The World Bank, 2010), 1.
36) Ibid, 8.
37) Mangahas.
38) WB and IFC. *Doing Business in the Philippines*, 26.
39) Ibid, 8-9.
40) Rosario G. Manasan. "Local Public Finance in the Philippines: Lessons in Autonomy and Accountability." *Philippine Journal of Development,* 32, No. 2 (2005): 32-102 quoted in Gilberto M. Llanto, "Fiscal Decentralization and Local Finance Reforms in the Philippines," Philippine Institute of Development Studies Discussion Paper Series, No. 10 (2009): 8-9.
41) WB and ADB. Decentralization in the Philippines: Strengthening Local Government Financing and Resource Management in the Short Run (Manila, RP: WB and ADB, 2005) quoted in Llanto, 9.
42) Joseph J. Capuno. "The Quality of Local Governance and Development under Decentralization," in *The Dynamics of Regional Development, the Philippines in East Asia* (ed.). Arsenio Balisacan and Hal Hill (Cheltenham, UK: Edward Elgar Publishing, 2007), 204-244 quoted in Llanto, 14.
43) WB and ADB in Llanto, 9.
44) Glenford Leonillo. "PODER Study: Weak Policies Cannot Curb Election-Related Violence in the Country," Ateneo School of Government, http://www.asg.ateneo.-edu/news2.php?newsid=193 (accessed April 8, 2011).
45) Arsenio Balisacan and Nobuhiko Fuwa. "Going Beyond Cross-Country Averages: Growth, Inequality and Poverty Reduction in the Philippines," *World Development,* 32, No. 11 (2004).
46) See http://comelec.wordpress.com/2011/05/16/local-initiative-in-a-qc-barangay-successful.
47) See http://www.baguiocity.com/news_article/sadanga-folk-choose-name-festival-referendum.
48) UNDP, *Human Development Report 2010 (20th Anniversary Edition): The Real Wealth of Nations: Pathways to Human Development* (New York, NY: UNDP, 2010).
49) Data culled from Republic of the Philippines, Progress Report on the Millennium Development Goals (Manila, RP: Republic of the Philippines, 2010).
50) Traditional midwives with no formal medical training.

References

Andvig, Jens Chr. et al. (2000). *Research on Corruption: A Policy Oriented Survey.* Oslo: Norwegian Agency for Development Co-operation.

Asian Development Bank (1995). *Governance Sound Development: Management.* Manila, RP: ADB.

Balisacan, Arsenio and Nobuhiko Fuwa (2004). Going Beyond Cross-Country Averages: Growth, Inequality and Poverty Reduction in the Philippines. *World Development,* 32, No. 11.

Boutros-Ghali, Boutros (1996). *An Agenda for Democratization.* New York, NY: United Nations.

Brillantes, Alex Jr. B. and Maricel T. Fernandez (2008). Is There a Philippine Public Administration? Or Better Still, *For Whom* Is Philippine Public Administration? *Philippine Journal of Public Administration,* 52, Nos. 2-4.

____(2010). Toward a Reform Framework for Good Governance Focus on Anti-Corruption. *Philippine Journal of Public Administration,* 54, Nos. 1-2.

Capuno, Joseph J. (2007). The Quality of Local Governance and Development under Decentralization. In *The Dynamics of Regional Development, the Philippines in East Asia,* edited by Arsenio Balisacan and Hal Hill, 204-244. Cheltenham, UK: Edward Elgar Publishing.

City of Manila et al. v. Hon. Perfecto A.S. Laguio, Jr. et al. (2005). GR No. 118127 Republic of the Philippines.

Harris-White, B. and G. White ed.(1996). Liberalization and the new corruption, *IDS Bulletin,* 27, No. 2.

Jurado, Gonzalo M. (2003). Growth Models, Development Planning, and Implementation in the Philippines, *Philippine Journal of Development,* 30, No. 1.

Kaufmann, Daniel, Aart Kraay and Massimo Mastruzzi (2009). Governance Matters VIII: Aggregate and Individual Governance Indicators 1996-2008, *Policy Research Working Paper,* No. 4978.

_____(2010). The Worldwide Governance Indicators: Methodology and

Analytical Issues, *Policy Research Working Paper,* No. 5430.

Leonillo, Glenford (2011). PODER Study: Weak Policies Cannot Curb Election-Related Violence in the Country, Ateneo School of Government. http://www.asg.ateneo.edu/news2.php?newsid=193

Llanto, Gilberto M.(2009). Fiscal Decentralization and Local Finance Reforms in the Philippines, *Philippine Institute for Development Studies Discussion Paper Series,* No. 10.

Local Government Code of 1991 (1991). Republic Act No. 7160.

Manasan, Rosario G. (2005). Local Public Finance in the Philippines: Lessons in Autonomy and Accountability, *Philippine Journal of Development,* 32, No. 2: 32-102.

Mangahas, Mahar (2010). Transparent and Accountable Governance: The 2009 SWS Surveys on Corruption, A presentation for the "Forum on the SWS 2009 Surveys of Enterprises on Corruption and Anti-Corruption Strategies" held on 19 February 2010 at the AIM Conference Center, Makati City.

North, Douglass C. (2011). Prize Lecture: Economic Performance through Time, Nobelprize.org. http://www.nobelprize.org/nobel_prizes/economics/laureates/1993/north-lecture.html

Republic of the Philippines (2009). *White Light Corporation, Titanium Corporation, and Sta. Mesa Tourist and Development Corporation v. City of Manila, represented by De Castro, Mayor Alfredo S. Lim.* GR No. 122846.

Republic of the Philippines (2010). *Progress Report on the Millennium Development Goals.* Manila: Republic of the Philippines.

Republic of the Philippines Constitution of 1987.

Saley, Juliet (2011). Sadanga Folk Choose Name of Festival in a Referendum, Baguio City.com http://www.baguiocity.com/news_article/sadanga-folk-choose-name-festival-referendum

Tapales, Proserpina D., Perfecto L. Padilla and Ma. Ernita T. Joaquin (1998). Human Resources Development and Management in Local Government, In *Local Government in the Philippines: A Book of Readings Volume I,* edited by Proserpina D. Tapales, Jocelyn C. Cuaresma, and Wilhelmina Cabo, 203-219. Quezon City, RP: Center for Local and Regional Governance and National College of Public Administration and Governance, University of the Philippines.

Transparency and Accountability Network (TAN)(2011). Corruption and Anti-Corruption in the Philippines, A paper prepared by TAN for GTZ Philippines.

UNDP(United Nations Development Programme)(2003). *Public Administration Reform Practice Note*. New York, NY: UNDP.

UNDP(2010). *Human Development Report 2010 20th Anniversary Edition The Real Wealth of Nations: Pathways to Human Development*. New York, NY: UNDP.

UNDP(2011). "The Human Development Concept." UNDP http://hdr.undp.org/en/humandev (accessed April 8, 2011).

World Bank(WB) and Asian Development Bank(ADB)(2005). *Decentralization in the Philippines: Strengthening Local Government Financing and Resource Management in the Short Run*. Manila: WB and ADB.

World Bank and International Finance Corporation(2010a). *Doing Business 2011: Making a Difference for Entrepreneurs*. Washington, DC: The International Bank for Reconstruction and Development/ The World Bank.

World Bank and International Finance Corporation(2010b). *Doing Business in the Philippines 2011*. Washington, DC: The International Bank for Reconstruction and Development/ The World Bank.

Chapter 9 Singapore-Style Public Sector Reforms

Jon S.T. Quah

Introduction

When Singapore attained self-government from the British in June 1959, the newly-elected People's Action Party (PAP) government inherited a civil service whose members had "a colonial mentality."[1] As they had to solve the problems of a serious housing shortage, rampant corruption, and a high unemployment rate of 14 percent, the PAP leaders realized that they had to change the attitudes of the civil servants so that they would cooperate and contribute to the solution of these problems.

Accordingly, the PAP government introduced six public sector reforms to tackle the problems encountered during 1959-1995, as summarized in Table 1 below.

The purpose of this chapter is twofold. First, to analyze and evaluate the effectiveness of the six public sector reforms introduced by the PAP government to solve the problems encountered. The second aim of this chapter is to identify the six lessons which other Asian countries can learn from Singapore's experience in implementing public sector reforms.

Table 1. Public Sector Reforms introduced by the PAP Government, 1959-1995

Problems	Reforms Introduced
1. "Colonial mentality" of civil servants.	Formation of Political Study Center in August 1959 to change the attitudes of the civil servants.
2. Housing shortage as half of the population was living in squatter huts, and only 9 percent were living in public housing.	Creation of the Housing and Development Board (HDB) in February 1960 as the first statutory board to provide low-cost public housing.
3. Widespread corruption.	Enactment of the Prevention of Corruption Act (POCA) in June 1960 to empower the Corrupt Practices Investigation Bureau (CPIB) to curb corruption effectively.
4. Unemployment rate of 14 percent.	Establishment of the Economic Development Board (EDB) in August 1961 to provide jobs by attracting foreign investment to Singapore.
5. The Increasing workload of the Public Service Commission (PSC).	Reduction of PSC's workload by increasing its size and creating the Education Service Commission and Police and Civil Defense Services Commission in 1990, and the system of 31 personnel boards in 1995.
6. Brain drain of talented senior civil servants to the private sector.	Periodic salary increases of civil servants from 1972 to 1994, and benchmarking of public sector salaries to private sector salaries from 1995.

Political Study Center to Change Values of Civil Servants

The Political Study Center was officially opened by Prime Minister Lee Kuan Yew on August 15, 1959. In his opening speech, Lee hoped that the senior civil servants would change their "colonial mentality" once they became aware of the problems facing the country after attending the two-week part-time, non-residential political study course. He stressed that it was the civil servants' responsibility to ensure that the civil service was efficient by working with the elected ministers to translate their plans and policies into reality (Lee, 1959: 219-220). In other words, the purpose of the Political Study Center was "to orientate senior civil servants to their new role in government" (Bogaars, 1973: 78).

According to George Bogaars (1973: 80), who was the Permanent Secretary in the Ministry of Foreign Affairs, "the doctrine and methods taught by the Political Study Center to fulfillits objectives were, by and large, successful" because

> there was a gradual transformation in the understanding and perception of the civil service of political matters and the issues which concerned the electorate and influenced Government policy.

Moreover, the fact that the PAP leaders and the senior civil servants shared a common English-educated and middle-class background and did not have any deep cleavages contributed a great deal to the Political Study Center's success (Quah, 1975: 328).

In addition to the Political Study Center, the PAP government also relied on four other methods to transform the attitudes and behavior of the senior civil servants. First, civil servants were encouraged to voluntarily participate in mass civic projects during the weekends to provide them with an opportunity to engage in manual activities. Apart from exposing the civil servants to other values, these weekend activities were also designed to improve their personal relationships with the political leaders (Seah, 1971: 86).

Second, the PAP government resocialized the English-educated civil servants by recruiting Chinese-educated graduates to reduce the former's predominance in the Singapore Civil Service (SCS) and to rectify its negative public image as "a preserve of the English-educated, and not representative of the local population"(Quah, 1975: 329). This recruitment policy was initiated in 1960 with the recruitment of 26 Nanyang University graduates for the education service and subordinate grades in the SCS.[2]

Third, the PAP government introduced tougher disciplinary measures to deal with those civil servants found guilty of misconduct. In 1961, the Central Complaints Bureau (CCB) was created to provide the non-English-educated public (who-constituted the majority) with an opportunity to complain against those civil servants who had been rude or unfair in their interactions with them. The CCB was also staffed with Chinese-educated personnel to make the agency more accessible to those members of the public with complaints against the English-educated civil servants (Quah, 1975: 330-331).

The fourth method employed by the PAP government in attitudinal reform was the policy of selective retention and earlier retirement of senior civil servants. This meant that those expatriate civil servants, who were competent and due for retirement, were urged to stay on, while their incompetent colleagues were retired prematurely. The combined impact of this policy and the reduction in the variable allowances of senior civil servants in June 1959 resulted in a high turnover rate among them.

In short, the PAP government's efforts in attitudinal reform were concerned with breaking the SCS's "isolationist and anachronistic outlook" (Seah, 1971: 88). The PAP leaders needed the support of the civil servants to implement the government's programs. However, they also knew that they had to first demonstrate to the civil servants that they were firmly in control before the latter would give their support.

Housing and Development Board to Solve the Housing Shortage

The Singapore Improvement Trust (SIT) was established as a statutory board by the British colonial government on July 1, 1927 to perform these six functions: (1) the preparation of the General Improvement Plan; (2) the eradication of insanitary buildings; (3) the formulation and implementation of improvement schemes; (4) the provision of housing for those dislocated by improvement schemes; (5) the acquisition and management of land; and (6) the construction of back lanes in slum areas (HDB, 1965: 16). In other words, the SIT was created as a *de jure* town-planning authority but not as a public housing authority.

However, in 1932, the SIT was given the power to build, and it constructed its first houses at Lorong Limau during the same year. The SIT's Board of Trustees was forced by the aggravation of the housing problem in Singapore to decide that the SIT should provide public housing for the "poorer classes." During its 32.5 years of existence, the SIT constructed a total of 23,264 housing units or an annual average of 716 housing units from July 1927 to January 1960. Even though the SIT built 20,683 housing units during 1948-1959, it could not meet the demand for housing generated by the population increase of 640,000 during the same period (Quah, 1985a: 234-235).

The SIT's failure to solve the housing shortage in Singapore transformed housing into a volatile political issue. Consequently, the PAP promised to provide more low-cost public housing for the population if it were elected in the May 1959 general election (Quah, 1985a: 239). In their campaign for that election, the PAP leaders identified the implementation of a low-cost public housing program as the eighth objective of their electoral platform (Quah, 2010: 200).

Learning from the SIT's failure and mistakes in solving the housing problem, the PAP government established the HDB on February 1, 1960 as a statutory board and the *de jure* public housing authority in Singapore. Lim Kim San was recruited from the private sector and appointed as the HDB's Chairman by Prime Minister Lee Kuan Yew who observed that Lim's "keen business sense" enabled him to build "the homes we needed speedily and economically with the labor skills and technology of that era" (Lee, 2009: viii). Unlike the British colonial government, which had an indifferent attitude toward public housing and an unenthusiastic response to the housing crisis (Quah, 1975: 218-219), the PAP government was committed to solving the housing problem in order to ensure that it would be reelected in the next general election.

Table 2. HDB's Performance in Public Housing, 1960-2009

Period	Total Number of Units	Average Building Rate
1960-1965	54,430	9,072
1966-1970	66,239	13,248
1971-1975	113,819	22,764
1976-1980	137,670	27,534
1981-1985	200,377	40,075
1986-1990	121,400	24,280
1991-1995	99,557	19,911
1996-2000	158,621	31,724
2001-2005	55,515	11,103
2006-2009	16,266	4,067
Total	1,023,894	—

Source: HDB (2010: 2).

The HDB has succeeded in solving the housing problem in Singapore because it constructed an impressive total of 1,023,894 housing units from 1960-2009, as shown in Table 2. Consequently, the proportion of the population living in public housing has increased from 9 percent to 82 percent during the same period (Department of Statistics, 2010a: 13). Why has the HDB succeeded when its predecessor—the SIT—failed to solve the housing shortage in Singapore?

The most important reason for the HDB's success is the PAP government's commitment to solving the housing problem as reflected in the following decisions:

1. The formation of the HDB as the first statutory board and the *de jure* public housing authority on February 1, 1960 to implement the low-cost public housing program.
2. The provision of adequate funds and personnel to enable the HDB to perform its functions effectively.
3. The enactment of the Land Acquisition Act of 1966 which empowered the HDB to evict squatters and pig farmers from land required for its building activities.

Second, unlike the SIT, the HDB capitalized on Singapore's assets and modified the policy context to facilitate the attainment of its goals. Instead of building apartments of three or four floors high like the SIT, the HDB built apartments with a maximum of 25 floors during its first 20 years as Singapore is not affected by earthquakes. Furthermore, the PAP government's massive allocation of funds for public housing enabled the HDB to build on a much larger scale and at a faster pace than the SIT. Indeed, the availability of government loans for public housing and the construction industry's rapid growth meant that the HDB was not handicapped by the scarcity of capital and shortage of building and construction capacity, which had plagued the SIT (Quah, 2011a: 127).

The third reason for the HDB's effectiveness was its ability to solve the squatter problem, which had adversely affected the SIT because it did not have the legal powers to evict squatters and pig farmers from land required for its building activities. The

HDB is empowered by section 5 (1) of the Land Acquisition Act of 1966 to compulsorily acquire land "for any residential, commercial or industrial purposes." In 1964 and 1971, the HDB revised its resettlement policy to provide those persons being resettled with attractive compensation rates and benefits. Consequently, the HDB resettled 74,327 families during its first 15 years (HDB, 1975: 146).

The fourth reason for the HDB's success is the better quality of its personnel and the anti-corruption measures adopted by it. In contrast to the SIT, the HDB has adopted a stricter and more elaborate recruitment procedure to ensure that only qualified personnel are recruited. The HDB recruited its senior officers on the basis of merit unlike the SIT, which had recruited its expatriate officers on the basis of race instead of educational background as European candidates were preferred even if they were unqualified (Quah, 1975: 148). In short, the HDB's recruitment procedures were superior and did not suffer from the same weaknesses of the SIT.

In terms of preventing corruption among its personnel, the HDB introduced greater control by revising the contracts procedure and the Chief Architect ensured strict adherence to the revised contracts procedure by closely supervising the work of senior officers in the Building Department. The HDB also abolished the SIT's points system of allocating apartments because it provided ample opportunities for corruption among those SIT officers administering this system. It introduced a balloting system for allocating apartments under the Home Ownership for the People Scheme.

All senior appointments to the HDB are screened by three government agencies—the Internal Security Department, Criminal Record Office, and the CPIB—before letters of appointment are issued to the successful candidates (HDB, 1973: 9). The rationale for this security screening is to prevent persons who are internal security risks, criminals or guilty of corrupt practices in the past, from being recruited by the HDB or any other public agency in Singapore.

In sum, the HDB's success in providing public housing for 82 percent of the population can be attributed to the PAP government's commitment to public housing and the HDB's ability to solve the problems encountered in implementing its public housing program. As the HDB was the first statutory board established by the PAP government in February 1960, the HDB's success in solving the serious housing shortage has not only enhanced the PAP government's legitimacy but also vindicated its reliance on statutory boards as important instruments for national development in Singapore.

Relying on the POCA and CPIB to Curb Corruption

Corruption was a serious problem in Singapore during the British colonial period because of the British colonial government's lack of political will and the ineffective anti-corruption measures adopted to curb corruption. Police corruption was rampant because of the low salaries of policemen, the ample opportunities for corruption, and the ineffective Anti-Corruption Branch (ACB) of the Criminal Investigation Department (CID), which was made responsible for corruption control with the enactment of the Prevention of Corruption Ordinance (POCO) in December 1937 (Quah, 2007: 9-16).

The problem of corruption deteriorated during the Japanese Occupation (February 1942 to August 1945) for two reasons. First, the high inflation rate made it difficult for the civil servants to live on their low salaries. Second, the scarcity of food and other basic commodities forced many people to trade in the black market. The Japanese Occupation had exacerbated the problem of corruption because "bribery, blackmail, and extortion grew out of the violence and fear" that the Japanese used to govern Singapore (Lee, 2005: 205).

Conditions did not improve during the post-war period and corruption was widespread among civil servants because their low salaries, high inflation, and inadequate supervision by their superiors provided them with ample opportunities for corruption with a low probability of being caught (Quah, 1982a: 161-162). Consequently, corruption was a way of life for many Singaporeans, and the British Military Administration, which took over after the Japanese surrender in August 1945, was referred to derisively as the "Black Market Administration" (Yoong, 1972: 55-56).

The POCO was ineffective because it limited the powers of arrest, search and investigation of police officers as warrants were required before arrests could be made. Furthermore, the penalty of imprisonment for two years and/or a fine of S$10,000 for those found guilty of corruption did not deter corrupt behavior (Quah, 1978a: 9). As the ACB was part of the CID of the Singapore Police Force (SPF), it was not surprising that the ACB was ineffective in curbing corruption, especially among policemen. Moreover, the ACB was inadequately staffed with only 17 personnel and its function of fighting corruption was given lower priority by the CID, whose top priority was to solve serious crimes like murder and kidnapping rather than corruption. It should also be noted that corruption control was only one of the ACB's 16 duties (Quah, 1978a: 14-15). Faced with these constraints, it was not surprising that the ACB failed to curb the problem of corruption.

The British colonial government only realized the folly of making the ACB responsible for curbing corruption when it discovered that three police detectives and some senior police officers were involved in the robbery of 1,800 pounds of opium worth S$400,000 (US$133,333) in October 1951 (Tan, 1999: 59).

This Opium Hijacking scandal exposed the ACB's weaknesses and its inability to curb police corruption. Consequently, the British colonial government established the CPIB as an independent agency outside the SPF in October 1952 to replace the ineffective ACB.

Corruption was a way of life in Singapore in June 1959 when the PAP government assumed office. Learning from the mistakes made by the British colonial government in curbing corruption, the PAP government demonstrated its commitment by enacting the POCA on June 17, 1960 to replace the ineffective POCO and to strengthen the CPIB by providing it with more legal powers, personnel and funding.

The POCA has three important features to rectify the POCO's weaknesses and to enhance the CPIB's legal powers and increase its personnel. First, the penalty for corruption was increased to imprisonment for five years and/or a fine of S$10,000 to enhance the POCA's deterrent effect. Second, according to section 13, a person found guilty of accepting an illegal gratification has to pay the amount he had taken as a bribe in addition to any other punishment imposed by a court. The third and most important feature of the POCA is that it has given the CPIB more powers and a new lease of life. For example, section 15 gives the CPIB officers powers of arrest and search of arrested persons. Furthermore, CPIB officers are empowered by section 18 to investigate the bank account, share account or purchase account of any person suspected of committing a corruption offence. Section 24 is perhaps the most important asset for the CPIB in its investigation of corruption offences because "the fact that an accused person is in possession, for which he [or she] cannot satisfactorily account, of pecuniary resources or property disproportionate to his [or her] known sources of income" is evidence that he or she had obtained these pecuniary resources or property "corruptly as an inducement or reward" (Quah, 2010: 176-177).

To ensure the POCA's continued effectiveness, the PAP government has introduced whenever necessary, amendments or new legislation to deal with unanticipated problems or to plug legal loopholes. The POCA was amended in 1966 to ensure that a person could be found guilty of corruption without actually receiving the bribe as long as he had shown the intention of doing so (section 9). The second amendment of the POCA in 1966 was section 37, which indicated that Singapore citizens working for their government in embassies and other government agencies abroad would be prosecuted for corrupt offenses committed outside Singapore and would be dealt with as if such offences had occurred in Singapore. To further enhance the POCA's deterrent effect, the fine for corrupt offenses was increased tenfold from S$10,000 to S$100,000 (US$82,950[3]) in 1989. On March 3, 1989, the Corruption (Confiscation of Benefits) Act 1989 was enacted to enable the court to issue a confiscation order against the estate of a deceased defendant (Quah, 2010: 177-178).

Unlike the British colonial government, the PAP government has also demonstrated its political will in curbing corruption not only by enhancing the CPIB's legal powers but also by providing the CPIB with more personnel and budget during the past 52 years. Table 3 shows that the CPIB's personnel have grown by 17 times from eight officers in 1959 to 138 officers in 2011. Similarly, as indicated in Table 4, the CPIB's budget has increased by 33 times from S$1,024,370 in 1978 to S$34,073,400 in 2011(Quah, 2010: 179-180; Republic of Singapore, 2011: 378).

The CPIB's effectiveness in curbing corruption is reflected in Singapore's consistently high ranking on these three indicators: (1) Transparency International's Corruption Perceptions Index (CPI) from 1995-2010; (2) Political Economic Risk Consultancy's

(PERC's) annual survey on corruption from 1995-2011 and (3) World Bank's control of corruption governance indicator from 1996-2009. Table 5 shows that Singapore's rank on the CPI ranges from 1st position in 2010 to 9th position in 1997. Its CPI score varies from 8.66 in 1997 to 9.4 in 2003 and 2005. Singapore has also retained its first position on PERC's surveys from 1995-2011. Similarly, Singapore's percentile rank on the control of corruption varies from 97.6 in 1996 to 100.0 in 1998.

Table 3. Growth of CPIB's Personnel, 1952-2011

Year	Number of Personnel	Year	Number of Personnel
1952	5	2000	84
1959	8	2005	82
1963	33	2007	89
1965	36	2008	86
1970	50	2009	90
1976	61	2010	138
1980	69	2011	138
1998	79		

Sources: Quah (1978a: 17) and Republic of Singapore (2011: 378).

Table 4. CPIB's Budget, 1978-2011

Year	Budget (S$)
1978	1,024,370
1987	4,147,230
1997	10,225,463
2007	14,619,718
2008	15,790,811
2009	16,135,696
2010	21,087,600
2011	34,073,400

Sources: Quah (2010: 180) and Republic of Singapore (2011: 378).

Table 5. Singapore's Performance on the CPI, PERC and Control of Corruption, 1995-2011

Year	CPI Rank and Score	PERC Rank and Score	Control of Corruption Percentile Rank
1995	3rd (9.26)	1st (1.20)	NA
1996	7th (8.80)	1st (1.09)	97.6
1997	9th (8.66)	1st (1.05)	NA
1998	7th (9.1)	1st (1.43)	100.0
1999	7th (9.1)	1st (1.55)	NA
2000	6th (9.1)	1st (0.71)	99.5
2001	4th (9.2)	1st (0.83)	NA
2002	5th (9.3)	1st (0.90)	99.5
2003	5th (9.4)	1st (0.38)	99.0
2004	5th (9.3)	1st (0.50)	99.5
2005	5th (9.4)	1st (0.65)	99.0
2006	5th (9.3)	1st (1.30)	98.1
2007	4th (9.3)	1st (1.20)	96.1
2008	4th (9.2)	1st (1.13)	99.5
2009	3rd (9.2)	1st (1.07)	99.0
2010	1st (9.3)	1st (1.42)	NA
2011	NA	1st (0.37)	NA

Sources: Quah (2011b: 225) and Business World (2011).

Using the Economic Development Board to Attract Foreign Investment

When the PAP leaders assumed office in June 1959, they faced many problems, including a high unemployment rate of 14 percent and the need to provide more jobs for the population (Chan, 2002: 15). Apart from providing more jobs, the PAP leaders realized the importance of improving the economic conditions in Singapore to minimize the communist threat by preventing the communists from exploiting the grievances of the unemployed or discontented Singaporeans. Furthermore, they also realized that economic development was needed to enhance the commitment of the citizens to Singapore and thereby reduce the effect of the competing loyalties of race, language, and religion (Quah, 1985b: 198-199).

The declining entrepot trade, high unemployment, and the lack of natural resources forced the PAP government to rely on industrialization to create more jobs. The EDB was formed in August 1961 as a statutory board to spearhead and implement the PAP government's strategy of promoting economic development through planned industrialization. During its first seven years, the EDB was responsible for promoting investment, financing industries, and developing Jurong, Singapore's first industrial town. However, because of its heavy workload, the EDB relinquished its second and third functions to the Development Bank of Singapore and the Jurong Town Corporation respectively, in 1968.

To promote investment, the EDB has provided various incentives to foreign firms to invest in Singapore. In his study of the EDB's culture, Edgar H. Schein (1996: 250) concluded that the EDB was "a very effective organization" because "the various elements of its culture align with each other and produce a whole that is greater than the sum of its parts." With a well-developed infrastructure, attractive tax incentives, stable industrial relations, and political stability, it is not surprising that Singapore has been selected by foreign companies as a preferred country for investing their money. In 1983, a survey conducted by the Association of Political Risk Analysis in New York placed Singapore among the top five countries in the world as a safe haven for investment because of its political stability (Quah, 1984: 184).

The EDB's success in attracting foreign investment has contributed significantly to Singapore's rapid economic developmentby broadening its economic base and bringing the latest skills and technology to its industries (Department of Statistics, 1992: 1.)

Table 6. Foreign Equity Investment in Singapore, 1980-2008

Year	Foreign Equity Investment
1980	S$13,002.4 million
1981	S$16,681.4 million
1982	S$20,355.3 million
1983	S$22,120.3 million
1984	S$24,801.2 million
1985	S$25,502.7 million
1986	S$28,584.0 million
1987	S$34,540.3 million
1988	S$41,276.7 million
1989	S$47,030.1 million
1990	S$57,935.2 million
1991	S$62,910.5 million
1992	S$65,351.0 million
1993	S$73,285.2 million
1994	S$85,843.5 million
1995	S$99,215.7 million
1996	S$115,648.0 million
1997	S$138,960.7 million
1998	S$156,859.5 million
1999	S$170,820.8 million
2000	S$191,452.5 million
2001	S$207,258.0 million
2002	S$225,705.0 million
2003	S$237,391.0 million
2004	S$263,819.0 million
2005	S$316,651.2 million
2006	S$372,367.6 million
2007	S$461,726.9 million
2008	S$464,347.5 million

Sources: Department of Statistics (1992: 17; 1995: 29; 1999: xi; 2001: xi; 2007: ix; 2010b: ix).

Table 6 shows that the foreign equity investment in Singapore has increased by almost 36 times from S$13,002.4 million in 1980 to S$464,347.5 million in 2008.

Decentralizing the Public Service Commission to Reduce Its Workload

The British colonial government introduced meritocracy in Singapore with the establishment of the PSC on January 1, 1951. The PSC was established in Singapore to "keep politics out of the SCS and to accelerate the latter's pace of localization" (Quah, 1982b: 50). The second objective is no longer important as the localization of the SCS was completed with the attainment of self-government in Singapore in June 1959. However, the primary objective of keeping politics out of the SCS remains relevant as the purpose of the PSC's program as stated in the national budget is "to meet the staffing requirements of the government in accordance with the merit principle" (Republic of Singapore, 1980: 78).

When the PSC was formed in 1951, it had three members who were assisted in their duties by a small secretariat of nine persons. In 1961, the PSC assumed responsibility for the disciplinary control of all civil servants from the Establishment Branch of the Ministry of Finance and for interviewing and selecting candidates for all scholarships, fellowships and training courses offered or sponsored by the government (PSC, 1964: 2). As the PSC has relied solely on interviews to select qualified candidates for the SCS, the performance of these two additional functions has increased its workload considerably. The number of interviews conducted by the PSC members increased from 14,625 in 1966 to 21,734 in 1969. This meant that the PSC and selection boards interviewed an average of 72 candidates per working day for appointments and promotions (PSC, 1970: 2).

To cope with its heavier workload, the number of PSC members was increased from three to ten and the size of the PSC secretariat was also expanded from nine to 286 persons during 1951-1982 (PSC, 1983: 1). According to Professor Gloria

Lim, who was a PSC member from 1982-1996:

> The volume of work was tremendous. I would spend hours before the interviews poring over the thick files that came. Then, on interview days, we would be there [at the PSC] from 2 pm to 9 pm, sometimes 10 pm (quoted in Fernandez, 2001: 40).

Furthermore, Larry Chong, a higher executive officer who worked in the PSC's secretariat from 1957-1990, revealed that interviews were also conducted on Sundays "when the PSC wanted to catch the crop of university graduates before other employers got to them" (Fernandez, 2001: 40).

In 1983, the PSC delegated to permanent secretaries and department heads its authority to recruit Division IV officers and to confirm officers in all the four divisions. However, in spite of this delegation, the PSC's workload increased tremendously during 1983-1989. Table 7 confirms that the PSC and selection boards interviewed a total of 50,274 candidates for appointments and promotions from 1983 to 1989. During the same period, the PSC dealt with 1,148 disciplinary cases and granted 1,543 scholarships and training awards.

Table 7. The PSC's Workload, 1983-1989

Year	Candidates Interviewed for Appointments and Promotions	Disciplinary Cases Completed	Scholarships and Training Awards Granted
1983	8,738	156	231
1984	6,933	161	173
1985	10,402	153	175
1986	6,414	174	215
1987	5,690	184	250
1988	5,512	154	238
1989	6,585	166	261
Total	50,274	1,148	1,543

Sources: PSC (1984-1990).

In March 1990, the Constitution of Singapore was amended to help the PSC cope with its heavy workload by increasing its membership from 11 to 15, including the chairman, and by creating two new subcommissions: the Education Service Commission (ESC) and the Police and Civil Defense Services Commission (PCDSC) for the police and civil defense services. Richard Hu, the then Minister for Finance, explained that these two agencies were formed to reduce "the current heavy workload borne by individual [PSC] members" and to "improve the responsiveness and effectiveness of civil service personnel management." He further admitted that the government had encountered difficulty in recruiting suitable candidates to serve on the PSC because it had "difficulty coping with its heavy workload, with members spending an average of 100 afternoons per year on commission matters" (*Straits Times*, 1990: 27).

On August 16, 1990, teachers in the Education Service, police officers of the rank of Inspector and above, and other officers in the Police and Civil Defense Services came under the purview of the ESC and PCDSC, respectively. The formation of these two agencies has reduced the PSC's workload to some extent because the PSC is no longer responsible for recruiting and promoting teachers, police officers, and civil defense officers. However, an examination of the workloads of the PSC, ESC and PCDSC during 1990-1994 indicates that, contrary to expectations, the PSC's workload has not been reduced substantially. Table 8 shows that the PSC interviewed 9,993 candidates (67.4 percent) compared to 4,254 candidates (28.7 percent) for the ESC and 573 candidates (3.9 percent) for the PCDSC during 1990-1994.

On August 25, 1994, the Constitution of Singapore was amended to devolve the specified powers of the PSC, ESC and PCDSC to a system of 31 personnel boards consisting of civil servants to recruit, promote and discipline officers. Accordingly,

Table 8. Workloads of the PSC, ESC, and PCDSC in Selecting Candidates to the Singapore Civil Service, 1990–1994

Year	PSC	ESC	PCDSC	Total
1990	2,604	655	30	3,289
1991	2,602	6	102	2,710
1992	2,235	1,160	139	3,534
1993	1,289	1,272	147	2,708
1994	1,263	1,161	155	2,579
Total	9,993 (67.4%)	4,254 (28.7%)	573 (3.9%)	14,820 (100.0%)

Sources: PSC (1991-1995).

from January 1995, the functions of recruitment and promotion of these officers were handled by these 31 personnel boards:

1. A special personnel board consisting of the Head of the SCS (Chairman), the Commissioner of the Internal Revenue Authority of Singapore, the Permanent Secretary of the Prime Minister's Office, and the Permanent Secretary of the Ministry of Finance, to deal with all administrative officers at Superscale E1 and below.
2. Six personnel boards consisting of 21 members to handle all Division I officers below superscale status. Each personnel board consists of six members each and its composition varies according to the ministries and agencies under its purview. There are 21 members for the six senior personnel boards as eight members serve on more than one board.
3. Twenty-four personnel boards made up of 103 members to take charge of Divisions II, III and IV officers (PSD, 1994: 1-2, 4).

On April 1, 1998, the PSC, ESC and PCDSC were amalgamated into a single PSC (PSC, 1999: 9). No official reason was given for this reversal of the 1990 decision. The creation of the ESC and PCDSC in August 1990 was designed to reduce the PSC's workload by removing from its jurisdiction more than 31,000 teachers and police and civil defense officers. Nevertheless, in spite of this change, the PSC's workload during 1990-1994 was still heavy as indicated in Table 8. On the other hand, the PSC's workload during 1995-2009 was reduced considerably by the introduction of the system of 31 personnel boards in January 1995 as shown in Table 9. In short, the ESC and PCDSC were dissolved in April 1998 as they were ineffective in lowering the PSC's workload during 1990-1994.

Table 9. PSC's Workload, 1995-2009

Year	Candidates Interviewed for Appointment	Officers Interviewed for Promotion	Disciplinary Cases completed	Scholarships and Training Awards Given
1995	70	45	83	231
1996	47	17	33	231
1997	53	16	45	214
1998	71	21	34	257
1999	96	24	37	332
2000	126	28	52	258
2001	126	9	59	253
2002	134	7	56	74
2003	175	17	52	50
2004	165	13	60	34
2005	192	18	52	49
2006	116	13	31	39
2007	203	18	30	57
2008	102	23	55	72
2009	13	32	69	85
Total	1,689	301	748	2,236

Sources: PSC (1996-2010).

Paying Competitive Salaries to Retain Talented Civil Servants

On assuming office in June 1959, the PAP government faced a budgetary deficit of S$14 million if it did not reduce public service expenditure (Quah, 2003: 148). To balance the budget and reduce the budgetary deficit, the Cabinet Budget Committee on Expenditure recommended "drastic cuts" in public service expenditures, including the removal of the variable allowances for senior civil servants, which resulted in a savings of S$10 million (Bogaars, 1973: 80). The PAP government restored the variable allowances in September 1961 with the improvement in Singapore's budgetary situation (Seah, 1971: 94).

In 1968, the Harvey Report on public sector salaries recommended salary increases for five grades in the Division I superscale salaries. However, the PAP government did not implement this recommendation until 1973 for two reasons: the economy could not afford a major salary revision and the private sector was not considered a serious threatas talented senior civil servants were promoted rapidly to retain them in the SCS (Lee, 1995: 21-22).

As the Singapore economy prospered in the 1970s, the higher salaries in the private sector contributed to a brain drain of talented senior civil servants from the SCS to the private sector. To curb the loss of talent from the SCS, the National Wages Council (NWC) recommended the payment of the Annual Wage Supplement or "13th month pay" in 1972 to minimize the gap between salaries in the public and private sectors in Singapore (Quah, 2010: 104-105). The salaries of senior civil servants were further increased in 1973, 1979, 1982, 1988, 1989 and 1994 to reduce the gap with private sector salaries.[4]

In 1989, the Minister for Trade and Industry, Lee Hsien Loong, promised that asthe PAP government's fundamental philosophy was to "pay civil servants market rates for their abilities and responsibilities," it "will offer whatever salaries are necessary to attract and retain the talent that it needs." He explained that the salary revision was "designed to catch up with several years of rising private sector incomes, and to make public service careers more competitive with the private sector." He concluded by promising that the government "will continue to carry out regular surveys of private sector salaries to stay competitive" because "paying civil servants adequate salaries is *absolutely essential* to maintain the quality of public administration which Singaporeans have come to expect" (Republic of Singapore, 1989: cols 382-383, emphasis added).

In October 1994, a White Paper on *Competitive Salaries for Competent and Honest Government* was presented to Parliament to justify the pegging of the salaries of ministers and senior civil servants to the average salaries of the top four earners in six private sector professions namely: accounting, banking, engineering, law, local manufacturing companies, and multinational corporations. More specifically, the White Paper recommended the introduction of formal salary benchmarks for ministers and senior civil servants, additional salary grades for political appointments and annual salary reviews for the SCS. The adoption of the long-term formula suggested in the White Paper removed the need to justify the salaries of ministers and senior civil servants "from scratch with each salary revision" (Republic of Singapore, 1994: 7-17).

Table 10. Salaries of Key Appointments in Singapore, 2008

Appointment	Monthly Salary	Annual Salary
President	S$119,520 (US$84,478)	S$3,870,000 (US$2,735,369)
Prime Minister	S$115,920 (US$81,934)	S$3,760,000 (US$2,657,619)
Minister/Permanent Secretary (MR4 Grade)	S$59,760 (US$42,239)	S$1,940,000 (US$1,371,219)
Superscale Civil Servant (Entry SR9 Grade)	S$18,240 (US$12,892)	S$398,000 (US$281,312)
Member of Parliament	S$13,710 (US$9,690)	S$225,000 (US$159,033)

N.B.: The exchange rate in 2008 was US$1 = S$1.4148.
Source: Lee (2007).

An International Labor Office expert has observed that "the high salaries [in Singapore] send a clear signal to civil servants in particular, and society generally, that the Government values greatly and is prepared to pay very generously a few key bureaucrats for their services to the country" (Chew, 1997: 37). In December 2007, the Public Service Division (PSD) announced that the salaries of ministers and senior civil servants would be increased from 4 percent to 21 percent from January 2008. Table 10 shows the salaries of the President, Prime Minister, Ministers, Permanent Secretaries, superscale civil servants at the entry grade, and Members of Parliament after the January 2008 revision. However, on November 24, 2008, the PSD announced that the salaries of administrative officers, political, judicial, and statutory appointment holders would be reduced by 19 percent in 2009 because of the economic recession. This meant that the President's annual salary was reduced from S$3.87 million to S$3.14 million. Similarly, the Prime Minister's annual salary was decreased from S$3.76 million to S$3.04 million in 2009 (Li, 2008).

In short, the PAP government's policy of paying competitive salaries for ministers and senior civil servants by benchmarking their salaries with those of six private sector professions has enabled the SCS to minimize the brain drain of talented civil servants to the private sector.

Evaluation of Public Sector Reforms in Singapore

How effective are the six public sector reforms introduced in Singapore from 1959-1995? Table 11 summarizes the effectiveness of these reforms in terms of solving the six problems addressed by them. The PAP government initiated the comprehensive reform of the SCS after assuming office in June 1959 because of the favorable timing after nearly 140 years of

Table 11. Effectiveness of Public Sector Reforms in Singapore

Reforms	Effectiveness of Reforms
1. Political Study Centre (August 1959)	The SCS and statutory boards have played an important role in national development in Singapore since June 1959.
2. Housing and Development Board (HDB) (February 1960)	The HDB has built 1,023,894 housing units from 1960-2009 and provides public housing for 82 percent of the population.
3. Prevention of Corruption Act (POCA) (June 1960)	The CPIB's impartial implementation of the POCA has minimized corruption as reflected in Singapore's first ranking on Transparency International's Corruption Perceptions Index in 2010, and its first ranking on PERC's corruption surveys from 1995-2011.
4. Economic Development Board (EDB) (August 1961)	The EDB has increased the foreign equity investment in Singapore by 36 times from S$13,002.4 million in 1980 to S$464,347.5 million in 2008. The unemployment rate has also been reduced from 14 percent in 1960 to 3.2 percent in 2009.
5. Decentralizing the Public Service Commission (PSC)	Unlike the ESC and PCDSC which were ineffective, the 31 personnel boards established in January 1995 were effective in reducing the PSC's workload.
6. Paying civil servants competitive salaries from 1972-1994 and benchmarking their salaries to six private sector professions from 1995.	Competitive salaries are effective in retaining top civil servants and scholar bureaucrats but not Division I officers who are not scholars.

British colonial rule. The PAP leaders emphasized both the institutional and attitudinal aspects of public sector reform because they were not only concerned with reorganizing the SCS and creating statutory boards, but also with changing the "colonial mentality" of the civil servants and their insensitivity to the population's needs (Quah, 1975: 325).

Apart from the right timing, the PAP leaders also had a positive attitude towards public sector reforms and this was clearly manifested in their critical speeches in the Legislative Assembly on various aspects of the administration of the colony. Perhaps the most important reason for the PAP government's decision to initiate the comprehensive reform of the SCS was that the degree of risk involved in not implementing the reform was greater than the risk accompanying the implementation of the reform. The PAP leaders realized that they had nothing to lose if the hostile and alienated civil servants were reoriented and "persuaded" to contribute towards the attainment of national development goals. On the other hand, the PAP government was also uncertain of its long-term survival and its ability to deliver the goods if the status quo was maintained and if the civil servants were allowed to behave as they did during the colonial period (Quah, 1975: 345).

During the British colonial period, the SCS did not play an important role in national development because it was preoccupied with enforcing colonial rule in Singapore and the economic exploitation of the natural resources of the region for the benefit of the home government in Britain (Quah, 1978b: 424). Consequently, the SCS focused on performing the traditional "housekeeping" functions of maintaining law and order, building public works and collecting taxes. In contrast, the important role of the SCS and statutory boards in Singapore's national development during the past 52 years under the PAP government indicates that the Political Study Centre was successful in eroding the "colonial mentality" of the civil servants.

Second, the PAP government established statutory boards in

Singapore from February 1960 with the creation of the HDB for three reasons. First, statutory boards were formed in response to the constraints faced by the SCS in implementing development programs. As the SCS is handicapped by its rigid regulations and lack of flexibility, it is more concerned with regulative and routine matters (Seah, 1976: 57). In view of the SCS's limitations, the PAP leaders decided to rely instead on statutory boards to accelerate the implementation of socio-economic development programs. This means that there is a division of labor between the SCS and the statutory boards: with the SCS being responsible for performing the regulatory and routine functions while the statutory boards, which are not affected by the procedural delays and regulations of the SCS, have been created to expedite the implementation of socio-economic development programs in Singapore.

The second reason for the formation of statutory boards was the reduction of the SCS's workload. Fred W. Riggs (1970: 130) identified two methods for improving an organization's performance: "administrative capacities can be enhanced by reducing the number of problems to be solved by government as well as by strengthening the capacity of government to solve problems." In other words, an organization's effectiveness can be improved by strengthening its capabilities or by reducing its workload. Thus, statutory boards have been created to reduce the SCS's workload through the implementation of many socio-economic development programs.

The third reason for establishing statutory boards in Singapore was the reduction of the brain drain of talented civil servants to the private sector by offering more favorable salaries and working conditions than the SCS. This means that instead of leaving the SCS for private sector jobs, talented civil servants had the additional option of being seconded for a few years to the statutory boards.

As the HDB was the first statutory board established by the PAP government eight months after its assumption of power in June 1959, the HDB's success in solving the serious housing shortage has not only enhanced the PAP government's legitimacy but also ensured its political survival. Similarly, the EDB's effectiveness in attracting foreign investment during the past 50 years has further reinforced the importance of statutory boards in Singapore's national development. The effectiveness of the HDB and EDB has vindicated the PAP government's reliance on statutory boards to accelerate the implementation of socio-economic development programs and led to the proliferation of 64 statutory boards in Singapore today.[5]

Corruption was a way of life when the PAP government assumed office in June 1959. The preceding Lim Yew Hock administration was "corrupt from head to toe" and "bribes and kickbacks were part of the way of life" in Singapore during the 1950s because "people had to grease palms to obtain licenses, permits, immigration papers, public housing and coveted places in schools" (Yap, Lim, and Leong, 2009: 555). Unlike its predecessors, the PAP leaders were committed to keeping Singapore free from corruption when they assumed power because:

> We were sickened by the greed, corruption and decadence of many Asian leaders. … When we took the oath of office … in June 1959, we all wore white shirts and white slacks to symbolize purity and honesty in our personal behavior and our public life. … We made sure from the day we took office in June 1959 that every dollar in revenue would be properly accounted for and would reach the beneficiaries at the grass roots as one dollar, without being siphoned off along the way. So from thevery beginning we gave special attention to the areas where discretionary powers had been exploited for personal gain and sharpened the instruments that could prevent, detect or deter such practices (Lee, 2000: 182-184).

Learning from the mistakes of the British colonial government in curbing corruption, the PAP government's top priority was to strengthen the anti-corruption measures it inherited by enacting the POCA in June 1960 to empower the CPIB, which was also provided with more personnel and budget to enable it to curb corruption effectively. As shown earlier, the CPIB's effectiveness in minimizing corruption is manifested in Singapore's first ranking on the 2010 CPI and 2011 PERC survey and its 99 percentile rank on the 2009 control of corruption indicator (see Table 5 above).

Perhaps the most important legacy of British colonial rule is the introduction of meritocracy to Singapore in January 1951 with the formation of the PSC. Since its assumption of office in June 1959, the PAP government has maintained its reliance on meritocracy by reducing the PSC's heavy workload through the creation of the ESC and PCDSC in 1990 and the 31 personnel boards in 1995. While the establishment of the ESC and PCDSC failed to reduce the PSC's workload significantly during 1990-1994, the system of 31 personnel boards created in January 1995 has succeeded in reducing the PSC's workload drastically from interviewing 9,993 candidates from 1990-1994 to interviewing 1,689 candidates from 1995-2009 (see Tables 8 and 9 above). Hence, it is not surprising that on November 15, 1992, Prime Minister Goh Chok Tong had attributed Singapore's success to the "practice of meritocracy in the civil service, in politics, in business and in schools, which has allowed Singaporeans to achieve excellence and to compete against others" (Goh, 1992: 15).

Finally, to compete for talent with the private sector and to retain talented civil servants from leaving for private sector jobs, the PAP government has relied on periodic salary revisions from 1972 to1994 to minimize the wage gap between the public and private sectors. However, from 1995 onwards, the salaries of ministers and senior civil servants have been benchmarked to the salaries of top earners in six private sector professions in Singapore.

How effective is the policy of paying competitive salaries in curbing the brain drain of talented civil servants in Singapore to the private sector? High salaries for permanent secretaries and heads of departments have been effective in retaining them in the SCS since none of them have left for private sector jobs before their retirement. However, an analysis of the resignation rates of Division I officers in the SCS from 1971 to 1984 has shown that the periodic salary revisions were ineffective in preventing Division I officers below the head of department level from leaving the SCS (Quah, 2003: 158-159). This is not surprising as the competitive salaries and accelerated promotion of the high-flyers or the scholar bureaucrats (those recruited into the SCS by the PSC through the award of scholarships) have alienated many civil servants, especially those who are non-scholars and low-flyers (Quah, 2010: 93).

Lessons for Other Asian Countries

The effectiveness of the SCS and statutory boards is reflected in Singapore's consistently high rankings on several indicators from 2002-2011 as shown in Table 12 below.

Singapore's rapid transformation from being a poor third world country in 1959 to a first world nation today has attracted a great deal of attention across the world. Consequently, it is not surprising that policymakers from many countries have visited Singapore to ascertain the reasons for its success including the effectiveness of its public bureaucracy, and to consider whether they could draw useful lessons for their own countries (Quah, 1998: 119). What lessons can other Asian countries learn from Singapore's experience in implementing the six public sector reforms discussed above?

Table 12. Effectiveness of Singapore's Public Bureaucracy, 2002–2011

Indicator	Rank	Score
World Bank's Government Effectiveness indicator, 2009	100.0	+2.19
World Bank's Control of Corruption indicator, 2009	99.0	+2.26
World Bank's Ease of Doing Business, 2011	1st	—
Transparency International's Corruption Perceptions Index, 2010	1st	9.3
Political Economic Risk Consultancy's (PERC) corruption survey, 2011	1st	0.37
PERC's Effectiveness of Asian Bureaucracies, 2010	1st	2.53
Global Competitiveness Report (GCR) Public Sector Competence, 2002	1st	5.1
GCR Public Trust of Politicians, 2010-2011	1st	6.4

Sources: http://info.worldbank.org/governance/wgi/sc_chart.asp World Bank (2010: 4); http://www.transparency.org/policy_research/surveys_indices/cpi/2010/results Business- World (2011); Lanka Business Online (2010); Cornelius (2003: 64); and Schwab (2010: 369).

Before proceeding further, it is necessary to note the significant contextual differences between Singapore and other Asian countries. As Singapore is a city-state with a land area of 712.4 sq km, a population of 5,076,700 and a GDP per capita of S$59,813 (US$43,867) in 2010 (Department of Statistics, 2011), its policy context is more conducive for implementing public sector reforms thanthe policy contexts in those Asian countries, which are larger in size, with bigger populations and lower GDP per capita. While it might not be possible to transplant *in toto* Singapore's public sector reforms to other Asian countries, there are nevertheless six lessons which these countries can learn from Singapore's experience.

Perhaps, the most important lesson to be learnt is that Singapore's success in implementing public sector reforms can be attributed to the commitment of the political leadership to these reforms, which is manifested in the provision of legislation, sufficient manpower and adequate budgets to enable the relevant agencies to implement the reforms effectively. We have seen above that the HDB, CPIB and EDB have been effective in providing public housing, curbing corruption, and attracting foreign investment to Singapore respectively, because the PAP government has been committed to their success through the enactment of legislation and the provision of adequate personnel and budgets to these agencies. In other words, strong political support and sponsorship is an indispensable prerequisite for the successful implementation of public sector reforms.

The second lesson is that public sector reforms must not focus only on the reorganization of the public bureaucracy but must also include the attitudinal transformation of the civil servants from their "colonial mentality" to their willingness to contribute to national development. This explains why the PAP leaders initiated their efforts in public sector reforms with the establishment of the Political Study Center on August 15, 1959, two and a half months after assuming office on June 3, 1959. Thus, apart from the political will of the leaders, public sector reforms will not succeed without the cooperation of the civil servants in the country. In short, reorganizing the civil services without changing the attitudes of their civil servants towards national development is a major cause of the failure of public sector reforms in many Asian countries.

The third lesson that can be learnt is the necessity to establish statutory boards to accelerate the implementation of socio-economic development programs because of the constraints and lack of flexibility of the civil service to perform this function. The PAP government relied on the HDB and EDB respectively to solve the housing shortage and provide jobs for the population by attracting foreign investment to Singapore as the SCS was not able to perform these two functions effectively because of its constraints. In other words, there should be a division of labor between the civil service and the statutory boards with the civil service taking care of the housekeeping functions and the statutory boards being responsible for implementing the socio-economic development programs like public housing and industrialization.

The fourth lesson is the importance of learning from the past mistakes in implementing public sector reforms in a country. For example, in terms of combating corruption in Singapore, the PAP government retained the CPIB as an independent anti-corruption agency and did not repeat the mistake of the British colonial government of not providing sufficient legal powers, personnel and financial resources to the CPIB during its first seven years. As discussed above, the POCA was enacted in June 1960, one year after the PAP government assumed office, to provide the CPIB with the legal powers to perform its functions effectively. Furthermore, the CPIB has also been provided with adequate personnel and funding by the PAP government to implement the POCA impartially. Table 3 shows that the growth of the CPIB's personnel from 8 to 138 officers from 1959-2011. Similarly, Table 4 indicates that the CPIB's budget has increased by 33 times from S$1.024 million to S$34.073 million during 1978-2011.

The PAP government has also succeeded in solving the housing shortage in Singapore by not repeating the mistake of the British colonial government in relying on the SIT to provide low-cost public housing when it was established as a town planning authority. Accordingly, the HDB was created as a statutory board in February 1960 as the de jure public housing authority and provided with sufficient personnel and funding, and empowered by the Land Acquisition Act of 1966 to acquire land and evict squatters for its public housing program. The HDB has built a total of 1,023,894 housing units during 1960-2009 and provides housing for 82 percent of the population today.

The fifth lesson that can be learnt from Singapore's experience in implementing public sector reforms is that the PAP government has enhanced the legacy of British colonial rule by maintaining the tradition of meritocracy in the SCS by retaining the PSC and ensuring its continued effectiveness by reducing its heavy workload through the establishment of the ESC and PCDSC in 1990 and the creation of 31 personnel boards in January 1995 after the ESC and PCDSC had failed to reduce the PSC's workload. Indeed, the emphasis on meritocracy by the PSC in recruiting and promoting civil servants has resulted in attracting "the best and the brightest" citizens to join the SCS, and the policy of accelerated promotion and payment of competitive salaries has minimized the brain drain of the scholar civil servants to the private sector.

Edgar H. Schein (1996: 221-222) has identified as one of Singapore's "major strengths" the policy of recruiting and retaining "the best and the brightest" citizens in government because "they are potentially the most able to invent what the country needs to survive and grow and to overcome the kinds of biases and blind spots." Similarly, Lee Kuan Yew has contended that Singapore's success in spite of its lack of resources can be attributed to four "basic values," one of which is meritocracy because "people get to where they are on merit; not *guanxi* (connections), not nepotism, not corruption. Hence, all are capable and competent" (Li and Teo, 2010: A5).

The final lesson is that Singapore's experience in implementing public sector reforms illustrates the importance of the policy context in terms of the absence of obstacles to these reforms.[6] Unlike many Asian countries, Singapore has a favorable policy context because its small land area and population, low level of corruption, economic affluence, political stability and the commitment of its political leaders to reform have contributed to the successful implementation of public sector reforms. In other words, Singapore has succeeded in implementing public sector reforms because of the absence of serious obstacles to such reforms.

In closing, it should also be noted that the SCS is not perfect in spite of its effectiveness and success in implementing public sector reforms. A serious problem which needs to be redressed is the unequal treatment of civil servants, as the scholar bureaucrats, who constitute less than one percent, are paid higher salaries and promoted rapidly to retain them in the SCS. However, the special treatment of these high-flyers has alienated the majority of the civil servants, who are non-scholars and low-flyers. The low morale of the non-scholar bureaucrats is the major reason for their premature departure from the SCS (Quah, 2010: 93-94).

Finally, in view of the rising expectations of the younger Singaporeans, the SCS has to maintain and improve on its high level of performance because, as Peter Ho, the former head of the SCS, has observed astutely: "maintaining a first-class Public Service, worthy of Singapore, is a journey without end" (Chua, 2010: 13). Thus, the SCS should not rest on its laurels, but should initiate appropriate measures to improve the low morale of the non-scholar civil servants on the one hand, and to change the arrogant attitude of the scholar civil servants as soon as possible, on the other hand. If these two problems are not resolved in the near future, there will be serious repercussions on the effectiveness of the SCS in the long run.

Notes

1) This refers to the civil servants' aloofness from the members of the public in Singapore during the colonial period and their insensitivity to their needs.
2) The language of instruction used in Nanyang University was Mandarin.
3) This conversion is based on the exchange rate of US$1 = S$1.20554 on August 24, 2011.
4) For a detailed analysis of these salary revisions, see Quah (2003: 149-153).

5) The complete list of statutory boards in Singapore in 2011 is available at the online government directory at http://www.sgdi.gov.sg/index.asp?cat=2.
6) Caiden (1969: 166-183) has identified these seven obstacles to administrative reforms namely: geography, history, technology, culture, economy, society and polity.

References

Bogaars, George E. (1973). Public Services. In *Towards Tomorrow: Essays on Development and Social Transformation in Singapore* (pp. 73-83). Singapore: National Trades Union Congress.

Business World(2011). Philippines' corruption score worsens. March 29. Available at http://www.bworldonline.com/content.php?title=Philippines'_corruption_score_worsens&id=28896.

Caiden, Gerald E. (1969). *Administrative Reform*. London: Penguin Press.

Chan, Chin Bock (2002). *Heart Work*. Singapore: Economic Development Board and EDB Society.

Chew, David C. E. (1997). Economic Restructuring and Flexible Civil Service Pay in Singapore. In Colclough, Christopher (ed.), *Public-Sector Pay and Adjustment: Lessons from Five Countries* (Chapter 2, pp. 22-45). London: Routledge.

Chua, Mui Hong (2010). *Pioneers Once More: The Singapore Public Service 1959-2009*. Singapore: Straits Times Press and Public Service Division.

Cornelius, Peter K.(ed.) (2003). *The Global Competitiveness Report 2002-2003*. New York: Oxford University Press.

Department of Statistics (1992). *Foreign Equity Investment, 1980-1989*. Singapore.

Department of Statistics (1995). *Foreign Equity Investment in Singapore 1987-1994*. Singapore.

Department of Statistics (1999). *Foreign Equity Investment in Singapore 1996-1997*. Singapore.

Department of Statistics (2001). *Foreign Equity Investment in Singapore 1998-1999*. Singapore.

Department of Statistics (2007). *Foreign Equity Investment in Singapore 2005*. Singapore.

Department of Statistics (2010a). *Yearbook of Statistics, Singapore 2010*. Singapore.

Department of Statistics (2010b). *Foreign Equity Investment in Singapore 2008*. Singapore.

Department of Statistics (2011). Key Annual Indicators. Singapore. Available at http://www.singstat.gov.sg/stats/keyind.html.

Fernandez, Warren (2001). *Without Fear or Favour: 50 Years of Singapore's Public Service Commission*. Singapore: Times Media for the Public Service Commission.

Goh, Chok Tong (1992). My Urgent Mission. *Petir, 11-12/92* (November/December): 10-19.

HDB(Housing and Development Board) (1965). *50,000 Up: Homes for the People*. Singapore: Straits Times Press.

HDB (1973). *Recruitment Section Procedure Manual*. Singapore.

HDB (1975). *Annual Report 1974/1975*. Singapore.

HDB (2010). *Annual Report 2009/2010*. Singapore.

Lanka Business Online (2010). Civil Service: India, Indonesia Worst for Red Tape in Asia: Survey. June 2. Available at http://www.lbo.lk/fullstory.php?nid=455805111.

Lee, Geok Boi (2005). *The Synonan Years: Singapore under Japanese Rule 1942-1945*. Singapore: National Archives of Singapore and Epigram Private Ltd.

Lee, Kuan Yew (1959). Speech at the official opening of the Political Study Centre. Singapore, August 15. The text of this speech is reprinted in Seah (1971), Appendix E, pp. 219-221.

Lee, Kuan Yew (2000). *From Third World to First, The Singapore Story: 1965-2000*. Singapore: Times Media.

Lee, Kuan Yew (2009). Foreword. In Asad-ul Iqbal Latif, *Lim Kim San: A Builder of Singapore*. Singapore: Institute of Southeast Asian Studies, pp. vii-ix.

Lee, Lynn (2007). Ministers, top civil servants to get 4% to 21% pay rise in January. *Straits Times*, December 13.

Lee, Matthew K. W. (1995). *Competing forthe Best and Brightest: The Strategic Use of Compensation in the Singapore Administrative Service*. B. Soc. Sc. Honors thesis, Department of Political Science, National University of Singapore, Singapore.

Li, Xueying (2008). Civil service to cut pay. *Straits Times*, November 24.

Li, Xueying and Teo, Wan Gek (2010). How Singapore turned improbable into reality. *Straits Times*, August 16: A1 and A5.

PSC (Public Service Commission) (1964). *Annual Report 1963.* Singapore.

PSC (1970). *Annual Report 1969.* Singapore.

PSC (1983). *Annual Report 1982.* Singapore.

PSC (1984-1990). *Annual Reports 1983-1989.* Singapore.

PSC (1996-2010). *Annual Reports 1995-2009.* Singapore.

PSD (Public Service Division) (1994). Devolution of Personnel Management Authority in the Civil Service–Subsidiary Legislation and Composition of Special and Senior Personnel Boards. Singapore: Press Statement.

Quah, Jon S.T. (1975). *Administrative Reform and Development Administration in Singapore: A Comparative Study of the Singapore Improvement Trust and the Housing and Development Board.* Ph.D. dissertation, Department of Government, Florida State University, USA.

Quah, Jon S.T. (1978a). *Administrative and Legal Measures for Combating Bureaucratic Corruption in Singapore.* Singapore: Department of Political Science, University of Singapore, Occasional Paper, No. 34.

Quah, Jon S.T. (1978b). The Origins of the Public Bureaucracies in the ASEAN Countries. *Indian Journal of Public Administration,* 24 (2) (April-June): 400-429.

Quah, Jon S.T. (1982a). Bureaucratic Corruption in the ASEAN Countries: A Comparative Analysis of Their Anti-Corruption Strategies." *Journal of Southeast Asian Studies*, 13 (1) (March): 153-177.

Quah, Jon S.T. (1982b). The Public Bureaucracy and National Development in Singapore. In Tummala, Krishna K. (ed.), *Administrative Systems Abroad* (Chapter 4, pp. 42-75). Washington, D.C.: University Press of America.

Quah, Jon S.T. (1984). Singapore in 1983: The Continuing Search for Talent. *Asian Survey*, 24(2) (February): 178-186.

Quah, Jon S.T. (1985a). Public Housing. In Jon Quah, S.T. Chan Heng Chee and Seah Chee Meow (eds), *Government and Politics of Singapore* (Chapter 10, pp. 233-258). Singapore: Oxford University Press.

Quah, Jon S.T. (1985b). Meeting the Twin Threats of Communism and Communalism: The Singapore Response. In Chandran Jeshurun (ed.), *Governments and Rebellions in Southeast Asia* (pp. 186-217). Singapore: Institute of Southeast Asian Studies.

Quah, Jon S.T. (1998). Singapore's Model of Development: Is it Transferable? In Henry S. Rowen (ed.), *Behind East Asian Growth: The Political and Social Foundations of Prosperity* (Chapter 5, pp. 105-125). London: Routledge.

Quah, Jon S.T. (2003). Paying for the 'best and brightest': Rewards for high public office in Singapore. In Christopher Hood and B. Guy Peters with Grace O. M. Lee (eds.), *Reward for High Public Office: Asian and Pacific Rim States* (Chapter 9, pp. 145-162). London: Routledge.

Quah, Jon S.T. (2007). *Combating Corruption Singapore-Style: Lessons for Other Asian Countries*. Baltimore: School of Law, University of Maryland.

Quah, Jon S.T. (2010). *Public Administration Singapore-Style*. Bingley: Emerald Group Publishing.

Quah, Jon S.T. (2011a). Innovation in Public Governance in Singapore: Solving the Housing Shortage and Curbing Corruption. In Anttiroiko, Ari-Veikko Bailey, Stephen J., and Valkama, Pekka (eds.), *Innovative Trends in Public Governance in Asia* (pp. 121-136). Amsterdam: IOS Press.

Quah, Jon S.T. (2011b). *Curbing Corruption in Asian Countries: An Impossible Dream?*, Bingley: Emerald Group Publishing.

Republic of Singapore (1980). *The Budget for the Financial Year 1980/1981*. Singapore: Budget Division, Ministry of Finance.

Republic of Singapore (1989). *Parliamentary Debates Singapore Official Report*, 53 (6) (March 17).

Republic of Singapore (1994). *Competitive Salaries for Competent and Honest Government: Benchmarks for Ministers and Senior Public Officers*. Command 13 of 1994. White Paper presented to the

Parliament of Singapore, October 21, 1994. Singapore: Prime Minister's Office.

Republic of Singapore (2011). *Singapore Budget 2011: Annex to the Expenditure Estimates*. Singapore: Budget Division, Ministry of Finance.

Riggs, Fred W. (1970). Administrative reform as a problem of dynamic balancing. *Philippine Journal of Public Administration,* 14 (2) (April): 101-135.

Schwab, Klaus (ed.) (2010). *The Global Competitiveness Report 2010-2011*. Geneva: World Economic Forum.

Seah, Chee Meow (1971). *Bureaucratic Evolution and Political Change in an Emerging Nation: A Case Study of Singapore*. Ph.D. thesis, Faculty of Economic and Social Studies, Victoria University of Manchester, UK.

Schein, Edgar H. (1996). *Strategic Pragmatism: The Culture of Singapore's Economic Development Board*. Cambridge: MIT Press.

Straits Times (1990), March 30, p. 27.

Tan, Ah Leak (1999). The Experience of Singapore in Combating Corruption. In Stapenhurst, Richard and Kpundeh, Sahr J. (eds.), *Curbing Corruption: Toward a Model for Building National Integrity* (Chapter 4, pp. 59-66). Washington, D.C.: World Bank.

Yap, Sonny, Lim, Richard, and Leong, Weng Kam (2009). *Men in White: The Untold Story of Singapore's Ruling Political Party*. Singapore: Singapore Press Holdings.

Yoong, Siew Wah (1972). Some Aspects of Corruption. *National Youth Leadership Training Institute Journal* (January): 54-59.

Chapter 10 Public Sector Reform and Governance in Thailand

Pairote Pathranarakul

Introduction

Public sector reform is one key government strategy which plays a significant role in management arrangements and a country's development. Public sector reform in Thailand has been realized amid a long passage of changes and revolutions. The first reform in the ancient period was acknowledged in the early *Ayudhya* era. The main reasons for reform were due to the necessity for the formation and unification of the Thai state during the process of nation building (Rojanawan, 2003). The structural arrangement for anational centralized administrative system was designed comprising of four main departments (Hongsanant, 1980: 5) called *Jatusadomp* which means the four pillars, namely *Wiang, Wang*, Khlang and Na. Significant reform was made during the reign of King Rama V when a modern administrative system was fully established in response to social and economic changes, especially in response to threats in the colonization era (Samudavanija, 1976).

The regime shift from an absolute monarchy to a constitutional government system led to several major reforms in the Thai administrative system. Most of such reforms were characterized by the disjointed incremental changes with discontinuity. Public sector reforms in Thailand, by nature, proceed along with the constitutional process and oscillate with several coups resulting indiscontinuity amid political conflict and instability.

Since 2002 the discourse on public sector reform in Thailand has changed from "public sector reform" to "public sector development." Public sector development has become key to bureaucratic efficiency and effectiveness in government policy. During the past decade, two Strategic Plans for Public Sector Development were formulated and implemented across the country. Changes and development, from 2002 until the present, have modernized the Thai public sector with higher capacity for providing public services to all target groups. New Public Management with governance principles are employed as basic guidelines for public sector development as well as for long-term reform directions.

The implementation of the Strategic Plan on Public Sector Development is carried out through devising diverse management tools and techniques such as the public service agreement (PSA), standard public services, a blueprint for change, performance evaluation with a balanced score card, knowledge management, competency enhancement, a new personnel management system, the Public Sector Management Quality Award (PMQA), management innovation, e-Government and e-Services, and an incentives scheme. The outcomes of public sector development are obvious in many areas: improvement of public service delivery, reduction in work processes, and more responsiveness to people's needs. Overall, public sector organizations under all ministries have made progressive changes in effectiveness, public service quality, efficient operation, and organization development. Several agencies have developed management innovation and initiated innovative services. These contribute to an increase in people's satisfaction as well as the country's competitiveness.

However, improvement in ethics, governance and social accountability dimensions remains a challenge. Thailand, as with other countries in transition, needs to enhance public sector capacity and prepare its readiness for new threats arising from various types of crisis, in particular social conflict, political instability, socio-economic inequality, energy crisis, and natural disasters. These critical factors have pressured continued reform for sustainable development in the public sector.

The main purpose of this paper is to propose a new paradigm in public sector reform based on sustainable development concepts. The author examines progress and outcomes of public sector reform then suggests a new perspective in changing the reform unit from the public sector organization to the local community. Under the new paradigm, the ultimate goal of public sector reform is sustained human well-being. This can be achieved through systematic arrangements of interrelated components, namely, social equity, economic viability, institutional capacity, resource conservation, ecological stability, and technological acceptability.

The prime objectives of public sector reform are geared toward building social harmony and political stability, inequality and poverty eradication, and strengthening the institutional capacity for the recovery of crises arising from internal and external factors. Concepts of governance and reform, and sustainable development are discussed. Recent progress and outcomes of public sector reform under the Strategic Plan for Public Sector Development are presented, followed by a review of development strategies and outcomes and National Social and Economic Development plans. Finally, a new reform paradigm and strategic measures toward sustainability is proposed for future actions.

Governance, Reform and Sustainable Development

Governance and Reform

Rhodes (1996) classified the uses of governance into six aspects: (1) as the minimal state; (2) as corporate governance; (3) as the new public management; (4) as "good governance"; (5) as a socio-cybernetic system; and (6) as self-organizing networks. According to Rhodes (1996), the minimal state and New Public Management (NPM) are more relevant to the discussion of governance since policy decisions (steering) is central to the analysis of public management while service delivery (rowing) is about how bureaucracy gets things done in effective and efficient ways.

Thus, the transformation of the public sector as part of the reforming processes involves "less government" but "more governance." Essentially, governance as self-organizing networks is useful in a broader scope and a dynamic situation. In accordance with this trend, the shared characteristics of governance include: interdependence between public, private, and voluntary organizations; continuing interactions between network members; interaction among participants; and a significant degree of autonomy from the state (Rhodes, 2000).

Governance implies the process of decision-making and the process by which decisions are implemented through involvement of diverse actors, both from public, private and civil sectors. Governance is normative in conception and its values depend on the actors and partners involved with playing active roles in such processes. Good governance is envisaged upon mutually supportive and cooperative relationship between government, the private sector, civil society, people's networks and voluntary organizations.

ESCAP[1] proposed eight characteristics of good governance: participatory, consensus oriented, accountable, transparent, responsive, effective and efficient, equitable and inclusive and follows the rule of law. Good governance is a key component of the Asian Development Bank's (ADB) Poverty Reduction Strategy[2] which recognizes the importance of capacity development. Four key interrelated elements that are considered necessary to ensure results are accountability, participation, transparency and predictability.

The idea of reinventing government (Osborne and Gabler, 1992) provides a new perspective for public sector reform (PSR), which is technically referred to as "New Public Management" (NPM).[3] NPM has been embraced as the contemporary paradigm through which governments need to be reformed and the public sector reengineered (Antwi and Analoui, 2008a as quoted in Analoui, 2009). This new management concept tends to challenge public managers to act as entrepreneurs who push efforts toward a privatized government that places values on the use of public money (Denhart and Denhart, 2000).

NPM is a global approach to reform in public sector management. NPM's principles include a shift away from an emphasis on policy toward an emphasis on measurable performance; a shift away from reliance on traditional bureaucracies toward loosely coupled, quasi-autonomous units and competitively tendered services; a shift away from an emphasis on development and investment toward cost-cutting; allowing public managers greater "freedom to manage" according to private sector practice; and a shift away from classic command and control regulation toward self-regulation (Lynn, Jr., 2006: 107).

Reform is used to describe many changes from minor, to management arrangements, to fundamental changes in ownership, governance, and management arrangements. It can be defined as change that has produced a measurable improvement in services or a noticeable change in the relationships between institutions of the state and the citizens (EU, 2009: 17).

Public sector reform is considered an integral part of the changing role of government in response to problems arising from internal and external threats. Reform is important in achieving improvements in public sector management. It is also conceived as a deliberate policy and action to alter organizational structures, process and behavior in order to improve administrative capacity for efficient and effective performance. Public sector reform requires public service to focus less on the procedures used traditionally by the bureaucracy and more on outcomes or outputs consistent with the policy intentions of government. A management style of getting results, rather than consistency in following traditional procedures, defines public sector reform advocates. Essentially, such reform involves inducing and managing change and is seen and used as a strategy for achieving improved performance within the public sector.[4]

A new framework of governing arises from changes in the relationship between government, private sector and society. The "governance without government" is becoming the dominant pattern for management of advanced industrial democracies (Rhodes, 1997). Guy Peters (1988) examined the governance debate in public administration then illustrated the dominant feature of the governance model which gives importance on strengthening networks and capacity for self-organizing, blending public and private resources, increasing emphasis on output rather input, and developing new instruments of control and accountability. A paradigm shift for public sector reform is characterized by: a greater focus on result and increased value for money, devolution of authority and enhanced flexibility, strengthened accountability and control, a client and service orientation, strengthened capacity for developing strategy and policy, introducing competition and other market elements, and changed relationships with other levels of government (OECD,

1995).

Sustainable Development Concepts

The Brundtland Commission's wide ranging discussion of sustainable development concepts includes the following statements (WCED, 1987): (1) sustainable development is development that meets the needs of the present without compromising the ability of future generations to meet their own needs; (2) it requires meeting basic needs of all and extending to all the opportunity to satisfy their aspirations for a better life; and (3) the concept of sustainable development provides a framework for the integration of environmental policies and development strategies… In essence, sustainable development is a process of change in which the exploitation of resources, the direction of investments, the orientation of technological development, and institutional change are in harmony and enhance both current and future potential to meet human needs and aspirations.

The pursuit of sustainable development requires: (1) a political system that secures effective citizen participation in decision-making; (2) an economic system that is able to generate surpluses and technical knowledge on a self-reliance and sustained basis; (3) a social system that provides solutions to tensions arising from disharmonious development; (4) a production system that respects the obligation to preserve the ecological base for development; (5) a technological system that can search continuously for new solutions; (6) an international system that fosters sustainable patterns of trade and finance; and (7) an administrative system that is flexible and has the capacity for self-correction (WCED, 1987: 65).

Sustainable development implies a new concept of economic growth, one that offers fairness and opportunity for all, not just the privileged few, without further destroying the world's finite natural resources and without compromising the world's carrying capacity (UNDP, 1992: 17). The minimum requirements for achieving sustainable development include: the elimination of poverty; more equitable distribution of resources; healthier, more educated and better trained people; decentralized, more participatory government; better understanding of the diversity of ecosystems, and better monitoring of the environmental impact of development activities (UNDP, 1992).

Barde (1990: 33-36) distinguished the concept of sustainable development into two types of approach: a global economic approach and an environmental or ecological approach. The economic approach involves many aspects of economic activity, in particular, the control of population growth; encouragement of technical change; and a change in the patterns of reproduction and consumption in order to maintain the stock of scarce resources. The ecological approach relies on the maintenance and transmission of management principles that foster the potential for growth and well-being.

Progress and Outcomes of Public Sector Reform

Public Sector Reform in the Classical and Transitional Period

Public sector reform in Thailand began during the *Ayudhya* period in which the central administrative system covered four departments (commonly known as *jatusadomp* or the four pillars), namely, *Wieng or Muang* which was accountable for criminal (law?) and justice; *Wang* which was responsible for internal affairs; *Khlang* which was responsible for trade and foreign affairs; and *Na* which took care of irrigation and agriculture (Hongsanant, 1980: 5).

The great reform was made during the reign of King Rama V (1868-1910). Departments were upgraded into ministries and civil servants were given the status of public service officials.

The main reform goals were to bring about unity and stability of the nation as well as a modernized bureaucratic system. Key reform areas included designing the central administrative system, reassessing the structure to avoid the overlapping mission and protecting the country from threats arising from colonialism during that time (Samudavanija, 1976).

After the regime shift from an absolute monarchy to democracy in 1932, there were several dimensional changes; political, social, economic, and administrative. In this period, there was a revision of laws on civil service which divide the administrative system into central, regional and local administration. Central administration was comprised of responsible ministries while regional administration was classified into provincial and district administration. A municipality system was established for the first time at the local administration level. Public sector reform has become a prime mission of all governments past to present. Vision and framework on the bureaucratic system and public sector reform was discussed and highlighted on a decentralized system and the changing roles of public sector organizations (Office of Bureaucratic System Reform Committee, 2001).

The big public sector reform was made in 2002. During the Thaksin Shinawatra's regime, public sector reform[5] was declared one key government policy for improving public service efficiency. Its policy directions covered five main areas: (1) changing the roles, mission and process of public sector management; (2) changing in budgeting, finance and procurement systems; (3) planning for the improvement of the civil service system; (4) reforming laws and regulations, in particular legal drafting and improvement processes; and (5) enhancing the values and cultural system for improving standard public service.

In order to implement the public sector reform policy, the new National Administration Act B. E. 2545 (2002) was promulgated and the Public Sector Development Commission (PSDC) was initiated. Under this Commission, the Office of the Public Sector Reform Development Commission (OPDC) acts as a strategic body in driving public sector reform.

The strategic goals of Thai Public Sector Development can be classified into four reform areas: better service quality, right-sizing, high performance, and democratic governance (OPDC, 2006). Better service quality aimed to improve the service delivery pattern of the public sector to be more diversified, convenient and responsive to the people's needs. Efforts were made toward providing the convergent service in one place in the form of government counter services (GCS); devolution of authority in giving orders, as well as granting permission and approval; and setting up the mechanisms to obtain public opinions and the information on the level of people's satisfaction.

Mission revision and rightsizing governmental organizations were implemented through amending the law concerning the public administration, restructuring of government organizations by transferring duties and officers to regional and local agencies. In addition, vertical and horizontal integration was encouraged in the organization of the public administration structure order to link bureaucratic systems among agencies.

Leveraging work processes and competencies to international standards was considered one salient component toward high performance organization. In order to achieve this goal, various efforts were proposed including: (1) increasing efficiency of public sector management through change management; (2) designing for more flexible and responsive action to the immediate problems of the country; (3) improving the competency, organization culture and core values; (4) developing the quality standard for the performance of the public sector in accordance with good governance guidelines; and (5) creating mechanisms for implementation and evaluation systems according to the

Performance Agreement (PA) of the public sector.

Organizational capacity development was also enhanced through the promotion of personnel competence in line with the organization's strategic direction, restructuring the bureaucratic structure for being more flexible, dynamic and self-organized in the forms of matrix pattern, task force and cross-functional team, and implementing anti-corruption measures and risk management.

Opening the public system to democratic governance was encouraged by strengthening the mechanisms for the participatory administration, creating networks for upgrading the public sector development and stimulating the processes of people's auditing as part of governance measures.

Strategic Plan for the Thai Public Sector Development

In order to develop an effective Thai public sector system while supporting the country's development in the era of change and globalization, the Strategic Plan for Public Sector Development (2003-2007) was formulated. Its vision was set toward "*facilitating the continuous development of the Thai public sector for sustainable results.*"

Seven major strategies have been initiated as follows: reengineering the work process, developing the public administrative structure, reforming the financial and budgeting system, improving personnel and remuneration system, promoting changes in paradigm, culture and values, modernizing the public sector, and opening bureaucracy for people's participation.

Reengineering the work process attempts to increase effectiveness and the standard delivery system, and to improve auditing and evaluation system. Progress has been made by adjusting the working process and changing behaviors in line with the principles of good governance. One-stop service and the internal control unit of government agencies have been promoted, especially risk management and value-for-money auditing.

The public administrative structure was developed to increase its capacity and flexibility. The main objective is to arrange the structure of public administration in an integrated manner. At the same time, the relations between the different levels of public administration have been appropriately arranged. This provides a shared link among different working dimensions and sectors. The regional administrative system and structure were revised and developed in order to strengthen the provinces, making them more capable to implement the National Agenda, government policies, and public projects.

The financial and budgeting system was reformed by transferring the decision making power and national budget responsibility to operational agencies. In connection with this system, an attempt has been made to encourage officials to change and develop their work performance under the new pattern of financial and budgetary management.

Improving personnel and remuneration systems have been made through various initiatives. Programs have been launched to promote capacity building and changes have been made to hiring methods. A performance-based payment means more competitive capacity in the domestic labor market through the adjustment of position classification and remuneration. Other progress schemes promote capacity building among government officials and open the opportunity for highly-qualified people to move easily into various levels of the governmental system.

Promoting changes in paradigms, culture and values is vital to Thai public sector reform. Public sector organizations are encouraged to create an environment favorable to the effective learning process, the support of managerial resources and deregulation. The expansion of knowledge networking and the promotion of public participation are crucial to changing paradigms, culture and values. In this implementation phase, the promotion and dissemination of a new paradigm is part of the national agenda to enhance public sector development.

Modernizing the public sector system has been made through the application of an information system and communication technology. This helps in increasing work efficiency and providing public services to a large number of people. The establishment of an e-Government system focuses on citizen-centered service delivery. A comprehensive e-online service center has been promoted, with exchange of information among public agencies to serve the general public 24 hours a day.

Opening bureaucracy for people's participation is one of the salient components in the Thai public sector reform. Although political change and the guiding principles of the Constitution of the Kingdom of Thailand B. E. 2540 (1997) and B. E. 2550 (2007) aim at increasing people participation in public sector management, the Thai public sector system has not adapted well to a rapidly changing situation. Officials are still attached to the status quo and patron-client relationships, particularly serving politicians and their bosses rather than the public. It is therefore, a move toward democratization of the public sector system by allowing the people to voice their opinions, and actively participate in public policy implementation and evaluation. It is essential that development programs and project activities that affect people's quality of life must be assessed, prior to making decisions and implementation, for the impact both environmental (EIA) and social (SIA), which also includes health impact assessment (HIA).

Progress and outcomes of public sector reform under the Strategic Plan on Public Sector Development (2001-2005) are summarized in four main aspects (OPDC: 2001):

1) Better service quality, a reduction in the hierarchic

structure, and a more decentralized system of decision making in project approval was set up. Standard time for service delivery as well as development of a one-stop system and joint counter services in response to needs has significantly increased customer satisfaction. Key reform results included: the development of a new public service in the form of a mobile unit, service link, government counter service (GCS), and e-services; the amendment of laws and legal procedures in order to support public services; the public service award for excellence and innovative organizations; and the enhancement of values for all officials through the campaign "I AM READY."[6]

2) Mission revision and rightsizing of the public organizations has led to a more unique structure with clusters among ministries and departments. Some departments were dissolved and merged while the Regional Operation Center (ROC) and the Office of Strategic Management (OSM) were established for strengthening regional administration. More than twenty public organizations were established and the Special Delivery Unit (SDU) was expanded for special public management. Strategic performance based, and an integrated approach was initiated in the budgeting process covering agenda, area, and function. At the same time rightsizing for human resources in the public sector was implemented resulting in about a 5 percent decline in manpower each fiscal year.

3) Enhancing managerial capacities of the public sector was another key result. Public management with annual action plans were prepared and implemented under the public service agreement (PSA) and self-assessment report. At the organizational and individual levels, a blueprint for change was encouraged among public agencies and incentive schemes to promote achievement in line with key

performance indicators. Development of capability and competency of public sector organizations was implemented through various activities including change leaders program, knowledge management through e-learning, information exchanges among public agencies and their stakeholders.

4) Opening the public system to democratic governance was emphasized by promoting public involvement in public sector management. Various communication channels were established for promoting public participation, including special committees which comprised of representatives, information dissemination, public forum and public hearings on development programs, public consultation, and an attitude survey.

The New Strategic Plan for Public Sector Development (2008-2012) has shifted its vision from people's well-being, national interest, competency and learning capacity, responsiveness to reform, and upholding ethics and governance. Four strategic issues include (OPDC, 2008: 1) enhancing public service that is responsive to people's need in a rapid and dynamic change; (2) reforming through the integration and collaboration with all parties through networks and people participation; (3) developing high performance organization (HPO) through increasing capability of officials in learning, initiative and adaptive change in different situations; and (4) building a system of self-governance, transparency, and accountability as well as raising officials' awareness and social accountability.

The progress and outcomes of public sector development are summarized into two main aspects (OPDC, 2009). First, performance evaluation based on a public service agreement shows improvement in effectiveness, quality of service, efficiency, and organization development. Second, there has been an effort to make public sector development more responsive to people's need and expectation. Development tools and techniques are applied in management processes which contribute to higher performance. Key performance areas from pushing efforts in public sector development include: (1) better quality public services have been expanded into district and local administration; (2) development of an integrated approach with networks and a partnership system. People participation and cluster management at the provincial level was encouraged; (3) high performance organization was promoted through management initiatives such as Public Sector Management Quality Award (PMQA), e-service and virtual office, and the Government Strategic Management System (GSMS). Preparation for the readiness of officials for adaptive changes was also arranged; and (4) self-governing and auditing systems gained the public's trust and respect. Policy and guidelines on governance and auditing were designed, and the provincial committee on good governance was set up.

The Public Services Development Award Scheme was promoted as an incentive for improving excellent public services among government agencies. Table 1 shows the proposed and awarded government agencies on public services development during 2003-2009. E-Services channels under e-Government development in cooperation with the Ministry of Information Technology and Communication are expanded in responsive to people's needs (Table 2).

Overall, the two Strategic Plans for Public Sector Development have contributed to the improvement of public management processes and quality of public services (OPDC, 2009). Public service agreement and management reform tools such as knowledge management, change leader and competency enhancement, and Public Sector Management Quality Award are

Table 1. Proposed and Awarded Government Agencies on Public Services Development, 2003–2009

Year	Proposed		Awarded	
	Agency	Work Process	Agency	Work Process
2003	50	169	19	25
2004	48	285	7	16
2005	62	250	12	21
2006	68	250	7	11
2007	53	133	31	46
2008	69	172	47	61
2009	61	162	45	79
Total	1,421 Work Processes		259 Work Processes	

Source: OPDC (2009: 104).

Table 2. List of e-Services Channels under e-Government Development

e-Services	Website	Purpose and Feature
Government Contact Center (GCC111)	http://www.1111.go.th	Center for public notation supplemented by Government hotline 1111
Khonthai CA	http://wwwca.khonthai.com/	Public registration for e-business
Thailand Gateway	http://www.khonthai.com/thailandgateway/	General service through e-mail
e-citizen	http://e-citizen.go.th/index.php	Central public service
Ombudsman	http://www.ombudsman.go.th	Complain on ethical and political issues
Secretariat Office of the Parliament	http://www.parliament.go.th/help/index2.php	General public service
Office of Permanent Secretary of PM	http://www.opmInter/link/sbc/index.asp	General public service
Government Counter Service	http://www.opdc.go.th/gcs/gcs_test/about1.php	Joint one stop service and counter service
Ministry of Foreign Affairs	http://www.mfa.go.th/web/2301.php	Center for public complaints

National Commission on Counter Corruption	http://www.nccc.thaigov.net/nccc/call.php	Information on corruption issues
Metropolitan Police Bureau	http://www.police.go.th/cpl/cpl_n.htmi	Information on legal and criminal issue
Ministry of Culture	http://www.m-cultutre.go.th/detail_page.php?sub_id=798	Cultural affairs information service
Customer Department	http://www.customs.go.th/feedback/feedback_center.jsp	Information on custom and legal violation
News on Drugs	http://dais.oncb.go.th	Information on drug trafficking
Department of Pollution Control	http://www.pcd.go.th/callcenter/	Information service on pollution control
National Park, Wildlife and Plant Species	http://www.dnp.go.th/service/main_service.htm	Information service on technical and recreation matters
Ministry of Public Health	http://www.moph.go.th/prac/complain/complain.shtml	Information service on heath products complain
District Office	http://www.amphoe.com/main.php	District information service
Joint District Center	http:ago.dopa.go.th/Eoutlet/index.php	District helping service with smile
Local Administrative Information Center (DhamrongthamCenter)	http://www.thailocaladmin.go.th/justice/justice.jsp	Center of justice service at local level

Source: OPDC (2009: 108).

promising a good reforming direction. In parallel, civil service reform has been driven by the Office of Civil Service Commission (OCSC) and many initiatives have been implemented. The Thai civil service system has become modernized due to the implementation of a strategic human resource and development program. The new civil service system has brought about positive results, in particular, in the areas of recruitment and selection, efficiency enhancement and motivation, and standard practice for performance evaluation (Pathranarakul, 2010).

In 2007, the Political and Economic Risk Consultancy (PERC)

ranked Thailand third in Asia for public services. Twelve countries in the Asian economic region with the most efficient bureaucracy were Singapore, Hong Kong, Thailand, Korea, Japan, Taiwan, Viet Nam, China, the Philippines, Indonesia, and India. Thai government officials continued to provide good service amid pressures and difficulties during the political turmoil. However, the corruption perception among government officials is still a painful one for Thai people as well as foreign investors.

Performance outcomes, in terms of competency and competitiveness, show that Thailand is ranked 13 out of 20 countries for ease of doing business (Tables 3 and 4). There was a slight improvement in the competitiveness score which reflects economic performance, government efficiency, business efficiency, and infrastructure (Tables 5 and 6). The global competitiveness in 2010 is illustrated in Appendix 1.

However, with regard to governance indicators, Thailand needs more political will, national commitment and mutual efforts to improve. The Worldwide Governance Indicators[7] have shown that between 1996 and 2009 Thailand remained in the same 50th–75th percentile rank. The country's performance trend for all available years between 1996 and 2009 in six governance

Table 3. Thailand's Rankings among Countries with Ease of Doing Business (2005–2009)

Year	Ranking	Number of Country
2005	20	145
2006	20	155
2007	18	175
2008	15	178
2009	13	181
2010	12	183

Source: World Bank (2010). The Doing Business, Report 2010.
(http://www.doingbusiness.org/documents/fullreport/2010/DB10-ful-report.pdf)

Table 4. Top Twenty Countries with Ease of Doing Business (2009)

Rank	Country	Rank	Country
1	Singapore	11	Iceland
2	New Zealand	12	Japan
3	United States of America	13	Thailand
4	Hong Kong	14	Finland
5	Denmark	15	Georgia
6	United Kingdom	16	Saudi Arabia
7	Ireland	17	Sweden
8	Canada	18	Bahrain
9	Australia	19	Belgium
10	Norway	20	Malaysia

Source: http://www.doingbusiness.org/documents/DB09_Overview.pdf

Table 5. The World Competitiveness Scoreboard (2008 and 2009)

2008	Country	2009	2008	Country	2009	2008	Country	2009
1	USA	1	21	United Kingdom	21	34	Jordan	41
3	Hong Kong	2	24	Belgium	22	51	Indonesia	42
2	Singapore	3	13	Taiwan	23	40	Philippines	43
4	Switzerland	4	20	Israel	24	44	Poland	44
6	Denmark	5	26	Chile	25	50	Mexico	46
9	Sweden	6	27	Thailand	26	48	Turkey	47
7	Australia	7	31	Korea	27	53	South Africa	48
8	Canada	8	25	France	28	47	Russia	49
15	Finland	9	28	Czech Republic	29	46	Italy	50
10	Netherlands	10	29	India	30	41	Colombia	51
11	Norway	11	36	Lithuania	31	42	Greece	52
5	Luxemburg	12	32	Slovenia	32	49	Croatia	53
16	Germany	13	30	Slovak Republic	33	45	Romania	54
	Qatar	14	37	Portugal	34	52	Argentina	55
18	New Zealand	15	23	Estonia	35	54	Ukraine	56
14	Austria	16		Kazakhstan	36	55	Venezuela	57
22	Japan	17	35	Peru	37			
19	Malaysia	18	39	Bulgaria	38			
12	Ireland	19	33	Spain	39			
17	China	20	43	Brazil	40			

Source: The World Competitiveness Scoreboard 2009.
(http://www.imd.ch/research/publications/wcy)

Table 6. The World Competitiveness Scoreboard (2009 and 2010)

2009	Country	2010	2009	Country	2010	2009	Country	2010
3	Singapore	1	19	Ireland	21	37	Peru	41
2	Hong Kong	2	21	United Kingdom	22	45	Hungary	42
1	USA	3	27	Korea	23	31	Lithuania	43
4	Switzerland	4	28	France	24	48	South Africa	44
7	Australia	5	22	Belgium	25	51	Colombia	45
6	Sweden	6	26	Thailand	26	52	Greece	46
8	Canada	7	17	Japan	27	46	Mexico	47
23	Taiwan	8	25	Chile	28	47	Turkey	48
11	Norway	9	29	Czech Republic	29	33	Slovak Republic	49
18	Malaysia	10		Iceland	30	41	Jordan	50
12	Luxemburg	11	30	India	31	42	Russia	51
10	Netherlands	12	44	Poland	32	32	Slovenia	52
5	Denmark	13	36	Kazakhstan	33	38	Bulgaria	53
16	Austria	14	35	Estonia	34	54	Romania	54
14	Qatar	15	42	Indonesia	35	55	Argentina	55
13	Germany	16	39	Spain	36	53	Croatia	56
24	Israel	17	34	Portugal	37	56	Ukraine	57
20	China	18	40	Brazil	38	57	Venezuela	58
9	Finland	19	43	Philippines	39			
15	New Zealand	20	50	Italy	40			

Source: The World Competitiveness Scoreboard 2010.
(http://www.imd.ch/research/publications/wcy)

dimensions, namely, government effectiveness, regulatory equality, rule of law, voice and accountability, political stability, and control of corruption has declined overtime. In particular, the latter three dimensions have fallen into the lower percentile rank.

The World Economic Forum's Global Competitiveness Report ranked Thailand's competitiveness 36th in 2009 to 38th in 2010-2011[8] as a result of the global economic downturn and severe political turmoil in the country. The quality of public institutions continues to deteriorate to 63rd place and technological readiness also lags at 63.rd

The top five most problematic factors in doing business in Thailand were as follows: government instability/coups; policy instability; inefficient government bureaucracy; corruption and access to financing. It is serious that the most critical factors concern institutional and government bureaucracy. Therefore, all parties should cooperate to increase competitiveness and long-term economic growth. Essentially, public sector reform direction should be more focused on these problematic factors.

Public Sector Reform from the Past until the Present National Economic and Social Development Plans

The National Economic Development Board (NEDB) was first established in 1959 to recommend an integrated and economically sound development plan based on the appraisal of available resources. During the first plan period (1961-1966), the plan attempted to raise national income through increasing agricultural production of important crops and increasing capital accumulation in the form of financial investment in the purchase of capital goods mostly for expansion of basic infrastructure as well as public welfare (NEDB, 1964).

The second plan (1967-1971) focused on socio-economic activities and aimed to spread development to remote regions. The plan declared that its objective of reducing geographical imbalances and income inequalities would be reached through public investment in rural development. Increase in the standard of living was aimed at primarily by means of maximization of resource uses in order to expand productivity, increase national income and maintain economic stability. The plan reflected policies geared to establishing a more balanced economic structure, emphasizing social development especially human resource development through an employment scheme, stressing the role of the private sector in industrial and services development (NEDB, 1967).

During the 15 years of planned development under the first three plans (1961-1967), the mobilization of investment funds to finance various public development programs strengthened the country's socio-economic structure. Development performance based on public development strategy contributed to achieving a high growth rate at an average of about 7 percent per annum from 1961 to 1971. The nature of growth, however, led to further income disparities among various population groups and regions of the country (NESDB, 1972).

The fourth plan was influenced by the "new economic and social order" theme. The socio-politico-economic transitions in the country during the third plan period compelled the government to adopt a new set of development positions and priorities for the fourth plan (NESDB, 1977: 4). Several basic policy reforms were considered necessary for promoting greater economic security and creating a more equitable socio-economic development and eventual poverty eradication among certain groups of people.

Thus, instead of emphasizing just "economic growth," the fourth plan stressed the importance of promoting "social justice" by reducing socio-economic disparities and improving people's welfare. It also called for effective implementation of various key development policies and programs through better co-ordination and improvement of management capabilities among operating agencies.

During the fifth plan period (1982-1986), Thailand faced a national economic recession due to the depressed state of the world economy. Simultaneously, several problems that had been building up emerged in many areas, such as economic and financial instability, income distribution, and poverty. The fifth plan adopted a new approach to development which emphasized the adjustment of the economic structure rather than economic growth expansion; efforts to balance economic and social development; poverty eradication in lagging areas; the transformation of plans into implementation; and the role of the private sector (NESDB, 1982: 3-4). Although the new approach had considerable success, the implementation of programs had limited effectiveness mainly due to lack of public participation in the policymaking process, and lack of coordination among the government agencies concerned.

The sixth plan set its goals on advancement of national development through making progress and attaining prosperity, and solving socio-economic problems that had accumulated over the past. Development issues included an increase in employment opportunity and appropriate distribution of income and how to cope with the deterioration of natural resources and the environment. Key development guidelines covered three main areas: (1) increase the efficiency in regard to human resources, natural resources and integrated management systems; (2) improve the production system with more diversity of products and market expansion; and (3) increase the distribution of income into provincial regions and rural areas by focusing income population areas as the main target group (NESDB, 1987).

The seventh plan (1992-1996), for the first time, explicitly stressed the sustainable development approach. Its main objectives were to maintain economic growth so as to ensure sustainability, redistribute income, decentralize development into regions and areas, and accelerate development through human resources, quality of life, the environment, and natural resource management (NESDB, 1992).

Though the Thai economy has grown rapidly, thus reinforcing stability, and has become increasingly internationalized, the overall development pattern is still unbalanced in several aspects. Firstly, income disparities among households and between rural and urban areas have widened at an alarming rate. Secondly, the deterioration of natural resources and the environment have become ever more severe, thus adversely affecting the quality of life and posing serious constraints for future development. Thirdly, the bureaucratic system is unable to adjust itself to change and cannot adequately respond to national economic and social transformations; there are constraints in terms of manpower, legal framework, rules and regulations, the administrative system, and organizational structure (NESDB, 1992: 2-4).

The eighth plan (1997-2001) revised the development paradigm by adopting human resource development as a single objective for achieving sustainable development. The plan focused on a decentralized system of planning, development of the people for and by the people, and management for sustainable development. During the eighth plan period, the future scenario aimed to attain economic stability, management capacity and social harmony as well as a closer collaboration between public, private and civil sectors (NESDB, 1997).

The eighth plan was an important turning point in the country's development planning. The plan represented new values and thinking in Thai society that gave importance to participation by all elements of society, and that aimed for "people centered development." Deploying economics was considered as tool to help people achieve greater happiness and better quality of life. The plan switched from a segmented approach to a holistic and integrated approach in order to create a balance in the development of the economy, society, and environment.

However, in the first year of the plan, Thailand experienced a severe economic crisis (commonly known as the *1997 Tom Yam Kung Crisis*) with great impacts on individuals and society, including problems of increased unemployment and poverty. Restoring stability and reducing the impact of the crisis thus became a priority.

The ninth plan adopted the sufficiency economy philosophy as fundamental guidelines for sustainable development of the country. Its salient components addressed three interrelated principles, namely, reasonableness, moderation and self-immunity together with another two preconditions knowledge and integrity which contribute to stability and sustainability (NESDB, 2002).

Development strategies during the ninth plan included three main clusters: (1) promoting good governance with emphasis placed on transparency, checks and balances, transfer of mission into local administration, anti-corruption as well as corporate governance and consumer rights protection; (2) strengthening the foundations toward a happy and healthy society by enhancing social justice and people's quality of life, reducing poverty, and conserving natural resources and the environment; and (3) restructuring the economy for more balance.

The plan prioritized solutions to problems arising from the economic crisis in order to build an economy with strong internal foundations and resilience to external changes, while aiming for balanced development with respect to people, society, the economy, and the environment. The performance under the ninth plan was moderately successful, e.g., stability of economy and the quality of life of people improved. However, the Thai economy remains vulnerable to externalities, while problems persist including poverty, income distribution, quality of education, security of life and transparency, particularly policy corruption in government administration. These remain priorities and challenges for future solution.

Thailand still faces major changes under the present tenth plan period (2007-2011) that provide both threats and opportunities for the country's development. The plan pays serious attention to changes in a development context under the globalization that will significantly affect Thailand for long-term development. The five major trends are: (1) changes in global financial markets and capital movements that may affect currency values; (2) advances in technology and the application of appropriate technologies to Thailand's strengths; (3) social changes due to population growth and other related factors may lead to new problem issues, e.g., land use conflicts, intellectual capital, ageing societies, and new communicable diseases; (4) free movement of peoples in the knowledge society, shortage of skilled labor and migration of undocumented labor; and (5) changes in the environment and natural resources, especially the depletion of natural resources that have negative effects on climate change, and the incidence of natural disasters.

In a time of rapid change and globalization, it is imperative to set appropriate strategies for national development. The plan attempts to build a knowledge base for resilience in a dynamic change, spread equitable development, promote good governance in national administration at all levels, promote the equality among diverse groups in society, strengthen local communities, and rehabilitate and conserve natural resources and the environment as a foundation for securing development, and as the basis of livelihoods for communities and society. Key development strategies are as follows: (1) development of human quality towards a knowledge-based and learning society by promoting integrity and knowledge, health in a livable environment, and peaceful coexistence in society; (2) strengthening community and society as the basis of national security by enhancing strong communities and their economies as well as securing community rights to manage, utilize, and protect natural resources and the environment; (3) reforming the structure of the economy for balance and sustainability through adjustment of production structure and productivity, resilience into the economy, and promotion of a fair distribution of the benefits; (4) development of biodiversity and conservation of the natural resource base for ecological balance; and (5) promoting good governance aimed at social justice and sustainability through developing a democratic culture and system of governance, encouraging people's participation in national administration, creating a public management with efficiency, governance, and cooperation with development partners, and managing national security and sustainability as well as responding to treats in all forms of emergency.

During the past five years the assessment of public institutions continues to decline due the recent problems of social unrest and political instability (World Economic Forum, 2010), as mentioned in the previous part. Sustainability and inequality issues are top priorities for all concerned parties in Thai society. The study of Phongpaijit (2001) on inequality and inequity in access to resources and public service points out that the recent political crises in Thailand are linked with fundamental problems of inequalities in society. These are income inequality and unequal accessibility to power and assets as well as poor quality of life. Political conflicts during 2006 and 2010 were related with structural problems and changes in peoples' way of life amid social dynamism. Thailand has shifted into a modernized and industrialized society but without developing basic social infrastructure for sustaining and securing its well-being. Institutional changes to eradicate various form of inequalities in society becomes an urgent agenda for future reform.

Recently, the Prime Minister Abhisit Vejjajiva's government has appointed two National Reform Committees for searching viable strategies toward social harmony as well as the long-term development of the country. The first National Reform Committee is chaired by the former Prime Minister Anand Panyarachun while the second, called National Reform Assembly, is chaired by scholar Praves Wasi. The twin committees call for a holistic reform framework for Thailand and initially propose a blueprint for changes addressing key strategic issues such as local governance and an administrative reform system, civil politics development, decentralizing the system into communities, and people empowerment.

In addition, the National Reform Assembly advocates for an integrated approach for the country's reform through building people's networks, strengthening healthy communities, and raising public awareness. Key issues raised for new reforms of the country include: more equitable and justice in land and natural resources allocation; welfare and socials security reform; a safety net and health care system for aging citizens; strategies and mechanisms toward a peaceful society; a decentralized and self-governing system for local communities; and cultural and aesthetic value enhancement for reconciliation in the country. These reform issues are in the scrutinizing process and expect to be synthesized and prepared into public policy proposal for the government and all concerned parties.

A New Reform Paradigm and Strategic Measures for Sustainability

Thailand, as with other countries in a transition, is now facing new challenges and constraints that could affect national development in the future. These are democratization and political instability; socio-economic inequality and poverty; imbalance in the development of rural communities; increase in the senior population group leading into an aging society; energy crisis; conflict over use of natural resources; natural disaster; and food security. Thus, public sector reform in Thailand needs a new paradigm with a holistic framework that can be adaptive for crisis mitigation and recovery during a transitional stage. The Thai public sector needs a system of governance and reform mechanisms in transforming both political and administrative dimensions to ensure sustainable public welfare.

Thus, a new paradigm based on sustainable development concepts is proposed. A new framework with new public spirit, empowering people and encouraging public involvement in the reform efforts are vital for a sustainable future. The reform unit should be shifted from public sector organizations to communities. Reform schemes should incorporate area and function, and implement both in vertical and horizontal directions with greater devolution into local administration. A system of governance at both political and administrative levels, public involvement, people empowerment, equity and equality enhancement, crisis and disaster management, and management innovation are among key promising strategies for new reform.

In this new paradigm, sustained human well-being is considered the ultimate goal for public sector reform. Yet, this goal would be achieved by the interaction of vital factors, such as social equity, economic viability, institutional capacity, resources conservation, environmental stability, and technological acceptability. If systematically addressed, these interlinked factors might contribute to the achievement of the ultimate goal of sustainable development in the sense of "sustained human well-being" (WCED, 1987; Barde, 1990; Barbier, 1987; Brown et al., 1987).

Social equity is one of the major preconditions for sustaining human well-being. Social and economic inequalities refer to a situation in which individuals in a society do not have equal status. Potential social inequalities include citizen or human rights, freedom of speech and assembly, the extent of property rights and access to education, health care, public services, natural resources and other social goals. Economic inequality refers to income disparity in the distribution of economic assets.

While economic inequality is caused by the unequal accumulation of wealth, social inequality exits because the lack of wealth in certain areas prohibits these people from obtaining the same quality of welfare as the wealthy in societies when access to these social goods depends on wealth. For instance, in natural resources management, severe social inequalities cause major resource constraints and environmental degradation from two sides. They lead to overexploitation of natural resources for short-term economic gains by the powers-that-be and simultaneous encroachment of impoverished rural populations in remote, yet ecologically sensitive areas for economic survival.

Significantly, indigenous Asian development philosophies such as Gandhianism, the Savodhaya movement, and the concept of a Buddhist economy, and sufficiency economy philosophy stress the need for a balanced socio-economic development. Poverty and inequality cannot be eradicated, indeed, without a certain measure of economic growth. It is essential that growth is fairly distributed, socially and regionally, and that it does not place great strains on natural resources and the environment.

Economic viability is vital for a sustainable society. Sustainable development aims at natural resource use together with and for the environment, with a concern to meet human dedicated needs and eradicate poverty. Economic growth with fair distribution is vital for national development and, indeed, required to sustain that growth. Thus, the need for economic growth to provide a socio-economic base to allow needs to be met is not "no-growth" or "high-growth" but rather "green growth," i.e., moderate economic growth which seeks to enhance and protect the environment. In this sense the sufficiency economy philosophy could serve as a basic guideline for public management and public sector reform for ensuring a sustainable and balanced economic growth with a better common future (Pathranarakul, 2008).

Resource conservation through sustained yield management will assure the carrying capacity for long-term development.

Sustained yield implies a recurrent increment of the biological resource in such a way that the portion removed by one harvest is replaced by growth or reproduction before the next harvest. For instance, sustainable development in forestry can be defined in terms of sustainability the ability to manage our forest resources without prejudice to its future productivity, ecological diversity and capacity for regeneration (Winpenny, 1991).

Technological acceptability means the need to use appropriate technologies. Technologies should strike a balance between human resource inputs, capital inputs, and environmental impacts. Green and clean technology like biotechnology and other advanced technologies, that are not harmful to mankind and the environment, could be promoted as an alternative for a sustainable society. Importantly, intermediate technology is a technology with a human face enhancing skillful hand and creative brain help uplift all human beings to be masters. New technology that makes use of the best of modern knowledge and experience is conducive to decentralization, compatible with the laws of ecology, gentle in its use of scarce resources, and designed to serve the human person instead of making him the servant of machine (Schumacher, 1974).

Institutional capacities are crucial to plan, implement, steer and manage toward sustainable development. As this development concept stresses an integrative approach, great importance is placed on managerial capabilities and institutional building. If sustainable development is understood as "people-centered development"(Korten and Klauss, 1984), it must be based on decentralized planning, people's participation, collaboration, and systematic processes of interaction between government agencies, people's representatives, private sector organizations, civil society organizations and other voluntary associations. Competency enhancement and people empowerment is vital for strengthening capacity to achieve the common goal of public sector reform (Pathranarakul, 1997).

Based on the new reform paradigm, the future direction of public sector reform moving toward a better system of governance is characterized by "less government, increased capacity for community self-reliance, and greater people empowerment" (Pathranarakul, 2002). Reform strategies include: (1) sustaining people's well being through inequality and poverty eradication and promoting socio-economic activities guided by the sufficiency economy philosophy; (2) enhancing local wisdom, community rights, and cultural diversity; (3) redesigning the power structure and relationships between public sector organizations and local communities; (4) promoting a self-governing system and self-reliance communities under the support of academic institutions and public agencies; (5) encouraging a decentralized scheme and empowering people and the community for sustainable management of natural resources; (6) strengthening people's networks and local mechanisms for solving community problems; (7) securing natural resources management and utilization on a sustained yield basis; and (8) rehabilitation of natural resources and the environment by conserving biological diversity and ecological system.

Conclusion and Recommendations

Public sector reform in Thailand during the past decade has been focused on public service quality through restructuring public organizations, strengthening managerial capability of officials and improving legal mechanisms. Yet the reform outcomes in terms of the sustained human well-being are still far from being achieved. Most of managerial resources were utilized for modernizing public sector organizations both the directional and operational units. Reform efforts like re-engineering the work process, designing for performance-based management and applying information technology and e-Government have contributed to better public services in all ministries. However, the issues of ethics and governance still constrain the Thai public sector development and country development as a whole.

The public sector and bureaucratic system should adjust itself to dynamic change and adequately respond to national economic and social transformations. Thereis, therefore, an urgent need to change and search for a new paradigm for public sector reform by gearing the ultimate outcomes toward sustainable development. This means putting our reform efforts and managing change for sustained human well-being and sets new priority on social equity, socio-economic equality, and quality of life. Public administration in transition needs efforts, as well as ethical supports, in fulfilling the desired goals including equality and justice (Argyriades et al., 2007).

Strategic measures in transforming the Thai public sector to be more responsive to dynamic changes and in accord with the sustainable framework are suggested as the following.

First, public sector reform should be implemented in accord with political reform. Essentially, a strategic development plan for public sector development must be aligned with the National Social and Economic Development Plan. Making public sector management more responsive to people's need, and encouraging active participation of private entities and civil society organizations (SCOs) to provide services effectively and efficiently could be promoted through civil forum and consensus building. More dialogue and communication to all those involved in public sector reform is necessary for ensuring sustainable results.

Second, sustainability indicators both in economic, social, and institutional dimensions should be designed and incorporated as goals for reform. Eradication of poverty and inequalities in society should be placed as top priorities on public sector reform agenda. Government agencies must collaborate with other institutions and delegate operational responsibilities to lower organizational levels, particularly the municipalities and district administrations.

Third, a sufficiency economy philosophy as guiding principles for balanced development should be applied to public sector reform. New public spirit, ethics and integrity enhancement among officials at all levels should be promoted and monitored through public campaign and mass media including on-line social networking. At the same time, encouraging transformational leaders, especially ethical leaders, should be implemented to act as catalysts for change in line with national shared values.

Fourth, strengthening judicial institutions and improving law enforcement to ensure social equity and justice for people affected by the reform and development processes is needed. People empowerment and inspiring citizens, especially at the grass-roots, are vital to secure faithfulness and act as consensus among stakeholders in analyzing the common causes of problems. There should be a specific committee comprising people representatives and other key stakeholders on monitoring and evaluation for ensuring continuous improvement and reform results.

Fifth, there should be more collaborative research and study focusing on key issues including transparent government, and the impact of corruption on governance and public sector reform. Comparative studies on public sector reform regarding best practices, i.e., among ASEAN member countries under the ASEAN community initiatives, as well as joint studies between academics, practitioners, and civic groups on governance and reform in international forum in the rapid and dynamic change regions.

Notes

1) The EU White Paper on Public Sector Reform; Europe's 500 Entrepreneurs for Growth, White Paper 2011. (http://www.europes500.eu/documents/europes500-whitepaper-03022011.pdf)
2) http://www.adb.org/governance/
3) The term "New Public Management(NPM)" was coined by Christopher Hood (Hood, 1989; 1991) and has come to characterize what many scholars of public management regard as a "universal administrative reform movement" (Aucoin, 1990: 115).
4) The EU White Paper on Public Sector Reform; Europe's 500 Entrepreneurs for Growth, White Paper 2011. (http://www.europes500.eu/documents/europes500-whitepaper-03022011.pdf).
5) use the new term "public sector" development instead of public sector reform.
6) I AM READY is a set of shared values as means for managing changes in new values and culture among officials. It comprises of Integrity, Activeness, Morality, Relevancy, Efficiency, Accountability, Democracy, and Yield.
7) Governance Matters 2010. Worldwide Governance Indicators, 1996-2009. (http://info.worldbank.org/governance/wi/sc_chart.asp)
8) Among the other Asia, Singapore (3rd), Taiwan (13rd), Korea (22nd), China (27th), Hong Kong (11st), Japan (6th), Malaysia (26th), and India (51st).

References

Allen, Hubert J. B. (1989). *Cultivating the Grassroots: Why Local Government Matters*. International Union of Local Authorities (IULA), The Hague.

Analoui, Farhad (2009). Challenges of Successful Reform: An International Perspective, *Journal of Management Development,* Vol. 28, No. 6, pp. 489-494.

Argyriades, Demetrios et al. (eds.) (2007). *Public Administration in Transition: Essay in Honor of Gerald E. Caiden*. London: Vallentine Mitchell.

Aucoin, Peter (1990). Administrative Reform in Public Management: Paradigms, Principles, Paradoxes and Pendulums, *Governance*, (3) : 115-37.

Barbier, Edward B. (1987). The Concept of Sustainable Economic Development, *Environmental Conservation,* Vol. 14, No. 3, pp. 425-459.

Barde, Jean-Philippe (1990). The Path to Sustainable Development, *The OECD Observer*, 164 (June/July): 33-37.

Batley, Richard and Larbi, George (2004). *The Changing Role of Government: The Reform of Public Services in Developing Countries*. Houndmills: Palgrave.

Brown, Becky J. et al. (1987). Global Sustainability: Toward Definition, *Environmental Management*. Vol. 11, No. 6, pp. 713-719.

Drucker, Peter F. (1994). *Post-Capitalist Society*. New York: Harper Business.

EU (2009). *Public Sector Reform: An Introduction*. Concept Paper, Tools and Method Series. European Commission.

Hammer, Michael and Champy, James (1993). *Reengineering the Corporation: A Manifesto for Business Revolution*. USA: HarperCollins Publishers.

Hongsanant, Kesinee (1980). *Evolution of Thai Civil Service*: A *Comparative Study on Civil Service Acts B.E. 2475-2515*. Bangkok: Mongkhol Printing (in Thai).

Hood, Christopher (1989). Public Administration and Public Policy: Intellectual Challenges for the 1990s. *Australian journal of Public Administration,* 48: 346-58.

Hood, Christopher (1991). A Public Management for All Seasons. *Public Administration,* 69: 3-19.

Johnson, Craig E. (2009). *Meeting Ethical Challenges of Leadership: Casting Light or Shadow*. Los Angeles: SAGE.

Korten, David C. and Klauss, Rudi (eds.)(1984). *People-Centered Development: Contributions toward Theory and Planning Frameworks*. West Hartford, Conn.: Kumarin Press.

Lynn, Jr., Laurence E. (2006). *Public Management: Old and New*. New York: Routledge.

NEDB (1964). *The First National Economic Development Plan (1961-1966)*. National Economic Development Board, Office of the Prime Minister, Government of Thailand.

NEDB (1967). *The Second National Economic Development Plan (1967-1971)*. National Economic Development Board, Office of the Prime Minister, Government of Thailand.

NESDB (1972). *The Third National Economic and Social Development*

Plan (1972-1976). National Economic and Social Development Board, Office of the Prime Minister, Government of Thailand.

NESDB (1977). *The Fourth National Economic and Social Development Plan* (1977-1981). National Economic and Social Development Board, Office of the Prime Minister, Government of Thailand.

NESDB (1982). *The Fifth National Economic and Social Development Plan* (1982-1986). National Economic and Social Development Board, Office of the Prime Minister, Government of Thailand.

NESDB (1987). *The Sixth National Economic and Social Development Plan (1987-1991).* National Economic and Social Development Board, Office of the Prime Minister, Government of Thailand.

NESDB (1992). *The Seventh National Economic and Social Development Plan (1992-1996).* National Economic and Social Development Board, Office of the Prime Minister, Government of Thailand.

NESDB (1997). *The Eight National Economic and Social Development Plan (1997-2001).* National Economic and Social Development Board, Office of the Prime Minister, Government of Thailand.

NESDB (2002). *The Ninth National Economic and Social Development Plan (2002-2006).* National Economic and Social Development Board, Office of the Prime Minister, Government of Thailand.

NESDB (2007). *The Tenth National Economic and Social Development Plan (2007-2011).* National Economic and Social Development Board, Office of the Prime Minister, Government of Thailand.

Office of Public Sector Development Commission (OPDC) (2003). *Strategic Plan for Thai Public Sector Development* (B.E. 2545-2550). Bangkok: OPDC.

Office of Public Sector Development Commission (OPDC) (2006). *Report on the Four Years of Public Sector Development.* Bangkok: OPDC.

Office of Public Sector Development Commission (OPDC) (2008). *Strategic Plan for Thai Public Sector Development* (B.E. 2551-2555). Bangkok: OPDC.

Office of Public Sector Development Commission (OPDC) (2009). *Report on the Thai Public Sector Development.* Bangkok: OPDC.

Office of Bureaucratic System Reform Committee, Civil Service

Commission (2001). *Vision and Framework for Bureaucratic Reform.* Bangkok: Civil Service Commission.

Osborne, David and Gaebler, Ted (1992). *Reinventing Government.* USA.: Addison-Wesley Publishing Company.

Pathranarakul, Pairote (1997). Public Management and People Empowerment, *Public Administration Journal*, Vol. 1 (May-August), Graduate School of Public Administration, pp.87-122.

Pathranarakul, Pairote (1998). Sufficiency Economy Philosophy and Public Management, *Public and Private Management Journal*, Vol.1 (January-April), Graduate School of Public Administration, pp. 67-107.

Pathranarakul, Pairote (2002). Development Strategy through Self-reliant Community: Policy Framework and a Sustainable Management Model, *Thai Journal of Development Administration.* National Institution of Development Administration, Vol. 42, No. 3, pp. 1-73.

Pathranarakul, Pairote (2010). Civil Service Reform in Thailand: A Perspective in Transition. In Kim, Pan Suk (ed.), *Civil Service System and Civil Service Reform in ASEAN Member Countries and Korea.* Seoul: Daeyoung Moonhwasa Publishing.

Peters, B. Guy (1998). Governance Without Government?: Rethinking Public Administration, *Journal of Public Administration Research and Theory*, 2: 223-243.

Polkun, Phokhin (1996). *Bureaucratic System Reform in Globalization.* Bangkok: Committee on Bureaucratic System Reform.

Pollitt, Christopher (1993). *Managerialism and the Public Services: Cut or Cultural Change in the 1990s* (2nd ed.). Oxford: Blackwell Publishers.

Pongpaijit, Phasuk (2001). "The First Keynote on Inequality and Inequity in Access to Resources and Basic Public Services in Thailand, 2 February 2001, Chulalongkorn University and The Rockefeller Foundation. (http://www.cuurp.org/thaiequity/thaiequity4all.htmi)

Rojanawan, Jirawat (2003. *Political Reform and Bureaucratic System.* Bangkok: Phuengton Publishing.

Rondinelli, Dennis A. (2003). Promoting National Competitiveness in a Globalizing Economy: The State's Changing Roles. In Rondinelli,

Dennis A. and Cheema, G. Shabbir (eds.), *Reinventing Government for the Twenty-First Century: State Capacity in a Globalizing Society*. Kumarian Press.

Samudavanija, Chai-Anan (1976). *Politics and Thai Political Changes during B. E. 2411-2475 (1868-1932)*. Bangkok: Social Sciences Association of Thailand.

Schumacher, E. F. (1974). *Small is Beautiful: A Study of Economics as if People Mattered*. London: Blond & Briggs Ltd.

Streeten, Paul (1981). *Development Perspectives*. New York: St. Martin's Press.

Thanapornphan, Rangsan (1995). Politics of Income Distribution, *The Manager Daily*, January 13, 1995: 8. Bangkok (Thai Daily Newspaper).

Uniteds Nation Development Program (UNDP) (1992). *Human Development Report 1992*. New York: Oxford University Press.

Winpenny, James (1991). Environmental Values and their implications for Development, *Development Policy Review*, Vol. 9, No. 4 (December), pp.381-389.

World Commission on Environment and Development (WCED) (1987). *Our Common Future*. Oxford University Press.

Chapter 11 Reforming the Public Sector in Viet Nam

Jairo Acuña-Alfaro and Do Thanh Huyen*

Introduction[1)]

Public sector reform is a broad term in itself. In the context of a single-party ruled socialist state like Viet Nam, the public sector is inevitably large. It involves different actors, such as the political party and its arms, the executive, the judicial, the legislative, and the state economic sector—all of which take up a large part of public sector employment and public finance. It is as such not easy to examine how public sector reform fares with other ASEAN countries. With this in mind, this paper provides a brief overview of public sector reforms in Viet Nam and presents evidence-based assessments of outputs of these reform processes. It does not have the ambition to look into all different components of public sector reforms in Viet Nam, which has been embarked on over the course of 10 years along

* We would like to thank Dr. Đặng Ngọc Dinh and Dr. Đặng Hoàng Giang from the Centre for Community Support and Development Studies, and Dr. Edmund J. Maleskky and Dr. Pierre F. Landry, international expert on quantitaive methodology in measuring governancefor their inputs in thes joint research work. Thanks are also extended to Dr. Tran Thi Bich, for her advanced statistically support and analysis, some of which is presented in section two of this paper, in particular analysis around tables 1a, 1b and 1c.

the line with the Public Administration Reform Master Programme 2001-2010. Rather, the paper focuses on two components of administrative procedures and public service delivery reform.

A question that is worth exploring is what outputs public sector reform expects to achieve. The question is raised given the fact that the public sector covers a handful of components that involve both the government as controller, facilitator and/or provider of services and the society as intermediary and/or totality of end-users of the services. A conventional approach to examining public sector reform has been to look more at the former rather than the latter. In other words, the conventional approach cares more about which inputs governments invest in or plan to do in order to improve the platform and/or create means for better service delivery. Inputs in this case may involve, but are not limited to, *de jure* institutions, governmental structures, human resources for public employment, public finance, and public facilities and infrastructure for the public sector. The missing element is a demand-side evaluation of the performance of the public sector in order to examine whether different public sector reform arenas are delivering results and to inform future interventions for improvement.

This paper aims to fill in the discrepancy of information for policy interventions in two components of the public sector reform. The paper does that by presenting key findings from a large-scale survey that flips the coin to look at citizens' feedback on the performance of the public sector in Viet Nam.[1] We argue from the perspective that demand-side monitoring and evaluation of performance of the public sector will enable policy makers to understand better how policies are being implemented and evaluate benchmark performance against other sectors. We also show the usefulness of monitorable indicators to track the performance of public sector reforms.

This paper is divided into three sections. The first section presents a brief overview of public sector reforms in Viet Nam. The second section discusses key findings about the performance of the public sector from citizens' direct experiences from the Viet Nam Provincial Governance and Public Administration Performance Index (PAPI) 2010 and shows to what extent PAPI helps fill in the information gap to support future policy cycles. In this section, we discuss performance levels of provinces. This is done to test development impact of public sector reforms. The paper concludes by summarising key points made and gives some initial recommendations for enhancing public sector reforms in Viet Nam.

Background to Recent Attempts to Reform the Public Sector in Viet Nam

In the past three decades Viet Nam has engineered and implemented a remarkable economic and social transition that has put the country into the low middle-income category. The *doi moi* (renovation) reforms undertaken since the 1980's aimed to create a "socialist oriented market economy" by providing a less centrally managed framework for realizing human development objectives and improving people's living conditions. Through this reform process, Viet Nam made impressive gains in poverty reduction and substantially improved social development indicators at the aggregate levels, notably in health and education. With its socialist-oriented market economy approach, Viet Nam has witnessed the strong emergence of the private sector, GDP income per capita in 2010 at approximately 1,200USD,[2] and GDP per capita at purchase parity power (PPP) in 2010 at 3,150USD.[3]

Within this reform process, Viet Nam has also undertaken an ambitious and comprehensive set of public sector reforms. In the context of a single-party socialist state, the public sector is inevitably large. It covers different players, including the political party and its political-social arms, the executive, the judicial, the legislative, and the state economic sector. All of these players take up a considerably large proportion of total employment and state budget. Almost 5 million people, equivalent to 10 percent of Viet Nam's workforce are classified as state employees, with education taking up 32 percent, public administration 3 percent, and health & social work 7.7 percent.[4] The state budget for the public sector in 2010 is projected to be at approximately 38 percent (excluding expenditures for national defense, public security and special sectors).[5]

Improving the performance of such a large public system requires multi-fold reforms, including public administration reforms, judicial reforms, legislative reforms, as well as political reforms.[6] This paper focuses on public administration reform, the leverage for the executive branch or the government, to improve the performance of the public administration system within Viet Nam's specific political context.

It is widely understood that government agencies and, as an extension, the public administration system have the mandate to strive to provide the highest quality service possible. In this regards, the "New Public Service" international literature assumes that there is a complexity of issues ranging from sophisticated regulatory reform efforts to the simplest provision of administrative services (i.e. the registration of a birth, an identity card, a driving license, or a construction permit).[7] The range of administrative services that must be provided by different government agencies varies, and efforts are constantly made.

In this context, it is assumed that the following is a comprehensive list of elements to consider administrative service provision: (1) *convenience* referring to the extent to which public administrative procedures are easily accessible and available to citizens; (2) *security*, referring to the degree in which administrative services are provided in a way that makes citizens feel safe and confident using them; (3) *reliability*, understood as the extent to which public administrative procedures are provided correctly and timely; (4) *personal attention and problem solving approaches*, regarding the extent to which civil servants provide information to citizens and work with them to help meet their demands; (5) *fairness*, referring to the degree to which citizens believe the government services are provided in a way that is equitable to all; and (6) *fiscal responsibility*, referring to the degree to which citizens believe government agencies are providing services in a way that uses financial public resources responsibly and rationally.[8]

When discussing the public administration system in general, it is important to note that "the majority of employees of government are not paper-pushers one usually associates with public administration, but rather are responsible for delivering public services to the public."[9] In that sense, many civil servants and public employees at central and local levels are responsible for providing public services that go beyond policymaking, regulatory public administrative procedures or implementation of legal normative documentation. The ultimate objective of the constant reform and modernization of a public sector apparatus is to provide better quality public services to citizens.

Viet Nam has taken on board all those agendas and elements in its public sector reform. Take its broad Public Administration Reform (PAR) Master Plan for 2001-2010 as an example. The overall objective of the PAR Master Plan puts it that "*democratic, clean, strong, professionalized, modernized, effective and efficient public administration system which operates in line with the principle of the socialist State rule of law under the leadership of the Party; public cadres and civil servants will have appropriate capacities and ethical qualities able to respond to the requirements of the cause of national building and development."*[10] In other words, the PAR Master Program aimed to reorganize its governmental organizations structures, modernize and professionalize the civil service system, enhance public finance management mechanisms, simplify bureaucracy and reduce corruption and nepotism.

Improvements have been noticed in each of these areas as noted in the 2010 Government's review report of the 10 year implementation of the PAR Master Plan.[11] However, the speed and pace of reform is uneven, and little evidence exist in terms of to what extent these efforts have helped advance socio-economic development through delivering better quality public and administrative services to citizens. In addition, despite political rhetoric for PAR and high-level discourse on importance and levels of priority for public administration reforms, there has been a constant fluctuation in the budgetary allocation for the implementation of the PAR Master Programme. This has led to an unequal distribution of resources between government bodies and provinces and in turn affected performance levels across both the public administrative system and public services.

Reforming Public Administrative Procedures

A critical element of the comprehensive objective set forth in the 2001-2010 PAR MP for reform of the Public Administration System (PAS), is to "proactively serve the people in their everyday life." Through more than a decade of implementation, the Government of Viet Nam has made renewed calls to reform public administrative procedures, in particular related to the six elements listed above. In short, the reform arguably has had two key moments. The first moment started with the initial years of piloting and testing in the early 2000s and in a limited number of Southern provinces (Ho Chi Minh City in particular) embarked on an innovative reform effort called "One-stop Shop" (OSS). The OSS model was developed with the aim of providing citizens with a centralized place to process and acquire a wide range of administrative documents necessary for their daily lives. The OSS model was further rolled out and is currently being implemented on a nationwide scale. Some initial improvements were achieved. For instance, the OSS, to some extent, has greatly contributed to improving the efficiency and effectiveness of public administrative services and in line with some basic principles of service provision.

Subsequently, in a continued effort to improve the provision of public administrative procedures, the Government of Viet Nam embarked on the second wave of reforms.[12] In this second wave, or the ongoing comprehensive reform efforts to document, it carries out streamlining and simplifying public administrative procedures at the national and local levels. Having identified the places where public administrative procedures were bound to be handled physically, the reform turns towards the elimination of bureaucratic, cumbersome and inconvenient procedures.

On both reform efforts, several recent studies and reviews have been conducted to document progress and bottlenecks. For instance, reviews of implementation of the PAR MP have shown mixed results regarding these two areas.[13] Public administrative procedures that are directly related to citizens and businesses remain cumbersome because of the subsequent reemergence of "sub-procedures" despite several reviews and increasing government attempts to simplify procedures through the Project 30 since 2007.[14] Recent government stock-taking and review of existing public administrative procedures shows that more efforts are needed in the reform of public administrative procedures to ensure their simplicity, clarity and legality.[15] On OSS mechanisms, evaluated to have "initially changed" the relationship between public administrators and citizens and organizations, OSSs have been put in place "in a formalistic way" with poor coordination across and within OSSs, and poor sense of responsibility of civil servants in charge.[16] In addition, not all provinces have fully implemented OSSs at the commune level.

Although those pitfalls have been recognized internally by the PAS, there remains a gap in information about how citizens at large, experience interacting with the system in order to get their paperwork processed. In other words, it is worthwhile reviewing the OSS model and administrative procedure reform from the demand-side point of view with the hope to have more objective assessment of what the public administration system has provided to citizens, in line with the reforms. Some snapshots of citizens' experience in dealing with selective public administrative procedures will be presented in Section 2.

Reforming Public Service Delivery

Viet Nam, as a socialist state, by definition, is obligated to provide basic services to its citizens. Healthcare, education, basic infrastructure and public security are state priorities, since they are sectors that involve the most frequent and direct interaction between the state and citizens. Since economic reforms in the early 1990s, public service providers have received increasing autonomy with respect to finance and managerial aspects through increasing delegation of administration tasks[17] in the hope that the equilibrium approach to the provision of the public services of the central planning era would be removed to pave the way for improved service quality through increased revenues, larger savings, and stronger incentives for good performance in public service delivery agencies.[18] Although improvements resulting from the autonomy in the services have been noted,[19] they are unevenly distributed across provinces, administrative units and different population strata.[20]

In the health sector for instance, there are differences in terms of autonomy, and as a result, performance, when health facilities at different levels are compared. According to the Viet Nam Development Report 2010,[21] district level and lower level public health facilities do not seem to benefit evenly from increasing autonomy. This has resulted in poorer performance of district facilities since they can hardly afford providing high quality services and attracting qualified healthcare staff. Healthcare takers or users prefer going to central and provincial level facilities where they expect better service and this has resulted in constant overcapacity of higher level hospitals.[22]

Greater autonomy does not seem to provide a one-size-fit-all solution to good quality education for all either. Concerns about the quality of education institutions at different levels have been noted in the current Education Development Strategy. Problematic areas include overcrowded classes, unqualified teachers, extra-curriculular classes for additional compensation, poor school infrastructure and so forth. The 2009-2020 Education Development Strategy specifically notes some of these problems, stating that education quality has failed to meet the increasing needs for learning related to socio-economic development and that there is discrepancy between quantity and quality in the education sector.[23] It also reports that the number of classrooms that are either temporary or are torn-out venues accounts for 11 percent of the total education facilities as of 2007.

Reforms to Monitor Performance of Public Sector

The transition towards higher development levels for Viet Nam requires that the public administration system to create opportunities for citizens to engage effectively in the realization of their full potential and capabilities. This implies that there are differentiated roles in economic development that go beyond simply putting efforts in reducing poverty, but enlarge citizens' potentials to play increasingly more dynamic roles that are not fulfilled by economic growth alone. This poses a challenge for the next stage of public administration reforms in Viet Nam. The challenge is to move towards modernizing the public sector by ensuring a more active monitoring role for non-state actors in the evaluation of public administration performance, in addition to strengthening the public sector's responsibilities in implementation of policies.[24]

On the role of non-state actors in monitoring and evaluating the public sector performance, the PAR Master Programme, in addition to several laws and ordinances in Viet Nam, had provisions for citizens' monitoring and assessment of public services to combat corruption and promote transparency, efficiency and accountability of the public sector. Yet, when it comes to monitoring and assessing the overall public sector performance from the perspective of a citizen as an end-user there are neither regular mechanisms nor any instruments to gauge the perceptions and experiences of citizens and non-state actors regarding the performance and efficiency of the public sector at the provincial level.

Ongoing efforts at different levels are led by the Viet Nam Fatherland Front (VFF)[25] through its central role of supporting implementation of public policies and monitoring of public sector performance at local level.[26] In addition, different policy instruments mention the importance of monitoring and measuring the performance of the public sector and its reform progress.[27] Although the intention of all these policy frameworks is noted, implementation remains problematic. The following key questions may arise: How far has Viet Nam progressed in its public sector reform? What is the current situation? How is Viet Nam's public sector performing at the provincial level and how much still needs to be further reformed? What are some recommendations on how to continue addressing these reforms effectively, and what options are worth considering regarding future directions?

Answers to these questions are more manifold than is often assumed, as public sector reform is a complex process aimed at improving the public administration system and the provision of public services. To address them, instruments that receive feedback from citizens on the quality of provincial-level policy making, administration, and service delivery, and motivate provincial governments to improve all of these areas are relevant. A number of internationally designed tools have been introduced into Viet Nam to assess the performance of public administration and enable comparisons between countries. However, these instruments often do not reflect representative perceptions of end-users, and do not involve major local stakeholders in the assessment.[28] In order to achieve higher impact in the local context of Viet Nam, it is essential to move beyond these international instruments to ones that provide provincial governments with more objective and detailed information.

In line with these motivations, the incipient Viet Nam Governance and Public Administration Performance Index (PAPI) measures governance and public administration performance at the provincial level from the perspective of citizens as end-users of public and administrative services. PAPI, constructed on the basis of a rigorous nation-wide survey that involved face-to-face interviews with 5,568 citizens randomly selected from different demographic backgrounds,[29] highlights how citizens experience the outputs provided by public administration agencies in their localities. Apart from measuring citizens' own experiences in participating in policy making, implementation and oversight as their rights, PAPI looks into different aspects of citizens' accessibility to public and administrative services such as health care and education. While the government-led reviews and monitoring processes look more at the supply side (i.e. institutions that shape the environment for and provide public services for citizens), PAPI provides insights from the demand side. It reveals how citizens are participating and interacting with the public administration system and how they are being enabled to enhance their potentials and capabilities by doing so. Practical experience and empirical perspectives of citizens provide snapshots of what the public administration system in Viet Nam has or has not done for their end-users, who have too often been absent in most of policy implementation reviews.

As such, PAPI gives a metric to evaluate inherently multidimensional and mutually reinforcing processes of governance and public administration. It also allows different parties and stakeholders to take and digest information that affect them most directly in their everyday governance, since dimensions can be disentangled. Considering that governance and public administration reforms also involve the provision of public services in more efficient and effective ways, PAPI looks at six different dimensions of provincial governance and public administration, including: (1) participation at local levels; (2) transparency; (3) vertical accountability; (4) control of corruption; (5) public administrative procedures; and (6) public service delivery. While the dimensions are presented separately for ease of asssessment, they are both mutually inclusive and complementary.

While all of the six dimensions are interlinked in the public sector considering the aim, objectives and philosophy that PAPI is pursuing, this paper specifically presents findings of two dimensions, including: (1) Public Administrative Procedures, and (2) Public Service Delivery. These dimensions directly show how effective, efficient, responsive and accessible the public sector is in delivering services to citizens. While analysing these two dimensions, this paper shows the correlation between them and other four dimensions, considering the importance of the end purpose of the public sector that is participatory, transparent, accountable and free of corruption.[30]

A Demand-side View of Reforms in the Public Sector

The following section presents key findings from PAPI 2010 on two dimensions measuring the performance of the public sector: (1) public administrative procedures, and (2) public service delivery. The key findings are discussed within the context of Viet Nam's public sector that is mandated to deal with public administrative procedures and provide public services to citizens. This section also briefly depicts the correlation between these two dimensions with other dimensions of governance and the public administration that PAPI measures.

Public Administrative Procedures

On administrative procedure reform, PAPI looks into a selection of public administrative procedures that are considered important to citizens' lives, and how they are dealt with at the One-stop Shops (OSSs). PAPI studies citizens' direct experiencees in interacting with local public administrators to see how responsive they are to demands for simpler and friendlier public administrative procedures and improved delivery of administrative services.

Figure 1 provides a visual picture of aggregate provincial performance regarding citizens' experience on public administrative procedures. This figure highlights results from three types of public administrative services and procedures, including public notary services, construction permits and land use rights certificates (LURCs), and it also hints to the performance levels of provinces.

Figure 1. Performance Levels on Public Administrative Procedures

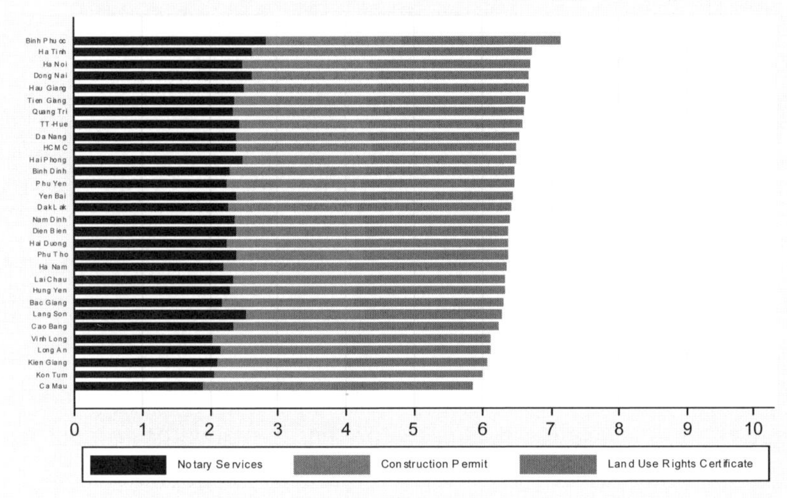

On the aggregates, Binh Phuoc stands out as the best performing province. But Binh Phuoc still has room for improvement, as very few of its citizens have used notary services or applied for construction permits. Ca Mau is at the bottom of the overall performance and the attributive factors are with its minimum scores in terms of total public notary quality and the number of respondents who applied for new LURC over the past three years (see Table 1 below).

The overall performance suggests that citizens' experiences with administrative procedures have the lowest variation across provinces. This low variance can be interpreted as depicting uniformity across provinces in dealing with public administrative procedures in the three services selected for monitoring. Moreover, the PAPI data makes clear that very few citizens actually utilize these procedures. Of the total number of respondents, 53 percent used notary services, 23.8 percent have applied for LURCs, and only 7 percent have applied for construction permits if national mean values are taken into

Table 1. Performance Indicators for Public Administrative Procedures

Dimension	Name of Indicator	PAPI Question	National Mean	National 90% CI	Provincial Scores	Score	Province
1) Notary Services	Respondent used notary service (%)	D501	53.23%	(52.14% 54.33%)	*Minimum* *Median* *Maximum*	22.89% 47.27% 80.49%	Kon Tum Binh Dinh/Dien Bien Binh Phuoc
1) Notary Services	Total notary quality score (Sum of 8 items)	D503	6.57	(6.48 6.65)	*Minimum* *Median* *Maximum*	1.80 6.81 7.59	Ca Mau Hau Giang/Quang Tri Ha Noi
2) Construction Permit	Respondent, who improved house in last 3 years, applied for construction permit (%)	D505	6.72%	(5.48% 7.96%)	*Minimum* *Median* *Maximum*	0.29% 4.25% 15.50%	Cao Bang TT-Hue/Ca Mau Quang Tri
2) Construction Permit	Total construction application quality score (Sum of 8 items)	D506	6.00	(5.96 6.03)	*Minimum* *Median* *Maximum*	4.16 5.84 7.80	Ha Noi Binh Dinh/Hung Yen Kon Tum
2) Construction Permit	If he/she applied for construction permit, respondent did not go to more than one window (%)	D505d	78.85%	(78.18% 79.52%)	*Minimum* *Median* *Maximum*	14.52% 77.84% 100.00%	Lang Son TT-Hue/Binh Phuoc Multiple Provinces
3) Land Use Rights Certificate (LURC)	Percentage of respondents who applied for new LURC in last 3 years (%)	D507	23.76%	(22.70% 24.81%)	*Minimum* *Median* *Maximum*	3.31% 20.68% 51.01%	Ca Mau Dong Nai/Hung Yen Binh Phuoc
3) Land Use Rights Certificate (LURC)	Total LURC application process quality (Sum of 8 items)	D508	5.51	(5.43 5.59)	*Minimum* *Median* *Maximum*	4.12 5.26 6.87	Lang Son Kien Giang/Binh Dinh HCMC
3) Land Use Rights Certificate (LURC)	If he/she applied for LURC, respondent did not go to more than one window (%)	D507c	78.85%	(78.18% 79.52%)	*Minimum* *Median* *Maximum*	14.52% 77.84% 100.00%	Lang Son TT-Hue/Binh Phuoc Multiple Provinces
3) Land Use Rights Certificate (LURC)	LURC application process has been simplified in past 3 year (% agree)	D509	77.56%	(76.63% 78.50%)	*Minimum* *Median* *Maximum*	45.78% 78.99% 95.94%	Cao Bang Ca Mau/Dak Lak Lang Son

account. Construction permits and LURCs are more frequently requested by citizens from middle-class or wealthy households.

Table 1 displays the individual indicators used for each one of the three subdimensions of administrative procedures. Each of the indicators in Table 1 were normalized to a 1-10 scale, with '10' representing the best outcome, and '1' representing the worst outcome observed in a Vietnamese province.[31] Each subdimension score represents the average score across the indicators thatcomprise it. Finally, the three subdimensions were averaged into an aggregate measure of public administrative procedures, so that each subdimension represents one third of the final score.

Public Notary Services

Public notary service is one area that has received a great deal of attention from public authorities, and significant steps have been taken to reform its provision. Therefore, we look to test whether or not it has become more accessible and friendlier to citizens, given the competition from privately provided notary services that are emerging as part of privatization[32] of notary services,[33] and given that commune/ward authorities have been delegated with a great deal of authority over this important job. As shown in Table 1, citizens' experiences in using public notary services that were made available in their localities. Citizens have an opportunity to give their feedback on the accessibility and quality of the service by giving their views based on their actual experience from visiting commune's or other public notary services, the clarity of procedures, publicity of fees, behaviour of civil servants receiving them, competence of civil servants serving them, paper work loads, notification of deadlines, receipt of results as appointed, and their overall satisfaction level of the provided service.[34]

Public notary services are a most commonly used service. Of the total surveyed respondents, 2,626 individuals used public notary services with 88.8 percent getting their documents notarized at the commune/ward level, and 11 percent going to district or provincial-level public notary services. This reflects the effect of decentralization of the services to the commune level as well as their privatization, which make them more available and accessible to citizens.

The star graphs in Figure 1a show the levels of agreement of respondents with statements about quality of services. Generally, public notary services are of good quality across 30 provinces with the exception of Ca Mau, Lai Chau and Dak Lak. Ca Mau is perceived as performing exceptionally poorly for this service, with its provincial score being only 1.80 for all eight sub-indicators measured. Hau Giang, Ca Mau's neighbor in the Mekong Delta, and Quang Tri, are close to the median score at 6.81. Ha Noi obtains the highest score of 7.59, with its star graph coming quite close to the perfect one (Figure 1a). This is possibly owing to the co-existence of privately-provided notary services that makes public notary services more convenient and accessible to citizens in Ha Noi.

Figure 1a. Measured Aspects of Quality of Public Notary Services(Branch Size= % of Respondents Agreeing to the Statements; Perfect =100%)

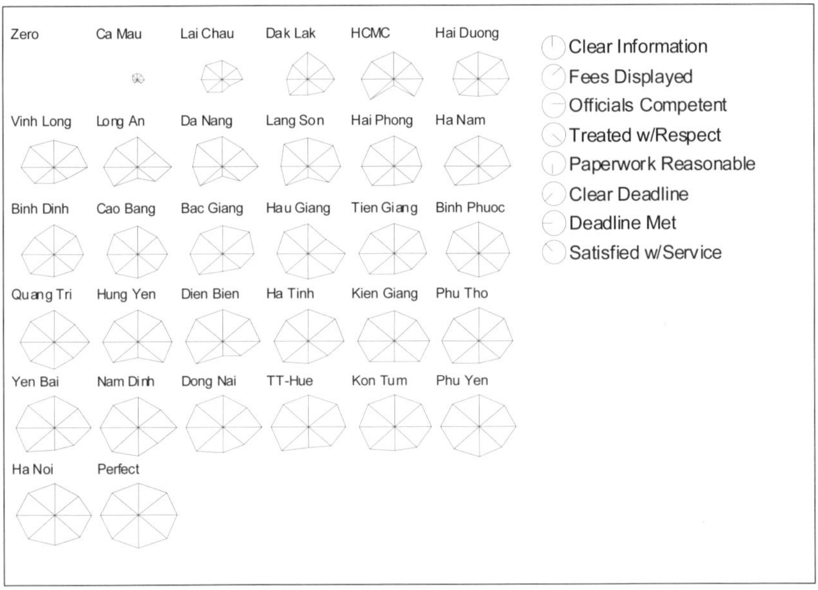

Meanwhile, Ho Chi Minh City tends to perform poorer in this service compared to Ha Noi despite the availability of private notary services. Unreasonable paperwork may have dragged Ho Chi Minh City down on the scale, making it just fare better than Ca Mau, Lai Chau and Dak Lak (Figure 1a). Respondents from Da Nang, Long An, Hung Yen and Thua Thien-Hue, also agreed that notary procedures are complicated in terms of paperwork. Notary fees, according to respondents from Hau Giang, are not publicly displayed.

Application Procedures for Construction Permits

According to the 2003 Law on Construction (No. 16/2003/QH11) and Government Decree 12/2009/ND-CP on Management of Construction Projects,[35] construction permits are required for construction project owners who wish to build new housing, expand or alter their existing property in more than a basic way (with some exceptions for citizens in remote, unplanned areas as described in Articles 19-21 of Decree No. 12/2009/ND-CP).[36] House construction and renovation are common for most citizens in both urban and rural areas in Viet Nam. With respect the effectiveness and efficiency of the offices where citizens go for their applications processed, respondents were queried about their views of the clarity of procedures, publicity of fees, behaviour of civil servants receiving them, competence of civil servants serving them, paperwork loads, notification of deadlines, receipt of results as appointed, and their overall satisfaction level of the provided service.

Very few respondents (7 percent) said they had applied for construction permits when building or renovating their houses over the past three years. The reasons why respondents did not apply for construction permits vary considerably. They either did not need them, for they did not build new houses or did major renovations during the time span asked, or they did not have finance to do so yet, or citizens in their localities were not required to get construction permits. More worrisome, only 35 percent of the 1,227 respondents who engaged in housing construction that would require a permit chose to apply for one. This implies something more problematic - that is citizens are actively avoiding using the service, either because of the complexity of the procedures, cost, waiting periods, or the limited effect of Decree No. 12/2009/ND-CP.

The star graphs in Figure 1b show the levels of agreement

of respondents with given statements designed for an examination of the total quality of the service. Among those who applied for construction permits, concerns were heard from big cities like Ha Noi, Hai Phong, Da Nang and Thua Thien-Hue. Ho Chi Minh City does a little better overall, but not regarding unnecessary paperwork, which was seen as highly problematic. The level of satisfaction with the overall quality is also low in rural provinces, such as Yen Bai and Dak Lak. Ca Mau again sees almost zero agreement to the statement that the paperwork for construction permits is reasonable. Contrary to Ha Noi, which scores minimum on the total quality in this service (4.16), Kon Tum gets the maximum score on this indicator (7.80), possibly because the demand for construction permits in the Central Highland province is low, and such as, quicker administrative services can be provided.

Figure 1b. Assessment of Construction Permit Application Procedures (Branch Size= % of respondents agreeing to the statements; Perfect =100%)

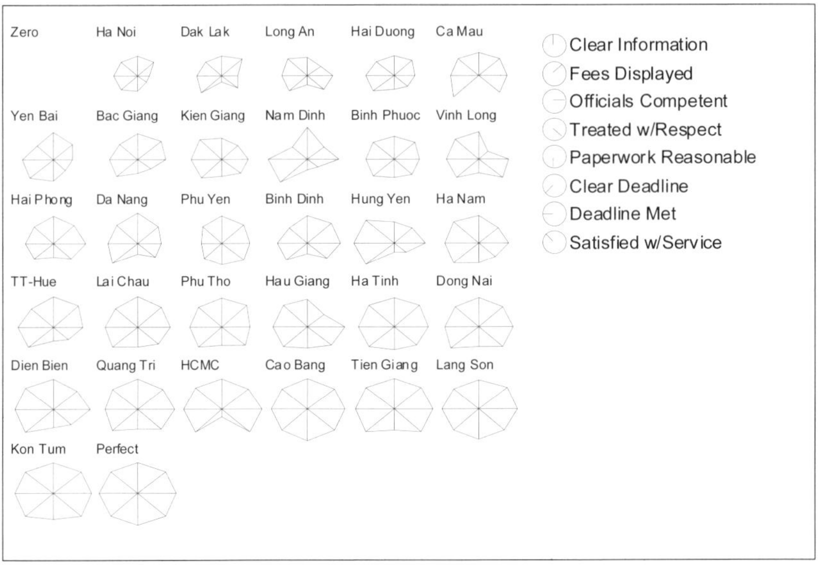

Application Procedures for Land Use Rights Certificates (LURC)

A LURC, by definition in the 2003 Land Law (No. 13/2003/QH11), is the certification that is issued by a competent state agency and granted to a land user in order to protect the legitimate rights and benefits of land users in the context of collective land ownership under uniform state management of land. Owners of LURCs have the right to sell, exchange, and mortgage the property for bank loans. More importantly, LURCs provide citizens with the comfort in knowing that their homes will not be taken from them without a legitimate public interest motivation and without just compensation.

As a result, international evidence has shown that citizens of any income strata with an enforceable land title are more likely to invest in home improvements, small businesses, and even in the education of their children.[37]

With their importance in definition of citizens' ability to enjoy the rights and benefit of land-use, LURCs are constantly the subject of discussion, especially in terms of how accessible they are to citizens from different geographical locations of administrative units (i.e. urban, rural and mountainous areas).

Data show that application for LURCs is not popular for the whole population sample, revealing the nature of low frequency of such events occuring in one's lifetime or at the household level. The percentage of respondents who applied for new or renewed LURCs over the past three years is at approximately 23.8 percent (see Table 1 above).

The total LURCs application process quality has a slight difference between minimum, median and maximum scores. Lang Son scored the minimum at 4.12, while Ho Chi Minh City scored the maximum at 6.87. Provinces like Kien Giang and Binh Dinh performed at the median level on this indicator. When asked if they had to go to more than one window in order to apply for new LURCs, 78.85 percent of respondents that experienced this service said they did not. However, there is a large variation among provinces. The number of respondents who did not have to go to more than one window ranges from 14.5 percent in Lang Son to 100 percent in Ho Chi Minh City.

The star graphs in Figure 1c show in a greater detail different levels of agreement of respondents with statements about those aspects. Respondents in Lang Son, Phu Tho, Binh Phuoc, Hai Phong and Ha Noi were not satisfied with the LURC application procedures. In provinces with bigger stars, such as Da Nang, Ho Chi Minh City, Hai Duong, Thua Thien-Hue and Hau Giang, respondents experienced that the procedures require too much paperwork. Other problems that surveyed provinces need to pay attention to include behaviours of civil servants receiving citizens, deadlines for LURCs to be granted, and publicity of

Figure 1c. Assessment of LURCs Application Procedures (Branch Size= % of Respondents Agreeing to the Statements in the Legend; Perfect =100%)

application fees.

We also look at the correlation between the satisfaction of respondents as an indicator for citizens'assessment of the total quality of application procedures and demographic characteristics of respondents. Table 1a below documents the estimated probit model where the dependent variable is citizens' satisfaction.[38]

Table 1a. Probability of Satisfaction when using LURCs Procedures

Dependent variable: satisfaction *Estimation method: binomial probit*			
		Coefficient	Std. Err.
Number of observations	*1052*		
Male		-0.089	0.093
Urban location		-0.013	0.105
Ethnicity: Kinh		0.018	0.162
Work in the government sector		-0.106	0.123
Education level			
Primary		-0.378*	0.219
Secondary		-0.269	0.214
High school		-0.485**	0.218
College and above		-0.491**	0.241
Perceived economic condition			
Normal		0.253*	0.150
Good		0.093	0.178
Hanoi		-0.420**	0.212
Ho Chi Minh City		-0.291	0.234
Intercept		1.201	0.255
Pseudo R-squared		*0.02*	
Log likelihood		*-482.66*	
LR Chi^2		*22.36*	

Note: '***' '**', '*' are significant at 1%, 5% and 10%, respectively.

Results in Table 1a show that, with the exception of people with secondary education, educated people are less satisfied with the LURCs procedures. Furthermore, Hanoi citizens are less satisfied with the service compared to citizens in other provinces. Specifically, a female educated Hanoian who is in normal economic condition and works in the private or foreign sectors has 16 percentage points less satisfaction than citizens with the same condition in other provinces. Contrarily, living in Ho Chi Minh City does not make the satisfaction with the service different from other provinces. Results from Table 1a also reveal that people with normal economic condition are more satisfied than those in bad economic condition holding other factors constant.

Factor analysis of citizens' experiences with different quality criteria of the public administrative services and procedures also reveals interesting findings. As depicted in Table 1b, we measured eight aspects of the quality of the administrative services. These aspects are reduced to one main dimension (see Eigenvalue column–those with Eigen value>=1 are kept as main dimensions). We name this dimension as satisfaction with the service or performance level of the service.

The factor analysis results in Table 1c reveal that citizens' satisfaction with the performance of the administrative services is determined by the reliability of administrative service provision (timeliness in service delivery), as well as problem solving (or competence) and fairness (or good attitude) of civil servants when providing the services.

In particular, on public notary service, Table 1c shows that receiving clear deadline and getting the result within deadline, overall satisfaction, clear information and good attitude from officials contribute the most to service users' satisfaction with public notary service. Similarly, good application procedures and service for construction permits require five factors, classified

Tables 1b. Factors Determining citizens' Satisfaction with Public Notary Service, Construction Permits and Land use Rights Certificates (LURCs)

Factors	Factor Description	Public Notary Service				Procedures on Application for Construction Permits				Procedures on Application for LURCs			
		Eigen value	Differ-ence	Propor-tion	Cumu lative	Eigen value	Differe-nce	Propor-rtion	Cumula-tive	Eigenv alue	Differ-ence	Propor-tion	Cumul-ative
Factor 1	Clear information about the procedures was available.	5.83746	5.70816	1.0009	1.0009	2.33995	1.90982	0.9583	0.9583	2.51708	1.87013	0.9193	0.09193
Factor 2	The amount I would have to pay in fees for the service was publicly displayed.	0.12930	0.06823	0.0222	1.0231	0.43014	0.16310	0.1762	1.1345	0.64695	0.47960	0.2363	1.1556
Factor 3	The officials were competent.	0.06107	0.07426	0.0105	1.0335	0.26704	0.24721	0.1094	1.2438	0.16735	0.15406	0.0611	1.2167
Factor 4	The officials treated me with respect	-0.01319	0.01055	-0.0023	1.0313	0.01982	0.05463	0.0081	1.2520	0.01329	0.07578	0.0049	1.2216
Factor 5	The procedure required too much paperwork.	-0.02374	0.0557	-0.0041	1.0272	-0.03480	0.07975	-0.0143	1.2377	-0.06249	0.08094	-0.0228	1.1987
Factor 6	I was provided with a clear deadline by which the service would be performed.	-0.02931	0.01347	-0.0050	1.0222	-0.11455	0.06434	-0.0469	1.1908	-0.14342	0.04999	-0.0524	1.1464
Factor 7	The service was performed within the stated deadline.	-0.04278	0.04373	-0.0073	1.0148	-0.17888	0.10808	-0.07133	1.1175	-0.19341	0.01391	-0.0706	1.0757
Factor 8	I am satisfied with the service I received.	-0.08651	-	-0.0148	1.0000	-0.28697	-	-0.1175	1.0000	-020732	-	-0.0757	1.0000

Note: LR test: independent vs. saturated: chi2(28) = 2.5e+04 Prob>chi2 = 0.0000

Tables 1c. Variables Determining Citizens' Satisfaction with Public Notary Service, Construction Permits and Land use Rights Certificates (LURCs)

Variables	Public Notary Service				Procedures on Application for Construction Permits					Procedures on Application for LURCs				
	Factor 1	Factor 2	Factor 3	Unique-ness	Factor 1	Factor 2	Factor 3	Factor 4	Unique-ness	Factor 1	Factor 2	Factor 3	Factor 4	Uniqu-eness
a. Clear information about the procedures was available.	0.8781	0.0206	-0.1418	0.2085	0.4096	0.1162	-0.2486	0.0221	0.7564	0.4132	0.883	0.2442	-0.0014	0.7341
b. The amount I would have to pay in fees for the service was publicly displayed.	0.7611	0.0892	0.0129	0.4127	0.4151	0.1573	-0.2491	0.0730	0.7355	0.4549	0.0005	0.2709	0.0034	0.7197
c. The officials were competent.	0.8665	0.1292	-0.0330	0.2315	0.6340	0.2225	0.2272	0.0199	0.4965	0.5256	0.4360	-0.0456	-0.0093	0.5315
d. The officials treated me with respect	0.5582	0.1529	0.1458	0.6438	0.5011	0.3361	0.2006	-0.0235	0.5952	0.5415	0.3713	-0.1207	0.0265	0.5536
f. The procedure required too much paperwork.	0.8529	0.0714	0.0647	0.2633	-01581	-0.1205	0.1845	0.1076	0.9149	-0.1226	-0.0921	0.0315	0.1100	0.9634
g. I was provided with a clear deadline by which the service wouldbe performed.	0.9653	-0.1830	0.0698	0.0298	0.5663	-0.3102	0.0904	0.0183	0.5746	0.6129	-0.3894	0.0063	-0.0035	0.4727
f. The service was performed within the stated deadline.	0.9630	-0.2032	0.0257	0.0307	0.6922	-0.3422	0.0099	-0.0204	0.4032	0.7678	-0.3510	-0.0634	-0.0100	0.2831
h. I am satisfied with the service I received.	0.9156	0.0308	-0.0933	0.1520	0.7225	-0.0399	-0.0945	-0.0270	0.4667	0.7680	-0.0149	-0.1122	0.0168	0.3971

Note: Scores above 0.5 demonstrate the statistical significance of the variable by their decreasing importance order as overall satisfaction, getting the result within deadline, good attitude from officials, receiving clear deadline, and competence of official. On LURC application procedures, Table 1c tells us that the main dimension (satisfaction of service users or performance of the service) is contributed by the following factors (classified by their decreasing importance order): overall satisfaction, getting the result within deadline, receiving clear deadline, competence of officials, and good attitude from officials.

We note that public administrative services and procedures other than notary service, construction permits and LURCs (e.g. birth certificates, death certificates, identification cards, marriage certificates, vehicle licenses, and so forth) are also critical to citizens. However, these procedures were not included in the PAPI survey because application for such certificates rarely occurs within an individual's life, and may not take place with the frequency required to assess improved performance over time. Moreover, because long and repetitive questionnaires can damage response rates, and the quality of responses, it was important to provide a parsimonious instrument that focused primarily on a selectived number of procedures.

Public Service Delivery

PAPI focuses on understanding citizens' experiences in using and benefiting from these services, in order to measure how authorities are responsive to citizens' most basic needs and demands. Respondents were queried regarding their experiences with accessibility and availability of basic public services in their communes, wards and/or provinces according to the national level policy frameworks which governs these services. For instance, this Dimension measures whether or not schooling of children at public primary schools is tuition-free as required by the Law on Universalisation of Primary Education in 1991.

Public health care is a critical basic service that any state must provide to its citizens. Four areas selected for analysis include overall accessibility to public health insurance; poor households' access to subsidized health insurance; availability of free medical checks for children under six years old; and, the overall quality of public hospitals at the district level. Given that social security policies are in place to facilitate delivery of those services, feedback from the society through means of media and everyday conversations reveals a mixed picture of the real effect of these policies.

Public health insurance, for instance, has been frequently reflected as one of the most problematic areas in public health. The secondary source of data covered by key news outlets in 2008 and 2009 shows that the poor and the disadvantaged with health insurance tend to be more vulnerable to biased treatment at public hospitals.[39]

On the quality of public hospitals at the district level, a criteria of seven "good-practices" were used, including patients not sharing beds, electric fans made available in sick-rooms, clean rest rooms, regular checkups, patients treated with respect, reasonable expenses, and reasonable waiting periods. These are examined by asking respondents about their direct experience when going to district public hospitals or having beloved people go to district public hospitals for checkups or treatment. Measurements are limited to those who had direct experience with the service, so that the indicators reflect direct experience and are most reliable. In addition, respondents were also asked if they are aware of the policy of free healthcare for children under six years old, to accommodate concerns about whether or not this vital policy is well-known by the general public.

Based on the understanding that primary education for all has been effective in Viet Nam for over two decades,[40] the overall quality of public primary education in order to measure the minimum standards of facilities (and teaching staff) for satisfactory primary education is examined. Because universal lower-secondary education for children between the ages of 11 to 18 years old has been effective since 2001,[41] the focus is framed within the primary school education, as not every commune/ward has its own lower-secondary school and in some localities lower secondary schools are shared by separate commune/ward units.[42]

Basic infrastructure is a straight forward subdimension in its own right as it looks at household accessibility to electricity, the quality of roads nearest to the house, the frequency of garbage pickups in residential groups, and the quality of drinking water. By asking respondents about the availability and quality of those public services, PAPI seeks to understand the contribution of local government to the infrastructure which affects citizens' fundamental living conditions.

Law and order at the residential level means the level of safety that citizens experience in everyday life. In this aspect, respondents were asked if they have experienced theft of vehicles (including cars, motorbikes, canoes, etc.), pick-pocketing, house break-in's and violence committed by robbers in the past one year. This sub-dimension aims at measuring whether fears about safety affect the quality of citizens' lives.

Figure 2 reveals the final scores, while Table 2 shows the indicators used to make the assessment. Figure 4 depicts an interesting but unsurprising finding from the collected data. Big cities tend to perform better in public service delivery, evident from national-level municipalities including Hai Phong, Da Nang, Ho Chi Minh City among the top ten provinces. However, from this group Ha Noi lags behind the other national-level municipalities. Its scores are significantly below its peers, implying that the difference is not the result of random chance and therefore reveals fundamental dissatisfaction with public service delivery among its citizens. Provinces that are far from the these big urban centres tend to perform worse, mainly due to poorer basic infrastructure, suggesting that in many areas rural residents do not have access to tap water or daily garbage collection.

Figure 2. Performance Levels on Public Services Delivery

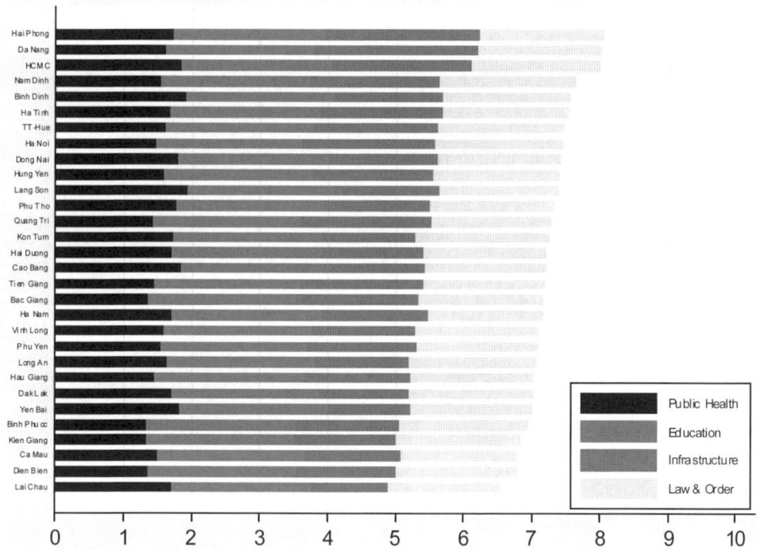

There seems to be little regional difference evident from the data that provinces from different regions (i.e. northern, central and southern) are distributed across the scale. The difference in performance is more visible when comparing provinces that are similar in terms of economic and geographical conditions (i.e. northern mountainous provinces like Lang Son, Cao Bang, Yen Bai and Lai Chau). The large difference between the top and bottom provinces is attributed to variance in the scores on infrastructure and law and order subdimensions. In a nutshell, poorer provinces may need to make more efforts in realizing national policies and provision of better public services and facilities for their citizens.

Table 2. Performance Indicators for Public Service Delivery

Dimension	Name of Indicator	PAPI Question	National Mean	National 90% CI	Provincial Scores	Score	Province
1) Education	Total quality of education (Sum of 8 items)	D607	4.63	(4.59 4.66)	*Minimum* *Median* *Maximum*	3.70 4.59 5.14	Lang Son Tien Giang/Ha Tinh Yen Bai
1) Education	Distance from home to nearest primary school (km)	D609b	1.23	(1.19 1.27)	*Minimum* *Median* *Maximum*	0.43 1.19 4.24	Ha Tinh Ca Mau/Dien Bien Lai Chau
2) Public Health	Total quality of hospitals (Sum of 7 items)	D605	5.13	(5.07 5.19)	*Minimum* *Median* *Maximum*	4.23 5.17 5.89	Da Nang Hung Yen/Binh Phuoc Long An
2) Public Health	Respondents with health insurance (%)	D601	53.29%	(51.76% 54.81%)	*Minimum* *Median* *Maximum*	29.82% 41.94% 95.91%	Ha Nam Phu Tho/Quang Tri Cao Bang
2) Public Health	Do poor households receive subsidized health insurance? (% Yes)	D602	74.16%	(72.84% 75.49%)	*Minimum* *Median* *Maximum*	53.57% 72.63% 91.86%	Kien Giang TT-Hue/Ca Mau Phu Tho
2) Public Health	Are medical checks for children under 6 free? (% Yes)?	D603	87.44%	(86.39% 88.49%)	*Minimum* *Median* *Maximum*	61.98% 85.64% 97.79%	Hau Giang Nam Dinh/Hung Yen Ha Tinh
3) Infrastructure	Households with electricity (%)	D610	97.05%	(96.55% 97.56%)	*Minimum* *Median* *Maximum*	33.03% 98.12% 100.00%	Lai Chau Dak Lak/Lang Son Ha Noi/HCMC/Da Nang
3) Infrastructure	Quality of road nearest to house (1. Dirt; 2. Gravel; 3. Concrete; 4. Paved)	D611	2.82	(2.78 2.87)	*Minimum* *Median* *Maximum*	1.75 2.77 3.84	Lai Chau Ca Mau/Kien Giang Hai Phong
3) Infrastructure	Frequency of garbage pick-up (0. Never to 5. Every Day)	D612b	1.97	(1.91 2.03)	*Minimum* *Median* *Maximum*	0.17 1.15 3.81	Ca Mau Ha Nam/TT-Hue Da Nang
3) Infrastructure	Respondents drinking tap water in home as primary drinking water (%)	D613	37.09%	(34.76% 39.42%)	*Minimum* *Median* *Maximum*	3.79% 24.83% 97.94%	Kon Tum Hau Giang/Ha Tinh Da Nang
3) Infrastructure	Respondents drinking rain or river water as primary source (%)	D613	6.27%	(4.92% 7.62%)	*Minimum* *Median* *Maximum*	0.00% 2.24% 33.79%	Multiple Provinces Hai Phong/Lang Son Hai Duong
4) Law & Order	Crimes experienced in last year by respondents (% vehicle theft, pick-pocket, break-in, violence)	D511a-D511d	17.42%	(15.87% 18.97%)	*Minimum* *Median* *Maximum*	1.52% 18.45% 50.54%	Kien Giang Hai Duong/Hai Phong Ha Nam
4) Law & Order	Assessment of safety in village (0 Very Unsafe; 3 Very Safe)	D510	2.19	(2.17 2.21)	*Minimum* *Median* *Maximum*	1.71 2.11 2.68	Lai Chau Hai Duong/Hung Yen Kon Tum
4) Law & Order	Safety improvement in past 3 years (% Agree)	D510-D510a	0.09	(0.08 0.10)	*Minimum* *Median* *Maximum*	-0.11 0.07 0.31	Ha Nam Lai Chau/Phu Tho Hung Yen

Public Healthcare

The performance of public healthcare includes insurance for general citizens and for the poor, the overall quality of district hospitals and free medical checks for children under six. Respondents were asked about their direct experience in using the services. Results show that 52 percent of respondents had direct experience with a public hospital in the past year. Of those, 64 percent accompanied a close household member to the hospital, while 36 percent were themselves treated.

Table 2 above shows large variation in people's access to public health insurance, with provincial scores ranging from only 29.82 percent (of the number of respondents with public health insurance) in Ha Nam to as high as 95.9 percent in Cao Bang. As high as 74 percent of the sampled population said that poor households receive subsidised health insurance in their respective communes/wards, while there is a big difference between Kien Giang (53.57 percent) and Phu Tho (91.86 percent). Regarding under six children's access to free health checkups, data shows a national mean score of 87.44 percent with small 90 percent confidence intervals. More than 60 percent of respondents asked in Hau Giang (minimum) and more than 97 percent in Ha Tinh (maximum) confirmed that the policy is in effect in respective provinces.

Figure 2a. Citizens' Assessment of District Public Hospitals (Branch Size= % of Respondents Agreeing to the Statements in the Legend; Perfect =100%)

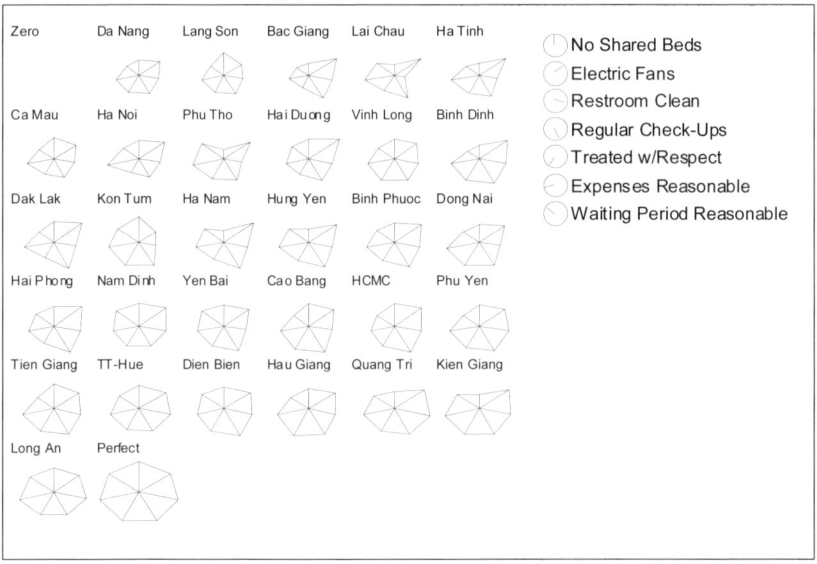

On quality of district hospitals, Figure 2a above reveals that provinces score differently in those indicators. The diamonds show levels of agreement of respondents with health care in district/ward public hospitals. Municipalities (in particular Da Nang and Ha Noi) do not score high on this indicator. The province of Long An seems to fare better than other provinces in all criteria measured. Figure 2a also tends to confirm public observation that patients have to share beds at public hospitals within districts. Another common observation from respondents is that health care expenses in district hospitals and waiting times are not reasonable and the quality of sick-rooms remains poor. This may open up a research question for the health sector to study why sharing beds is a problem in district hospitals, even in the least expected incidences like Lai Chau, Ha Nam and Hung Yen.

Public Primary Education

When compared with the national mean at 4.63 (see Table 2 above), most provinces perform at a modest level in their delivery of public primary education in general. Yen Bai tends to perform the best among the 30 provinces, scoring at 5.15 at provincial scores on the overall quality of primary education, while Lang Son scored poorly, 3.70.

If examined from specific criteria for measuring the quality (Figure 2b),[43] there seems to be large variations in terms of performance in provinces. Infrastructure of public primary schools and quality of teachers are generally good. However, teachers tend to favour school children participating in extra classes, and classes remain crowded in general. Also, provinces need to look into the problems of informal payments and bribery to teachers since these phenomena are reflected regardless of provinces being urban, rural, or mountainous.

Data also show that the mean distance from home to the nearest primary schools is at 1.23 km across provinces, reasonable for primary school children to walk to class. However, there is a large variation between mountainous provinces and lowland ones. In Ha Tinh, public primary schools are at 0.4 km on the average in sampled communes/wards, while those in Lai Chau are at over 4 km way. Geographical conditions need to be taken into account when comparing provinces regarding this indicator.

Figure 2b. Citizens' Assessment of Public Primary Schools (Branch Size= % of Respondents Agreeing to the Statements in the Legend; Perfect =100%)

Infrastructure

Infrastructure attributes greatly to the difference across provinces. The reason is that there is a large variance between urban and rural provinces in terms of access to electricity, paved roads, frequency of garbage pickups and access to tap water. Table 2 above reveals the differences in provincial scores in these areas. For instance, for households with electricity, only 33 percent of respondents in Lai Chau said they have access to electricity while the percentage in Ha Noi, Ho Chi Minh City, and Da Nang equals 100 percent. The quality of roads nearest to houses also hints difference between urban and rural provinces. In Lai Chau, there are more dirt and gravel roads, while in Hai Phong respondents use exclusively paved roads. On the frequency of garbage collection services, Da Nang's citizens stands far better than other provinces with most residents reporting garbage collection every day, compared to almost zero frequency in Ca Mau.

On drinking water, 37 percent of the whole sampled population said they get access to tap water in home as primary source of drinking water, as opposed to 6.27 percent to rain or river water. Only 3.79 percent of surveyed respondents in Kon Tum said they have tap water for drinking, against 97.94 percent in Da Nang.

Figure 2c. Experience with Petty Corruption in Accessing Public Services (Branch Size= % of Respondents who Claim Type DOES NOT take Place; Perfect =100%)

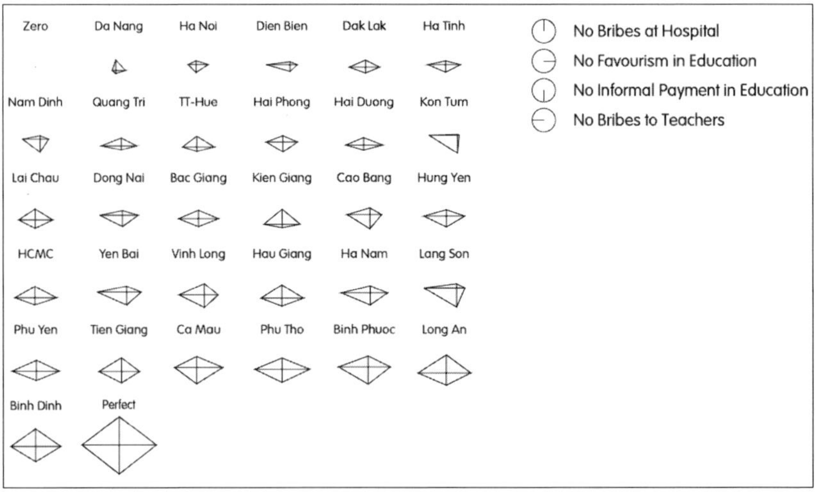

We also look at the fairness in public service delivery. Figure 2c depicts that no province comes close to matching the perfect score of denials on all indicators. There is a significantly high variance across provincial units on these questions. Respondents in Binh Dinh, Long An, and Binh Phuoc have over half of their respondents denying the existence these corrupt activities on every indicator. On the other hand, Da Nang, Ha Noi, and Dien Bien have very few respondents denying the existence of informal fees when accessing health and education services. Da Nang has particularly problematic scores in the area of education, where only 20 percent of respondents deny paying extra to primary education institutions and give bribes to teachers.

Conclusions

Viet Nam's public sector will continue playing a key role in narrowing the rich-poor gap and ensuring just provision of services to all citizens beyond the alleviation brought about directly by economic growth itself. Research findings presented in this paper have shown evidence of rich-poor gaps between people with different demographic backgrounds. Poorer performing provinces are those with high density of ethnic minority people and with more difficult geo-economic conditions. Therefore, development of institutions and processes that are more responsive to the needs of ordinary citizens, including the poor and the disadvantaged, remains a top priority for Viet Nam in its transition towards a higher development level.

The way ahead to overall public sector reforms in Viet Nam is to focus on improving the performance of the public sector through professionalization and modernisation. Areas of priority for reform in the public sector, therefore, include: (1) competence and ethics of civil servants and public employees; (2) responsiveness and reliability of public services, apart from convenience; (3) transparency of the public sector to ensure fairness to every end-user; (4) increasing accountability towards end-users using physical and electronic means (one-stop shop facilities and local government portals); and, (5) shaping the public sector into a convenient, responsive institution, seen as an essential bridge between government and society.

As findings from PAPI suggest, citizens' satisfaction with the public administrative area of the public sector is more likely to be determined by the reliability of administrative service provision, competence of public service providers, and behaviours of civil servants in providing services. This poses new challenges for a modern, professional public administration system in Viet Nam, other than physical facilities in place to service end-users like the One-stop Shops. With respect to public services, including health care and education, more work needs to be done at both national and provincial levels to improve the equality in access and the quality of these critical basic services for all citizens. Variances across provinces hint areas where national and provincial governments need significant improvement and where they can do better.

The transition towards a middle-income country also implies a shift in the relationship between the public sector and citizens in the way they interact with each other. Understanding each other's requirements and needs is essential in any smooth interaction given new social, economic and institutional challenges. To reform in this direction, the public sector needs to be fed with evidence-based information from different sources rather than relying its own anecdotal self-assessments. For the public sector to service them better, citizens require being engaged in monitoring the performance of the public sector by giving feedback on the quality of the services they receive. Demand-side monitoring tools that adopt a rigorous, scientific and objective methodology are therefore necessary as they help the public sector detect and leverage areas for change.

Notes

1) The Viet Nam Provincial Governance and Public Administration Performance Index (PAPI) is an incipient and ongoing joint collaboration partnership between the Center for Community Support Development Studies (CECODES, a Vietnamese NGO under the Viet Nam Union of Science and Technology Association, VUSTA), the Department of Democracy and Law and the Center for Theory Works at the Viet Nam Fatherland Front (VFF), and the United Nations Development Programme (UNDP). Fieldwork was possible thanks to the facilitation and collaboration of the VFF district, commune/ward and local level chapters. For detailed presentation and analysis of PAPI, see CECODES, VFF & UNDP (2011). The Viet Nam Provincial Governance and Public Administration Performance Index (PAPI): Measuring citizens' experiences. Hanoi, also available at www.papi.vn.
2) According to official data from the General Statistics Office in 2010.
3) According to Economic Intelligence Unit data in July 2011.
4) According to the Viet Nam Labour Force Survey conducted in 2009.
5) Projected state budget expenditure by sector in 2010 for the public sector, excluding that for national defence, public security and special sectors, issued as an annex for Decision 3234/QD-BTC dated 21 December 2010 by the Minister of the Ministry of Finance on publicizing state budget estimates for 2010.
6) Viet Nam is implementing different sectoral reforms in the public sector. Public administration reform has completed its first 10-year phase (see Decision 136/2001/QD-TTg dated September 17, 2001 deciding the Overall Program on State Administrative Reform in the 2001-2010 period). Judicial reform started in 2005 upon Resolution No. 49-NQ/TW dated June 2, 2005 of the Politburo of the Communist Party of Viet Nam on the Strategy on Judicial Reform towards 2020. State owned enterprise reform has been in its process for two decades since 1990 upon Decision No. 143/HDBT of the Ministers Council on May 10, 1990 and later legislated in the Law on Enterprises 2005.
7) For a discussion on the "New Public Service" literature see Denhardt and Denhardt (2007) and Peters and Pierre (eds.) (2007).
8) Based on Denhardt and Denhardt (2007), p. 61.
9) Peters and Pierre (2007), p. 1.
10) The overall objective of the PAR Master Programme as stipulated in Decision 136/2001/QD-TTg (September 17, 2001) Overall Program on State Administrative Reform in the 2001-2010 period.
11) See Ministry of Home Affaires of Viet Nam (2010).
12) Decision No. 93/2007/QĐ-TTg dated 22/6/2007 of the Prime Minister on the One-stop Shops and Decision No. 94/2006/QĐ-TTg dated 27/4/2006 of the Prime Minister on Action Plan for Public Administration Reform for the period of 2006-2010. Article 17 of Regulation on Implementation of One-stop Shop Mechanism, an enclosure to Decision 181/2003/QĐ-TTg of the Prime Minister requesting for implementation at the provincial and district levels in January 2004,

and at the commune level in January 2005.

13) See MOHA (2010).

14) The Project on Simplification of Administrative Procedures in All State Management Areas for the period of 2007-2010, better known as Project 30, was approved for implementation under Decision 30/QĐ-TTg dated January 10, 2007.

15) It is reported by the Government that after the first phase of stock-taking and review of administrative procedures of the Project 30, over 5,500 administrative procedures (AP) have been checked, 453 AP have been requested to be removed, 3,749 are proposed to be revised, 288 APs are proposed to be replaced so as to create more favorable conditions for citizens and enterprises (See MOHA, 2010).

16) Painter et al. (2009), pp. 344-348 presents a discussion of the mid-term review of the implementation of the PAR Master Programme 2001-2010., Also, see MOHA (2010) most recently highlighting the same deficiencies.

17) See Resolution No. 08/2004/NQ-CP of the Government of Viet Nam on continued delegation of state management functions from the central government to provincial government

18) See Government Decree No. 71/2003/ND-CP on delegation of tasks on administration of staffing quotas in public administration agencies and public service delivery agencies.

19) A review of delegation of management tasks by Ha Noi People's Committee shows a mixed picture of what have and have not been achieved through the exercise (See Ha Noi Moi Online (17/11/2010), Phân cãả khẩụẵậồộệảegation of Administration Tasks: Resolving problems, increasing synergy and effectiveness. URL: http://www.hanoimoi.com.vn/newsdetail/Kinh-te/399693/phan-cap-quan-ly-khac-phuc-bat-cap-tang-dong-bo-hieu-qua.htm[Accessed on 01/12/2010])

20) See World Bank (2009), pp. 64-65.

21) Ibid.

22) A research conducted in six central level hospitals in Ha Noi, Thua Thien-Hue and Ho Chi Minh City in 2008 found that bed occupation rates in these provinces range between 150 and 200 percent while each medical doctor in these facilities has to check from 70-130 patients a day and spends barely nine minutes for each patient on average (see Xuyen, N. T. and Cuong, L. Q. (2008).

23) See Government of Viet Nam (2009).

24) See Acuña-Alfaro (ed.). (2009), p. 40.

25) The Vietnamese Fatherland Front (VFF), founded in 1977, is a largest politico-social organisation that consists of many mass organisations in Vietnam. The Front and its member organisations are described as "the political base of people's power." It is intended to have a significant role in the society, promoting "national solidarity" and "unity of mindsin political and spiritual matters." Many of the government's social programs are conducted through the Front. One of the most important mandates of the Front is to oversee the activities of government organizations, elected deputies, political officials and civil servants. The Front plays a particularly significant role in elections of members of the National Assembly and People's Councils at all levels.

26) In particular the Viet Nam Fatherland Front Law (June 12, 1999) states in article

12 that the supervision by VFF "aims to contribute to safeguarding and building the Socialist Republic of Viet Nam into a clean and strong one operating effectively and efficiently, and to protect the legitimate rights and interests of the people." In addition, see Government and Central VFF Committee Inter-agency Resolution No. 05/2006/NQLT-CP-UBTWMTTQVN dated April 21, 2006 on the issuance of Regulation on VFF's oversight of cadres, civil servants and Party members at their respective residential places.

27) They include, but are not limited to, Decision No. 136/2001/QD-TTg on September 17, 2001 on Overall Program on State Administration Reform in the 2001-2010 period, Resolution No. 17/2007/NQ-TW on August 1, 2007 on the Acceleration of Administrative Reform and increase of the effect and effectiveness of the State Management; the Ministry of Planning and Investment's (MPI) Decision No. 555/2007/QD-BKH on issuing the results-based M&E framework for 2006-2010 SEDP, to name a few. Resolution No. 21/2009/NQ-CP on May 12, 2009 on National Anti-Corruption Strategy towards 2020 and the supplementary governmental decisions on building criteria for monitoring corruption and anti-corruption work. As well as the current Socio-Economic Development Strategy (2011-2020) on people's mastery of development process and draft Proposal on State Administration Reform in the 2011-2020 period.

28) An exception in Viet Nam is the ongoing efforts of measuring economic governance for private sector development through the Provincial Competitiveness Index (PCI). The Provincial Competitiveness Index (PCI) is the result of a major collaborative effort of the Viet Nam Competitiveness Initiative (VNCI) and the Viet Nam Chamber of Commerce and Industry (VCCI). For information see www.pcivietnam.org/ and Malesky (2009). Appendix B also provides a comparative table of differences and similarities between PAPI and PCI.

29) See CECODES, VFF & UNDP (2011), Chapter 3 for more details.

30) See CECODES, VFF & UNDP (2011).

31) See CECODES, VFF & UNDP (2011), Chapter 3 for more details.

32) In official documents in Viet Nam, the term "xa hoi hoa" (literally translated into English as "socialization") is coined to refer to the process of involving or mobilizing the private sector in the provision of public services like education, healthcare, vocational training, culture, sports and environment (see Decree No. 69/2008/ND-CP of the Government dated 30/05/2008 providing for policy to encourage "socialization" in those areas).

33) "Socialization" of notary services is underway in accordance with the Law on Notarisation of 2007 (Article 26). Privately provided notary services are available mainly in Ha Noi and Ho Chi Minh City. Some can be found in other centrally managed cities like Can Tho, Hai Phong and Da Nang, as well as in other provinces like Nghe An and Thanh Hoa and Son La. This initiative, however, has not been replicated across the country.

34) See questions D501 and D503 in the Questionnaire (Appendix C), CECODES, VFF & UNDP, 2011.

35) See Government Decree No. 12/2009/ND-CP on Management of Construction

Projects dated 12 February 2009. (Available at www.chinhphu.vn/portal/page?_pageid=578,33345598&_dad=portal&_schema=PORTAL&docid=83485. [Accessed on 16/12/2010]).

36) Exceptions for application for construction permits are housing construction projects in remote areas, in areas where no urbanization plans are in place, housing renovation that does not cause negative impact on overall architecture and structure of the entire building, and private houses in remote, sparsely populated and unplanned areas (Articles 19-21, Government Decree 12/2009/ND-CP on Management of Construction Projects, a by-law document of Law on Construction 2003).

37) See for instance Galiani and Schargrodsky (2010).

38) Analysis done by Tran Thi Bich (2011). In-depth quantitative analysis of the Dimension 5 data of "The Viet Nam Provincial Governance and Public Administration Performance Index (PAPI) 2010" for inputs for Working Paper "Citizens' Experiences with Public Administrative Procedures Reform: Some In-depth Analysis and Case Studies" commissioned by UNDP Viet Nam. [Work in progress]

39) See Acuña-Alfaro (2009b).

40) Law on Universalisation of Primary Education in 1991 mandates primary education for all children between the ages of 6 and 14. Under this Law, children attending public primary schools do not have to pay tuition (Article 13). Children at the age of primary education set forth above attend primary schools or classes in their residential groups or wherever convenient to them.

41) Decree No. 88/2001/NĐ-CP of the Government dated 22 November 2001 on implementation of lower secondary for all.

42) Circular No. 17/2003/TT-BGDĐT dated 28 April 2003 giving guidance on Articles 3, 7 and 8 of Decree No. 88/2001/NĐ-CP with definition of who are the subjects to universal lower secondary education.

43) The diamonds show levels of agreement of respondents with above statements about public primary schools at the commune/ward level.

References

Acuña-Alfaro, Jairo (ed.) (2009a). *Reforming Public Administration in Viet Nam: Current Situation and Recommendations.* United Nations Development Programme (UNDP), Viet Nam Fatherland Front (VFF) and Center for Community Support Development Studies (CECODES) joint publication. Ha Noi, Viet Nam: National Political Publishing House.

Acuña-Alfaro, Jairo (2009b). Media coverage on corruption in the health sector in Viet Nam: The tip of the ice-berg? *Presentation at the Anti-corruption Dialogue*, November, Hanoi.

Acuña-Alfaro, Jairo, Dang, Giang and Thanh, Huyen Do (2010), Measuring Governance and Public Administration for Human Development: A Demand-Side Approach. *Background Paper for 2010 National Human Development Report - UNDP -VASS*, September. Ha Noi, Viet Nam.

Center for Community Support and Development Studies (CECODES). Vietnam Fatherland Front (VFF) and United Nations Development Programme (UNDP) (2011), The Viet Nam Provincial Governance and Public Administration Performance Index (PAPI): Measuring citizens' experiences. Hanoi. Also available at www.papi.vn.

Denhardt, Janet V. and Denhardt, Robert B. (2007). *The New Public Service: Serving, not Steering.* Armonk, New York: M. E. Sharpe.

Galiani and Schargrodsky (2010), Property Rights for the Poor: The Effects of Land Titling. *Journal of Public Economics*, Elsevier, Vol. 94(9-10), pp. 700-729, October.

Government of Viet Nam (2009), *Viet Nam Education Development Strategy 2009-2020.* Hanoi.

Kaufmann, Daniel Kraay, Aart and Mastruzzi, Massimo (2009). *Governance Matters VIII: Aggregate and Individual Governance Indicators for 1996-2008.* Washington, D.C.

Ministry of Home Affairs of Viet Nam (MOHA)(2010). Report on review of the implementation of the Public Administration Reform Master Plan (2001-2010) and Orientation and Tasks for Public Administration Reform for the period of 2011-2020. *Draft Report for Submission to the Government for approval of issuance*. Hanoi.

Malesky, Edmund(2009). *The Viet Nam Provincial Competitiveness Index: Measuring economic governance for private sector development. 2009 Final Report*. Viet Nam Competitiveness Initiative Policy Paper 14. Viet Nam Chamber of Commerce and Industry (VCCI) and United States Agency for International Development's Viet Nam Competitiveness Initiative (VNCI). Ha Noi, Viet Nam. For electronic information see http://www.pcivietnam.org/reports.php

Painter, Martin, Hop, Ha Hoang and Khoi, Chu Quang (2009). Institutional Reform for Public Administration in Contemporary Viet Nam. In Acuña-Alfaro, Jairo (editor). *Reforming Public Administration in Viet Nam: Current Situation and Recommendations*. UNDP, VFF and CECODES. pp.318-376. Ha Noi, Viet Nam.

Peters, B. Guy and Pierre, Jon (eds.) (2007). *The Handbook of Public Administration*. Los Angeles: SAGE Publications.

United Nations Development Programme (UNDP) (2002). *Human Development Report: Deepening Democracy in a Fragmented World*. United Nations Development Programme, New York and London: Oxford University Press.

World Bank (2009). *Viet Nam Development Report 2010: Modern Institutions*.

Xuyen, N. T. and Cuong, L. Q. (2008), Research on current situation and reasons for over-capacity public hospitals at the centre level, *Journal of Practical Medicine*. Hanoi.

Chapter 12 Major Issues of Government Innovation in South Korea

Pan Suk Kim and Kil Pyo Hong

Introduction

Present governments all over the world not only have to solve the lingering problems of government policy failures from the previous generations, but also have to develop reform measures to effectively respond to the changes of environment on a macroscopic level, such as globalization, informatization, and localization. In order to find solutions to such governmental crises, governments worldwide are pushing for sustainable government innovation with new administrative paradigms different from those of the past.

The scope and the concept of government innovation differ by whom the matter is discussed, and this case will look into a narrow part of it, focusing on the administrative system. Recent use of the term innovation or reform in the government and the public sector has various meanings and different applications, so it comes as no surprise that the definition of government innovation or reform becomes vague at times. In the past, each regime has established a reform agency and named it differently, but its meaning was not significantly different. Literally speaking, there might be some degree of difference between the term innovation and reform, but this chapter uses it interchangeably. Government innovation or reform could imply a broad range of transformation in the area of public administration. It is a journey of continuous improvement of service delivery and management as shown in Figure 1.

Figure 1. A Journey of Public Sector Reform

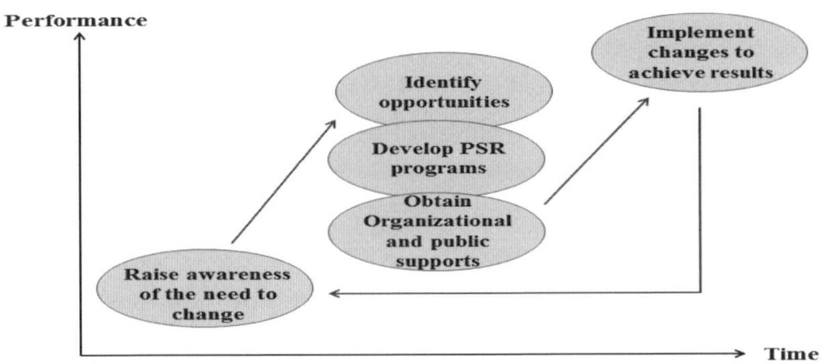

We often witness debates using the same phrase to explain fundamentally different innovative phenomena. Then, the debate itself is bound to be fruitless, without any productive or agreeable conclusion, if such debate does not have a specific focus. With this being said, therefore, this chapter will only focus on the discussion of government innovation activities centered on the administrative system, which can be said is the conventional field of government innovation. Also, this research will pay close attention to the methods and the controversial issues of such methods that surface during the innovation.

The option of maximizing administrative outcome through various innovation methods has had different results as the administrative paradigm and the situation in which each nation is, has continuously changed. After the 1980's, Western nations, such as the United Kingdom and the United States, adopted the

New Public Management (NPM) paradigm to develop government innovation methods. During this period, members of the British Commonwealth such as the United Kingdom, Canada, and New Zealand, emphasized the structural reform of governments and improving the quality of public service. The United States followed a similar path, but it is unique in emphasizing marketization and efficiency of administration (Kettl, 2000).

Nations like the United Kingdom and Canada acknowledged the limits of the structural reform methods under the NPM paradigm, and therefore adopted the New Governance paradigm to institutionalize the participation of the citizens and other stakeholders, emphasizing government innovation methods that promote a more rapid response system of the government. In the case of the United States, the Reinventing Government (REGO) initiative during the Clinton Administration is maintained at a certain level, it has emphasized the New Public Services (NPS) paradigm, which was offered to be an alternative of the NPM (Denhardt & Denhardt, 2000).

After the 1990s, new paradigms such as the New Governance and the NPS were emphasized. On the other hand, neo-liberalism-based NPM was criticized. Yet, that is not to say the NPM is no longer in use. It can be said that many nations have adopted the NPM in their own way (Christensen and Lægreid, 2007). In fact, administrative paradigms are not disconnected from one paradigm to the next, but rather are overlapping each other. In other words, traditional public administration, NPM, and New Governance are all related to some degree, and the level of such connection varies from government to government.

In the case of South Korea, the transition of the government innovation paradigm has been rather dynamic. The Kim Dae-Jung Government (from 1998 to 2003), which was the government in power during the IMF-Bailout and the Asian financial crisis in the late 1990s, drastically accepted many key policy paradigms of the NPM, such as privatization, reducing the size of the public sector, and customer-oriented administration. Also, it can be said that the succeeding Roh Moo-Hyun Government pursued complex government innovation activities under the NPM in conjunction with the New Governance paradigm. Then again, since the more pragmatic Lee Myung-Bak Government came to power in 2008, the characteristics of the market-friendly NPM has been on the rise. Retrospectively, there is no innovation method that has absolute superiority across time and situation. Therefore, it is usually the case where governments take the given situation and each nation's distinctiveness into account and develop a more relevant innovation method (OECD, 2005).

Table 1. Major Trajectories of Public Sector Reform

Major Trajectories of Public Sector Reform
Civil Service Reform
Anti-Corruption
Decentralization and Local Autonomy (deconcentration-delegation-devolution)
Corporatization or Privatization (Separating public service delivery from government)
Financial and Budgetary Reform
Regulatory Reform (Deregulation)
Informatization (Electronic and Mobile Government)
Public Enterprise Reform
Public Private Partnership (PPP), etc.

Generally speaking, there are many trajectories of public sector reform as shown in Table 1. Among many attempts at innovation from different governments of the past, this chapter reviews the government innovation initiatives under the Roh Moo-Hyun Government (2003-2008) and the key issues around many methodologies. The Roh Moo-Hyun Government put government innovation as one of its priorities on the president's agenda for a relatively long-time during his administration. Towards the end of its regime, the effort of government innovation became somewhat controversial as public servants were exhausted by such effort and consequently felt fatigued. Nonetheless, it is impossible to look into all of the issues, although those issues are interesting enough. Therefore, this research focuses on the issues related to government size and efficiency and the issues of visible innovation and performance. This research also attempts to identify key tasks ahead in order to promote an appropriate government innovation for sustainable government innovation.

The Process of Government Innovation in the Roh Moo-Hyun Government

It has not been long since the term "government innovation" has had a wide range of uses. In the case of Korea, terms such as "reform" were taboo under the authoritarian governments in the past. It can be said that the use of the term "reform" has been in use since the Roh Tae-Woo Government, and the succeeding governments since then began to apply similar terms. The Kim Young-Sam Government used the term "renovation," the Kim Dae-Jung Government used the terms "reform" and "innovation," and the Roh Moo-Hyun Government used the term "innovation." "Innovation" was a term most usually used in businesses of the private sector, not in the context of government and public administration. However, the term gained popular use during the Kim Dae-Jung Government and then subsequent use during the Roh Moo-Hyun Government. The dictionary definition of each term might be different, but it can be said that their uses in the administrative field are the same.

After the Asian financial crisis, the Kim Dae-Jung Government had no choice but to reform various sectors including corporatization, privatization, outsourcing and downsizing in order to overcome the financial crisis. Reform measures implemented during the Kim Dae-Jung have been well documented so that there is no need to repeat here (Kim, 2000). After that, the Roh Moo-Hyun Government was unique in its continuous, though excessive at times, efforts of government innovation through the mobilization of various innovation methods and of a stepwise change management of government innovation. From the beginning, President Roh Moo-Hyun was seriously committed to government innovation and his key assistants also made a master plan-like "roadmap to government innovation." With its vision of innovation in mind, the roadmap to government innovation provided a guide to suggest the direction of policies and enabled the government to track and monitor the progress of innovation. By doing so, it served as an extended plan to carry out innovation in a more consistent manner. In order to execute the plan, the government pursued a stepwise implementation strategy: (1) establishing the foundation of government innovation with dynamic energy for innovation; (2) implementation and expansion of government innovation with the introduction of change management; and (3) internalization of government innovation with the expansion of systematic innovation and promotion of innovation culture, and the integration of task and innovation.

In order to enhance the efficiency in the public sector, the Roh Moo-Hyun Government had not only implemented methods of the private sector, but also devised new methods more suitable to the public sector. For example, the government was active in implementing to the public sector management techniques developed in the private sector, such as the Balanced Score Card (BSC), change management, Business Process Management (BPM), and talent management. Also, taking the distinct characteristics of the public sector into account, the government attempted to devise new methods, such as agenda management, conflict management, and policy quality management. Although not all efforts were successful, it was a good learning experience for the public sector to study more about the methods of the private sector.

Meanwhile, in order to spread the strategic change management method for government innovation, the Roh Moo-Hyun Government developed and utilized various performance management systems and innovation assessment systems. Innovation assessment is to assess the level of the innovation implementation, and through such a system, the government intended to add tension to the implementation of innovation, promote a more competitive environment among public organizations through a ranking system, and simultaneously set the direction for the innovation itself. For a sustainable government innovation, the government attempted to internalize the innovation with a system of performance management and innovation assessment.

As mentioned above, the Roh Moo-Hyun Government developed various government innovation activities, yet it put less emphasis on some relatively key factors of NPM, such as reducing the size of the government, privatization, and outsourcing. On the other hand, the government emphasized quality improvement and rightsizing of the government (Eun Jae-Ho et al., 2005). Due to such a characteristic, later towards the end of the regime, the government was accused of being weaker in performance, yet larger in government size. Since the purpose of this case study is not to assess the government innovation of the Roh Moo-Hyun Administration, so the assessment of whether the Roh Moo-Hyun Administration was a success or a failure is beyond the scope of this study.

The Lee Myung-Bak Government which has succeeded the Roh Moo-Hyun Administration since 2008, did not highly value the efforts of government innovation from the previous government, and therefore was reluctant to pursue the projects or courses of the previous government. Due to the ideological gap, transition from the old to new government created a disconnection of government policies. In other words, the previous government's innovation policy was disconnected during the Lee administration. The Lee Myung-Bak Government established the Presidential Council on National Competitiveness as the advisory council to the President, and internally planned regulatory reforms, attraction of foreign direct investment, regulatory reform, and public sector reform. However, public sector reform has not been executed to the extent the citizens expected, and the government seemed to only focus on revitalizing the economy. Some degree of public enterprise reform might have been executed, but government innovation has not taken place seriously during the Lee administration.

Due to the disconnection of innovation policies by the latter government, the performance of the Roh Moo-Hyun Government's effort for government innovation cannot be appropriately assessed. Especially, the Lee Myung-Bak Government concluded that the previous government was a failure because the government innovation from the Roh Moo-Hyun Government increased the size of the public sector by increasing the number of public servants and the size of the national budget. On the basis of the NPM paradigm's idea of efficiency, the Lee Myung-Bak Government pushed for measures whose key factors are downsizing of government and privatization. It is yet too early to make solid conclusions on the result of such measures, but it can be said that the tangible results expected during early stages of the regime have not been achieved. Therefore, there is a need to review issues over government innovation methodologies relating to government size and efficiency. In addition, there is a need to review the relationship between innovation methods and innovation performance at this point.

This study attempts to identify the characteristics of government innovation methods carried out by the Roh Moo-Hyun Government, find out if changing how the public servants work will correlate to the increase in government efficiency, and answer the question of why innovation performance cannot be measured promptly in the public sector. In order to do so, this chapter addresses key issues relating to government innovation, and then attempts to identify future tasks.

Issues on Government Size and Efficiency

The Logic of Government Innovation Based on Market-Friendly Restructuring

One of the representative structural reform methodologies of the NPM paradigm is the market-friendly restructuring by means of privatization, outsourcing, government size reduction, and agencification. It might be an innovative methodology that ultimately attempts to improve the quality of service and achieve government efficiency through a market-friendly structural reform. Government reformation under market-friendly structural reform can be simplified as the diagram shown in Figure 2.

Through a market-friendly structural reform method, such as privatization and outsourcing, this methodology focuses on simultaneously reducing the size of government organizations and implementing market principle into the government. Under the market principle, this method is under the assumption that, by eliminating the consequences of government monopolies, the quality of public services can be improved. Also, the method is under the assumption that the competitive principle applied within an organization will undermine the stagnant nature of bureaucracy by promoting a personnel management system closer to what we can see as "survival of the fittest," hence increasing government efficiency. If market-friendly structural

Figure 2. Logical Structure of Market-Friendly Restructuring

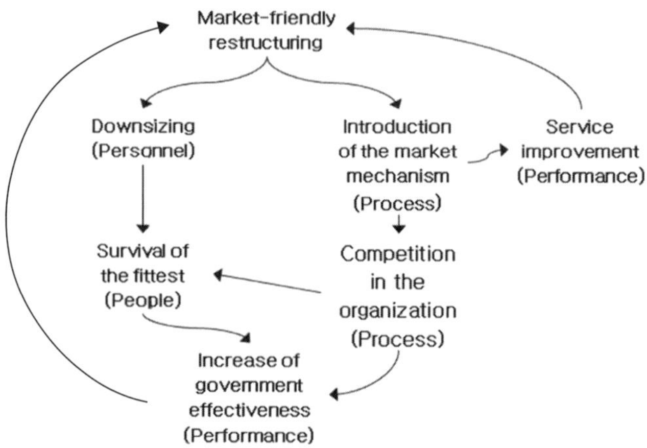

reform can contribute to improvement of public service and increase in government efficiency, market-friendly structural reform will be accelerated through the self-reinforcement loop within the innovation system.

According to the experience of the Kim Dae-Jung Government and of developed nations, such as the United States, the United Kingdom and New Zealand, it cannot be said that the NPM paradigm was a complete or total failure. Many nations including many European countries have partially reduced the size of the public sector, and were successful in mitigating parts of the bureaucratic ills by implementing the market competition principle. It is undeniable that Korea was also a beneficiary of the reformative paradigm as it allowed the overcoming of the national economic crisis in 1997 within a short period. Despite such benefits, however it does not answer the initial topics of discussion, namely if the steady, market-friendly restructuring yielded steady supply and quality of public service, if government efficiency was improved through government size-reduction and a performance-based system, and if the increase in government efficiency contributed to resolving the newly surfacing socio-economic problems.

Meanwhile, the NPM methodology which attempted to achieve government efficiency through government size reduction has been going through a transition phase all over the world since the new millennium. Western nations which are the very origin of the "small government" method are said to be trending towards increasing the size of their government (Eun et al., 2005). Although New Zealand had a drastic cut in its number of public servants in the mid 1990's, there has been a steady increase in the number since 2001. Allen Schick warned that most developing countries should not follow the New Zealand's way of reform. The United Kingdom under the Thatcher Government also drastically reduced the size of her government, yet there has been a steady increase of the size since the end of the 1990's. Furthermore, there is skepticism as to whether Korea can achieve similar results to the developed nations under the NPM paradigm given Korea's distinctiveness.

All nations, inclusive of developed nations, have pushed for government innovation methods that most suit their historical background and situational factors. Therefore, it is hard to say that choosing the innovation methodologies used in the United States or the United Kingdom will yield the same result in Korea, whose historical path of development and situational factors are quite different (Schick, 1998). The Kim Dae-Jung Government was successful in reducing the size of public organizations, public enterprises and public institutions.

However, parts of the public sector that were not under a direct monitoring had a tendency of becoming larger. The reason and background for such results are as follows. First, the experience and legacy of developing the national economy under the structure of free market competition affects the efficiency of government innovation methodologies based on the NPM. The United States and the United Kingdom already have some experience developing the national economy with limited roles of government and free market competition. On the other hand, from the point of liberation until the 1990's, Korea has followed an economic path primarily led by the government. Therefore, the natural free market competition mechanism is not fully embedded within the Korean economic system.

Second, the private market and industries have to be well-developed for a market-friendly restructuring reform such as privatization and outsourcing to demonstrate its effect. Nations like Korea lack a well-developed structure for social division of labor due to the size of its national economy and its monopolistic industrial structure. Rash efforts for privatization and outsourcing will ultimately increase the semi-public sector that will live off government subsidies. Also, such efforts might end up transforming the state monopolistic structure to a private monopoly. Lastly, such efforts might have the public service market occupied by foreign capitals due to its weak domestic capital. Therefore, an incomplete market substitution will only cause a down trend in the supply and quality of public service.

Third, it is questionable whether Korea has the labor market structure that is capable of naturally laying off of public servants. Recently, the Korean labor market is partially demonstrating traits of a cross-sectional labor market with a more horizontal mobility. However, this phenomenon is ultimately a segmented labor market structure divided by age, limited to the labor market mostly consisted of laborers in their 20s and 30s. For those who are over 40, being laid off would mean a semi-permanent unemployment, or working in a temporary position. The act of forcibly laying off public servants can ignite more resistance and produce side effects, such as causing the public servants to create and then to glide themselves into more affiliated organizations that are socially less important.

Fourth, there is the problem of whether the government can

fulfill the public's high expectations. Most people will be two-faced, where they will agree to the government size reduction, but then will go against any effort that hinders the public services that directly affect them. If such a socio-economic problem were to surface, popular opinion through the media is that the state should step up and resolve the issue. However, any reduction of public services or substitution to private service against the will of the public is a risky political decision. Therefore, the state has its hands tied when coming up with any solution.

The Logic of Government Innovation Valuing the People and Process

If a government pushes for a result-oriented government reform in the form of restructuring of the public sector and improvement of services, it can achieve various visible results, such as the reduction of government organizations and personnel, and the diversification of the means of providing public service. However, those efforts do not change the fundamental problem within the administrative agents and the administrative system, and therefore will not be able to secure internal sustainability. There will be a cycle where once the external factors weaken through modifications in the direction of policy or changes of regime, the government will be back to where it was before the reform. Once caught in this "yo-yo effect," public servants themselves might fall into innovation cynicism and lose the motive for any kind of internal change.

The Roh Moo-Hyun Government in 2003 was not obsessed with the short-term results of government reform. Instead, it chose a more difficult course of innovation that attempted to mitigate the fundamental causes through innovation efforts valuing the people and the process. In other words, instead of the physically-visible restructuring reform, it focused its efforts on innovation activities that value the people and the process.

This type of government innovation starts in the upper echelon, meaning from the president to ministers, vice-ministers, and other heads of various organizations. Among these, the innovation leadership from the president is the starting point of government innovation that plays a pioneer role in bringing the kind of changes emphasized in transformative leadership theories. In other words, one is to set good examples of change before emphasizing how others should change. Before focusing on the innovation of the public institutions in the lower echelon, it is easier to get the message of the innovation across by starting with the innovation of the presidential executive office and the central government.

Under the innovative leadership of the heads, beginning with that of the President, the Roh Moo-Hyun Government developed and implemented new methods of performance management systems while pushing forth an innovation process in the form of improving how the government works. Simultaneously, the government attempted to change the ethics and actions of the public servants through training and learning (Park, 2007). These personnel and process-oriented efforts of government innovation share many characteristics with the fundamental transforming methods of the government system and organizations emphasized in the government-recreation theories from the United States. Theoretically, the Reinventing Government initiatives may seem to have progressed, yet as can be seen through the results from Feldman (1999), activities in the actual field are limited to just cost-reduction and improvement of efficiency using the market principles. On this matter, the government innovation of the Roh Moo-Hyun Government stands out that it was not just table talk, but it developed innovation methodologies through action.

On the basis of innovation of the process and the people, the

Roh Moo-Hyun Government had put much effort into producing a difficult-to-reverse system of reform that would change the very constitution of the system and the culture. Here, system innovation represents the phase in which the embeddedness principle of government innovation is realized. In social network theories, embeddedness is the degree to which individuals or agencies are enmeshed in a social network. The concept was introduced by sociologist Mark Granovetter and the term embeddedness involves the overlap between social and economic ties within and between organizations (Granovetter, 1985; Kim, Yong Hak, 2003). Granovtter (1985) states that under the embeddedness theory, the relationship of the interactions among actors could be reproduced. Embeddedness under the perspective of innovation states that an individual innovation activity exists in relation to other innovation activities, and the patterns of these innovation activities will then affect individual innovations (Hong and Chang, 2000).

Also, the embeddedness principle places a psychological limit to the actions of the transacting members so that they are compelled to follow such rules of innovation. In other words, they have no other choice than to go through a structural innovation in order to survive in the organization. A system innovation phase can be said to be the most appropriate state of innovation, yet it will not be achieved easily. In accordance with the electronic knowledge management system (i.e., the "*E-jiwon*" system was developed by President Roh for efficient task and knowledge management), the Roh Moo-Hyun Government produced cases of successful examples, such as the wider use of the integrated government task management system and the integrated innovation system of the Korea Customs Service based on the customs administrative information system and the performance management system. However, such innovations did not expand to the extent of the government as a whole, not to mention the disconnection to the next regime. While explaining the reforms of the public service after 1997, a report (Cabinet Office, 2006) of the public service reform team in the United Kingdom's Cabinet Office suggests a similar concept; the self-improving system. Here, a self-improving system is coined after a system with embedded continuity of improvements (capability development, improvement of performance management) and incentives for innovation (Pawson and Jacobs, 2010).

The last phase to creating a dynamically-balanced innovation system can be completed by activating a self-reinforcement loop, reinforcing the innovation leadership with feedback, from recovering government trust, through system innovation-based results, such as improvements of public service and policy efficiency and increase in government efficiency. The problem here is that the phase of system innovation, furthermore the phase of system innovation with continuous innovation results, takes a long time and faces many obstacles during the process. Especially, at the most vulnerable point of this innovation methodology, there is a time-lag between the exertion of innovation leadership and the manifestation of the results.

Nonetheless, process innovation and efforts to change work ethics and actions of public servants will not produce visible results in the early phases of innovation, and instead can cause an increase in the input cost, which might then lead to a temporary decrease in government efficiency. This is because process innovation and change of work ethics and actions themselves are not matters that will directly produce results. As discussed earlier, full-scale innovation results cannot be achieved until the system innovation phase is reached. Compared to the results, when there is an increase in the visible costs during process and personnel innovation, there might even be a degradation of organization efficiency. Also, because new methods are susceptible to failure, more so than they are to success, they are recognized as being more troublesome than preceding methods.

Chung, Jung-Gil and his associates (2005) take administrative time-lag to look further into such a phenomenon. They emphasize that in order for a complex cause-and-effect relationship to work, one must take the time-lag of policy into consideration. Especially, for a new system or policy to produce the anticipated effects, there must be enough time for the new method to adjust internally and externally. During this adjustment period, the input cost of the new system can exceed the outcome, but once the new system settles in there becomes a higher chance that the outcome will exceed the input cost.

This is the same relationship that one can see between R&D investment and its result, where one will expect to produce continuous R&D results after having acquired the internal capabilities and system through enough investment. Given the chance, one can develop a ground breaking technology once in a while, yet we must not overlook the lesson that continuous development of technology comes from the major companies like 3M, Intel, and Samsung well-equipped with their internal capabilities and systems. Jim Collins (2001) calls this the "Flywheel Effect." According to Collins, the major companies with capabilities incomparably higher than those of other mediocre companies in the market will reach an explosive grow that a certain point after continuous efforts and innovations. Such efforts are less likely to produce results in the short run, yet the growths they bring are table-turners. Instead of novel technologies or new products, what becomes the foothold to becoming a great company are assets like leadership and passion, securing well-trained human resources, awareness and hope, and a well-disciplined culture (Collins, 2001). Likewise, as innovation activities to bring big and small changes accrue, energies of innovation will continuously be accumulated, and at a certain point, lead to an explosive growth (KIPA, 2005).

In order to complete the self-reinforcement loop that strengthens the innovation leadership through system innovation, it is vital to secure stable governance. As can be seen in corporate cases of GE, Toyota, and Samsung, a stable innovation leadership that can be maintained over time has to be secured in order to realize a self-complete form of system innovation, which will then produce innovative results. In this matter, Korea with its single-term system faces hardship in securing this stable innovation leadership. This is because if the issue of time lag between activities and results is not solved in a timely manner, national support of the government innovation will be weakened, which will then put even more political pressure on the regime. Taking this into account, government innovation focusing on process and people requires a stable innovation leadership of at least 10 years. In the case of Korea, although the Roh Moo-Hyun Government decided to follow the methods it did, there was not enough time for the innovation to be fruitful as the proceeding regime chose not to follow the same path.

System changes are important in the process of innovation, but it is also important to bring an end to any obstructive custom. The Roh Moo-Hyun Government emphasized the change in work ethics and behaviors of the public servants. However, during the process of innovation, the government seemed to prefer a more institutionalized method, and the introduction of a new system was criticized as being too official and institution-oriented (Park, 2007). Ideally, it is appropriate to pursue changes in both the system and customs. However, due to realistic limits, it seems like the Roh Moo-Hyun Government attempted to change the institution first, and go abreast the internalization or stabilization of that institution with the changes of practices and customs. This may be why the Roh Moo-Hyun Government was criticized for being focused solely on the system changes.

Promoting Visible Performance of Innovation and Related Issues

Although government innovation by the Roh Moo-Hyun Government was systematically processed with strategic visions and pre-planned roadmaps to innovation, there are still many who believe that results of government innovation were less than satisfactory. Therefore, there were many from the political administration and public offices, who showed much skepticism against the methodologies pursued by the Roh Government. Issues to be discussed regarding this problem are as below.

Input Cost of Government Innovation.

Innovation cannot come from ground-zero. Innovation requires corresponding resources and efforts. The different kinds of resources and efforts implemented compose the input cost. One of the many characteristics found in the process of innovation in the public sector is that, even though sensitive when it comes to producing results, the process is rather insensitive to input of human resourcese specially public servants. For example, there is a tendency to overlook the input of human resources when calculating the input for the final result.

When considering the input of public servants, it is important to divide the input into quantitative input and qualitative input. Quantitative input is measured by the number of public servants mobilized and the hours consumed during the innovation process. As seen, quantitative input can be categorized as consumable and definite. On the other hand, qualitative input refers to the mental energy consumed and the level of on-hand knowledge and capabilities put into use, and therefore indefinite. Qualitative input can cause negative and positive psychological conditions, such as innovation exhaustion or fatigue, cynicism, sense of accomplishment, confidence in task performance, and creativity.

These results from qualitative input are variables as they bring ripple effects upon other tasks outside innovation activities. In other words, negative psychological conditions, such as innovation exhaustion and cynicism, mean a qualitative input cost even more costly than the quantitative input cost. On the other hand, positive psychological conditions, such as sense of accomplishment, confidence in task performance, and creativity are used as a positive function by improving the effectiveness of the organization, and thus offsetting the quantitative input cost.

In order to appropriately assess the result of government innovation, one must consider the input of resources and efforts for the innovation, not just the final product. Coming to this matter, however, the government sector is not willing to put forth systematic data or information that will enable one to see how many resources were put into government innovation or reform. The private sector even came up with an unfamiliar concept of timetech for task innovation, and there is a need to integrate the experience and knowhows from the private sector into the public sector. Time-tech treats input time as an input resource, and establishes a plan to manage and administer the given limited time efficiently and there is a need to manage and assess the input cost of government innovation at such a level.

Performance Measurement of Government Innovation

In a lot of organization innovation research, variables for level of innovation or output of organization innovation are usually the adoption and the execution of innovation (Wolfe, 1994; Fichman, 2001). However, the only reason behind a government's effort to innovate is to improve effectiveness and outputs of the organization through adopting and resolving an innovation task. Therefore, there is a need to measure beyond the primary result of adoption and execution level of innovation task, and measure the secondary results, namely the outcome of the innovation.

The number of new products introduced within the last three years, the ratio of sales/profit for the new products, the number of new ideas adopted, the failure rate of the development process, the consumer satisfaction index, the cost and quality of products in comparison to other sectors, the time input of human resources for each new product, the average lead time for mass production of new products, and the number of new processes adopted within the last three years are indices used to determine the outcome of the final result of innovations in the private sector (Tidd, Bessant, and Pavitt, 2001). Unlike the private sector, the public sector, especially a government organization, faces difficulties in selecting its indices for outcome, and therefore difficulties in measuring outcome.

Solving the issue of how to measure the final outcome of government innovation is one of the most fundamental, and at the same time, most difficult tasks when applying concepts and techniques of innovation in the public sector. The general logic of performance measurement of government innovation is as follows. When method 'A' is used for conducting an ongoing task, let's assume that it will incur cost 'a' and produce 'c' level of performance. Similarly, when method 'B' is used for carrying out a given task, let's assume that it will incur cost 'b' and produce 'd' level of performance. Here, (d−c) expresses the proportion of change of performance based on the result of innovation, and (b−a) denotes the proportion of change of input cost. If the formula (d−c) > (b−a) holds true, then the difference is the benefit of innovation conducted once. Expressed in simple arithmetic terms, if this innovation activity is conducted f times during a certain period, the benefits of innovation will be expanded to the formula (d−c−b+a) × f.

The problem is that there are difficulties in applying such performance measurement. The reasons can be said as follows. First, it is difficult to measure the yielded outcome in the public sector. Second, information relating to costs and outcome is difficult to come up with or may not even be managed. Third, the concept of opportunity cost is seldom acknowledged. Opportunity cost is the cost of any activity measured in terms of the value of the best alternative that is not chosen so that it is the sacrifice related to the second best choice available to someone, or a group, who has picked among several mutually exclusive choices. The first and second problems are solvable depending on the methods of measurement and development of outcome management system. However, the third problem cannot be solved as easily. The reasons are as follows.

First, the problem of the final outcome being hard to measure can be improved with continuous efforts to measure. Public organizations usually feel negatively when it comes to measuring outcome, and even when they have to measure, they would prefer to measure simultaneously the amount of activities produced through policies and the quantity of the products deriving from the activities. For example, when imparting training for the unemployed, organizations tend to measure the effect of a policy based on the training activities and the number of trainees who have successfully completed the course. However, the fundamental reason for the training projects is to boost the rate of reemployment of the unemployed. The problem is that it is hard to distinguish if the reemployment is purely due to the effect of the training or just differences in personal capabilities. For this reason, organizations determine the effect for most training projects with the training activities actually executed and the number of trainees who have successfully finished the course. There arises a self-contradiction that the higher the unemployment, the size of the training project has to grow regardless of the actual effectiveness of the training. As explained, when public organizations measure the amount of activities and the quantity of products because it is hard to measure the final outcome of a public organization, then there is a problem. There is a contradiction that for the sake of policies, there would not be any problem if organizations continue to put efforts in the training projects for the unemployed that do not even merely reflect the real demand from the labor market. Osborne and Gaebler (1992) recognize this problem and emphasize the need to put efforts into coming up with an approximate value closest to the final outcome even if it may not be perfect. In other words, they are saying that implementing good enough methods of measuring is better than not measuring at all. Those incomplete methods can be improved as needed and become closer to being complete. This is because this can then prevent dissipation of resources which will have the final outcome of unfolding more favorably.

Second, the problem of cost and outcome related information being difficult to compile, or not being managed at all, can be gradually mitigated through development of an administrative information system and performance management system. One of the obstacles that hinder the public sector from devising an appropriate index to measure outcome is that due to a lack of past data, it takes a long time to devise an effective index (Popovich, 1998). However, current information technologies and the following development of information systems have changed the management process tremendously, and those activities and contents are converted digitally and managed systematically. Especially, in countries like Korea with developed information communication technologies where the rate at which digital administrative systems are developed and spread is rapid, accumulation of digital data can be carried out easily. Also, as there is a trend for digital convergence where different kinds of system information are inter-connected and can be put into use, the shortage of basic information will no longer be a limiting factor in measuring outcome in the public sector.

As mentioned earlier, the third problem of measuring and acknowledging the innovation outcome using the concept of opportunity cost is difficult to overcome with the government's sheer effort. It is a matter that can be solved when groups such as the board of audit and inspection, the national assembly, civic groups, and media who could monitor and put checks on the administration, all give their social consent. Additionally, principles such as the need to combine quantitative and qualitative analysis relating to the measuring issue of government innovation, pushing for the participation of informants and public servants in order to devise an effective measuring method, putting forth efforts to continuously review and revise measuring methods, applying an appropriate number of measuring methods, ensuring fairness of the measuring institutions, and maximizing the use of performance data (Osborne and Gaebler, 1992), all have to be taken into account for further consideration.

Time-Lag and Policy Effectiveness

One of the main problems that the government innovation under the Roh Moo-Hyun Government faced was the internal limit within the method itself. The Roh Moo-Hyun Government attempted to bring a fundamental change based on an autonomous administrative system and innovation of the culture within public offices. However, the 5-year term (usually under 3 to 4 years considering the effect on the regime towards the end of its term) acts as the underlying limit in producing a ground breaking innovation outcome that people can actually perceive in the public sector. The Roh Moo-Hyun Government's innovation was focused on establishing infrastructure for innovation and changes in behaviors, which suggests that there has to be enough time for any real innovation outcome or effect to take place. Also, correlation between improvement of administrative services and its causes, namely improvement of infrastructure, and innovations in behavior and culture, is rather unclear, making it even more difficult for the general public to perceive the effects of government innovation. On the other hand, innovation outcome in the private sector can be confirmed in a relatively short-period. This is because response from the market acts as a mechanism to confirm outcome in the private sector. Conversely, government innovation outcome has to be applied to policy outcome in the public sector, which will require the time factor to be taken into consideration. Chung et al.(2005) take administrative time lag into account when studying the relationship between process of changes in policy and systems, system reforms, and outcome. In doing so, they emphasize the need to apply the time lag in a multilateral way.

Alongside, in order to judge the outcome of policy innovation (success or failure of the innovation), the time lag issue of policy effect should be taken into account. Let us further analyze why it should be using the following three different cases: (1) Case of Model A shows good performance in a short term, but government effectiveness does not last long; (2) Case of Model B shows good performance in a short term and government effectiveness does not decline even in a medium term; and (3) Case of Model C looks like a government failure in a short term, but government effectiveness increases over the time continuously. Case A seems to bethe successful case of innovation and case C the failure in the short run, but the opposite may hold true in the mid to long run.

This is because when predicting the relationship between implementing a new system and its outcome, there is a complex cause-and-effect relationship, and it is also because there is a time lag between the time at which a new system is implemented and at which it takes effect (Chung et al., 2005). Therefore, there can be a huge mistake in the future of public policy effectiveness if innovation outcome is taken on in a hastily manner, or if the success and failure of an innovation is decided on the short-run. Having said this, when selecting cases of success and failure for innovation, one must consider the issue of policy effectiveness on the basis of the outlook of time.

Future Tasks for Sustainable Government Innovation

For a sustainable government innovation, there has to be practical solutions for the problems of government innovation methodologies, and simultaneously the establishment of a theoretical foundation in order to support continuous innovation.

Searching for a Rightsize of the Public Sector and Autonomous Restructuring Measures

For sustainable government innovation, it is important to find the solution for the issue of rightsizing the government and the public sector, inclusive of their restructuring. Although government size itself is not a topic of discussion, it is not a matter to be dismissed. This is because the final outcome expected from government innovation contributes to the people's confidence level of the government, and this is strictly connected to the appropriateness and credibility of the tax burden to the people. In-depth research and multilateral and comprehensive discussions on the matters of public institutions inclusive of the central government and its affiliated organizations, local governments and their affiliated organizations, public enterprises and subordinate institutions are to be conducted in the future. This issue is beyond a simple matter of size, and goes beyond the issue of the government's function and effective intervention measures of the government. This issue is to be treated with a comprehensive review of matters such as the issue of overlapping functions and allocation of tasks within the public sector as a whole, beyond just the scope of internal central ministries and agencies, the issue of downsizing of functions of the public sector utilizing market mechanisms, and the possibility of solving the issue of social problems through partnerships with a third sector. This is why there is a need for innovative visions for the overall administration of the nation beyond just the administration innovation of government.

This complex issue of government size and responsibility of performance should not focus on who is to blame, but rather should focus on seeking new measures together. First of all, the central government and public institutions need to develop and execute autonomous restructuring measures. A uniform restructuring all across government organizations and public institutions under the central government is behind the times, and yields a high chance for side effects during the process. Therefore, there is a need for new measures to guide government organizations and public institutions to an autonomous and voluntary restructuring. In order to devise such measures, organizational management like adjustment of functions, and strategic human resource management that would lead to early leaving or switching of positions, and assessment management, relating to a system of budget coordination and total personnel expenses, are to be closely coordinated.

Also, if the central government does not have direct control over the public sector like its affiliated or subordinate institutions, measures that would otherwise promote competition principles in the public sector and have the institutions responsible for its performance should be considered. The problem here in promoting this is that there are still misconceptions in the public offices that implementing competition principles is not the same concept as privatization. Implementing competition principles is a matter of administration, rather than a matter of action. Therefore, inefficiency from a monopolistic administration can be solved to a certain extent with just the implementation of competition principles. Also, the misconception of performance responsibilities being transferred to the hands of the private sector upon privatization should be rectified. Privatization means reassigning the function of providing services, and should not be taken as transferring all of the government's responsibilities. Also, we are to set aside the dichotomy of market regulation versus abolition of market regulation, and need to seek measures to solve social issues utilizing the market mechanism. Taking the aging society as an example, the government can directly intervene through the means of taxing, welfare, or pension, but there are also means to mitigate the issue through the market mechanism, such as expanding the personal pension market or promoting "silver" industries considering the rise of aging society.

In addition, instead of the affiliated or subordinate institutions that are under the direct control of the government, a trilateral partnership among government, private, and a third sector should be established actively. The Roh Moo-Hyun Administration, from the stand point of governance, sought to promote direct participation of civic groups and many other stakeholders, but was not enthusiastic in introducing partnerships through co-determination and co-responsibility in the field. However, the responsibility for such a weak link in the public-private partnership with private enterprises and the third sector does not solely lie in the hands of the government, yet the government, with its authority to make policy decisions and with its sufficient resources, should step up and solve the issue proactively.

Reinforcing a Theoretical Foundation for Sustainable Government Innovation: Value-Oriented Public Management

The government should not hesitate in implementing multiple theories and methodologies to solve details of problems and not be tangled by a certain administrative paradigm. One might criticize that there are no principles or a clear philosophy behind this kind of innovation, yet the originally existing paradigms or theories, and methodologies do not solve the complex and multi-natured problems of a government. It is worthy to integrate the newly constructed ideologies and principles, given that they are appropriate, into one theoretical model.

This chapter suggests an alternative theoretical model to a new government innovation that puts the Korean government's experience and knowhow into use. Tentatively, we will call government innovation "Value-oriented Public Management (VPM)" as government innovation is to establish and execute strategic management systems in order to realize the desirable values of public management. VPM has three characteristics: (1) searching for goals that seek measurable public values; (2) establishment and implementation of strategic public management systems; and (3) as a networked open system, government model and administrative systems based methodologies.

First, the goals of public values should be measurable. Government innovation is recognized as a means to realize the set of public values that the government should pursue and be responsible for. Generally, the NPM paradigm focuses on economic values such as performance and efficiency. In other words, NPM emphasizes that efficiency in the public sector is improved through management improvements, such as the cases of the entrepreneurial roles of public officials, organization reform, decentralization, introduction of market mechanism in the public sector, respecting the needs of customers, improvement of quality (Zifcak, 1994). However, the outcome of government activities should be decided taking into account economic values, such as performance and efficiency along with social values, such as fairness of allocation or reallocation of resources, correspondence relating to the people's demand, and the diversity and representation of human resources.

Public values involve a complex chain relation between ultimate values and instrumental values. Generally, the ultimate public values are expressed as abstract ideologies such as freedom, equality, justice, and democracy, whereas instrumental public values are expressed as the administrative ideologies or values in order to realize the ultimate values. Legitimacy, democracy, efficiency, effectiveness, fairness, equity, responsibility, transparency, and neutrality would fall under such a category. VPM emphasizes that these instrumental values are core values of good governance that are to be manifested.

The ultimate values of a state and its government exist as an abstract ideology, and therefore, are known to be difficult to measure. On the other hand, instrumental values (administrative values) reflect and selectively materialize the regime's ideological goals, the situation in which each state is placed, and the administrative paradigm best-suited for the given time. Efficiency (an efficient government), transparency (a transparent government), participation (a participatory government), service (a serving government), decentralization (a decentralized government) that are reflected in the government's innovation visions of the participatory state are examples of such selective instrumental values, and many other states advocate these values in order to achieve good governance.

Up until now, ultimate values as well as instrumental values were known to be difficult to measure in the public sector. In the private sector, there are profitability indices measured in the currency units, where there are none for the public sector. Even if there is one, it would be considered incomplete as it is able to only measure partial portions. For instance, it is realistically impossible to operate administrative outcome in a measurable form, and some critics say that doing so would blur the very meaning of administrative activities that seek common good

(Mier, 1993; Park, 2007).

Strictly put however, the lesson behind the immeasurability and consequences of administrative actions is that there is a problem with management. Having gone through the series of implementation processes, only after being able to recognize and measure the status, outcome, and difference with the goal can there be the corresponding goal-oriented control and management. If one looks at the development path of business administration focusing on the private sector, it used to heavily rely on the quantitative values and indices, focusing on the monetary issues and productivity. However, there have been recent efforts to measure qualitative values such as intangible assets and intellectual assets. As can be seen in the process of development of BSC, although it may be incomplete in the early stages, through improvement of indices and modifications of the relationship of indices it will produce a complex-value system appropriate for individual organizations. Goal-oriented administrative actions can be much reinforced if the instrumental values of the administration can be measured in the form of indices based on the systematic concept (Boland and Fowler, 2000).

Therefore, the VPM model aims to establish measurable and manageable public values and supports public management to improve the effort. Of course, the administration should be careful and should put in constant efforts in improving the measuring indices of public values, as an inappropriate measurement index can bring about erroneous management actions. It has become less difficult nowadays to measure public values due to the measuring-friendly administrative environment that underwent remarkable development of various information systems, accumulation of research on outcome measurement in the public sector, and improvement on the techniques of performance management, such as activity-based accounting and measuring intangible assets. Here, keep in mind the earlier claim by Osborne and Gaebler (1992) that there still is a need for efforts to get the closest approximate value of the final outcome, although it may not be perfect. Incomplete means of measurement can be improved as needed and worked towards becoming complete, and therefore it is better than not measuring in the first place. Not measuring and assessing are only as good as praising failure.

Second, strategic public management systems are to be established and utilized. The VPM mode emphasizes establishment and use of strategic management systems suitable to the public sector. The word "strategic" in the phrase strategic management means focusing on situation suitability that promotes adaptation to changes in environment, securing and effectively allocating required resources, and focusing on planning an integration of implementation processes. The public sector actually has recognized the importance of strategic concepts and strategic planning and has put them into partial use, yet the strategic standpoint could not be applied to the overall establishment and operation of the administrative system. Thus, the VPM model emphasizes the establishment and the application of a strategic management system applied across the overall public sector.

From the standpoint of integration between planning and implementation, and also for suitability of the situation, the VPM model emphasizes internal and external coordination. Internal coordination is the complementary relationship among internal factors that constitute administrative institutions and management practices, and external coordination is the compatibility of institutions and their environmental contexts (Chung et al., 2005). In order to enforce internal coordination, there should be a constant coordination and integration of government functions and planning. In order to coordinate and integrate without invading the autonomy of agencies and institutions, mid-to-long term plans and strategic measures to manage goal setting are to be devised. In order to maintain external coordination, any changes in the environmental context should be detected in a timely manner, and then establish a system within the government to sensitively respond to external demands.

Even with the VPM model, external coordination is hardly solved, and this is because of the checks and balances between administrative and legislative bodies of the government. The idea of the separation of the three powers and its principles of the modern state create the foundation of the current-day democracy. The problem here is executing administrative activities on the basis of legislation. In order to ensure timeliness of the administration, timeliness of the legislations has to be ensured. In other words, in order to complete the innovation process and finally make it institutionalized, the National Assembly has to create or make amendments to the related regulations, yet there are many cases where this process fails to come through at the right time. With this being said, if the ultimate purpose of government innovation is the restoration of the people's confidence, then one must not overlook the corporate responsibility of the legislative body in relation to the timeliness of government policies. One of the biggest problems for government innovation is finding a solution to mitigate this issue without disturbing the ideologies and principles of the separation of the three powers, especially the checks and balances between administration and legislation.

In relation to this problem, there is a need to devise measures to help solve the issue of legislation-based administration with governance through participation. Referendums and monitoring the legislative activities would be examples of such measures. Legislative activities of members of the National Assembly or members of the local councilsare to be respected, yet if their activities do not reflect the will of the public, then the issue should be solved through complementary measures such as the referendum system. Also, if elected officials do not represent the will of the constituents, then there should be restrictions imposed upon their political actions through referendums and monitoring of their legislative activities. The ultimate responsibility of VPM is not just being responsible for the methods, but rather being responsible for the final values of serving the people.

Third, as a networked open system, the VPM emphasizes government models, administrative systems, and methodologies based on the models and systems. The VPM model does not limit the administrative system to a closed government organization, and instead regards it as an open network (Joo, 2003). This has a thread of connection with Rhodes' assessment (1996) on the weaknesses of the NPM paradigm. Rhodes called the NPM a kind of managerialism and identifies its weakness into four categories (focusing much on the internal problems of an organization and not being able to manage external problems; excessive obsession on the goal, overlooking the importance of maintaining relationships and confidence; focusing solely on the outcome without being able to fulfill public obligations; and excessive emphasis on competition, which is contradictory to the co-ordination principle vital to policy networking).

The VPM model focuses on the trilateral cooperation and joint efforts among public-private-third sector when confronting the current social issues. Therefore, when solving the social issues the government is facing, one should not be confined to the dichotomous classification, namely government to civil, or public to private. Also, VPM focuses on the function and roles of the third sector. Third sectors are organizations owned and controlled by the private sector or civil society, yet the purpose of the organizations is not to accumulate wealth for a certain individual, but rather is to fulfill the social needs of the public. The VPM model includes the roles and functions of the third sector as a vital means to solving public problems. This is because the roles and functions of the third sector can be effective as the realized agent of the desired values. Government is well versed when it comes to policy administration, regulation, ensuring fairness, preventing discrimination or exploitation, ensuring the sustainability of an enterprise, and ensuring social unity. Private enterprises are best in executing of economic tasks, innovation, commercialization, adaptation to sudden changes, discontinuing of obsolete activities, and executing complex and technical tasks. Although relatively low in profit, third sector is better suited for tasks that require a high maintenance of confidence from the customers, requires direct and personal attention, and requires the organization to abide by moral guidance and individual responsibilities. The VPM aims for a triangulation system among the public-civil-third sector to achieve the desired values to the highest extent.

Conclusions

When pushing forth a government innovation, it is necessary to refer to similar cases in other nations, yet it is even more important to develop models and theories that best suit our own situation. Governments of each nation, inclusive of that of Korea, actively sought for innovation activities to yield better outcomes of the government since the 1990s. The Kim Young-Sam Government achieved improvements in civil affairs administration and deregulation through the Administration Renovation Committee, the Kim Dae-Jung Government pushed for reforms in four different fields (finance, business, labor, and public sector) and spread innovation in the public sector through the Administrative Reform Committee (later it was renamed as the

Presidential Committee for Government Innovation), and the Roh Moo-Hyun Government sought for a multilateral government innovation through the Presidential Committee on Government Innovation and Decentralization.

There can be different assessments on each of the government innovations by different regimes, and this research is not about innovation assessment, and therefore it is difficult to provide specific details of assessment on the success and failure of a particular administrative reform or government innovation sought by previous governments. Yet, it can be said that there is a mix of positives and negatives of the Roh Moo-Hyun in this paper. The positive side of the government innovation by the Roh Moo-Hyun Government is the efforts and genuine intention of its government innovation. Unlike its predecessors, the Roh Moo-Hyun Government established a roadmap to innovation in the early stages of its term, and pushed for innovation based on the basic outline. It pushed for innovation in many different fields such as administrative reform, personnel reform, localization, fiscal reform, electronic government, and democratic good governance. Especially, the central personnel commission, at the time, actively sought for innovation in the field of human resource management and human resource development.

However, the assessment of individual innovation initiative might be quite diverse depending upon its context and content as well as who is assessing what and whom. Nevertheless, one of the overarching criticisms is that the frontlines of the innovation had been excessively expanded and caused innovation exhaustion by promoting large-scale innovation during the whole term. The zealous efforts of establishing related organizations pushing forth the innovation, and allocating teams for innovation in different agencies are well appreciated, yet the fact that there is a fundamental limit to government innovations, based on market-friendly restructuring for government efficiency, had been overlooked. Also, although the Roh Administration attempted to push for government innovation based on the innovation of human and process, there was a limit to applying embeddedness to the scene. In addition, the regime attempted to produce a visible innovation outcome before the end of the term, the input cost of the government innovation was high, there were difficulties in measuring the outcome, and the time-lag for policies to be effective limited the opportunity for people to experience the effects of the innovation. Therefore, for a sustainable and an effective government innovation, there has to be a new theoretical foundation to support the cause, and this research suggested the value-oriented public management paradigm. The VPM promotes measurable public values, establishes and utilizes a strategic public management system, and, as a networked open system, emphasizes government models, administrative systems, and methodologies based on the models and systems.

It is not an easy task to take all of the principles and methods promoted by the Korean government for government innovation and characteristics of the respective implementation process, and consolidate them to develop one theoretical model. Even then, in order for government innovation to be continued effectively, the various methodologies should be maintained and be applicable to the reality we are facing, and simultaneously have to have a systematic theoretical foundation to respond to much criticism. Therefore, regardless of the faction, the Korean public administration academia should approach these issues in-depth, from a neutral standpoint.

The Lee Myung-Bak Government has focused its efforts on revitalizing the economy upon the global economic recession and financial crisis. In the early stages of the regime, the government sought to partially promote development of public institutions and deregulation, yet it is difficult to say that such were the core issues of the current government agenda. Therefore, it can be said that unlike the preceding regimes, the Lee Myung-Bak Government did not have government innovation as the government's high priority. Then what will the new regime in 2013 do? Although revitalizing the economy will still be an important issue, it can be expected that social policies around welfare, and other government innovations not pursued by the current government will become the core priorities in the public sector. When it comes to values, economic values are bound to be continuously emphasized as the economy is following a downward trend. However, taking into account the deepening polarization of the society and overflowing demand for welfare, it is possible that social values will be important measures of values, and therefore academia is to come together and hold in-depth and fierce debates on the issue of new government innovation.

References

Acar, W., Chaganti, R., and Joglekar, P. (1985). Mode of Strategy Formulation: the content-focused and process-focused modes can and must meet, *American Business Review,* January: 1-9.

Bateson, G. (1979). *Mind and Nature.* New York: Bantam Books.

Bennett, R. J. (ed.) (1994). *Local Government and Market Decentralization: experiences in industrialized, developing and former eastern bloc countries.* Tokyo: United Nations University Press.

Boland, T. and Fowler, A. (2000). A Systems Perspective of Performance Management in Public Sector Organizations, *International Journal of Public Sector Management,* 13(5): 417-446.

[UK] Cabinet Office (2006). *The UK Government's Approach to Public Service Reform: A Discussion Paper.* London: Cabinet Office.

Carnevale, D. G. (1995). *Trustworthy Government: Leadership and Management Strategies for Building Trust and High Performance.* San

Francisco: Jossey-Bass.

Christensen, T. and Lægreid, P. (2007). *Transcending New Public Management: the transformation of public sector reforms*. London: Ashgate Publishing.

Chung et al. (2005). *Time-Lag Approach in Public Administration.* Seoul: Pakyoungsa (in Korean).

Chung, Jung Gil and Chung, Joon Geum (2005), Time-Lag Factors in Public Policy and Institutional Change. In Chung et al.. *Time-Lag Approach in Public Administration*. Seoul: Pakyoungsa (in Korean).

Chung, Myung Ho and Chang, Seung Kwon (1998). Complexity Theory and Organization Theory: Self-Organizational Order and Manifested Learning, *Korean Journal of Management,* 6(2): 37-80 (in Korean).

Collins, J. (2001). *Good to Great: Why Some Companies Make the Leap and Others Don't.* New York: HarperCollins.

Eun et al. (2005). *Universality and Speciality of Government Innovation in the Participatory Government*. Seoul: Korea Institute of Public Administration (in Korean).

Fichman, R. G. (2001). The Role of Aggregation in the Measurement of IT-related Innovation, *MIS Quarterly,* 25(4): 427-455.

Granovetter, M. (1985). Economic Action, Social Structure and Embeddedness, *American Journal of Sociology,* 91(3): 481-510.

Halachimi, A. (2005). Governance and Risk Management: Challenges and Public Productivity, *International Journal of Public Sector Management,* 18(4): 300-317.

Hong, Kil Pyo (2006). Methodological Issues of Government Innovation in the Participatory Government and Future Tasks. Paper presented at the Winter Conference of the Korea Institute of Public Administration (in Korean).

Hong, Kil Pyo and Chang, Seung Kwon (2000). Restructuring Mechanism of Reproduction in Management Innovation. Paper presented at the Spring Conference of the Korea Productivity Association (in Korean).

Joo, Sung Soo (2003). *Governance of Public Policy*. Seoul: Hanyang University Press (in Korean).

Kettl, D. F. (2000). *The Global Public Management Revolution.* Washington DC: Brookings Institution.

Kim, Pan Suk (2000). Administrative Reform in the Korean Central

Government, *Public Performance and Management Review,* 24 (2): 145-160

Kim, Pan Suk and Hong, Kil Pyo (2011). Issues of Government Innovation and Searching for a New Direction for Further Development: A Case of Government Innovation in the Roh Moo-Hyun Government, *Korean Public Personnel Administration Review,* 10(3): 20-35 (in Korean).

Kim, Yong Hak (2003). *Social Structure and Behavior* (3rd ed.). Seoul: Nanam (in Korean).

Koller, T. (1994). What is Value-based Management, *McKinsey Quarterly,* 3: 87-101.

Korea Institute of Public Administration (KIPA) (2005), *Understanding Government Innovation: Innovation Strategies and Implementation Logics of the Participatory Government.* Seoul: Korea Institute of Public Administration (in Korean).

Marquardt, M. (1999). *Action Learning in Action.* Palo Alto, CA: Davies-Black.

Mastenbroek, W. F. G. (1996). Organizational Innovation in Historical Perspective: Change as Duality Management, *Business Horizons,* 39(4): 5-14.

Meier, Kenneth (1993). *Politics and the Bureaucracy: Policy-making in the Fourth Branch of Government* (3rd ed.). Pacific Grove, CA: Brooks/Cole.

[UK] National Audit Office (NAO) (2006). *Achieving Innovation in Central Government Organizations: Detailed Research Findings.* Great Britain: Her Majesty's Stationery Office.

OECD (2005). *Modernising Government: the Way Forward.* Paris: OECD.

Olson, P. D. and Bokor, D. W. (1995). Strategy process-content interaction : Effects on growth performance in small, start-up firms, *Journal of Small Business Management,* 33(1): 4-44.

Osborne, D. and Gaebler, T. (1992). *Reinventing Government: How to Entrepreneurial Spirit is Transforming the Public Sector from Schoolhouse to Statehouse, City Hall to Pentagon,* Reading, MA: Addison-Wesley.

Osborne, D. and Plastrik, P. (1998). *Banishing Bureaucracy.* NY: Plume.

Park, Soo Kyung (2007). Characteristics of Administrative Reform in the Roh Moo-Hyun Government, *Journal of Government Studies,* 13(2): 213-249 (in Korean).

Pawson, H. and Jacobs, K. (2010). Policy Intervention and Its Impact: New Labour's public service reform model as applied to local authority housing, *Housing, Theory and Society,* 76(1): 76-94.

Popovich, M. G. (ed.). (1998). *Creating High-Performance Government Organization.* San Francisco: Jossey-Bass.

Ott, J. S. and Dicke, L. A. (2001). Challenges Facing Public Sector Management in Era of Downsizing, Devolution, Dispersion, Empowerment, and Accountability, *Public Organization Review: A Global Journal,* 1(3): 321-339.

Rhodes, R. A. W. (1996). The New Governance: governing without government, *Political Studies,* 44(4): 652-667.

Schick, A. (1998). Why Most Developing Countries Should Not Try New Zealand's Reform, *World Bank Research Observer,* 13(1): 123-131.

Tidd, J., Bessant, J., and Pavitt, K. (2005). *Managing Innovation: Integrating Technological, Market and Organizational Change* (3rd ed.). New York: John Wiley.

Wolfe, R. A. (1994). Organizational Innovation: Review, Critique and Suggested Research Directions, *Journal of Management Studies,* 31(3): 405-431.

Zifcak, S. (1994). *New Managerialism: Administrative Reform in Whitehall and Canberra.* Buckingham, UK: Open University Press.

Index

D

E

M

Q

R

S

T

V

W

Y

List of Contributors
(Listed by the alphabetical order of the author's last name)

Nik Rosnah Wan Abdullah is Professor and Deputy Dean of the Tun Abdul Razak School of Government at University Tun Abdul Razak in Kuala Lumpur, Malaysia. She had been Associate Professor and Head of the Department of Adminsitrative Studies and Politics in the Faculty of Economics and Administration, at the University of Malaya. She received her Ph.D. degree from Sussex University and MPA degree from Universityof Liverpool in the United Kingdom. She was a Senior International Fellow at the Johns Hopkins University and the Lee Kuan Yew School of Public Policy in Singapore. Her area of expertise includes regulatory reform, public policy, public sector management, health sector reform, human resource management, and administrative reform.

Jairo Acuña-Alfaro has been a Policy Advisor on Public Administration Reform and Anti-Corruption at UND, Viet Nam since October 2007. He has a Ph.D. in Development Studies at the University of Oxford, and an MA in Political Economy from the University of Essex. He is editor of the book, *Reforming Public Administration in Vietnam: Current Situation and Recommendations* in 2009. Team leader of "The Viet Nam Provincial Governance and Public Administration Performance Index" Research.

Suresh Balakrishnan is Chief Technical Advisor with the United Nations Development Programme for the Governance and Public Administration Reform: Support for Better Service Delivery Programme for Laos. He previously served as Executive Director of the Public Affairs Centre, a nonprofit think tank based in Bangalore, India, that is devoted to improving governance by strengthening civil society in its interface with the state. He has more than two decades of experience with monitoring and evaluation in the governance and development sectors, which spans training, research, and consulting. He has worked closely with national, provincial, and city governments and nongovernmental organizations in Asia and Africa to strengthen service delivery. He has been closely involved in the evolution of citizen report cards, which are now being mainstreamed into public administration reform initiatives in several countries.

Alain Benicy is an Advisor to the Royal Government of Cambodia with responsibility for administrative reform in 2007 and a former senior executive of the Canadian Federal Public Service. His career evolved around planning and managing reforms in central agencies and ministries. He has been a senior consultant since 1993 with projects in Cambodia and South America. Between 2000 and 2007, he was a technical advisor at the Secretariat to the Council for Administrative Reform.

Alex B. Brillantes, Jr. is a professor at the National College of Public Administration and Governance, University of the Philippines (UP-NCPAG). He is also Secretary General of the Association of Schools of Public Administration of the Philippines (ASPAP) and Deputy Secretary General of the Eastern Regional Organization for Public Administration (EROPA).

He served as Executive Director of the Local Government Academy (LGA) of the Department of Interiorand Local Government (DILG), and Director of the Center of Local and Regional Governance (CLRG) of the UP- NCPAG. He got his Ph.D. and M.A. degrees from the University of Hawaii, and an MPA from the University of the Philippines. He has written three books and has published papers on local government, development administration and civil society in local and international journals.

Herisadel P. Flores is a lecturer in the National College of Public Administration and Governance (NCPAG) of the University of the Philippines (UP). He is concurrently a researcher in the Center for Local and Regional Governance (CLRG) of the same college. He has a master's degree in Development Economics and a B.A. in Public Administration from the University of the Philippines. At present, he is pursuing his doctorate in Public Administration at the University of the Philippines.

Kil Pyo Hong is Professor of Business Administration at Baekseok University in South Korea. He received his B.A. M. A. and Ph.D. degrees from Seoul National University. He teaches organization theory, innovation strategy, and human resource management. He has been a member of the advisory committee on management assessment in the Ministry of Strategy and Finance and the Ministry of Government Administration and Home Affairs. He is currently a member of the Board of Directors of the Korean Academy of Management.

Ngo Hongly is a former senior executive of an international IT firm operating in France. Upon returning to Cambodia in 1994, Mr. Ngo worked at the Cambodian Development Council as a UNDP consultant. He subsequently undertook a long-term consulting assignment with the Office of the Council of Ministers advising of matters relating to administrative reform. In 1999, he became a senior technical advisor to the Council for Administrative Reform (CAR). He became Secretary General to the CAR in 2004.

Do Thanh Huyen is a Policy Analyst, UNDP, Viet Nam since July 2008 and team member of "The Viet Nam Provincial Governance and Public Administration Performance Index" Research. She has an M.A. in Development Studies from the University of Auckland, New Zealand.

David Jones is a member of staff in the Faculty of Business, Economics and Policy Studies, University of Brunei Darussalam. Previously he held various academic posts in Singapore and elsewhere. These included Associate Professor, Department of Political Science, National University of Singapore, Adjunct Professor, School of Economics, Singapore Management University, Local Director in Singapore, Masters in Public Administration Programme, Australian National University. He was awarded his doctorate at Queen's University of Belfast. His research interests cover public sector reform, public service management, public budgeting, government procurement, land administration and agrarian reform. He has published numerous articles in these fields in international journals and in edited collections, as well as a book on land reform in Ireland.

Pan Suk Kim is an Underwood Distinguished Professor of Public Administration and the Director of the Institute for Poverty Alleviation and International Development (IPAID) at Yonsei University in Korea. He is currently President of the

International Institute of Administrative Sciences (IIAS) and Vice Chairman of the UN Committee of Experts on Public Administration (UNCEPA). He worked in the Korean government as a Secretary to the President for Personnel Policy in the Office of the President. He earned his doctoral degree in public administration from the American University in Washington, DC. His areas of research interests are public sector reform, governance innovation, human resource management, international development, and organizational change. He was a member of the IIAS Executive Committee and the IASIA Board of Management. He was Deputy Editor of the *International Review of Administrative Sciences* and sits on the editorial board of several international journals. He is currently Editor-in-Chief of the *Asian Review of Public Administration*. In 2009, he received the International Public Administrating Award from the American Society for Public Administration (ASPA).

Htay Htay Lwin is a Professor and Head of the Department of Applied Economics and a Director of the Master of Public Administration (MPA/EMPA) Programme at the Yangon Institute of Economics, Myanmar since 2007. She was previously a Professor and Head of the Department of Applied Economics and a Director of the Master of Public Administration (MPA) Programme at the Meikhtila Institute of Economics, Mandalay Division, Myanmar. She also served as an Associate Professor and Head of Department of Applied Economics, at the Meikhtila Institute of Economics from June 2001 to April 2003.

Pairote Pathranarakul is Assistant Professor and Vice President for Administration of the National Institute of Development Administration (NIDA) in Bangkok, Thailand. He served as Associate Dean for Planning and Development and Associate

Dean for Administration at the Graduate School of Public Administration (GSPA/NIDA). Holding an MPA (Hons.) in Public Policy and Project Management, Graduate School of Public Administration, NIDA and a Ph.D. in Regional and Rural Development Planning, Asian Institute of Technology, he currently teaches graduate courses in public management, project planning and management, and crisis and disaster management at NIDA. He has published papers on governance and public management, development administration, development strategies for self-reliant communities. His research interest areas are public management, governance and reform, sustainable development, innovation management, and crisis and disaster management.

Eko Prasojo is head of the Postgraduate Program for Public Administration, University of Indonesia and a member of staff in the Faculty of Social and Political Sciences at the University of Indonesia. He graduated from the Faculty of Social and Political Sciences at the University of Indonesia and has a Master's and Doctorate in Public Administration from Deutsche Hochschule fuer Verwaltungswissenschaften Speyer Germany. Eko Prasojo is a member of the Steering Committee within the executive council of Eastern Regional Organization of Public Administration (EROPA), Chairman of Expert Commission, Indonesian Association of Public Administration (IAPA) and Member of the Asian Association for Public Administration (AAPA). His research interests include federalism and decentralization, democratization and local democracy, political economics in bureaucracy, Administrative Reform, and Public Policy Studies.

Jon S.T. Quah was Professor of Political Science at the National University of Singapore and the co-editor of *the Asian Journal* *of Political Science* until his retirement in June 2007. He is now based in Singapore as a consultant on anti-corruption strategies and civil service reforms in Asian countries. His most recent publications include: *Curbing Corruption in Asian Countries: An Impossible Dream* (Bingley, UK: Emerald Group Publishing, 2011); *Taiwan's Anti-Corruption Strategy: Suggestions for Reform* (Baltimore: Schoolof Law, University of Maryland, 2010); *Public Administration Singapore-Style* (Bingley, UK: Emerald Group Publishing, 2010); *Combating Corruption Singapore-Style: Lessons for Other Asian Countries* (Baltimore: School of Law, University of Maryland, 2007); and *Curbing Corruption in Asia: A Comparative Study of Six Countries* (Singapore: Eastern Universities Press, 2003).

Khammoune Viphongxay was Vice Chairperson of the Public Administration and Civil Service Authority in the Prime Minister's Office, Lao PDR. He is currently Deputy Minister of the Ministry of Home Affairs. His recent areas of work include decentralization reforms, development of civil society and creation of local councils. He is alsoon the faculty of the National Academy of Politics and Public Administration. He is a member of several key committees including the State Committee for Organizational Improvement. He is also the Project Director for UNDP's Governance and Civil Service Reform Project, as well as the Civil Society Project.